C

FOR

DUMMIES™

VOLUME I

by Dan Gookin

IDG BOOKS

IDG Books Worldwide, Inc.
An International Data Group Company

San Mateo, California ♦ Indianapolis, Indiana ♦ Boston, Massachusetts

C For Dummies, Volume I

Published by
IDG Books Worldwide, Inc.
An International Data Group Company
155 Bovet Road, Suite 310
San Mateo, CA 94402

Library of Congress Catalog Card No: 94-77739

ISBN 1-878058-78-9

Printed in the United States of America

10 9 8 7 6 5 4 3 2 1

1B/QY/SS/ZU

Distributed in the United States by IDG Books Worldwide, Inc.

Distributed in Canada by Macmillan of Canada, a Division of Canada Publishing Corporation; by Computer and Technical Books in Miami, Florida, for South America and the Caribbean; by Longman Singapore in Singapore, Malaysia, Thailand, and Korea; by Toppan Co. Ltd. in Japan; by Asia Computerworld in Hong Kong; by Woodslane Pty. Ltd. in Australia and New Zealand; and by Transworld Publishers Ltd. in the U.K. and Europe.

For general information on IDG Books in the U.S., including information on discounts and premiums, contact IDG Books at 800-434-3422 or 415-312-0650.

For information on where to purchase IDG Books outside the U.S., contact Christina Turner at 415-312-0633.

For information on translations, contact Marc Jeffrey Mikulich, Foreign Rights Manager, at IDG Books Worldwide; FAX NUMBER 415-286-2747.

For sales inquiries and special prices for bulk quantities, write to the address above or call IDG Books Worldwide at 415-312-0650.

For information on using IDG Books in the classroom or ordering examination copies, contact Jim Kelly at 800-434-2086.

 is a registered trademark of
IDG IDG Books Worldwide, Inc.
BOOKS

About the Author

Dan Gookin

Dan Gookin got started with computers back in the post-slide-rule age of computing: 1982. His first intention was to buy a computer to replace his aged and constantly breaking typewriter. Working as slave laborer in a restaurant, however, Gookin was unable to afford the full "word processor" setup and settled on a computer that had a monitor, keyboard, and little else. Soon his writing career was under way with several submissions to fiction magazines and lots of rejections.

His big break came in 1984, when he began writing about computers. Applying his flair for fiction with a self-taught knowledge of computers, Gookin was able to demystify the subject and explain technology in a relaxed and understandable voice. He even dared to add humor, which eventually won him a column in a local computer magazine.

Eventually Gookin's talents came to roost as a ghost writer at a computer book publishing house. That was followed by an editing position at a San Diego computer magazine. During this time, he also regularly participated on a radio talk show about computers. In addition, Gookin kept writing books about computers, some of which became minor best-sellers.

In 1990, Gookin came to IDG Books with a book proposal. From that initial meeting unfolded an idea for an outrageous book: a long-overdue and original idea for the computer book for the rest of us. What became *DOS For Dummies* blossomed into an international best-seller with hundreds and thousands of copies in print and many translations.

Today, Gookin still considers himself a writer and computer "guru" whose job it is to remind everyone that computers are not to be taken too seriously. His approach to computers is light and humorous yet very informative. He knows that the complex beasts are important and can help people become productive and successful. Gookin mixes his knowledge of computers with a unique, dry sense of humor that keeps everyone informed — and awake. His favorite quote is "Computers are a notoriously dull subject, but that doesn't mean I have to write about them that way."

Gookin's titles for IDG Books include the best-selling *DOS For Dummies, WordPerfect For Dummies, WordPerfect 6 For Dummies, PCs For Dummies, Word For Windows For Dummies,* and the *Illustrated Computer Dictionary For Dummies.* All told, he's written more than 30 books on computers and contributes regularly to *DOS Resource Guide, InfoWorld,* and *PC Computing.* Gookin holds a degree in communications from the University of California-San Diego and currently lives with his wife and boys in the as-yet-untamed state of Idaho.

ABOUT IDG BOOKS WORLDWIDE

Welcome to the world of IDG Books Worldwide.

IDG Books Worldwide, Inc., is a subsidiary of International Data Group, the world's largest publisher of business and computer-related information and the leading global provider of information services on information technology. IDG was founded more than 25 years ago and now employs more than 5,700 people worldwide. IDG publishes more than 200 computer publications in 63 countries (see listing below). Forty million people read one or more IDG publications each month.

Launched in 1990, IDG Books is today the fastest-growing publisher of computer and business books in the United States. We are proud to have received 3 awards from the Computer Press Association in recognition of editorial excellence, and our best-selling ...*For Dummies* series has more than 7 million copies in print with translations in more than 20 languages. IDG Books, through a recent joint venture with IDG's Hi-Tech Beijing, became the first U.S. publisher to publish a computer book in the People's Republic of China. In record time, IDG Books has become the first choice for millions of readers around the world who want to learn how to better manage their businesses.

Our mission is simple: Every IDG book is designed to bring extra value and skill-building instructions to the reader. Our books are written by experts who understand and care about our readers. The knowledge base of our editorial staff comes from years of experience in publishing, education, and journalism — experience which we use to produce books for the '90s. In short, we care about books, so we attract the best people. We devote special attention to details such as audience, interior design, use of icons, and illustrations. And because we use an efficient process of authoring, editing, and desktop publishing our books electronically, we can spend more time ensuring superior content and spend less time on the technicalities of making books.

You can count on our commitment to deliver high-quality books at competitive prices on topics customers want to read about. At IDG, we value quality, and we have been delivering quality for more than 25 years. You'll find no better book on a subject than an IDG book.

John Kilcullen
President and CEO
IDG Books Worldwide, Inc.

VIII WINNER
*Eighth Annual
Computer Press
Awards 1992*

IX WINNER
*Ninth Annual
Computer Press
Awards 1993*

IDG BOOKS

Acknowledgments

The publisher would like to acknowledge the outstanding efforts of everyone who worked to make this book possible.

(The publisher would like to give special thanks to Patrick J. McGovern, without whom this book would not have been possible.)

A word from the author

The Author would like to acknowledge that no animals were harmed during the writing, editing, or production of this book.

Credits

Publisher
David Solomon

Managing Editor
Mary Bednarek

Acquisitions Editors
Janna Custer
Megg Bonar

Production Director
Beth Jenkins

Senior Editors
Sandra Blackthorn
Diane Graves Steele
Tracy L. Barr

Production Coordinator
Cindy L. Phipps

Production Quality Control
Steve Peake

Editorial Assistants
Beth Reynolds
Laura Schaible

**Assistant to
Managing Editor**
Jodi L. Thorn

Project Editor
Rebecca Whitney

Technical Reviewer
Ronald R. Dippold

Production Staff
Tony Augsburger
Valery Bourke
J. Tyler Connor
Angela Hunckler
Patricia R. Reynolds
Robert Simon
Gina Scott

Proofreader
Betty Kish

Indexer
Liz Cunningham

Book Design
University Graphics

Cover Design
Kavish + Kavish

Contents at a Glance

Cartoons at a Glance

By Rich Tennant

Table of Contents

● ●

The 5th Wave   By Rich Tennant

Re·al Pro·gram·mers

Real Programmers don't look stylish.
To do so would indicate a belief in
society.

Introduction

● ●

*W*elcome to *C For Dummies*, Volume I — your last, desperate, and final attempt to learn the C programming language.

Although I can't promise that you'll become a C guru after wading through this text, I can guarantee you the following:

❏ You will know how to recognize a C program and, when one is grouped with an IRS Form 1040, the morning stock report, baseball statistics, and anything written in Braille, you'll be able to pick out which one is the C program.

❏ You will be able to write C programs that no other publisher would let an author print in its C books.

❏ You will appreciate the following but be unable to use it at cocktail parties to impress your friends:

```
while(dead_horse)
    beat();
```

❏ You will learn to speak in C Talk, which is the ability to look at character groupings, such as printf, putch, and clock, and pronounce them as "print-f," "put-kar," and "see-lock."

❏ You will have fun.

I can't really guarantee that last point. However, this book was written minus the sword of mathematics hanging over anyone's head. Let's leave stern programming up to those who fuss over Avogadro's number and Fibonacci sequences and who debate the merits of how to indent their C program source code. Serious work is for the nerds. Fun happens when you learn *C For Dummies*, Volume I.

What Will Learning C Do for Me?

Look at your computer screen. Imagine something happening there. Anything. As long as you know how to program a computer, what you imagine will take place. OK, maybe not as fast as you like — but it can be done.

Programming is the ultimate way to get even with a computer. *You* are in charge. *You* tell the beast what to do. And it will obey you, even when you tell it to do something stupid. Computers are fast and obedient, not smart.

Anything your computer does, any devices it talks with or controls, can be manipulated by using a programming language and writing programs that pull the right levers. The C programming language has been crowned the best and most common way to program any personal computer. C may not be the easiest programming language to learn, but it's not the most difficult. It's tremendously popular and well supported, which makes it a good choice (though the BASIC programming language is really the easiest to learn).

About This Here Dummy Approach

Most *Dummies* books are references. That's a point I like to drive home to people who say, "I learned such-and-such in your *Dummies* books." No way! The *Dummies* book is out to remind, to console, to entertain. It's not designed to teach anything (though it doesn't hinder the learning process).

So how can I write a tutorial, *C For Dummies*?

The answer is to cheat. Most tutorials assume that you don't know anything. This approach is good and positive and all that, but it leads to some big pitfalls. Rather than give you a small bite of everything when you begin, for example, they make you finish your vegetables right away — one whole helping — all in tiny, baby bites. And what can vegetables do for you all at once? Why not nibble on some juicy steak? Or maybe have a taste of dessert before another chomp at the tepid and "Gosh, Mom, these carrots are awfully soft — how long did you steam them" vegetables?

My answer is this: You learn a little at a time, but not everything at once. Babies are born with all five senses to master, and they do so a little at a time. This book may toss some new concept your way and say, "Now here is such-and-such! Just type it in and nod your head (or babble and coo). I'll explain how it works in a later lesson." I feel that this approach works because it lets you create interesting programs right away, and it doesn't make you feel like you're stuck in one area more than you need to be.

For those with a more structured approach to learning, this book is divided into eight main chapters. Each chapter has several different lessons in it, each associated with the main chapter concept. But new ideas are laced throughout, all carefully cross-referenced in true *Dummies* style.

So although you don't get a reference (though there are plenty of tables and whatnot), you will be learning something. To prove it, each lesson ends with a quiz, and each chapter has a final exam. So there!

Programs in This Book

Part of the fun of learning to program by reading a book is that you type the programs yourself. This is the way I learned to program a computer. I sat down with Dr. David Lien's *Learning TRS-80 BASIC* book and, 36 solid hours later, I finished. Then I slept. Then I did it again because I completely forgot everything but remembered enjoying doing it the first time.

So you have to type stuff in. When you do, it looks like this:

```
Here I go, typing some stuff in. La, la, la.
```

Mostly you type complete programs, consisting of several lines like the one before this paragraph. Type them all in, and press Enter at the end of each line. Because this book is only so wide, however, occasionally you see a line split in two. It looks like this:

```
This is an example of a very long line that was painfully split in
            two by this book's cruel typesetters.
```

When you see that, *don't* type in two lines. Just keep typing, and everything will fit on one line on your screen. If you forget this, your programs will mess up, so I've tossed in several reminders throughout the book when such a thing happens.

In this book, the 0 in program listings has a slash through it (∅). Don't freak out, and don't type a capital O. It's just a zero.

"Omigosh — There Are Quizzes and Tests in This Book!"

I had to — I just had to — put in a quiz at the end of each lesson and a whopping-big final exam at the end of each chapter. It's necessary. You have to practice what you learn and know what you've been taught. The tried-and-true way to do this (modern education aside for a second) is to give tests.

Don't panic. You grade yourself. Answers are in Appendix A, along with any pertinent explanations. And although each lesson has at least 4 questions and each final exam has at least 16, I've made them goofy and somewhat entertaining for you. Heaven forbid that anyone actually use this tome as a textbook! (Oh, and I've included a new, nonoffensive, NEA-approved, color-coded grading system to keep up with the times.)

Foolish Assumptions

This book makes the following assumptions about you, your PC, your compiler, and — most important — your state of mind:

❑ You must be adept at using DOS. This book doesn't have time to teach you both C programming and using DOS. Besides, anyone crazy enough to try C programming should know DOS already, so I trust you to some extent on this one.

❑ I don't expect anyone to be a DOS guru here. Instead, know the following commands or terms and you'll be OK: COPY, DEL, FORMAT, REN, file, subdirectory, filename extension, and root directory. These terms and more are bandied about wantonly in this tome. Beware!

❑ You should be adept at using a text editor. I don't mean DOS's old EDLIN here — I mean a *real* editor — something like DOS's Edit program, QEdit, or one of the nifty editors that probably came with your C programming package. I can't teach you both the editor and C programming, so get to know your editor.

❑ You should already have a C programming language *compiler* at your ready. This book addresses the biggies: Borland C++ (also Turbo C) and Microsoft Visual C++ (also whatever else Microsoft has). Other compilers aren't directly addressed, though everything in here should work on them as well. Whatever the case, the compiler and its accompanying programs should be installed on your computer and ready to run. This book doesn't cover installation or setup of any compiler in particular.

❑ By the way, my main compiler while testing this stuff was Borland C++ Version 3.1.

❑ The plus-plus issue, as in C++, isn't an issue here. All compilers are C++ now because competition dictates it. Before you can learn C++, you have to learn the basic techniques of C programming anyway, and that's what's taught here. A follow-on to this series may cover C++ at some future date. Speaking of which . . . .

❑ This book has a sequel, *C For Dummies,* Volume II. It picks up right where this book leaves off, going into more detail about some subjects and offering the same, loving advice on the advanced issues. Look for it in your favorite bookstore soon!

Icons Used in This Book

 Technical information you can avoid

 Something you should remember to do

Something you should remember not to do

A suggestion worthy of note

A blow-by-blow description of how a program works

 Secret, aside information you can use to make programming easier

 Something fishy with the Microsoft Visual C++ compiler

Something fishy with the Borland C++ compiler

Generic compiler fishy stuff

You've worked long enough. Consider taking a break. Go outside, walk your dog, down a bag of munchies, trim your toenails — do anything — just give it a rest for awhile.

Same thing as the snack icon. Go take a break.

Icons Not Used in This Book

Indicates a deep glimpse into the psychology of Macintosh users

Alerts you to features of Excel 4.0 for Windows

Something that can be done from the menu

Final Thots

Learning C is an ongoing process. Only a dweeb would say, "I know everything about programming in C." There are new things to be learned every day and different approaches to the same problems. Nothing is perfect, but many things are close.

My thoughts on the matter are this: Sure, people who took 20 years of C programming and paid too much per semester at A Major University will have some C snobbishness in them. Whatever. Ask yourself this: Does my program run? OK. Does it do what I want? Better. Does it meet their artificial standards? Who cares? I'll be happy if your sloppy C program works. But keep this in mind: The more you learn, the better you get. You'll discover new tricks and adapt your programming style to them.

I hope that you enjoy the journey you are about to begin. So crack your knuckles, power up that compiler, and prepare yourself for a few solid hours of eyeball frazzle. You're going C programming!

Chapter 1
The (Sometimes Painless) Beginner Stuff

• •

In This Chapter

▶ An extremely short and cheap history of the C language

▶ How a meek and mild text file becomes a program

▶ Writing the traditional first C program

▶ The required woes of editing and recompiling

▶ Dealing with the heartbreak of errors

▶ What the C language looks like (or parts is parts)

▶ Input and output (with which we must up put)

▶ After the mess comes organization

▶ Important rules of C you'll never remember

Programs In This Chapter

GOODBYE.C   ERROR1.C   RULES.C

• •

*W*elcome to the introductory stuff. The lessons in this chapter provide the background material you need to get started with C programming. It's time for everyone to take that first brave, bold step off the cliff of fear and into the spongy, comfortable pit of programming.

Before hitting ground, I'd like to assure you — especially if you've never programmed a computer — that you're about to thoroughly enjoy telling it what to do. Prepare to have fun. This is easy. I promise. This book will never get over your head since I'm a mere mortal and not a C god.

Lesson 1-1: An Extremely Short and Cheap History of the C Language

First there was the B programming language. Then there was the C programming language.

No, I'm not being flip. C was developed at AT&T Bell Labs in the early '70s. At the time, Bell Labs had a programming language called B — B for Bell. The next language they did was C — one up on B.

The guy who created the C programming language at Bell Labs is Dennis Ritchie. I mention this in case you're ever walking on the street and you happen to bump into Mr. Ritchie. In that case, you can say, "Hey, aren't you Dennis Ritchie, the guy who invented C?" And he'll say, "Why — why, yes I am." And you can say "Cool."

Stuff you don't need to know about language levels

Programming languages have different levels. These levels describe how difficult or easy the programming language is to learn. The most difficult are the low-level languages; high-level languages are easier and more English-like. C is a mid-level language, which is somewhere (on a human scale) between fine English diction and grunting and pointing.

The lowest of the low-level programming languages is machine language. This is the primitive grunts and groans of the microprocessor itself. *Machine language* is essentially numbers and codes the microprocessor understands and executes. The plus is that a program written in machine language runs faster than programs written in other languages, and the programs are tiny.

Assembly language is a cousin of machine language. They're almost identical except that assembly language uses chopped-up English words rather than numbers. It's still considered a low-level language and, therefore, is difficult for humans to learn and master. And though

assembly language programs run faster than anything else, it takes an eternity to write them. Or at least part of an eternity.

C is a mid-level language. Parts of it are like assembly language — in fact, most DOS C compilers let you use assembly language within a C program, no sweat. Other parts of the C language are more high-level, bordering on the almost-comprehensible. C has the advantage of speed as well as being almost English-like to some extent.

High-level languages include the popular BASIC programming language as well as other languages that just aren't that popular anymore. BASIC reads almost like English and all its commands and instructions are English words — or at least English words missing a few vowels or severely disobeying the laws of spelling.

Although high-level languages are easy to read and understand by humans, they run slower than their C or assembly language counterparts. Also, the programs themselves tend to be larger.

Lesson 1-1 Quiz

1. C comes from a programming language called:

    A. A.

    B. B.

    C. Sea.

    D. Primordial C.

2. The B language stood for:

    A. Before C Language.

    B. Better than the A Programming Language.

    C. Bill & Ted's Excellent Programming Language.

    D. Bell Labs Programming Language.

3. If they came up with another language after C, it would probably be called:

    A. A.

    B. B.

    C. D.

    D. All of the above.

4. C is a:

    A. Low-level language.

    B. Mid-level language.

    C. High-level language.

    D. I thought we weren't required to know stuff in the Techy boxes.

Lesson 1-2: How a Meek and Mild Text File Becomes a Program

When you create a program, you become a programmer. I know, the term is new to you. Still, your relatives or people you know may refer to you as a "computer operator" or "wizard" even though your association with the beast is passing at best. So hang the title of Programmer on your shingle and swell with pride.

Ahhh . . . .

Now that you are a programmer, what's your job? Obviously, it's to write programs. But programs should have a purpose. The purpose is to make the computer do something.

The object of programming is to "make it happen." The C language is only a tool for communicating with the PC.

It's your job as a programmer to translate the intentions of users into something the computer understands and then give users what they want. And if you can't give them what they want, at least make it close enough so that they don't constantly complain or — worse — want their money back.

- ✔ I could offer a lot of philosophical advice about writing friendly programs and keeping in mind that the user isn't that smart, but, naaah.
- ✔ Concentrate on who's using the program and make sure that their needs are being met. Granted, this is advanced stuff; at this point, the struggle is just getting it to work.

The C development cycle

Here is how you create a C program in nine steps — in what's known as the *development cycle:*

1. Come up with idea for program.

2. Use editor to write source code.

3. Compile program by using C compiler.

4. Weep bitterly over errors (optional).

5. Link program with linker.

6. Weep bitterly over errors (optional).

7. Run program and test.

8. Pull out hair over bugs (optional).

9. Start over (required).

No need to memorize this list. It's like the instructions on a shampoo bottle (which are there, by the way, if you haven't been bored, as I was recently, and resorted to reading a shampoo bottle for lack of other reading materials in the place where you shower — and do other stuff). No one reads shampoo instructions because we all know how to shampoo our hair. You'll soon be working through these steps often enough that you won't have to memorize them.

(Knowing about the "development cycle" is neat, though. You can complain to your friends that you're woefully entrenched in the throes of a C language development cycle. Watch their eyes widen as you impress them with your programming knowledge!)

- ✔ Step 1 is the hardest. The rest fall naturally into place.
- ✔ This really will become shampoo-easy to you in just a few lessons.

The source code

When you create a program, you tell the computer what to do. Since the computer can't understand speech and since hitting it — no matter what emotional value that has for you — does little to the PC, your final line of communications is to write the computer a note — a file on disk.

To create the note, you use a program called a *text editor*. This is a primitive version of a word processor, minus all the fancy formatting and printing controls. The text editor lets you type text — that's about all.

Using your text editor, you create what's called a *source code file*. The only special thing about this file is that it contains instructions which tell the computer what to do. And although it would be nice to write instructions like "Make a funny noise," the truth is that you must write instructions in a tongue the computer understands. In this case, the instructions are written in the C language.

When you've finished writing the instructions, you save them in a file on disk. Have the first part of the filename be the name you want to give the final program. For example, if you were creating a game called UFO Kill, the source code file should have a first name of UFOKILL.

The second part of the filename, the extension, must be C, for the C language. This is important! Most text files end in TXT or sometimes DOC. For the C language, your files must end in .C (dot-C), such as UFOKILL.C.

- ✔ The source code file is a text file on disk. It contains instructions for the computer that are written in the C programming language.
- ✔ You use a text editor to create the source code file. Most C compilers come with their own text editors. If yours did not, you can use a third-party text editor to do the job. (Some programmers prefer third-party text editors.)

- ✔ It's possible to use a word processor to create your source code files. However, save the file as a "plain text" or "DOS text" or "ASCII" or "unformatted" file. (Using a word processor to create a source code file is a lot like using a 747 to drive to work; it's a little too much power for the job at hand.)
- ✔ The source code file ends with a C as its filename extension.

✔ The first part of the source code filename should be the name of the program you want to create.

The compiler

After the source code is created and saved to disk, it must be translated into a language the computer can understand. This job is tackled by the compiler.

The *compiler* is a special program that reads the instructions stored in the source code file. The compiler runs through each instruction and translates it into the secret code understood only by the computer's microprocessor.

If all goes well and the compiler is duly pleased with your source code, it produces an *object code file,* a second file that's saved on disk. The object code file has the same first name as the source code file, but it ends in .OBJ (dot-OBJ). So for that UFO game, it would be UFOKILL.OBJ.

If the compiler doesn't understand something, it displays an error message on the screen. At that point, you can gnash your teeth and sit and stew. Then go back and edit the source code file again, fixing whatever error the compiler found. (This isn't as tough as it sounds.) Then you attempt to compile the program again — you *recompile.*

After the compiler does its job, the program isn't finished. A third step is required: linking. This subject is covered in the next section.

✔ The compiler takes the information in the source code file and translates it into instructions the computer can understand. The result is a new file — the object file.

✔ The object file ends in OBJ. The first part of the object file name is the same as the source code filename.

✔ By the way, all these files are stored in the same directory. For information on cleaning them up, see Lesson 1-8.

✔ Errors happen. When the compiler sees something it can't understand, it stops compiling and displays an error message on the screen. Although this sounds dreadful, the errors are really quite easy to fix. Lesson 1-4 discusses how.

✔ Some of the C lords call an object file's contents *object code.* "The object file contains object code, you silly twit," they spit at you through their teeth.

TECHNICAL STUFF

Curious, but not required, information on object files

Are object files necessary? No, not really. They're an intermediate step. From your source code, the compiler creates machine-language instructions that are directly understandable by the microprocessor. It could at that point build the final program file for you, but an OBJ file is created instead.

The reasons for OBJ files come from when you have large programming projects. In those cases, you're usually working with multiple source code files. Why? Primarily to keep the program manageable. For example, your word processor can hold a 500-page novel as one file, but it's easier to deal with chapter-size files instead. For large programs, it makes sense to break them up into smaller pieces, or *modules.* Each module is compiled separately, and several OBJ files are created. It's the linker's job to string together, or *link,* the separate OBJ files into one EXE file.

At this point in your C programming career, the programs are too small to warrant creating separate source files and multiple OBJ files. The linker is still required, however, to convert the single OBJ file into the final program file.

The linker

The *linker* is a program, like the compiler. Its job is to create the final program file.

What the linker does is to take the OBJ file created by the compiler and spruce it up, producing the final program file. That file ends with either a COM or EXE extension — which is how program files are identified under DOS.

The first part of the program filename is the same as the first part of the source code filename. So if you start with UFOKILL.C, the compiler creates an object file, UFOKILL.OBJ, and then the linker creates the final program file, UFOKILL.EXE.

- In most DOS C compilers, both the compiler's and linker's jobs are done together, one after the other. You may occasionally see "compile" and "link" listed as two steps (which they are), but with your C compiler they may be combined into one.

- Like the compiler, when the linker sees something it can't figure out, it produces an error message. In that case, you have to decipher the error message and compile the program again (recompile). Lesson 1-4 deals with dealing with errors.

- Text editor ⇨ Compiler ⇨ Linker.

- Source code ⇨ Object code ⇨ Program.

✔ The program file ends in EXE, though it's possible to tell the linker to create COM files. You can refer to your linker's documentation for pulling off that trick.

✔ Yup, that's right: From starting with a single source code file, you end up with three files on disk: UFOKILL.C, UFOKILL.OBJ, and UFOKILL.EXE. Some compilers may anoint your hard drive with even more files. Refer to Lesson 1-7 for information about managing everything.

Lesson 1-2 Quiz

1. How does a programmer translate the intentions of the user?

   A. Barely.

   B. By creating a program that lets the user accomplish some task, hopefully the same task the user wants accomplished.

   C. Voodoo.

   D. Who said it was the programmer's job to translate the intentions of the user?

2. The C development cycle is:

   A. A stationary device you pedal to work off ugly fat.

   B. The steps required to create a program by using the C language.

   C. For older, more lethargic dogs.

   D. How our oceans were formed millions of years ago.

3. Match the file on the left with the thing that creates it on the right:

   A. Source code file   1. Text editor

   B. Object file   2. Compiler

   C. Program file   3. Linker

   D. Francophile   4. France

4. Which of the following describes the files used to create the STOMP program?

   A. STOMP.C - STOMP.OBJ - STOMP.EXE

   B. STOMP.C - STOMP.EXE

   C. STOMP.C - STOMP.COM - STOMP.EXE

   D. STOMP - LEFT, STOMP - RIGHT, STOMP, STOMP

Lesson 1-3: Writing the Traditional First C Program

Every C book since the time of the ancient Romans has the traditional first C program. This book follows that custom, though the *Dummies* C program has more of an attitude than other C books have. Here 'tis:

Name: GOODBYE.C

```
#include <stdio.h>

void main()
{
        printf("Goodbye, cruel world!\n");
}
```

Yikes! Step back and blink your eyes! But get used to this because this is the way programs are presented in this book.

Right away you should dwell on the recognizable. What's familiar to you? Yes, that is the English alphabet, A through Z, but mostly in lowercase. And some of those characters you may have seen lurking around on your keyboard: the parentheses and the curly brackets or braces, { and }. Save for printf and the \n thing, all the other words should be familiar to you:

```
include
void
main
"Goodbye, cruel world!"
```

(OK, you may not go walking around saying "void" a lot, but you get the idea.) This is good; so far, C only looks bad.

Your task is to take that monstrous text and transform it into a program that displays the following line on your screen:

```
Goodbye, cruel world!
```

I'll explain how everything works, what's important, and what's not in just a few pages. For now, you have two steps to accomplish:

1. Scurry off to the "Steps" section later in this lesson that's particular to your C compiler. For example, Microsoft Visual C++ users should read the "Steps" section written just for them.

2. Follow the individual steps outlined in each section. The end result is the GOODBYE program you can run on your computer.

- ✔ Cool programmers don't say that they're "writing a program." They say they're "coding." Nerds program; cool people *code*.

- ✔ Lesson 1-6 offers details about the GOODBYE program's source code and all the wondrous things it contains. Refer there if you need even more help typing it in.

- ✔ In *C For Dummies,* your first program is GOODBYE, and it displays the message Goodbye, cruel world. Other books about C — almost all of them, in fact — have HELLO as their first program. It displays the placid message Hello, world! I suppose that this is to prove either how "fun and friendly" C can be or that C programmers want to start their careers believing that everyone on planet Earth is watching his computer screen. My suggestion: How about a program that says Hello you introvert, get out and meet some girls! (Yes, you too can write such a program — keep reading.)

Entering the GOODBYE.C program's source code (everyone read this!)

Here are the line-by-line instructions for entering the GOODBYE.C program. Refer to the "Steps" section for your compiler before you start typing this stuff.

Start by typing the first line, which is shown in **bold** in the first step (type only the information you see on that line; descriptions of what you're typing follow):

1. The first line:

```
#include <stdio.h>
```

Type a pound sign, found above the 3 key on your keyboard, and then the word include and a space. Type a left angle bracket (above the comma key), then stdio, a period, h, and then a right angle bracket. Everything must be in lowercase — no capitals! Press Enter to end this line and start the second line.

2. The second line:

Press the Enter key. This line is blank, the easiest line in the program to type.

3. The third line:

```
void main()
```

Type the word void, a space, main, and then two parentheses hugging nothing. There is no space between main and the parentheses and no space inside the parentheses. Press Enter to start the fourth line.

4. The fourth line:

```
{
```

Type a left curly bracket or brace. (It's Shift+{ on your keyboard.) This character is on a line by itself, right at the start of the line. Press Enter to start the fifth line.

5. The fifth line:

Some editors may automatically indent this line for you. (That's because they're "C-aware.") If so, cool. If not, start this line by pressing the Tab key:

```
printf("Goodbye, cruel
     world!\n");
```

The Tab key should indent this line a few spaces. It doesn't matter how far. The idea is just to indent — to stand the text off from the left margin.

Type `printf`, the word *print* with a little *f* at the end. It's pronounced "print-eff." Type a left parenthesis. Type a double quote. Type `Goodbye, cruel world`, followed by an exclamation point.

After the exclamation point, type a backslash. This is the slash above the Enter key on your keyboard.

Following the backslash is the letter *n,* which must be a lowercase *n,* and then a double quote, a right parenthesis, and a semicolon. All these characters must be typed exactly as they appear in this book.

Press Enter to start the sixth line.

6. The sixth line:

The cursor returns to the beginning of the next line. If not — if it's still indented — press the Home key to move the cursor to the beginning of the line:

```
}
```

Type a right curly brace at the beginning of the fourth line. Press Enter to end this line.

You're done. Double-check your source code — what you see on the screen — with the listing for GOODBYE.C at the beginning of this lesson. Make sure that everything matches up. Now you're ready to use that text file to create a program by using your C compiler.

Steps: Creating the GOODBYE program in Microsoft Visual C++

Step 1. In Windows, start the Microsoft Visual C++ program, if you haven't already.

Step 2. From the File menu, choose New. An "Untitled" window appears.

Step 3. Type the GOODBYE.C source code, as shown at the beginning of this lesson.

Or follow the instructions in the sidebar titled "Entering the GOODBYE.C program's source code" (see Figure 1-1).

You'll notice that the words *include* and *void* appear in a different color after you type them. This is called *syntax coloring,* which is how the compiler displays special words (though not all the words) in the C programming language. You can shut off this option by choosing the View menu's Syntax Coloring item.

Step 4. Save your source code. Use the Save command on the File menu. Name the file GOODBYE.C.

```
┌──────────────────────────────────────────────────────────────┐
│ ─                    Microsoft Visual C++                ▼ ▲  │
├──────────────────────────────────────────────────────────────┤
│  File  Edit  View  Project  Browse  Debug  Tools  Options  Window  Help │
├──────────────────────────────────────────────────────────────┤
│ [toolbar icons]                                                │
├──────────────────────────────────────────────────────────────┤
│ ─                    <1> UNTITLED.1*                     ▼ ▲  │
├──────────────────────────────────────────────────────────────┤
│ #include <stdio.h>                                             │
│                                                                │
│ void main()                                                    │
│ {                                                              │
│      printf("Goodbye, cruel world!\n");                        │
│ }                                                              │
│                                                                │
│                                                                │
│                                                                │
│                                                                │
│                                                                │
│                                                                │
│                                                                │
│ ◄ ▌                                                         ► │
├──────────────────────────────────────────────────────────────┤
│                                                                │
│                                                                │
│                                                                │
│                                                  │00005│001│   │
└──────────────────────────────────────────────────────────────┘
```

Figure 1-1:
GOODBYE.C
in the
Visual C++
environment.

Step 5. From the Project menu, choose the menu item titled Build GOODBYE.EXE.

This step both compiles and links the program. A second window appears and displays messages detailing the conversion process from source-code text file, GOODBYE.C, to program file, GOODBYE.EXE.

If everything goes as planned — Ta da! — you see the following message displayed:

```
GOODBYE.EXE - 0 error(s), 0 warning(s)
```

Congratulations!

If you get an error message, return to the editing window, <1> GOODBYE.C, and double-check your work. Lesson 1-5 offers more information for dealing with the heartbreak of errors.

Step 6. On the Project menu, choose the menu item titled Execute GOODBYE.EXE.

This step displays a third window, GOODBYE, that displays the message Goodbye, cruel world.

The message displayed is the fruit of your labors. It was produced by a program you created and built yourself. The program file GOODBYE.EXE is now permanently stored on your PC's hard disk and can be run from now until when you accidentally erase it.

The program you created is actually a Windows-only program. You cannot run GOODBYE.EXE at the DOS prompt, only in Windows. To create DOS-prompt programs, refer to the next section, on using Microsoft Visual C++ at the DOS prompt.

Press Ctrl+C when you're done looking at the program, to return to Microsoft Visual C++.

Step 7. Skip ahead to the section titled "Save it! Compile it! Link it! Run it!"

Steps: Creating the GOODBYE program in Microsoft Visual C++ or Microsoft C/C++ at the DOS prompt

Obviously, Microsoft intends for you to run Visual C++ in the visual Windows environment; otherwise, they would have called it DOS-blind C++. Regardless, remember to run the MSVCVARS.BAT batch file program before you use Visual C++ at the DOS prompt. Otherwise, you get all tangled up in all sorts of errors I don't bother to explain.

Step 1. Using a text editor, such as DOS's EDIT program, QEdit, or something similar, type the GOODBYE.C source code, as shown at the beginning of this lesson.

You can follow the instructions in the sidebar titled "Entering the GOODBYE.C program's source code" if you need a little more help.

Step 2. Save your work to disk in a file named GOODBYE.C.

(You have to refer to your editor's documentation for the proper Save commands.)

Step 3. Quit your editor and return to the happy DOS prompt.

Step 4. At the DOS prompt, use the CL command to compile and link your program.

Type the following line:

```
C> CL GOODBYE.C
```

Remember to specify the full filename for the source code: GOODBYE.C. If you forget the dot-C, the final program will not be created.

Press Enter. The CL command both compiles and links the source code.

If everything goes as planned, you see something like the following lines displayed:

```
Microsoft (R) C/C++ Optimizing Compiler Version 8.00
Copyright (C) Microsoft Corp 1984-1993.  All rights reserved.

goodbye.c

Microsoft (R) Segmented Executable Linker  Version 5.50
Copyright (C) Microsoft Corp 1984-1993.  All rights reserved.

Object Modules [.obj]: goodbye.obj
Run File [goodbye.exe]: "goodbye.exe" /noi
List File [nul.map]: NUL
Libraries [.lib]:
Definitions File [nul.def]: ;
```

Congratulations! It worked.

If you get an error message, return to your text editor and double-check your work. Lesson 1-5 offers more information on dealing with the heartbreak of errors.

Step 5. The C compiler has created a program named GOODBYE.EXE. That's your program. To run it, type GOODBYE at the DOS prompt just as you would run any other program:

```
C> GOODBYE
```

Press Enter and you see the program's output displayed. It should look like this:

```
Goodbye, cruel world!
```

The message displayed is the fruit of your labors. It was produced by a program you created and built yourself. The program file GOODBYE.EXE is now permanently stored on your PC's hard disk and can be run from now until the earth's magnetic poles shift late next year and destroy all the data stored on our hard drives.

Step 6. Skip ahead to the section titled "Save it! Compile it! Link it! Run it!"

Steps: Creating the GOODBYE program in Borland C's integrated environment

These steps apply to Turbo C and Borland C++ up through Version 3.1. If you're using Borland C++ Version 4.0, please refer to Appendix C immediately!

Step 1. If you're not in the Borland C integrated environment, type BC at the DOS prompt to start it. Type:

```
C> BC
```

and press Enter. The Integrated Development Environment (IDE) appears, complete with an empty editing screen (titled NONAME00.CPP) awaiting your eager-to-type fingers.

If you've already been playing with Borland C, the program you previously worked on appears in the editing window. When this happens, choose New from the File menu, and you're given a blank window in which you can work. You can also choose New from the File menu when the NONAME00.CPP window doesn't appear as it should (obviously a bug).

Step 2. Type the GOODBYE.C source code, as shown at the beginning of this lesson, or follow the instructions in the sidebar titled "Entering the GOODBYE.C program's source code" (see Figure 1-2).

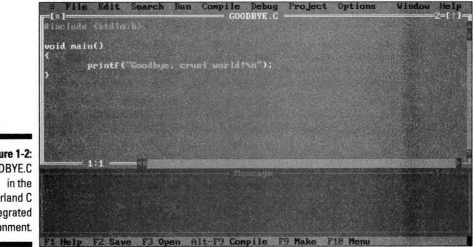

Figure 1-2: GOODBYE.C in the Borland C integrated environment.

Notice that various words you type appear in different colors. The first line shows up in green, and the words *main* and *printf* appear in yellow on my screen. This means that Borland C offers help on those words, which are central to the C programming language. The text you enter in double quotes may appear in a second color — light blue on my screen. Information about changing these colors and what they represent is carefully hidden in the Borland C documentation.

Step 3. Save your program. Use the Save command on the File menu. Name the file GOODBYE.C.

The Borland C compiler may save your file to disk with the CPP extension. Eh, big deal. That's the C++ extension, which is the same as C for this exercise.

Step 4. From the Run menu, choose the menu item titled Run.

Another window appears and displays messages way too fast for you to see. What you may catch at the top of the window are the words *Compiling* and then *Linking*. In the integrated environment, the compiling and linking steps are done one after the other when you choose the Run menu item.

The bottom window on the screen is the "Message" window, telling you what just happened. You'll probably see something like the following lines displayed in that window:

```
Compiling GOODBYE.CPP
Linking GOODBYE.EXE:
```

Everything has worked according to plan: The C compiler has taken your source-code text file and created the mighty program file GOODBYE.EXE. Congratulations are in order — the M&Ms and Diet Coke are on the house!

If you get an error message, Borland C stops compiling and rudely flashes the "Error" beacon. Return to the editing window, and the line containing the error is highlighted. Cross-check it with the listing at the beginning of this lesson to see whether you forgot anything and then try again. Lesson 1-5 offers more information about dealing with the heartbreak of errors.

The program has been created — and it has been run as well. If your computer is really fast, you probably missed the message being displayed.

Step 5. To see what you just did, press Alt+F5.

This step displays the "output screen," which looks like your typical DOS screen. Toward the bottom, you should see the following message:

```
Goodbye, cruel world!
```

Press Enter to return to the integrated environment.

A better way to test this program is to quit the integrated environment and type GOODBYE at the DOS prompt:

```
C> GOODBYE
```

Press Enter and DOS runs the program you just created. The output is the same, but at least this way you have time to marvel at it.

Step 6. Skip ahead to the section titled "Save it! Compile it! Link it! Run it!"

Steps: Creating the GOODBYE program by using Borland C at the DOS prompt

Step 1. Using a text editor, such as DOS's EDIT program, QEdit, or something else you enjoy, type the GOODBYE.C source code, as shown at the beginning of this lesson.

You can follow the instructions in the sidebar titled "Entering the GOODBYE.C program's source code" if you need a little more help.

Step 2. Save your work to disk in a file named GOODBYE.C.

(You have to refer to your editor's documentation for the proper Save commands.)

Step 3. Quit your editor and return to the friendly DOS prompt.

Step 4. At the DOS prompt, type the BCC command to compile and link your program.

Yes, both steps are done with one command. Type the following line:

```
C> BCC GOODBYE.C
```

Remember to specify the full filename for the source code: GOODBYE.C. If you forget the dot-C, the final program is not created.

Borland C also compiles C programs that end with the CPP extension. If you're using this extension, type **BCC GOODBYE.C** at the DOS prompt.

Step 5. Press Enter. If everything goes as planned, you see something like the following displayed:

```
Borland C++  Version 3.1 Copyright (c) 1992 Borland Interna-
      tional
goodbye.cpp
Turbo Link  Version 5.1 Copyright (c) 1992 Borland Interna-
      tional

      Available memory xxxxxxx
```

Any error messages are cause for concern; the program will not be created. If you see such an error message, return to your editor and double-check your source code with the code listed at the beginning of this lesson. Otherwise, everything worked. Congratulations!

Lesson 1-5 offers more information about dealing with the heartbreak of errors.

Step 6. The Borland C compiler has created a program named GOODBYE.EXE on disk — your program. To run it, type GOODBYE at the DOS prompt just as you would run any other program:

```
C> GOODBYE
```

Press Enter and you see the program's output displayed. It should look like this:

```
Goodbye, cruel world!
```

The message displayed is the fruit of your labors. It was produced by a program you created and built yourself. The program file GOODBYE.EXE is now permanently stored on your PC's hard disk and can be run from now until the next lightning bolt hits your house.

Step 7. Skip ahead to the section titled "Save it! Compile it! Link it! Run it!"

Steps: Creating the GOODBYE program generically

Step 1. Start your text editor.

In DOS it can be EDLIN, EDIT, or a third-party text editor, such as Brief, QEdit, the Norton Editor, and so on. Using a word processor is OK, but save the file in plain text, DOS text, or ASCII format.

To remember which command you use to edit your source file, write it in this blank line:

_____

Step 2. Type the GOODBYE.C source code, as shown at the beginning of this lesson, or refer to the sidebar titled "Entering the GOODBYE.C program's source code" if you need a little more help.

Step 3. Save the source code to disk as GOODBYE.C.

Step 4. Compile the source code.

This step requires your C compiler's compile command. Traditionally, the command is CC, which is what is used in UNIX, the mother operating system of the C programming tongue. For example:

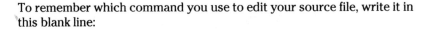

```
cc goodbye
```

The CC command is used in UNIX. Your C compiler may offer a similar command, though it may also have other options that have to be specified in addition to the source filename.

If, after pressing Enter, everything goes as planned, you should see a message displayed, informing you that the program compiled without errors.

If you get an error message, return to your text editor and double-check the GOODBYE.C program. Lesson 1-5 offers more information about dealing with the anxiety of errors.

To remember which command you use to compile your source file, write it in this blank line:

_____

Step 5. The next step is to link the program. This step may not be required, depending on the intelligence of your C compiler.

To see whether you have to link, use the DIR command and check for GOODBYE.EXE in the current directory. If it's there, skip down to step 6.

If you need to use the LINK program to create GOODBYE.EXE, it may look something like this:

```
link goodbye
```

LINK is the name of the C program linker. Its job is to create the GOODBYE.EXE file — the program that is the fruit of your labors. The preceding format is generic; most C compilers require additional options before a file can be "linked."

If you get an error message here, it may be because you forgot some linker option. If the LINK program mentions any "unknown" or "unrecognized" commands, however, return to the text editor and check over the GOODBYE.C program.

To help you remember which command you use to link your object file and create the final program file, write it in the following blank line (or if linking isn't required, write "I'm done!" in the blank):

_____

Step 6. Run your program. Type GOODBYE at the DOS prompt:

```
C> GOODBYE
Goodbye, cruel world.
```

The message displayed is produced by a program you created and built yourself. The program file GOODBYE.EXE is now permanently stored on your PC's hard disk and can be run from now until the IRS seizes your PC for failure to pay your back taxes.

Save it! Compile it! Link it! Run it!

Four steps are required in order to build any program in C. They are *save, compile, link,* and *run.* Most C programming language packages automatically perform the linking step, though whether or not it's done manually, it's still in there.

Saving means to save your source code. You create that source code in a text editor and save it as a text file with the C (single letter *C*) extension.

Compiling is the process of transforming the instructions in the text file into instructions the computer's microprocessor can understand.

The *linking* step is where the instructions are finally transformed into a program file. (Again, your compiler may do this automatically.)

Finally, you *run* the program you've created. Yes, it's a legitimate program, like any other on your hard drive.

You have completed all these steps in this lesson, culminating in the creation of GOODBYE.EXE. This is how C programs are built. At this stage, the hardest part is knowing what to put in the source file, which gets easier as you progress through this book. (But by then, getting your program to run correctly and without errors is the hardest part!)

✔ The program that compiles is the *compiler.* The program that links is the *linker.*

✔ In Microsoft Visual C++, use the Build command in the Project menu, not the Compile command. Build combines both the compiling and linking steps.

✔ In Borland C's integrated environment (BC), the command to make it all happen is Run, which is conveniently on the Run menu. You can also get into the habit of pressing Ctrl+F9 to run your programs.

✔ To see your program's output in the Borland C integrated environment, press Alt+F5. This keystroke displays the output screen. Press Enter to return to the integrated environment.

✔ Lesson 1-2 went over the save, compile (and link), and run steps in more detail than was presented here; refer to that lesson for a review if you're in the mood.

✔ See Lesson 1-8 for information about keeping all the various files, *.C and *.EXE, organized on your hard drive.

Lesson 1-3 Quiz

1. A source code file is:

    A. Produced by the C compiler.

    B. Transformed into a destination code file by the C compiler.

    C. A text file.

    D. Wait, let me turn back a few pages to find out.

2. Employee theft is most probably caused by:

    A. Future ex-employees.

    B. Management.

    C. A lack of supervision.

    D. Stealing.

3. C source code files end with the following filename extension:

    A. SC.

    B. C.

    C. SEA.

    D. SEE.

4. Pick the correct sentence:

    A. Save it, compile it, link it, run it.

    B. Run it, compile it, save it.

    C. Save it, defile it, eat it.

    D. Beat it, just beat it.

Lesson 1-4: The Required Woes of Editing and Recompiling

Not everything in your C program may go right the first time. You may have accidentally included a typo in your source code: `printf` becomes `prinft` or just `print`, for example. If so, the compiler spits out a vicious error and your program isn't created. Or maybe instead of `world`, the program displays `word1`. That kind of mistake isn't an error. It's more of a boo-boo. But still, it's something that has to be fixed.

To fix a broken program, you usually have to go through two steps:

1. Reedit your source code, and then save the fixed-up file to disk.

2. Recompile the source code, and produce the final repaired program file.

These are still steps in the C language development cycle, discussed in Lesson 1-2. As a programmer, you try to avoid them as much as possible. In real life, however, they happen way too often.

- ✔ It happens.

- ✔ Information on dealing with errors specifically is presented in Lesson 1-5. This lesson, however, tells you the necessary procedures for repairing your source file and then redoing the program.

Reediting your source code file

Your source code file isn't carved in stone — or silicon, for that matter. It can be changed. Sometimes the changes are necessary, in the case of errors and boo-boos. At other times, you may just want to modify your program, adding a feature or changing a message or prompt — what the hard-core C geeks call *tweaking*. To do that, you have to reedit your source code file.

The GOODBYE program, introduced in the preceding lesson, displays a message on the screen: Goodbye, cruel world! Actually, you can make it display almost any message you like. To do so, use your editor and change the source code file so that it displays a different message.

You should do this part now: Use your text editor to reedit the GOODBYE.C source code. If you're using an integrated environment, activate the window that contains the GOODBYE.C source code. (If you have a mouse, click on that window by using the mouse.) At the DOS prompt, use your text editor to reedit the file: Start your editor and load the GOODBYE.C source code file.

After you're in your editor and you see the GOODBYE.C source code on your screen, you can change the message that is displayed. You have to edit only the following line:

```
printf("Goodbye, cruel world!\n");
```

Replace the text Goodbye, cruel world! — and only that part of the line — with any other message. Don't mess with anything else — the \n or stuff outside the double quotes.

As an example, you can delete Goodbye, cruel world and replace it with Farewell, you ugly toad! Don't be afraid to do this! In fact, it's an order: Change the text in your GOODBYE.C source code file to read as follows:

```
printf("Farewell, you ugly toad!\n");
```

This modification changes the program's output to display `Farewell, you ugly toad!` This is such a charming computer message that no PC should start the day without it.

When you're done with your editing, double-check your work. Use your editor's commands to save the file to disk again. Now you're ready to recompile your source code, as covered in the next section.

> ✔ "Reediting your source code file" means to use your text editor to modify the source code, the text file that contains the C language instructions.
>
> ✔ You reedit the source code file to repair an error caught by the compiler or linker or to modify the program. This happens a lot.
>
> ✔ In the Microsoft Visual C++ and Borland C integrated environments, your source code appears in an editing window. Just click on that window by using the mouse or use whatever magic the program has, and make the necessary modifications to your source code.
>
> ✔ When the modifications are complete, save the file to disk again.

> ✔ Saving the file to disk again overwrites the original file. (When you saved GOODBYE.C to disk again in this section, the original file was replaced by the newer version.) So if you want to save the file to disk under a new name, use your editor's Save As command.

Recompiling (or the C equivalent of the "do-over")

Recompiling means to make the program one more time — to rework the steps you went through to create the program originally. This process usually happens after you modify or change the source code, such as was done in the preceding section. Because the source code is different, you have to feed it to the compiler again to generate the new, better (and hopefully bug-free) program.

To recompile, you use the steps outlined in the preceding lesson. In the Borland C integrated environment, for example, you press Alt+F9 to compile, link, and run the program. (Refer to Lesson 1-3 for details about your particular compiler.)

> ✔ After you reedit your source code file, you have to recompile to re-create the program file. This is how you fix an error or modify the program.
>
> ✔ Some C compilers may require relinking as the next step. Refer to Lesson 1-3 to see whether your compiler automatically links or requires you to manually use some sort of LINK command.
>
> ✔ If you see any errors after recompiling, you must re-reedit your source code and then re-recompile again. (Actually, there is only "reediting" and "recompiling"; no sense in getting re-happy.)

"But my compiler won't recompile!"

This is a strange condition, but I've seen it in a few compilers. Essentially, the compiler is looking at the files on disk and seeing that nothing's been changed — even though you've reedited your source code. There are two ways to solve the problem:

1. First, resave your source code to disk. That may do it for a number of compilers.

2. Second, choose a Rebuild or Rebuild All command from your compiler's integrated environment menu. The program should recompile at that point, no matter what.

Tossing out the old and in with the new

Reediting and recompiling are facts of life when you're programming in C. Note that though there is only one *re-* in each of those words, you may do a lot of re-reediting and re-recompiling. Forget about the extra *re-*s; just lie to all your friends and tell them that your C programs all work perfectly the first time.

Occasionally, you may just want to start over. If so, what you have to do is clean out your editor and give yourself some blank paper — or blank screen, in this case — on which to work. You can then build a new program, compile it, link it, run it, and be on with new and wondrous merriment, beating the computer into submission by using your mastery of the C programming language. (Well, maybe in a few more chapters.)

- To start a new program in either the Microsoft Visual C++ or Borland C integrated environments, choose the New menu item from the File menu. This gives you a new, clean editing slate on which to write down your next program. (You do this in the next lesson.)

- Your old projects hang around in the integrated environment until you close their windows. The following two check marks tell you how do that in each of the popular integrated environments.

- In Microsoft Visual C++, you can rid yourself of an old C project by highlighting its source code window and choosing Close from the File menu.

- In Borland C, you can rid yourself of an old C source file by closing its source code window: Click the box in the window's upper left corner or highlight the window and press Alt+F3.

- At the DOS prompt, you use your editor to create a new file. Just start your editor, and it should give you a blank screen on which to work. Then use a new name to save the file you enter to disk.

Lesson 1-4 Quiz

1. Reediting a source code file may be necessary because:

   A. There was an error.

   B. The program didn't do something it was supposed to do and you need to fix it.

   C. Tweaking is eternal.

   D. A, B, and soon C.

2. After you reedit your source code file, you should:

   A. Rerun the program to see whether you fixed the errors.

   B. Recompile and *then* rerun the program to see whether you fixed the errors.

   C. Watch "CNN Headline News" for three hours straight while you await inspiration.

   D. Make a backup in case of nuclear attack.

3. The capital of Nepal is:

   A. Katmandu.

   B. Fondue.

   C. Hairdo.

   D. Doggy doo.

4. To start a new C language program, you:

   A. Start working on a new source code file.

   B. Reformat your hard drive, reinstall your C compiler, and then start over with Lesson 1-1.

   C. Curl up in bed like a sick puppy while everyone who hates you passes by and hits you with a pool cue.

   D. Pray for inspiration and then do answer A.

Lesson 1-5: Dealing with the Heartbreak of Errors

Errors happen. Even the best of programmers get errors. The guys who wrote 1-2-3, WordPerfect, and any other famous software package? They get errors every day. Bill Gates? Errors all over the place. Peter Norton? Laugh while we count the errors together, my acolyte!

Errors are nothing to be embarrassed about. And the best thing is that the compiler tells you, with uncanny accuracy, just what the error is and where it is. Contrast this with your most nightmarish math class: They only wrote "WRONG!" by your calculations no matter how innocent a mistake you made. Yes, computers can be forgiving — and this can actually teach you something.

Yikes! An error! But before you shoot yourself....

Here is a new program, ERROR.C. Note the optimism in the name. This is a flawed C program, one that contains an error (albeit an on-purpose error):

Name: ERROR.C

```
#include <stdio.h>

void main()
{
    printf("This program will error.\n")
}
```

Your job is to type the source code for ERROR.C into your editor. If you're using an integrated environment, such as Microsoft's Visual C++ or Borland C's integrated environment, choose the New command from the File menu. This command starts you off editing in a new window.

Type the source code exactly as it appears. Use the following ERROR.C Cheat sidebar if you need extra assistance in entering the source code.

When you're done and everything looks OK, save the source code file to disk. Name it ERROR.C.

Your next task is to create the program, ERROR. This is done by compiling and then linking using the steps outlined in Lesson 1-3. Refer back there if you need to review the command (or commands). Compile and link now.

Unfortunately, when you compile this program, it produces an error. The next section provides the autopsy.

✔ You can close the GOODBYE.C window now, if you want. You won't be using that program again in this book, but feel free to run it as a demonstration to impress your friends.

✔ Please use the Cheat sidebars that offer extra help in entering the program if you need them. These boxes appear in this part of the book only to offer you extra help in typing programs. Later chapters offer "blow-by-blow" descriptions of how the programs run, plus a little information about typing stuff, but they aren't as generous as this first chapter is.

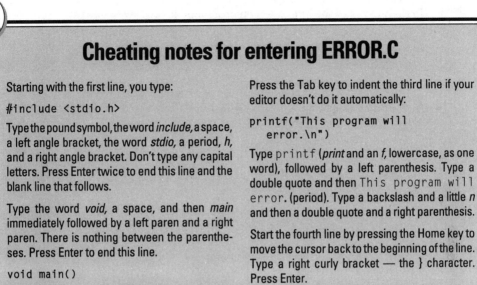

Cheating notes for entering ERROR.C

Starting with the first line, you type:

```
#include <stdio.h>
```

Type the pound symbol, the word *include,* a space, a left angle bracket, the word *stdio,* a period, *h,* and a right angle bracket. Don't type any capital letters. Press Enter twice to end this line and the blank line that follows.

Type the word *void,* a space, and then *main* immediately followed by a left paren and a right paren. There is nothing between the parentheses. Press Enter to end this line.

```
void main()
```

The second line is only one character: Type a left curly bracket — the { character. Press Enter.

```
{
```

Press the Tab key to indent the third line if your editor doesn't do it automatically:

```
printf("This program will
    error.\n")
```

Type printf (*print* and an *f,* lowercase, as one word), followed by a left parenthesis. Type a double quote and then This program will error. (period). Type a backslash and a little *n* and then a double quote and a right parenthesis.

Start the fourth line by pressing the Home key to move the cursor back to the beginning of the line. Type a right curly bracket — the } character. Press Enter.

```
}
```

✔ Throughout this book, you are directed to enter source code and compile various programs. The commands are terse: "Type this" and "Compile it" or just "Run the program." This is regrettably necessary because I can't document every C compiler every time a program has to be created. On the up side, your C compiler commands should become familiar to you in no time.

Boy, did I goof!

The ERROR.C program erred! What a shock.

Don't be alarmed — this was expected. (In fact, you may have seen this type of error before.) Depending on which compiler you're using, you may see some of the following as output:

```
...error.c(4) : error C2143: syntax error : missing ';' before '}'
```

Additional messages may be displayed by the Visual C++ compiler, though the preceding line is in there somewhere. The key to look for is the word *error.* That's followed by a secret error number (C2143, in this case).

Press any key in the integrated environment, if you haven't already.

```
Error ERROR.C 6: Statement missing ;
Error ERROR.C 6: Compound statement missing }
```

In the Borland C integrated environment, this text (or something similar) is displayed in the Message box. The flashing "Error" beacon alerts you to the error right after you press Alt+F9 to compile or run.

If you're using Borland C at the DOS prompt, each error message ends with the text in function main. This is the command line's way of helping you pinpoint where the error happened. (In the integrated environment, the error is highlighted on the screen.)

```
error.c:4: parse error before '}'
```

This error was generated on a UNIX machine. No matter which C compiler you're using, it produces an error message similar to this one or close to the error messages spewed forth from the Microsoft or Borland compilers.

Examining the error message

So far, the error message looks rather rude. It's not that reassuring hand on your shoulder and the kind voice explaining that you boo-booed. Still, what the error message lacks in personality, it makes up for in information.

On the up side, though it's cryptic, the error message is informative. Whatever your compiler, you should be able to single out the following bits of information:

> The program that contained the error, ERROR.C

> The line that contains the error, line 6 (though it may not be — you can't really trust computers too much)

> The type of error, *syntax error* (and possibly what was syntactically wrong)

> The location of the error (before the })

It still may not be clear exactly what's wrong, but you're given many clues. Most important, you're given a line number:

```
The error is in line 6.
```

OK, it's really in line 5, but the C programming language is flexible, and the compiler doesn't discover that "something's missing" until line 6. (We can cut the compiler some slack here.)

The error type is also important. A syntax error means a typo. *Syntax* refers to the way languages are put together. In the C language, a semicolon is required at the end of a sentence, just as periods are used at the end of sentences in English. ERROR.C is missing a semicolon. Your compiler may even tell you that directly:

```
Statement missing ;
```

The solution? You have to reedit the source code file and fix what's wrong. In this case, you would reedit ERROR.C and add the semicolon to the end of line 5. Even if you looked at line 6 (per the output's insistence), you would see nothing wrong there. If so, your eyes would wander back and — being aware of the Missing Semicolon Syndrome — you would see the problem and mend it.

- ✔ Errors are not the end of the world! Everyone gets them.

- ✔ The line number refers to a line in the source-code text file. This is why nearly all text editors use line numbers, which you can see at the top or bottom of the screen or editing window. (It may also be the "row" number.)

- ✔ The Borland integrated environment even positions the cursor — automagically — where the semicolon must be added. This is what you paid extra for.

- ✔ The line number may or may not be accurate. In the case of a missing semicolon, the next line may be the "error line." This holds true with other types of errors in C. Oh well, at least it's close and not a generic honk of the speaker and "ERRORS GALORE, YOU FOOL" plastered on-screen.

- ✔ Examples of syntax errors include forgetting to use the semicolon (which was demonstrated here); leaving off a parenthesis or a double quote mark (") or a curly bracket; forgetting a comma or putting one in the wrong place; and raising the tax on alcohol and cigarettes but not on ice cream.

- ✔ Of course, you may be thinking, "OK, smarty-pants computer, you know what's wrong — fix it!" But computers don't just jump to conclusions like that. This is the evil of "Do what I mean": Computers can't read minds, so *you* must be precise. They are champs, however, at pointing out what's wrong (and almost snobbishly so).

Repairing the malodorous program

To make the world right again, you have to fix the program. This requires editing the source code file, making the needed correction, saving the source code file back to disk, and then recompiling.

The ERROR.C program can be fixed by adding a semicolon. Edit line 5 and add a semicolon to the end of the line. It should read as follows:

```
printf("This program will no longer error.\n");
```

This line should still be indented. I've changed the text in addition to adding the semicolon to the end. Other than those two changes, everything else in the program remains untouched.

Save ERROR.C back to disk.

Recompile the program by using the instructions specific to your compiler, as presented in Lesson 1-3. Everything should go off without a hitch. (If there is a hitch, though, refer to the preceding two sections to find and repair any other errors that may have crept in.)

You can now run the final program and delight in its output:

```
This program will no longer error.
```

- ✔ Fix the file and recompile! Lesson 1-4 elaborates on this subject.

- ✔ You have to press Alt+F5 in the integrated environment to see the program's output. Press Enter to return to the integrated environment.

- ✔ Pull two *R*s out of ERRORS and you have Eros, the Greek god of love. The Roman god of love was Cupid. Replace the *C* in Cupid with *St* and you have Stupid. *Stupid errors* — how lovely!

  I can't always tell you where to fix your programs. ERROR.C is the only program listed in this book that contains an on-purpose error. When you get an error, you should check your error message to see where the error is in your source code. Then cross-check your source code with what's listed in the book. That way, you'll find what's wrong. But when you venture out on your own and experiment, you have only the error message to go by when you're hunting down your own errors.

No need to fill your head with this

There are two kinds of errors: warnings and errors. Some compilers may call the errors "critical" errors. (Sounds like a mistake Siskel and Ebert would make.) Other times, they may be "fatal" errors, like opening a creepy closet in one of those *Friday the 13th* movies.

The warning means "Ooo, this doesn't look tasty, but I'll serve it to you anyway." Chances are, your program will run, but it may not do what you intend. Or it may just be that the compiler is being

touchy. With most DOS C compilers, you can switch off some of the more persnickety warning error messages.

The error, or critical error, means "Dear Lordy, you tried to do something so criminal I cannot morally complete this program." OK, maybe not that severe. But the compiler is unable to complete its task because it just doesn't understand your instructions.

The dreaded linker errors

Don't dispense with the ERROR.C file just yet. Don't close the window, and don't zap the project. (If you did, use your editor to "load" the ERROR.C file and prepare to reedit.)

Change the third line in the ERROR.C source code file to read as follows:

```
pirntf("This program will error.\n");
```

In case you don't see it, the word printf has been edited to read pirntf — the *i* and *r* are transposed, which is a common typo. But this isn't a syntax error. The way C works is that it just assumes that pirntf is something you're serious about, and it goes about its business. However, the linker, which glues program files together, catches the error, wondering what pirntf is all about.

Save the ERROR.C file to disk. Then recompile it by using your compiler.

There will be an error! Refer to the following section to review the details of the error your particular linker displays:

```
...error.c(3) : warning C4013 'pirntf' undefined; assuming ...
Linking...
ERROR.OBJ(...error.c) : error L2029: '_pirntf' unresolved external
 LINK returned error code 2.
Creating browser database...
ERROR.EXE - 1 error(s), 1 warning(s)
```

Here you can see that an error takes place during the compiling stage, but that's considered OK. In fact, it's one of the "warning" errors mentioned in the Techy sidebar a few paragraphs ago. During the "Linking . . ." stage of the program is when the error's true fatalism is disclosed.

If you're using Microsoft C at the DOS prompt, the error message is displayed as follows:

```
ERROR.OBJ(...error.c) : error L2029: '_pirntf' unresolved external
There was 1 error detected.
```

It's harder to tell where the error took place here. However — *major hint time* — error message numbers in Visual C++ are prefixed with *C* and *L*. *C* means a compiler error, and *L* means a linker error. In the preceding lines, the enigmatic error number is L2029, a linker error.

(You are expected, of course, to contend with this confusion if you're using Visual C++ at the DOS prompt anyway.)

After pressing the "any" key (which is secretly the Enter key), the Borland integrated environment shows you the following line in the Message box:

```
Linker error: Undefined symbol _pirntf in module ERROR.C
```

At the DOS prompt, the error is displayed as follows:

```
Turbo Link  Version 5.1 Copyright (c) 1992 Borland International
Undefined symbol _pirntf in module error.c
```

Golly, there is also a dreaded warning error about a prototype. Obviously, the compiler has had its fill of your programming! Seriously, the critical error message involves the word *link,* which is your clue to a linker error.

```
Undefined symbols: _pirntf
```

The gist of what's going on here is the dreaded "undefined symbol," usually followed by the offensive and otherwise misspelled word, prefixed by an underline.

- ✔ A linker error is earmarked by the word *link* somewhere in the error message, though in Microsoft C at the DOS prompt, you must have a keen eye to spy the *L* in the error number.

- ✔ It's harder to accept linker errors when your compiler automatically links for you. Still, they happen. And unlike compiler errors, all linker errors are "fatal."

- ✔ Refer to Lesson 1-2 for additional information about the linker's role in creating a program.

Dealing with linker errors

The linker's job is to pull together different pieces of a program. If it spots something it doesn't recognize, such as `pirntf`, it assumes, "Hey, maybe this is something from another part of the program." So the error slides by with a "warning" initially. But when the linker tries to look for the unrecognized word, it hoists its error flags high in the full breeze.

To fix the linker errors, you follow the same steps as you did when you repaired compiler errors. Using the error message as a guide, locate the offending line in your source code. Then fix the typo or otherwise mend the line to make the program right.

In ERROR.C, second edition, you have to edit the line that contains the weird `pirntf` to read more properly as `printf`. Just move the *i* and the *r.* Use your text editor to make the change. You might want the final result to look like this:

```
printf("This program will not error.\n");
```

Save the change to disk.

Recompile the program again. This time, it should link up without any errors.

✔ Linker error dead giveaway: Underlines!

✔ With linker errors, you usually get the exact line number plus the odious word. If you don't get a line number, at least you get the offending word. Use your editor's Search command to locate that word in the source code. The fix is the same regardless of the cause: Edit the file and recompile.

✔ Linker errors usually mean that a program wasn't created. This is good because without the missing piece, the EXE program might crash your computer.

Lesson 1-5 Quiz

1. What could the following error message mean?

```
Error error.c 6: Statement missing ; in function main
```

    A. There is an error in line 6.

    B. There is an error in line 5.

    C. There is an error somewhere in the vicinity of your computer.

    D. Probably A and B, though C looks suspiciously true.

2. Why is the semicolon so important?

    A. You haven't told me yet.

    B. I'm just typing the programs.

    C. I assume that you'll clue me in to it in Lesson 1-6.

    D. But I'm still having fun in the meantime.

3. Why does the linker catch spelling errors?

    A. Because the compiler learned to spell in a California school.

    B. The spelling error may be another piece of the program, so when the linker can't find that piece, it displays an error.

    C. What else is there for the linker to do?

    D. The linker is really the essence of your third-grade English teacher and, though she has long since passed on, she still despises you.

4. How should you react to an error?

    A. Get mad at the guy who sold you the compiler.

    B. "I'm a failure! I'm stupid and ugly! Even my dog hates me! I just burned the rice."

    C. Fix the file, recompile.

    D. Zip off a résumé to Microsoft boasting of your prowess!

All about errors!

A common programming axiom is that you don't write computer programs as much as you remove errors from them. Errors are everywhere, and removing them is why it can take years to write good software.

Syntax errors: The most common and first found by the compiler as it tries to churn the text you write into instructions the computer can understand. Most syntax errors are typos and other faux pas. The compiler usually points them out for you and lists line numbers and categories of offense.

Linker errors: Primarily involve misspelled commands. In advanced C programming, when you're working with several source files, or modules, to create a larger program, linker errors may involve missing modules. Also, if your linker requires some "library" file and it can't be found, another type of error message is displayed.

Run-time errors: Generated by the program when it runs. They aren't bugs; instead, they're things that look totally acceptable to the compiler and linker but just don't do quite what you intended. (This happens often in C.) The most common run-time error is a *null pointer assignment.* You aggravate over this one later.

Bugs: The final type of error you encounter. The compiler diligently creates the program you wrote, but whether that program does what you intended is up to the test. If it doesn't, you must work on the source code some more. Bugs include everything from things that work slowly to ones that work unintentionally or not at all. These are the hardest things to figure out and are usually your highest source of frustration.

Lesson 1-6: Looking at the C Language (or Parts Is Parts)

Any new language will look weird to you. Your native tongue has a certain cadence or word pattern. And the letters all fit together in a certain way. Foreign languages, they have weird characters: ç, ü, ø, and letter combinations that look strange in English: Gwynedd, Zgierz, Qom, and Idaho.

Strange new things require getting used to. It requires a road map so that you know what's what. There's really no point in blindly typing in a C program unless you have a faint idea of what's going on.

The big picture

Figure 1-3 outlines the GOODBYE.C program's source code, which was used as an example in Lesson 1-3.

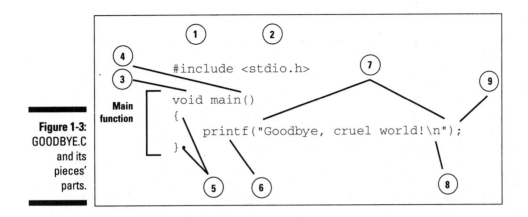

Figure 1-3:
GOODBYE.C
and its
pieces'
parts.

Each program must have a starting point. When you run a program, DOS sends it off on its way — like launching a ship. As its last dock-master duty, DOS hurls the microprocessor headlong into the program. The microprocessor then takes the program's helm at that specific starting point.

In all C programs, the starting point is the main() function. Every C program has one, even GOODBYE.C and the other C programs you have created thus far. The main() function is the engine that makes the program work, which displays the message on the screen.

Other C programs may carry out other tasks in their main() function. But whatever's there, it's the first instruction given to the computer when the program runs.

- main() is the name given to the first (or primary) function in every C program. C programs can have other functions, but main() is the first one.

- It's a common convention to follow a C language function name with parentheses, as in main(). It doesn't mean anything. Everyone does it, and I'm doing it here so that you don't freak when you see it elsewhere.

- In Borland C++, you may have seen the error message say "in function main." This message refers to the main function — the void main() thing that contains the C language instructions you've been writing.

- A function is a machine — it's a set of instructions that does something. C programs can have many functions in them, though the main function is the first function in a C program. It's required.

Function. Get used to that word.

Pieces' parts

Here are some interesting pieces of the C program shown in Figure 1-3:

1. #include is known as a preprocessor directive, which sounds impressive, and it may not be the correct term, but you're not required to memorize it anyhow. What it does is tell the compiler to "include" another program or file along with your source code, which generally avoids a lot of little, annoying errors that would otherwise occur.

2. <stdio.h> is a filename hugged by angle brackets (which is the C language's attempt to force you to use all sorts of brackets and whatnot). The whole statement #include <stdio.h> tells the compiler to use the file STDIO.H, which contains standard I/O, or input/output, commands required by most C programs.

3. void main identifies the name of the function main. The void identifies the type of function or what the function produces. In the case of main, it doesn't produce squat, and the C term for that is "void." (Lesson 6-3 elaborates on this.)

4. Two empty parentheses follow the function name. Sometimes there may be items in these parentheses, which is covered in Chapter 5.

5. The curly brackets or braces enclose the function, hugging in tight all its parts. Everything between { and } is part of the function main() in Figure 1-3.

6. printf is a C language instruction, part of the programming language that eventually tells the computer what to do.

7. Belonging to printf are more parentheses. In this case, the parentheses enclose text, or a "string" of text. Everything between the double quotes (") is part of printf's text string.

8. An interesting part of the text string is \n. That's the backslash character and a little *n*. What it represents is the character produced by pressing the Enter key. What it does is to end the text string with a "new line." (This is elaborated on in Lesson 2-5.)

9. Finally, the printf line, or statement, ends with a semicolon. The semicolon is how the C compiler knows when one statement ends and another begins — like a period at the end of a sentence. Even though printf is the only instruction in this program, the semicolon is still required.

✔ Text in a program is referred to as a *string*. For example, "la-de-da" is a string of text. The string is enclosed by double quotes.

✔ The C language is composed of keywords that appear in statements. The statements end in semicolons, just as sentences in English end in periods. (Don't frazzle your wires over memorizing this right yet.)

The C language itself — the keywords

The C language is really rather brief. There are only 33 *keywords* in C. If only French were that easy! Table 1-1 shows the keywords that make up the C language.

Table 1-1	C Language Keywords	
asm	enum	signed
auto	extern	sizeof
break	float	static
case	for	struct
char	goto	switch
const	if	typedef
continue	int	union
default	long	unsigned
do	register	void
double	return	volatile
else	short	while

Not bad, eh? But these aren't all the words you find in the C language. Other words or instructions are called *functions*. These includes jewels like printf and several dozen other common functions that assist the basic C language keywords in creating programs.

Since we're all using DOS, additional functions specific to DOS are piled on top of the standard C armada of functions. And if you get into Windows, you find hoards of Windows-specific functions that bring C's full vocabulary into the hundreds. And no, you don't really have to memorize any of them. This is why all C compilers come with a language reference, which you'll undoubtedly keep close to your PC's glowing bosom.

Languages are more than a collection of words. They also involve grammar, or properly sticking together the words so that understandable ideas are conveyed. This concept is completely beyond the grasp of the modern legal community.

In addition to grammar, languages require rules, exceptions, jots and tittles, and all sorts of fun and havoc. Programming languages are similar to spoken language in that they have various parts and lots of rules.

✔ You will never be required to memorize the 33 keywords.

✔ In fact, of the 33 keywords, you may end up using only half on a regular basis.

✔ Some of the keywords are real words! Others are abbreviations or combinations of two or more words. Still others are cryptograms of the programmer's girlfriends' names.

✔ Each of the keywords has its own set of problems. You don't just use the keyword else, for example; you must use it *in context.*

✔ Functions like printf require a set of parentheses and lots of stuff inside the parentheses. (Don't fret over this right now; just nod your head and smile in agreement, "Yes, printf does require lots of stuff.")

✔ By the way, the fact that printf is a C function and not a keyword is why the #include <stdio.h> thing is required at the beginning of a program. The STDIO.H file contains the instructions telling the compiler what exactly printf is and does. If you edit out the #include <stdio.h> line, the compiler produces a funky "I don't know that printf thing" type of error.

Other C language components

There are many other parts to the C language, making it look rather bizarre to the new programmer. But right now, all that's standing between ignorance and knowledge is *time,* so don't dwell on what you don't know. Instead, keep these few points rolling around in your mind like so many knowledge nuggets:

✔ The C language uses words — keywords, functions, and so forth — as its most basic elements.

✔ Included with the words are symbols. Sometimes these are called *operators,* and at other times they're called something else. For example, the plus sign (+) is used in C to add things.

✔ The words have options and rules about how they're used. These rules are all referenced in the C manuals that came with your compiler. You don't have to memorize all of them, though a few of them become second nature to you as you learn and use C.

✔ Parentheses are used to group some of the important items required by C words.

The words are put together to create *statements,* which are similar to sentences in English. The statements all end with a semicolon.

✔ Braces are used to group parts of a program. Some of the words use braces to group their belongings, and all the separate functions you create within a program are grouped by braces. In Figure 1-3 and in all your C programs so far, for example, the braces have been used to contain the belongings of the main function.

✔ All this stuff put together (and more stuff I dare not discuss at this point) makes up the syntax of the C language. Syntax is how languages are put together.

✔ Lesson 4-4 contains more information about formatting a C program.

Lesson 1-6 Quiz

1. The main function in every C language program is called:

   A. Numero uno.

   B. main.

   C. Primus.

   D. Survival.

2. C language keywords are:

   A. The "words" of the C language.

   B. Easier than French keywords but still as rude.

   C. Uttered only in candlelit reverence by the C Language Gurus.

   D. As numerous as the stars and nearly as distant.

3. In addition to the keywords are:

   A. Functions, such as `printf`.

   B. Functions that came with your compiler which do all sorts of fun things with DOS and Windows.

   C. Functions you can make up yourself.

   D. Probably all of the above.

4. Functions require parentheses because:

   A. They talk in whispers.

   B. The parentheses keep the function warm.

   C. The parentheses hold various things required by or belonging to the function.

   D. What's a function?

5. A telltale sign of any C program is the curly brackets or braces. Using what you know of C so far, draw in the braces where they should appear in the following program:

```
void main()

___
    printf("Goodbye, cruel world!\n");

___
```

Lesson 1-7: Input and Output (with Which We Must Up Put)

Computers are really all about input and output — the old I/O of days gone by. What cowboys used to sing about. The wimmin folk would want to dance real slow. Maybe cry. It was a sentimental thing, y'all. Something fancy, dooded-up city slickers read about in dime magazines.

A-hem!

Input and output: You type something in and get a response, ask a question and get an answer, put in 50 cents and get your pop — things along those lines. This goes along with what was presented in Lesson 1-2: It is your job as a programmer to write a program that does something. At this point in the learning process, triviality is OK. Soon, however, you'll be writing programs that really do something.

Introduce yourself to Mr. Computer

To meet the needs of input and output — the old I/O — you can try the following program, WHORU.C — which is "who are you," as well as can be stuffed into a DOS filename. Please don't go calling this program "horror-you" (which could be spelled another way, but this is a family book).

The purpose of this program is to type your name at the keyboard and then have the computer display your name on the screen, along with a nice, friendly greeting.

Name: WHORU.C

```
#include <stdio.h>

void main()
{
    char me[20];

    printf("What is your name?");
    scanf("%s",&me);
    printf("Darn glad to meet you, %s!\n",me);
}
```

Tips and stuff for entering the WHORU.C source code

WHORU.C starts with the #include thing, which you should type as follows:

```
#include <stdio.h>
```

Then comes a blank line (press Enter) and the all-important main function, the first function in any C program:

```
void main()
```

void is followed by a space and then main. Glued to the *n* in main are a left and right parenthesis with nothing between them. The next line (line 2) contains a sole curly bracket:

```
{
```

The left brace encloses all the commands and C language stuff that belong to the main function. Press Enter after typing the brace. (All the lines that follow this brace — up until the final left brace — are C language statements. Each ends in a semicolon.)

```
    char me[20];
```

Press the Tab key to indent this line if your editor doesn't do it automatically. The line begins with char, followed by a space, and then me and the number 20 in square brackets. (The square brackets are underneath the curly brackets on your keyboard.) The line ends in a semicolon.

Line 4 is blank:

Press Enter alone, making this a blank line.

Press Tab to indent the next line, line 5, if it's not automatically indented (and the same holds true for the next two lines):

```
    printf("What is your name?");
```

The line starts with printf. Then comes a left paren, (, and What is your name? is enclosed in double quotes. Then comes a right paren,), and then the semicolon. Press Enter to end the line.

Press the Tab key to indent line 6 if it's not indented automatically. Then type scanf, *scan* plus little *f*, which is another function like printf. It's followed by a left paren and then %s ("percent-s") in double quotes, a comma, an ampersand (&), the word *me,* and a right paren. The line ends in a semicolon. This is the most complex line in the program — watch what you type:

```
    scanf("%s",&me);
```

Line 7 starts with an indent and then another printf function. This time, notice that there are two items between its parentheses. The first item is in double quotes. Don't forget the double quotes or you'll get an error! The text in double quotes ends with %s (percent-s), an exclamation point (!), and then \n (backslash-n). The *s* and the *n* must be lowercase:

```
    printf("Darn glad to meet you,
    %s!\n",me);
```

After the final double quote comes a comma and then me. The line ends with the final paren and a semicolon. Press Enter.

Line 8 contains the final curly bracket enclosing the main function. Press the Home key to move the cursor to the beginning of the line if you need to. Press Enter after typing the } character:

```
}
```

To enter the WHORU.C source code, start off with a clean slate. In your integrated environment, choose New from the File menu. At the DOS prompt, use your editor to summon up a blank screen on which you can enter this new program.

Type the source code into your editor. You have my permission to browse over the detailed instructions in the WHORU.C Cheat sidebar for extra assistance. Double-check everything. Don't bother with any details just yet. Type and hum, if it pleases you.

Save the file to disk. Name it WHORU.C.

Don't compile this program just yet. That happens in the next section.

- ✔ Use the New command on the File menu to get a new editing window in Visual C++ or the Borland C integrated environment.

- ✔ Left paren is the (character. Right paren is the) character. *Paren* is short for parentheses or a type of steak sauce. (It's also not a "real" word and is frowned on by English teachers of the high-and-tight bun.)

- ✔ Line 6 may look complex — and it is. But soon, all those tidbits will become old friends to you. Lesson 2-5 tells you more (if you can't wait — but finish here first).

- ✔ A *variable* is a storage place, where you put information in a program. A string variable, such as me in WHORU.C, is used to hold text. Numeric variables hold numbers and values. Chapter 3 douses any burning curiosity you have about the subject.

Compiling and running WHORU.C

Compile the WHORU.C source code by using your compiler. Refer to Lesson 1-3 if you need to review the necessary steps. (If your compiler requires linking as a separate step, link the program as well.)

If there are syntax or other errors, double-check your source code with what is listed in this book. Review the preceding points to make sure that everything was entered properly or refer to the Cheat sidebar titled "Tips and stuff for entering the WHORU.C source code" for more information. Be on the lookout for jots and tittles — parentheses, double quotes, backslashes, percent signs, sneeze splotches, or other unusual things on your monitor's screen.

If the compiler meets with success, you will have a second file on disk, WHORU.OBJ. That object file is then linked by your linker to create the final program to run, WHORU.EXE.

Don't run the program just yet! That's covered in the next section.

- Fix any errors by reediting the source code and then recompile (refer to Lesson 1-6).

- A common beginner error: Unmatched double quotes! Make sure that you always use a set of "s (double quotes). If you miss one, you get an error. Also make sure that the parentheses and curly brackets are included in pairs; left one first, right one second.

- If you have any linking errors, take note of the line number and rework the source code if you need to.

The reward

If your compiler doesn't automatically run the WHORU program, run it now. Choose the Run command or type the name of the program — WHORU — at the DOS prompt:

```
C> WHORU
```

Your output should look like this:

```
What is your name?
```

The program is now waiting for you to type your name. Go ahead: Type your name! Press Enter.

If you typed **Buster**, the next line is displayed:

```
Darn glad to meet you, Buster!
```

- If the output looks different or the program doesn't work right or generates an error, review your source code again. Reedit to fix any errors and then recompile. Refer to Lesson 1-5 if you need extra help.

- You have to press Alt+F5 in the integrated environment to see that the program printed your name.

- I/O is input/output, what computers do best.

- I/O, I/O, it's off to program I go . . . .

- This is an example of a program that takes input and generates output. It doesn't do anything with the input, but it does qualify for I/O.

- In the nearby WHORU.C blow-by-blow sidebar, you find a full description of how WHORU.C works. These blow-by-blow boxes appear more frequently as you get deeper into this book. Use them to help you understand how the program works and what each individual whatchamacallit in the source code does.

Secret information about how the WHORU.C program works–shhh!

When your C program runs, the first thing the computer does is to carry out any instructions in the main function. (Other stuff may be done first, but that's not important at this stage.) In WHORU.C, there are four instructions in the main function. Here is how the computer deals with each one:

```
char me[20];
```

The preceding line tells the compiler to create a string variable. char, short for *char*acter, identifies a storage place for characters (as opposed to a storage place for numbers or old shoes your wife won't throw away). The name of the string variable is me. (You can name a variable almost anything; Lesson 3-3 posts the rules.) The number in the brackets tells the compiler to set aside 20 characters of storage space — which means 20 bytes — to be used by the me variable. You can store a string in me's cubbyhole that's 20 characters or fewer in length.

```
printf("What is your name?");
```

This line tells the compiler to execute the printf function. printf displays the text string, What

is your name?, in quotes. This is the program's prompt, begging for input.

```
scanf("%s",&me);
```

The preceding line tells the compiler to execute the scanf function. scanf reads the keyboard for a specific type of input. That input is defined by %s, which tells scanf to look for a string of text and to stop looking when you press the Enter key. The &me part of scanf's function tells the compiler to store the text entered in the me variable.

```
printf("Darn glad to meet you,
    %s!\n",me);
```

This final line tells the compiler to execute the printf function. The text in quotes is displayed, but printf spies the %s in those quotes. The %s means, "I'm a blank here. I need something to fill in the blank. A string of text is what I'm looking for." The string used is the contents of the me variable, which is specified after the text in quotes and a comma.

Believe it or not, all this stuff will make sense to you in just a few short lessons. You'll be a true, rebellious C programmer in no time flat.

Lesson 1-7 Quiz

1. Computers are really about:

    A. Driving normal, well-adjusted people into a slow, twisted fit of insanity.

    B. Doing math and other nerdy stuff.

    C. Input and output.

    D. Making Bill Gates even more money.

2. I/O is:

    A. Line 43 on your 1040 form.

    B. Flight 415 from Des Moines to Akron.

C. Not possible because you can't divide a letter of the alphabet by zero.

D. Input and output.

3. B&O is:

A. Binary output.

B. Baltimore and Ohio.

C. Body odor.

D. $200 a visit if you own all four railroads.

4. "Oops! I see a syntax error. This means that I should:"

A. Compare my source code with the one shown in this book, reedit, save it again to disk, and then recompile.

B. Sulk.

C. Return this book and buy a cheap and abject imitation.

D. Return this book and buy a technical book I'll never read, which will join the many other tomes I have of its ilk.

Bonus question — worth 50 points!

Name three of the most influential members of Congress during the Hoover administration.

A.

B.

C.

Lesson 1-8: After the Mess Comes Organization

This is a bonus lesson, thrown in now because you don't really notice the "mess" problem until it gets way out of hand. What I'm referring to is the detritus left on your hard drive when you develop C programs; the many companion files and whatnot the compiler creates when it transforms your source code into a program file.

> ✔ Detritus \di-'trit-es\ *n*. 1. Gravel or bits and pieces of nature that result from disintegration. 2. Crumbs, pebbles, shattered bits of your childhood dreams, anything small and meaningless, etc.

It's innocent to assume that writing C programs is a neat and tidy affair. But like that person who shows up at the park to feed just one pigeon, you soon learn how untidy the operation can be.

The C compiler produces lots of stuff

A C compiler spins through your hard drive like a tornado, spewing out files like toy trucks and pieces of stuffed animals from my son's crib. You need to keep that stuff organized. Furthermore, you have to know which of the files are worth keeping and which are so much flotsam that — like things the cat coughs up — just keep appearing all over the place.

For every C program you create, at least three files are left on your hard drive:

> The source code file, ending in C
>
> The object file, ending in OBJ
>
> The program file, ending in EXE

Some compilers may toss in even more files and stuff, which means that if you've written the few programs already introduced in this chapter, you may have 15 or more files lurking around on your hard disk.

> ✔ When you edit a source code file, your editor may copy the original file to a backup, which may have the extension BAK. Do not delete these files indiscriminately!
>
> ✔ Microsoft Visual C++ creates two additional intermittent files I've seen: a BSC file and an SBR file. BSC is a browser database file. The SBR is the source browser file. Other extensions you may see are VCW, WSP, ICO, BMP, MAP, and a host of others — though these extensions appear primarily when you're writing Windows-specific programs.
>
> ✔ Borland C++ may generate PRJ (project) files, but only when you're working with large projects or have created a project in the integrated environment. Don't delete the PRJ files!
>
> ✔ Larger C projects may also have files ending in H, MAK, and other assorted extensions. Do not delete these files! To keep them organized, I recommend putting these projects in their own subdirectories, which is covered later in this lesson.

What to keep, what to toss

I wouldn't recommend deleting any files right now. However, the two types of files that are the most important end in C and EXE. Everything else is suspect and may be deleted to save space on your hard drive — but, again, not at this stage in the learning process.

> ✔ As long as you have your source code (*.C) files up-to-date and intact, you can rebuild any program you've created.

✔ The OBJ files can be deleted after a program is created. (For larger programming projects, I recommend keeping them around. If you don't, the compiler has to re-create them all if you have to rebuild the program. This adds time to the whole process.)

✔ Don't delete any backup (*.BAK) source code files until after your project is finished and working fine. The reason is *voodoo*. Sometimes, changing some little thing in a source code file causes the program to just start acting weird. If you have the backup file handy, you can restore it to get the program working properly again. (Delete the original source code file, rename the BAK file to C, recompile.)

(I don't know why C programs do this, but it's true: You change one tiny thing and the program doesn't run anymore. With backup files, you can easily restore the program to the way it was before you started messing with it. Then carefully, *carefully,* try editing again.)

Organizing everything

Just like any other project on your computer, each C language project you create should have its own directory or maybe a branch of subdirectories.

For example, you should create a general directory for your C projects. Call it CPROJ or maybe PROJECTS or CSTUFF. Put this directory in the same "branch" as your C compiler or stick it right off the root directory.

Under the CSTUFF directory, you should create subdirectories, one for each of your C projects. The purpose here is to organize. You'll know that anything in CSTUFF is a C programming project, so any additional subdirectories indicate individual projects you may be working on or have worked on in the past.

The first directory you should create is a LEARN directory, in which you toss the projects outlined in this book plus any other work you do when you're experimenting. You may also want a KILL directory, in which you put projects that are OK to delete at a later time. (Some call this directory TEMP, but I'm a violent type and prefer KILL.)

Other directories should appear according to the projects you work on. Want to write a fancy file-sorting program? Put it in the FFSORT directory. (You can name the directories after the projects.) Writing a shoot-'em-up game? Put it into SHOOT.

Figure 1-4 shows how such a tree structure works. Note that this "branch" can go anywhere: under your compiler's directory, off the root directory, in a general PROJECTS or WORK directory, wherever.

✔ If you've already started putting files just anywhere, go ahead and move them to a permanent location in a CSTUFF or PROJECTS directory.

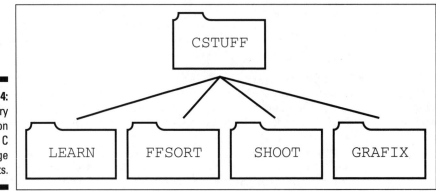

Figure 1-4:
Subdirectory organization for your C language projects.

✔ You create directories by using the MD command. Files are moved by using the MOVE command with DOS 6; to move files, you must use the COPY command and then the DEL command in versions before DOS 6.

✔ Why organize? Primarily because it helps keep your program files together. C creates a lot of file by-product. That stuff can easily get lost in a huge directory full of files. Especially when you move on to creating larger projects, it's just nicer to keep your project files in their own directories.

✔ All this file stuff is carefully explained in *DOS For Dummies*. Advanced subdirectory and organizational stuff is presented in *More DOS For Dummies*. Both are from IDG Books Worldwide.

Lesson 1-8 Quiz

1. For every program you write in C, several additional files are created. Among them:

   A. Files ending in C, OBJ, EXE, and maybe BAK.

   B. Files ending in WAM, BOO, LEE, and maybe UGH.

   C. They're breeding like rabbits! Please! Make them stop!

   D. Several responsible congressmen, who usually vote in the minority.

2. The most important files worth keeping are C and EXE because:

   A. A file ending in C is the source code file, and EXE is the program created from it.

   B. This is the C language, and it's pointless to keep PAS and ASM files in this instance.

   C. Those filename extensions can both easily be typed with the left hand.

   D. Everything else, it's just a trifle.

3. The capital of Manitoba is:

    A. Winnebago

    B. Winnipeg

    C. Whinypug

    D. Sasquatch

4. Creating a subdirectory structure for your C programs will help you:

    A. Learn more about DOS.

    B. Lose files and programs more efficiently than shoving everything into the root directory.

    C. Organize your C programs and keep you sane.

    D. Lower your cholesterol and lose that spare tire.

Bonus question — worth 1 gazillion points!

I'm thinking of a number between 1 and 10:

    A. Is it 5?

    B. Is it 3?

    C. Is it 9?

    D. Is it 2?

Lesson 1-9: Important Rules of C You'll Never Remember

C is full of rules. You learn this right away because you keep on forgetting them, which causes the compiler to spit nasty error messages at you. It's a fact of life — something you must put up with, like rude drivers, higher taxes, and funny noises your body makes in formal public settings.

A word of warning before starting: There's no need to memorize these rules! Most of them come into play later, when you write C programs that may actually violate them.

The helpful RULES program

To help you understand the most easily offendable C rules, I've summarized them in a program you can write, called RULES. It displays several lines of text reminding you of the basic rules of C:

Name: RULES.C

```
#include <stdio.h>

void main()
{
    printf("Braces come in pairs!\n");
    printf("Comments come in pairs!\n");
    printf("All statements end with a semicolon!\n");
    printf("Spaces are optional!\n");
    printf("Must have a main function!\n");
    printf("C is done mostly in lowercase.\
It's a case-sensitive language.\n");
    printf("Don't let the underlines bother you!\n");
    printf("Declare variables before you use them!\n");
}
```

Type the source code for RULES.C into your editor. If you're in an integrated environment, start off with a new editing window by choosing New from the File menu. (You can close any other open editing windows; save the files in them if you need to.)

Shallow information on entering the RULES.C source code

This program starts with #include<stdio.h> and the void main() — just like all the other C programs you've written thus far. The next line is the first curly bracket, the one that holds tight all the belongings of the main() function.

All those printf functions are followed by parentheses and a line of text — a *string* — in double quotes. All the strings end with the \n, the backslash little *n* character. All the lines — the *statements* — end in semicolons.

The eighth and ninth lines are actually one statement, both parts of a single printf function:

```
printf("C is done mostly in
    lowercase.\
It's a case-sensitive
    language.\n");
```

The line has been split in two using the backslash at the end of line 8. Line 9 starts off with the rest of the text string, which ends with the \n and then the double quote, paren, and semicolon.

Yes, these notes are getting brief. Indeed, this is the final Cheat box in this book. If you need additional help, scrutinize the program listing with those generic reading glasses you can get at any drugstore.

If you need extra help weaving your fingers around some of the rougher spots in RULES.C, use the nearby Cheat box. When you're done and you've double-checked what you've typed, save the file to disk as RULES.C.

Compile the program. Refer back to Lesson 1-3 if you need extra help remembering how to compile. If you get any errors, you have to reedit the source code and then recompile. Lesson 1-5 deals with errors; Lesson 1-4 tells you how to reedit and recompile.

Run the final program, RULES.EXE, if your compiler doesn't do that automatically. Your output should look like this:

```
Braces come in pairs!
Comments come in pairs!
All statements end with a semicolon!
Spaces are optional!
Must have a main function!
C is done mostly in lowercase. It's a case-sensitive language.
Don't let the underlines bother you!
Declare variables before you use them!
```

 ✔ Darn that integrated environment! Press Alt+F5 to see the rules displayed. Press Enter when you're done.

 ✔ Note that lines 8 and 9, though split in the source code, produce a single line of output. This is because only the \n characters tell the printf function to produce a new line of text. In fact, the \n combination is called a *newline*. (More combinations are shown in Lesson 2-5.)

 ✔ These are all the rules? Ha! You should be so lucky. Basically, you should follow the cockroach truism here: For every rule listed here, there are ten more lurking in your kitchen cabinets! Seriously, these rules are the most commonly violated — at least the ones I seem to goof up all the time.

Bonus program time!

Consider this string of text:

```
"This is a string of text."
```

String is the name of that thing. That thing is a string. It's text, nestled between two double quotes, and it's the way the C language deals with lines of text.

This chapter has used the printf function many times to display text, similar to the preceding string. In just about every case, the string ends with the following doodad:

```
\n
```

This is C-Greek for "gimme a new line of text." The n actually stands for *new* in "new line" (though they write it as one word: newline).

The program you just created, RULES.C, uses \n all over to keep each rule on its on line. This makes the output of the RULES program easy to read. To drive this home, edit the RULES.C source code file again.

In your editor, delete all the \n characters: search for \n and replace it with nothing (if you know how to work your editor's search-and-replace function).

Save the file to disk and recompile it. If any errors sprout, reedit your source code and recompile.

Run the program. Its output resembles this ugly clot of text:

```
Braces come in pairs!Comments come in pairs!All statements end
with a semicolon!Spaces are optional!Must have a main function!C
is done mostly in lowercase. It's a case-sensitive language. Don't
let the underlines bother you!Declare variables before you use
them!
```

Without the \n (newline ding-a-ling) in the text, all the lines print one after the other — a jumbled mess. With the \n, the printf function sticks a newline character — like pressing Enter — at the end of each line and makes it all look proper.

- ✔ In C, the \n character is used in a text string as though the Enter key were pressed.
- ✔ It's always \n with a little *n*. C is mostly lowercase.
- ✔ The \n is called *newline*, though calling it slash-n or backslash-n is acceptable, but as long as you don't say that aloud.
- ✔ Table 2-1 in Lesson 2-5 lists other characters of a similar nature to \n.

Lesson 1-9 Quiz

1. Which of the following is a C language rule you plan on goofing up the most?

   A. Forgetting to end a statement with a semicolon.

   B. Thinking that \n"); couldn't be part of a program and that the author's elbow must have somehow accidentally bopped the keyboard.

   C. Forgetting to save my files to disk.

D. Forgetting to pair up { and } as well as (and) and sometimes < and > but never [and].

2. Semicolons are required at the end of:

    A. A line.

    B. A C language statement, which may or may not be a line but is more of an ethereal thing at this stage in my understanding of the C language.

    C. An operation where they remove most of your colon.

    D. The first half of an independent clause or compound sentence.

3. Which is correct?

    A. A string of text.

    B. An agglomeration of text.

    C. A second helping of text, with double-quote topping.

    D. A semicolon of text.

4. When I see \n, I think:

    A. The n subdirectory.

    B. Lordy, can this get any more cryptic?

    C. Newline, like New Line Cinema and their wonderful Freddie Krueger films.

    D. There's an n lurking to the right of a backslash.

Chapter 1 Final Exam

1. Write a C program that displays the following message on the screen:

   ```
   10,000 years of human development so I could
   display this on my computer. Wow!
   ```

2. Approximately how many ways are there to write a C program that displays the message in question 1?

   A. Dozens.

   B. Hundreds.

   C. Thousands.

   D. Millions.

3. The C programs you've typed in so far start with:

   A. `#include <studio.h>`.

   B. `£include <stdio.hach>`.

   C. `#include <stdio.h>`.

   D. `#include <mr.pointy>`.

4. The next thing in a C program is:

   A. `main void()`.

   B. `avoid main()`.

   C. `void main()`.

   D. `Like, void man()`.

5. The main function in all C programs is called:

   A. `void`.

   B. `main`.

   C. `first`.

   D. `{ and }`.

6. Surrounding the main function — holding it together — are:

   A. Gluons.

   B. Curly brackets or braces.

   C. Parentheses.

   D. These little jobbies: A and Ω.

7. They can send a man to the moon, so why can't they:

    A. Do anything of consequence since then?

    B. Figure out that you need more women's restrooms than men's?

    C. Deliver mail across town in less than three days?

    D. Make a decent decaffeinated coffee?

8. C is composed of:

    A. Words, statements, functions, and other stuff I haven't learned yet.

    B. Random characters and text, making it look like a cat trying to type.

    C. Curly braces and stuff like that.

    D. Snakes and snails and puppy-dog tails.

9. Statements in C, similar to sentences in a human language, end with what character?

    A. Opus from Bloom County.

    B. The period.

    C. A semicolon.

    D. This character: } — I don't know what it's called.

10. Text enclosed in double quotes is referred to as a:

    A. String of text.

    B. Thing of text.

    C. Wingding of text.

    D. Rama-lama-ding-dong of text.

11. When you start writing a C program, you begin by making a:

    A. Nerd-compatible workplace, replete with pizza or Chinese food, carbonated and heavily caffeinated beverage, Doritos, and awful lighting conditions.

    B. Small sacrifice to the C lords.

    C. Program ending in EXE or COM, depending on the lingua franca.

    D. Text file.

12. What is another name for what you created in question 11?

    A. Geek feast.

    B. Token offering.

    C. Executable file.

    D. Source code file.

13. The compiler does what?

    A. It compiles — duh!

    B. It makes a text file flatter, effectively doubling the storage capacity of your hard drive.

    C. It converts the source code file into an object file.

    D. It takes the C words and makes them into commands for the computer.

14. What does the linker create?

    A. The final product — the EXE program file.

    B. Sausages.

    C. Lincoln Logs.

    D. Cuff links.

15. How do you deal with errors?

    A. Like a 10-year-old frustrated with a video game.

    B. Reedit the source code file and recompile.

    C. Stare blankly at the computer because it's definitely not your fault.

    D. Sausages.

16. How many lines of text will the following `printf` statement display:

```
printf("This is line one.\nAnd this is line two.");
```

    A. One.

    B. One and a half.

    C. Two.

    D. Between one and two.

Chapter 2

Building (and Stumbling) Blocks of Basic C Programs

• •

Lessons In This Chapter

▶ printf (or printing has nothing to do with your printer)

▶ scanf (which is pronounced "scan-eff")

▶ Remarks, comments, and suggestions

▶ gets and puts (or no more *f* suffixes, please!)

▶ More fun with printf

Programs in This Chapter

QUIT.C	DBLQUOTE.C	JUSTIFY.C	WHORU.C
COLOR.C	MADLIBL.C	INSULT1.C	STOP.C
INSULT2.C	PRINTFUN.C		

Vocabulary Introduced In This Chapter

printf	char	scanf	/* comments */
gets	puts		

• •

*S*peak to me, O great computer!

What's that? It can't hear you? Probably because you haven't yet learned how to tell the computer how to talk. Computers can talk. Sometimes, if you're not careful, it's hard to get them to shut up. And unlike some humans, they can also listen. This chapter's lessons address the basics of teaching a computer to talk and listen by using the C language.

Lesson 2-1: `printf` (or Printing Has Nothing to Do with Your Printer)

The `printf` function is used in the C programming language to display information on the screen. It's the basic, all-purpose, "Hey, I want to tell the user something" display text command. The format for using the basic `printf` function — the way you type `printf` when you write C programs — appears in the next box.

- ✔ The `printf` function is a complete statement. A semicolon always follows the last parenthesis. (OK, there may be an exception, but it's not worth fussing over at this point in the game.)

- ✔ I know: "print" usually means to send something to your printer. Well, in the olden days, computers didn't have them thar fancy monitors and such. Back then, the `printf` command really did print on a printer — a teletype machine. Rather than change the command name, they just changed the location of its output from the printer to the screen.

Function `printf` (display some text on the screen)

The `printf` function can get really fancy, but in its most basic mode of operation, it uses the following format:

```
printf("text");
```

`printf` is always written in lowercase. This is a must. It's followed by parentheses, which contain a quoted string of text. The final paren is always followed with a semicolon.

The italicized *text* in the preceding code line means that you can replace it with any string of text. `printf`'s job is then to display that text on the screen. Although the text is enclosed in double quotes, they aren't part of the message `printf` puts up on the screen.

There are special rules about the text you can display, all of which are covered in Lesson 2-5.

(This is the simple format, by the way. A more advanced format for `printf` appears later in this lesson.)

Another "printf *displays something humorous" program*

The printf function's job is to display a message on the screen. If you worked through Chapter 1, you did this many times. What say you do it again with the following program, QUIT.C? This program displays a totally hilarious message when you type it at the DOS prompt. Truly, I should be hired as a writer for the David Letterman show.

Name: QUIT.C

```
#include <stdio.h>

void main()
{
    printf("Quit from what? You're at the DOS prompt!");
}
```

Start out in your compiler with a new, blank window in which you can type the preceding source code. Choose New from the File menu. Or if you're at the DOS prompt, use your editor to give you some blank screen on which you can compose QUIT.C.

Carefully type the preceding source code into your editor. Be careful and double-check your typing. This is C scrawl at its best.

Save the source code file to disk and name it QUIT.C.

Compile the program. Build the final product, QUIT.EXE.

If you encounter any errors, reedit the source code file, QUIT.C. Just return to your text editor and double-check everything against the preceding text. Recompile to get the thing to work.

Here is what the program's output should look like — what you see if you type QUIT at the C> prompt:

```
Quit from what?  You're at the DOS prompt!
```

Ha, ha. This should be funny when you type it at the DOS prompt. "Oh, *your name*," they'll say, "You've become such a card since you've learned that C programming language."

✔ Whenever a new program is introduced, you should choose the New command from the File menu in your integrated environment. This way, you can create each program in its own editing window without confusing yourself with other programs in other editing windows.

✔ Also, it's OK to close any extra windows after you begin work on another program. This is the way it is from this point onward in this book. Remember to close old project or source code windows when a new program is introduced and to begin writing that new program in its own editing window.

✔ Lesson 1-2 offers instructions, particular to your compiler, for compiling QUIT.C.

✔ Obviously, this program makes no sense when you run it from within Windows. Refer to the Microsoft Visual C++ user's guide for instructions on creating DOS programs using Visual C++. Or just think of something you can display by using printf that would be thigh-slapping funny in Windows, as shown in this example:

```
printf("Bill Gates never wants you to quit Windows!");
```

✔ Because the integrated environment only flashes the output at you, the bombastity of this program is missed. Press Alt+F5 to see the output and then press Enter to return to the integrated environment. Or be a dude and quit the integrated environment to run the QUIT program at the DOS prompt as the good Lord intended.

Printing funky text

Ladies and gentlemen, I give you this text string:

```
"Ta da!  I am a text string."
```

It's a simple collection of text, numbers, letters, and other characters, all neatly enclosed in double quotes. Wrap it up in the bunlike parentheses:

```
("Ta da!  I am a text string.")
```

Put printf on one side and a semicolon on the other:

```
printf("Ta da!  I am a text string.");
```

And you have a hot dog of a C command to display said string on the screen. Neat and tidy.

But consider this string:

```
"He said, "Ta da! I am a text string.""
```

Is this criminal or what? It's still a text string, but it contains a double quote. Actually, it has four double quotes in all. That means eight tick marks hovering over this string's head. How can it morally cope with that?

```
""Damocles" if I know."
```

The C compiler never punishes you for "testing" anything. There is no large room in a hollowed-out mountain in the Rockies where a little man sits in a chair looking at millions of video screens, one of which contains your PC's output, and no, the little man doesn't snicker evilly when you get an error. Errors are safe! So why not experiment?

Please create the following program, DBLQUOTE.C. The program is yet another "printf displays something" example. But this time, what's displayed contains a double quote. Can you do that? This is your experiment for the day.

Name: DBLQUOTE.C

```
#include <stdio.h>

void main()
{
    printf("He said, "Ta da! I am a text string."");
}
```

Start off with a *new* slate in your editor and create this program. Type the source code exactly as it appears, including the double quotes — four in all. Compare what you have on your screen with what appears in the preceding lines to ensure that they match up. When you're satisfied, save the source code file to disk as DBLQUOTE.C.

Compile and run the preceding program — if you can. Chances are highly likely — definite, in fact — that you'll see one of the following error messages displayed when you attempt to compile:

```
missing ')' before identifier 'Ta'
```

```
Function call missing )
```

(At the DOS prompt, the text in function main is appended to this error message.)

```
parse error before 'Ta'
```

The deal is that printf requires a text string enclosed in double quotes (refer to the printf format at the beginning of this lesson). Your compiler knows that. After the second double quote, however, before the word *Ta*, the compiler expected something else, possibly the second parenthesis in the `printf` function or another valid C command or doohickey (see Figure 2-1). It didn't see that, so an error was produced. What luck.

Obviously, there is a need to have a double quote in a string. The secret is figuring out how the `printf` command can see a double quote without the compiler getting flustered over it. The answer is to use an escape sequence.

✔ A text string cannot contain a bald double-quote character or a few other verboten characters listed in the next section. It must begin and end with a double quote. But in the middle? No way!

✔ To print such weird characters, you must use an *escape sequence,* which is a special way of sticking said weird characters into a text string without fouling up the `printf` command.

✔ Your tip that something was wrong in the Borland C environment should have been the miscolored text as you typed it. That's one way to catch common errors, such as forgetting about double quotes and escape sequences. With all the things to hate about Borland C, this is one of the nicer aspects.

✔ In the olden days, programmers would have simply gone without certain characters. Rather than trip up a string with a double quote, they would have used two single quotes. Some ancient programmers who don't know about escape sequences still use these tricks.

Introducing a few escape sequences

Escape sequences are designed to sneak otherwise forbidden characters into text strings. The way they do this is with the backslash character (\). Locate this character on your keyboard. It should be above the Enter key, though they often hide it elsewhere. (Yes, it's the same backslash key DOS is fond of using.)

The backslash character becomes the first character in the escape sequence. When printf sees the backslash, it thinks, "Omigosh, there must be an escape sequence coming up," and it braces itself to accept an otherwise forbidden character.

To sneak in the double-quote character without getting printf in a tizzy fit, the escape sequence \" (backslash-double quote) is used. Behold the new, improved program.

Name: DBLQUOTE.C

```
#include <stdio.h>

void main()
{
    printf("He said, \"Ta da! I am a text string.\"");
}
```

The only change here is in line 5, the printf statement. Notice the \" escape sequences in the string. There are two of them, prefixing the two double quotes that appear in the string's midsection. The outside two double quotes, the ones that really are bookmarks to the entire string, remain intact. Looks weird, but it doesn't error.

Edit your DBLQUOTE.C source code file. Don't start over with a new slate; edit the source code sitting in your editor right now. Make the escape-sequence modification to line 5, as shown in the proper DBLQUOTE.C listing. All you have to do is insert two backslash characters before the rogue double quotes: \".

Save the changed source code file to disk. Just choose the Save command from the File menu to overwrite the original DBLQUOTE.C program. If you're using a DOS text editor, use whatever Save command resaves the file to disk. No need to change the name here.

Compile the program by using the commands you should have by now memorized for your compiler. This time it should work and display the following output:

```
He said, "Ta da! I am a text string."
```

- ✓ OK, you Borland people: Remember to press Alt+F5 to see the output from the integrated environment. Press Enter when you're done staring.

- ✓ The \" escape sequence produces the double-quote character in the middle of a string.

- ✓ Another handy escape sequence you may have used from Chapter 1 is \n. That produces a "new line" in a string, just like pressing the Enter key.

- ✓ All escape sequences start with the backslash character, so how do you stick a backslash character into a string? Use two of them: \\ is the escape sequence that sticks a backslash character into a string.

✔ An escape sequence can appear anywhere in a text string: beginning, middle, or end and as many times as you want to use them. Essentially, the \ thing is a shorthand notation for sticking forbidden characters into any string.

✔ Other escape sequences are listed in Lesson 2-5 (see Table 2-1).

The *f* means formatted

The function is called printf for a reason. The *f* stands for something. It doesn't mean print-fast or print-function. It means print *formatted.* The advantage of the printf function over other, similar display-this-or-that functions in C is that the output can be formatted.

Later lessons introduce you to the formatting aspect of the printf function. There's no need to worry about it at this stage, but I do need to show it to you because when it's used in that manner, printf takes on a different format, shown in the following function box.

More information about what variables are and what they do is in Chapter 3.

Function printf
(display formatted text and variables)

Yes, the printf function still tosses information up on the screen. But the text string displayed can also be a *format string,* one that can control or format your program's output:

printf("*format_string*"[,*var*[,...]]);

What appears in the double quotes is really a *formatting string.* It's still text that appears in printf's output. Intermingled in the text, however, are various *conversion characters,* or special "placeholders," that tell the printf function how to format its output. (They are discussed at length in Lesson 2-5.)

The extra items, shown in the square brackets in the preceding code line, are called *arguments.*

The argument shown in the line is *var,* which is short for *variable.* printf can be used to display the content or value of one or more variables. This is done by using special conversion characters in the format_string. Figure 2-2 illustrates this concept rather beautifully.

The [,...] doohickey means that you can have any number of *var* items specified in a single printf function (before the final paren). For each *var* item, however, there must be a corresponding conversion character in the format_string. They must match up or you get an error when the program compiles.

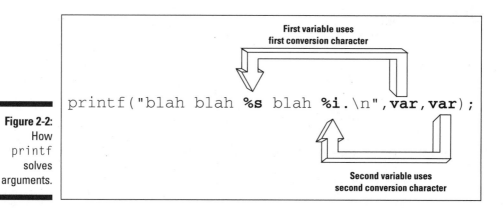

First variable uses
first conversion character

```
printf("blah blah %s blah %i.\n",var,var);
```

Second variable uses
second conversion character

Figure 2-2:
How
printf
solves
arguments.

A bit of justification

At this point in the game, there's no need to venture farther into the cold,
murky waters of the printf statement. Arguments and variables. Ecch! I'd
rather exist on a diet of brackish water and airline food.

On second thought, perhaps a program that demonstrates printf's formatting
powers is in order. Such a program is JUSTIFY.C, whose contents you are not
required to memorize but whose output you're completely allowed to marvel
at. What JUSTIFY.C does is to display two strings: right will be right-justified
and left will be left-justified. This makes more sense when you see the
program's output than by just looking at the source code.

Name: JUSTIFY.C

```c
#include <stdio.h>

void main()
{
    printf("%15s","right\n");
    printf("%-15s","left\n");
}
```

Enter this source code into your text editor. In the first printf statement, the
first string is %15s (percent, 15, little s). That's followed by a comma and then
right, followed by the newline escape sequence, \n (backslash, little n). The
second printf statement is nearly the same thing, though with a minus sign
before the 15 and the string left rather than right.

Use the nearby "Blow-by-blow" description box for more information about how JUSTIFY.C works or if you need more help typing the program.

This program contains more C doodads than any other program introduced so far in this book. Be careful with what you type! When you're certain that you have it right, save the file to disk as JUSTIFY.C.

Compile JUSTIFY.C. Fix any errors if you need to.

Run the program. Your output should look something like this:

```
              right
    left
```

The word `right` is right-justified 15 spaces over; `left` is left-justified. This was dictated by the `%15s` formatting command in `printf`. The `%15s` didn't print at all. Instead, it controlled how the string that was displayed appeared on the screen. That's the formatting power of `printf` at work.

The JUSTIFY.C program shows you only a hint of what the `printf` function can do. `printf` can also format numbers in a remarkable number of ways, which is a little overwhelming to present right now in this chapter.

- ✔ Did you remember semicolons at the end of the `printf` statements? That's a common boo-boo.

- ✔ The variables, `var`, are called "arguments." The term *argument* means another option, a doodad or thingamabob, required by a C language command.

- ✔ No it doesn't.

- ✔ Yes it does.

- ✔ More details on the formatting power of the `printf` function are offered in Lesson 2-5. However, this book doesn't dive into the details of formatting as shown in the JUSTIFY.C program. See your C language reference and look up `printf` for the details if you're interested.

Secret information about how JUSTIFY.C works (don't tell!)

The JUSTIFY program consists of two `printf` statements that use a special formatting string which tells `printf` to format its output:

`printf("%15s","right\n");`

The "control string" is listed first, which tells `printf` what to display. Before this program, `printf` was just displaying text. But the percent character holds special meaning to `printf`. It identifies a *conversion character*—what I call a "placeholder"—that tells `printf` how to format its output. In this case, the conversion character is `s`, which means string. The `15` tells `printf` to display a string using only 15 characters. The string to display is listed next, `right\n`, which is the word *right* and a newline escape sequence (like pressing Enter.)

If the 15 spaces were periods, here is the way `printf` would display the text *right*:

`........right` *(newline here)*

The newline character, `\n`, is the 15th character.

If you substitute the string "banana" for "right," you see the following line:

`........banana (newline here)`

The text is still right-justified. (However, any string longer than 15 characters in this example would not be cut short.)

The next line in the program looks the same, but a minus sign is stuck in front of the 15:

`printf("%-15s","left\n");`

The minus sign means to left-justify the output.

All this conversion-character stuff can get complex. Rest assured that seldom does anyone memorize it. Often advanced programmers have to consult their C language references and run some tests to see which formatting command does what. Most of the time you won't be bothered with this stuff, so don't panic.

Lesson 2-1 Quiz

1. Write a program, BYE.C, that displays the following message on the screen:

   `Goodbye? Ha! This is DOS. You can never leave!`

2. What is an "escape sequence?"

   A. That part of the film when Steven Seagal and his babe run away from the bad guys, but she trips because she's wearing high heels in the jungle.

   B. The event triggered by your pressing the Esc key.

   C. Any series of events that begins with "Hey look, there's Elvis!"

   D. A method of putting special characters into a text string.

3. Write a program, STOOGES.C, that uses one `printf` statement which displays the following three words, each of them on a line by itself:

```
Larry
Moe
Curly
```

Hint: Use the \n (newline) escape sequence.

4. Modify the program you wrote in question 3 so that each word is displayed surrounded by double quotes. Again, keep it all on one line — a single `printf` can do the job.

Hint: Use the \" (double quote) escape sequence. The final `printf` statement has numerous backslashes in it.

5. The old "Star Trek" episode where Kirk beams down to the planet, kisses the women, and kills the aliens:

A. I'm not sure, but it was on last Saturday.

B. A Private Little War.

C. Shore Leave.

D. Just about any third-season episode.

Lesson 2-2: `scanf` (Which Is Pronounced "Scan-Eff")

Output without input is like Desi without Lucy, yang without yin, Caesar salad without the garlic. It means that the seven dwarfs would be singing, "Oh, Oh, Oh" rather than "I/O, I/O." Besides — and this may be the most horrid aspect of all — without input, the computer just sits there and talks *at* you. That's just awful.

C has numerous tools for making the computer listen to you. A number of commands read input from the keyboard, from commands that scan for individual characters to the vaunted `scanf` function, which is used to snatch a string of text from the keyboard and save it in the cuddly, warm paws of a string variable.

✔ `scanf` is a function like `printf`. Its purpose is to read text from the keyboard. (`printf` displays text on the screen.)

✔ `scanf` can also read in numbers and do other amazing things, but for this lesson the theme is strings of text from the keyboard. Additional mumbo jumbo on using the `scanf` function is offered in Lesson 6-2.

✔ Like the *f* in `printf`, the *f* in `scanf` means "formatted." You can use `scanf` to read a specifically formatted bit of text from the keyboard. In this lesson, however, you just use `scanf` to read a line of text, nothing fancy.

✔ There are better ways to read text from the keyboard than using `scanf`. Lesson 2-4 shows you one technique that uses the humble `gets` function.

Putting `scanf` *together*

To make `scanf` work, you need two things. First, you need a storage place to hold the text you enter. Second, you need the `scanf` function itself.

The storage place is called a *string variable. String* means a string of characters — text. *Variable* means that the string isn't set — it can be whatever the user types. A string variable is a storage place for text in your programs. (Variables are discussed at length in Chapter 3.)

You create the variable by using the format illustrated in the next box.

Keyword `char` **(declaring a string variable)**

To create a variable, you need a C language keyword that tells the compiler, "OK, I'm giving you a variable here." For text, the keyword is `char`:

`char var[size];`

The `char` is followed by a space — or tab — and then the name of the variable, `var`. For strings of text (more than one character), the maximum length of the string also has to be specified in square brackets.

The `var` is the name of the variable. Rules and regulations for what you can and cannot name variables are offered in Lesson 3-3.

The `size` indicates the number of characters long the string can be. So if you are asking for a first name, figure that most first names (outside the Indian subcontinent) are 20 characters or fewer in size.

A semicolon follows the last bracket (after the `size`) because this is a complete C language statement.

The second thing you need is `scanf` itself. Its format is somewhat similar to the advanced, cryptic format for `printf`.

Function `scanf` (reading a text string)

The `scanf` function is used to read information from the keyboard. In the format shown here, `scanf` is configured to read a line of text from the keyboard:

```
scanf("%s",&var);
```

Like `printf`, the `scanf` function is followed by stuff in parentheses. Unlike `printf`, `scanf` does not display the text in quotes.

First comes the formatting string that tells `scanf` what type of text to look for. When `%s` is reading a line of text, `%s` is specified in double quotes. These characters tell `scanf` to look for a line of text ending with a press of the Enter key.

Following the formatting string is a comma, then an ampersand (&), and finally the name of a string variable. This is how you tell `scanf` where to put the text entered at the keyboard.

The `scanf` function is a complete statement in the C language, so it ends with a semicolon.

As an example of using `scanf` to read in someone's first name, first you create a storage place for the first name:

```
char firstname[20];
```

This C language statement sets aside storage for a string of text — like creating a safe for a huge sum of money you wish to have some day. And just like the safe, the variable is "empty" when you create it; it doesn't contain anything. As many as 20 characters can be typed into this storage area, which is set by the 20 in square brackets.

The next step is to use the `scanf` function later in the program to read in text from the keyboard. Something like the following line would work:

```
scanf("%s",&firstname);
```

Here is what `scanf` sees: "OK, I need to read a string of text from the keyboard, `%s`. And all that text I'm going to store in the string variable named `firstname`. Cool. Now if the user would just type something, I could go about my business."

Figure 2-3 illustrates this concept. First, a string variable is created — like a safe — used to store as many as 20 characters of text. The variable is named `firstname`. Then, later in the program, the `scanf` function reads the keyboard and stores the characters typed in `firstname`'s variable storage.

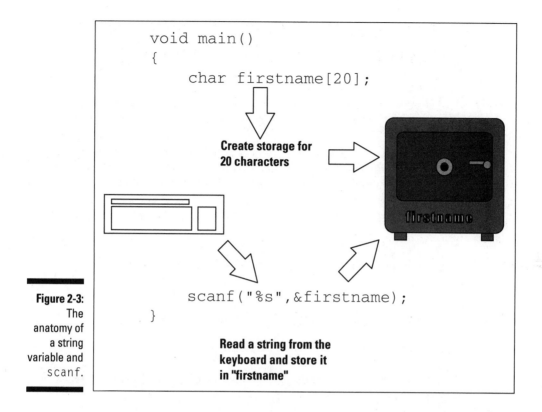

✔ If you're writing a C program that requires input, you must create a place to store it. For text input, that place is a string variable, which you create by using the char keyword. (Refer to the program at the end of this lesson for an example.)

✔ Variables used in a C program appear as the first items in a function, right after the initial curly bracket. They are official C language statements and require a semicolon.

✔ More on variables in Chapter 3.

✔ scanf works like printf, though it requires a variable in which the text will be stored. You can't just say "read the keyboard"; you need a place to store the text that is read.

✔ The string variable is a storage place where text entered from the keyboard is kept. The char keyword tells the compiler the variable's name and how much storage space is required.

✔ Chapter 3 discusses variables and how they work in detail. Lesson 3-5 offers information about string variables.

✔ The formatting codes used by scanf are identical to those used by printf. In real life, you use them mostly with printf, seeing as how there are better ways to read the keyboard than by using scanf. Refer to Table 2-2 in Lesson 2-5 for a list of the formatting percent-sign codes.

Plugging scanf *in to a program*

The following program, WHORU.C, you've probably seen before. It was demonstrated in Lesson 1-5. It uses scanf to read text from the keyboard. The printf statement then displays that text. This is an example of input and output.

Name: WHORU.C

```
#include <stdio.h>

void main()
{
   char me[20];

   printf("What is your name?");
   scanf("%s",&me);
   printf("Darn glad to meet you, %s!\n",me);
}
```

If you didn't enter and compile this program in Lesson 1-5, do so now. Refer back there for additional instructions and sample output.

✔ The char me[20]; statement tells the C compiler to set aside storage for 20 characters to be entered. The string variable is named me.

✔ The scanf function reads the keyboard, storing any text input in the variable me.

✔ The final printf function displays the result. Notice how both printf and the scanf function before it use a similar format:

```
scanf("%s",&me);
```

scanf has "%s" and then &me in its parentheses.

```
printf("Darn glad to meet you, %s!\n",me);
```

printf has "%s" (in addition to other text in the quotes) and then me in its parentheses.

Tweaking WHORU.C a bit

To show how similar `printf` and `scanf` are, make the following modification to WHORU.C. Change the final `printf` statement to read:

```
printf("%s",me);
```

This line makes `printf` and `scanf` use a nearly identical format. Both have a formatting string containing the %s conversion character, and both have the me variable specified as an "argument" (though it's pointless to argue with yourself).

Save the edited file and recompile it. Fix any errors if they sneak into the picture. Then run the final program.

The output is different because "Glad to meet you" isn't displayed. Yet this example illustrates how the two functions are similar and how they treat input and output.

Why the ampersand for `scanf` and not for `printf`?

To read text from the keyboard, you need storage space. That storage space is created with the `char` keyword, as described in this lesson. When the text is stored in a string variable, such as me, you can use the variable's name in your program to represent the stored text. This is how `printf` displays the same text read by `scanf`. But how come `scanf` sticks an & in front of me?

The answer, as you're probably suspecting, is cryptic. The & in front of a variable tells the C compiler to locate a variable's address in memory — the spot where the variable sits as opposed to the variable's value. I know what you're thinking: The computer should really do this kind of work

for you. But it's just one of those things that crops up in the C language, frustrating and confusing wrapped into one (and a subject touched on in the next volume of this book).

Forgetting to stick the & in front of `scanf`'s variable is a common mistake. Not doing so leads to some wonderful *null pointer assignment* errors that you'll relish in lessons to come. As a weird quirk, however, the ampersand is optional when you're dealing with string variables. To prove it, you can edit WHORU.C, stick an ampersand into either, both, or neither the `printf` and `scanf` functions, and then recompile and the program will run the same.

The miracle of %s

Lesson 2-6 goes into full-blown detail about using the printf function. So far, you've seen its formatting capacity only with regard to strings, using the %s placeholder. But %s can be used a number of times, not just once. And it can be used with multiple string variables.

Consider the following pointless program, COLOR.C, which uses two string variables, name and color. It asks for your name and then your favorite color. The final printf statement then displays what you entered.

Name: COLOR.C

```
#include <stdio.h>

void main()
{
    char name[20];
    char color[20];

    printf("What is your name?");
    scanf("%s",name);
    printf("What is your favorite color?");
    scanf("%s",color);
    printf("%s's favorite color is %s\n",name,color);
}
```

Enter this program into your editor. Choose the New command from the File menu if you're working in an integrated environment.

Save this file to disk as COLOR.C.

Compile COLOR.C, magically transforming it into the program COLOR.EXE. If you get any errors, double-check your source code and reedit the file. A common mistake: Forgetting that there are two commas in the final printf statement.

Your output should look something like this:

```
What is your name?dan
What is your favorite color?brown
dan's favorite color is brown
```

Some helpful hints for typing in the COLOR.C program

The program begins with #include<stdio.h>, a blank line, void main(), and then the sole curly bracket — just like every other C program you've written so far. This sets up the C compiler with its required main function and everyone should live happily ever after — providing that you don't forget the final curly bracket at the end of the source code listing.

Lines 5 and 6:

The char keyword is used to set aside storage for two string variables, name and color. Both have room for 20 characters. Notice how these two statements come first in the program. This is a must. They also both end in semicolons, a must-must.

The seventh line:

This is a blank line, traditionally used in C programs to separate where the variables are defined and the "meat" of the program.

Lines 8 and 9 and lines 10 and 11:

Two questions are posed by using printf-scanf combinations similar to those in the WHORU.C program. In the first question, the response is stored in the name variable by the scanf function. In the second question, scanf stores the response in the color variable.

The 12th line:

The final printf statement uses two %s place-holders to display the two string variables. The formatting string (with the two %s placeholders) comes first in double quotes. Because there are two variables that need displaying, they follow the string separated by commas.

- So I forgot the & in the scanf statement. Sue me! Seriously, read the box titled "Why the ampersand for scanf and not for printf?" for more information.

- This is the last time I need to remind users of Borland's integrated environment to press Alt+F5 to see the full output. Press Enter to return to the coziness of your integrated environment.

- Incidentally, % is a special character — like the double quote and backslash characters in a string. To display a percent sign in a string, you should specify it twice:

```
printf("Our bank's CDs have a lousy 2%% annual yield.\n");
```

This command displays the following string:

```
Our bank's CDs have a lousy 2% annual yield.
```

Experimentation time!

Which is more important: the order of the %s doodads or the order of the variables — the arguments — in a printf statement? Give up? I'm not going to tell you the answer. You're going to have to figure it out for yourself.

To solve the %s and variable dilemma, make the following modification to l ine 12 in the COLOR.C program:

```
printf("%s's favorite color is %s\n",color,name);
```

The order of the variables here is reversed; color comes first and then name. Save this change to disk and recompile. The program still runs, but the output is different because you changed the variable order. You may see something like this:

```
blue's favorite color is Bill.
```

See? Computers *are* stupid! Actually, the point here is that it's important to remember the order of the variables when you have more than one listed in a printf function. The %s thingies? They're just blanks.

How about making this change:

```
printf("%s's favorite color is %s\n",name,name);
```

This modification uses the name variable twice — perfectly allowable. All printf needs is two string variables to match the two %s signs in its formatting string. Save this change and recompile. Run the program and examine the output:

```
Lois's favorite color is Lois
```

OK, Lois, you been drinking again? Make that mistake on an IRS form and you'll spend years playing golf with former stockbrokers and congressmen. (Better learn to order your variables now.)

Finally, make the following modification:

```
printf("%s's favorite color is %s\n",name,"blue");
```

Rather than the color variable, a *string constant* is used. A string constant is simply a string enclosed in quotes. It doesn't change, unlike a variable, which can hold anything. (It isn't variable!)

Save the change to disk and recompile your efforts. The program still works, though no matter which color you type in, the computer always insists that it's "blue."

✔ The string constant "blue" works because printf's %s placeholder looks for a string of text. It doesn't matter whether the string is a variable or a "real" text string sitting there in double quotes. (Of course, the advantage to writing a program is to use variables that store input; using the constant is a little silly because the computer already knows what it's going to print. I mean, ladies and gentlemen, where is the I/O?)

✔ The %s placeholder in a printf function looks for a corresponding string variable and plugs it in to the text that is displayed.

✔ You need one string variable in the printf function for each %s that appears in printf's formatting string. If the variable is missing, a syntax boo-boo is generated by the compiler.

✔ In addition to string variables, you can also use string constants, often called *literal* strings. This is kind of dumb, though, because there's no point in wasting time with %s if you already know what you're going to display. (I have to demonstrate it here, however, or I'll go to C Teacher's Prison in Connecticut.)

✔ Make sure that you get the order of your variables correct. This is especially important when you use both numeric and string variables in printf. (Using numeric variables is covered in Lesson 3-4.)

✔ The percent sign (%) is a holy character. *Om!* If you want a percent sign (%) to appear in printf's output, use two of them: %%.

Lesson 2-2 Quiz

1. To read a line of text from the keyboard and display it, you need which two things:

    A. A keyboard and a C compiler.

    B. Yin and yang.

    C. Cheech and Chong.

    D. printf and scanf.

2. Which of the following creates a string variable, menutext, that's 48 characters long?

    A. char menutext;

    B. menutext[45];

    C. menutext;

    D. char menutext[48];

3. Write a program that accepts input from the keyboard and stores it in a variable called name. The program then displays the output twice on the same line. For example, the output should look something like this:

```
What is your name? Fred
Fred? My name is Fred too!
```

4. When I see %s in a printf function, I know that:

   A. It must have a corresponding string variable later in that same printf function.

   B. Something will be figured by percents.

   C. It's a variable thingamaboo.

   D. Gone, gone, gone are those carefree days of my youth.

5. Which of the following is a literal string?

   A. The thing William Shakespeare used to tie up his boots.

   B. \"This is a string constant.\"

   C. "No, I'm a literal string!"

   D. %s

It's time for a well-deserved rest. Please go take a break.

Lesson 2-3: Remarks, Comments, and Suggestions

An important part of programming is remembering what the heck it is you're doing. I'm not talking about the programming itself — that's easy to remember and there are books and references galore in case you don't. Instead, the thing you have to remember is what you are attempting to make a program do at a specific spot. This is done by inserting a *comment* in your source code.

Comments aren't really necessary for the small programs you're doing in this book. They don't begin to become necessary until you write larger programs — things on the scope of Excel or DOS — where it's easy to lose your train of thought. To remind yourself of what you're doing, you should stick a comment in the source code, explaining your approach. That way, when you look at the source code again, your eyes don't glaze over and the drool doesn't pour, because the comments remind you of what's going on.

Adding comments

Comments in a C program have a starting point and an ending point. Everything between those two points is ignored by the compiler, meaning that you can stick any text in there — anything — and it doesn't affect how the program runs.

```
/* This is how a comment looks in the C language */
```

This is a fine example of a comment. What follows is another example of a comment, but the type that gives this book its reputation:

```
/*
Hello compiler!  Hey, error on this: pirntf!
Ha! Ha! You can't see me!  Pbbtbtbt!
Nya! Nya! Nya!
*/
```

- The beginning of the comment is marked by the slash and asterisk: /*.

- The end of the comment is marked by the asterisk and slash: */.

- Yup, they're different.

- The comment is not a C language statement. You do not need a semicolon after the */.

A big, hairy program with comments

The following program is MADLIB1.C. It uses the printf and scanf functions described in Lesson 2-2 to create a short yet interesting story.

Name: MADLIB1.C

```
/*
MADLIB1.C Source Code
Written by (your name here)
*/

#include <stdio.h>
```

```
void main()
{
    char adjective[20];
    char food[20];
    char chore[20];
    char furniture[20];

/* Get the words to use in the madlib */

    printf("Enter an adjective:");          /* prompt */
    scanf("%s",adjective);                   /* input */
    printf("Enter a food:");
    scanf("%s",food);
    printf("Enter a household chore (past tense):");
    scanf("%s",chore);
    printf("Enter an item of furniture:");
    scanf("%s",furniture);

/* Display the output */

    printf("\n\nDon't touch that %s %s!\n",adjective,food);
    printf("I just %s the %s!\n",chore,furniture);
}
```

Quick hints for entering MADLIB1.C (if you still need them)

The only thing new to you in this program should be the comments. Each one begins with /* and ends with */. Make sure that you get those right: slash-asterisk begins the comment, and an asterisk-slash ends it. They're not both the same.

MADLIB1.C uses these four string variables: adjective, food, chore, and furniture. All four of them are created by the char keyword, and 20 characters of storage are set aside for each. Each of the string variables is filled by scanf with your keyboard input.

Each of the final printf functions contains two %s placeholders. Two string variables in each function supply the text for the %s placeholders.

The second-to-last printf function begins with two newline characters, \n \n. These characters separate the input section, where you enter the bits of text, from the program's output.

Type the program exactly as written earlier. Use the preceding Cheat sidebar to help you through it (if you need extra help).

Save the file to disk and name it MADLIB1.C.

Compile the file into MADLIB1.EXE. If you have any errors, double-check the source code, reedit, recompile.

Here is a sample of the program's output:

```
Enter an adjective:hairy
Enter a food:waffle
Enter a household chore (past tense):vacuumed
Enter an item of furniture:couch

Don't touch that hairy waffle!
I just vacuumed the couch!
```

✔ This program is long and looks complex, but it doesn't use any new tricks. Everything here you've seen already: the creation of string variables with char, printf to display text and string variables, and scanf to read the keyboard. Yawn.

✔ There are five comments in MADLIB1.C. Make sure that you can find each one. Notice that they're not all the same, yet each begins with /* and ends with */.

Comment styles of the nerdy and not-quite-yet-nerdy

The MADLIB1.C program contains five comments and uses three different commenting styles. Though there are many more ways of commenting your programs, these are the most common:

```
/*
MADLIB1.C Source Code
Written by Mike Rowsoft
*/
```

Ever popular is the multiline approach, shown here. The first line starts the comment with the /* all by itself. Lines following it are all comments, remarks, or such and are ignored by the compiler. The final line ends the comment with */ all by itself. Remember that final /*; otherwise, the C compiler thinks that your whole program is just one big, long comment (possible, but not recommended).

```
/* Get the words to use in the madlib */
```

This is a single-line comment, not to be confused with a C language statement. The comment begins with /* and ends with */ all on the same line. This is 100 percent okey-dokey, and because it's not a statement, you don't need a semicolon.

```
    printf("Enter an adjective:");              /* prompt */
```

Finally, there is the "end of line" comment. After the preceding printf statement plus a few taps of the Tab key, the /* starts a comment, and */ ends it on the same line.

Why are comments necessary?

Comments aren't necessary for the C compiler. It ignores them. Instead, comments are for you, the programmer. They offer bits of advice, suggestions for what you're trying to do, or hints on how the program works. You can put anything in the comments, though the more useful the information, the better it helps you later on.

Most C programs begin with a few lines of comments. All my C programs start with information such as the following:

```
/* MINICOM.C
Dan Gookin, 9/26/94 @ 2:45 a.m.
My latest attempt to write a communications
program in C.  Wish me luck.
*/
```

These lines tell me what the program is about and when I started working on it.

In the source code itself, comments can be used as notes to yourself, such as:

```
/* Find out why this doesn't work */
```

Or this:

```
save=itemv;  /* Save item value here */
```

Or even reminders to yourself in the future:

```
/*
Someday you will write the code here that makes
the computer remember what it did last time this
program ran.
*/
```

The point here is that the comments are notes *for yourself.* If you were learning C programming in school, you would write the comments to satiate the fixations of your professor. If you work on a large programming project, the comments placate your team leader. For programs you write, the comments are for you.

Bizzar-o comments

During my travels, I have seen many attempts to make comments in C programs look interesting. Here's an example:

```
/*****************************************
**  Bill & Ted's Most Excellent Program **
*****************************************/
```

This comment works. It contains lots of asterisks, but they're still stuck between /* and */, making it a viable comment.

```
/*
 * This is a long-winded introduction to an
 * obscure program written by someone at a
 * university who's really big on himself and
 * thinks no mere mortal can learn C — and who
 * has written three "C" books to prove it.
 */
```

The idea in this example is to create a "wall of asterisks" between the /* and */, making the comment stick out on the page.

```
//This is another style of comment, permitted with
//Borland C++ and Microsoft Visual C++
```

Here you see the newer style of C comment. Two slashes start the comment, which ends at the end of the line (there are no ending */ characters). This style has the advantage that you don't have to both begin and end a comment, making it ideal for placing comments at the end of a C language statement, as shown in this example:

```
    printf("Enter an adjective:");        // prompt
    scanf("%s",adjective);                // input
```

These modifications to the MADLIB1.C program still keep the comments intact. This method is preferred because it's quick; however, /* and */ have the advantage of being able to rope in a larger portion of text without typing // all over the place.

Using comments to disable

Comments are ignored by the compiler. No matter what lies between the /* and the */, it's skipped over. Even vital, lifesaving information, mass sums of cash, or the key to eternal youth — all these are ignored if they're nestled in a C language comment.

Modify the MADLIB1.C source code, changing the last part of the program to read as follows:

```
/* Display the output */

/*
    printf("\n\nDon't touch that %s %s!\n",adjective,food);
    printf("I just %s the %s!\n",chore,furniture);
*/
}
```

To make the modification, follow these cinchy steps:

1. Insert a line with /* on it before the first `printf` function in this example.

2. Insert a line with /* on it after the second `printf` function.

With the last two `printf` statements disabled, save the file to disk and recompile it. It runs as before, but the resulting "mad lib" isn't displayed. The reason is that the final two `printf` functions were "commented out."

✔ You can use comments to disable certain parts of your program. If something isn't working correctly, for example, you can "comment it out." You might also want to include a note to yourself, explaining why that section is commented out.

✔ Sometimes you may notice that something isn't working which should. The reason is that you might have *accidentally* commented it out. Always check your /* and */ comment bookends to make sure that they match up the way you want them to.

Avoiding "nested" comments

The most major of the faux pas you can commit with comments is to "nest" them, or to include one set of comments inside another. To wit, I present the following C program fragment:

```
if(all_else_fails)
    {
    display_error(erno);              /* erno is already set */
    walk_away();
    }
else
    get_mad();
```

Don't worry about understanding this example; it all comes clear to you later in this book. However, notice that the display_error function has a comment after it: erno is already set. But suppose that, in your advanced under-standing of C that is yet to come, you want to change the gist of this part of the program so that only the get_mad() function is executed. You comment out everything but that line to get it to work:

```
/*
if(all_else_fails)
    {
    display_error(erno);   /* erno is already set */
    walk_away();
    }
else
*/
    get_mad();
```

Here, the C compiler sees only the get_mad function, right?

Wrong! The comment begins on the first line with the /*. But it ends on the line with the display_error function. Because that line ends with */ — the comment bookend — that's the end of the "comment." The C compiler then starts again with the walk_away function and generates a syntax error on the rogue curly bracket floating in space. The second comment bookend (just above the get_mad function) also produces an error. Two errors! How heinous.

This is an example of a *nested comment,* a comment within a comment. It just doesn't work. Figure 2-4 illustrates how the C compiler interprets the nested comment.

To avoid the nested-comment trap, you have to be careful when you're dis-abling portions of your C program. The solution in this case is to uncomment the erno is already set comment. Or you can comment out each line individually, in which case that line would look like this:

```
/* display_error(erno);   /* erno is already set */
```

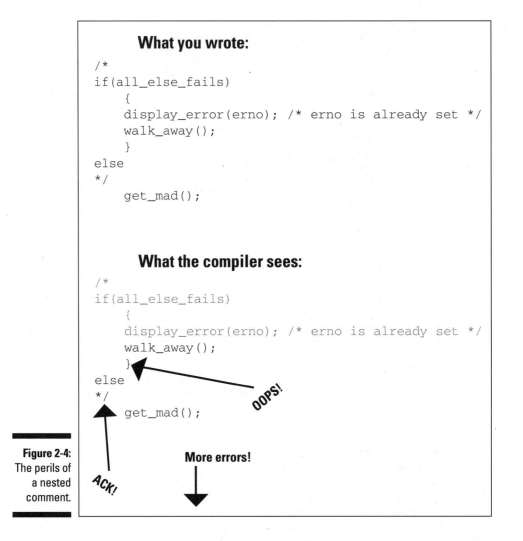

What you wrote:

```
/*
if(all_else_fails)
    {
    display_error(erno); /* erno is already set */
    walk_away();
    }
else
*/
    get_mad();
```

What the compiler sees:

```
/*
if(all_else_fails)
    {
    display_error(erno); /* erno is already set */
    walk_away();
    }
else
*/
    get_mad();
```

OOPS!

ACK!

More errors!

Figure 2-4:
The perils of
a nested
comment.

This method works because the comment still ends with */. The extra /* inside the comment is safely ignored.

✔ Yeah, nested comments are nasty but nothing you need to worry about at this point in the game.

Lesson 2-3 Quiz

1. Comments in a C program are:

    A. Silly little things you write to yourself.

    B. Ignored by the compiler.

    C. Musings of a befuddled programmer.

    D. Probably all of the above.

2. The characters that start and end a comment are:

    A. Different.

    B. /* and */.

    C. // and Enter (end of the line).

    D. Probably all of the above.

3. What is wrong with the following comment?

```
*/
printf("My project leader is a doodoo head.\n"); /*
```

    A. The text need not be commented out.

    B. The wrong combination is used to end the comment.

    C. The commenting characters do not appear on the same line.

    D. The wrong combinations are used to both start and end the comment.

4. In addition to jotting down notes for yourself, you can also use comments to:

    A. Block out parts of the program that don't run — called "commenting out."

    B. Write notes to the people who hide in the closet and use your computer when you finally pass out.

    C. Taunt the compiler.

    D. Fill the editorial page and annoy the Clinton administration.

5. Comments?

Lesson 2-4: gets *and* puts (or No More f Suffixes, Please!)

The printf and scanf functions aren't the only way you can display information or read text from the keyboard. No, no, no. The C language is full of tricks to meet this end. And when you find out how limited and lame they are, you will probably create your own functions that read the keyboard and display information just the way you like. Until then, you have to put up with what C offers.

For the most part, printf and scanf are just too fancy. They use many fancy codes and secret symbols to display and read information. On a more simple and elegant level are the gets and puts functions, from the vaunted *s* family of functions.

Goodbye scanf, hello gets

gets is nice and simple. scanf, well, that was crude by comparison (capable, but crude). Both do the same thing: They read characters from the keyboard and save them in a variable. gets only reads in text, however. scanf can read in numeric values and strings and in a number of combinations. That makes it valuable, but for reading in text, clunky.

The format for gets, which is really cinchy, appears in the next function box.

Function gets

The gets function reads characters you type at the keyboard, saving them in a string variable you must have already created by using the char keyword. It stops reading characters when you press the Enter key.

```
gets(var);
```

gets is followed by a set of parentheses and always ends in a semicolon. Inside the parentheses is *var*, the name of a string variable.

The gets function is a complete statement in the C language. It always ends in a semicolon.

Another completely rude program example

The following is the INSULT1.C program. This program is almost identical to the WHORU.C program introduced in Lesson 1-5. The differences are the text that is displayed and that gets is used rather than scanf.

Name: INSULT1.C

```
#include <stdio.h>

void main()
{
    char jerk[20];

    printf("Name some jerk you know:");
    gets(jerk);
    printf("Yeah, I think %s is a jerk, too.\n",jerk);
}
```

Enter INSULT1.C into your editor. If you're using an integrated environment, choose New from the File menu to start over with a new editing screen. Save the file to disk and name it INSULT1.C.

Compile the program. Reedit the text if you find any errors. Remember your semicolons and watch how the double quotes are used in the printf functions.

Quick notes to help you contend with this program

The fifth line creates the string variable jerk. There is room enough there for 20 characters.

In the eighth line, gets is used to read the keyboard. Type gets and then the string variable in parentheses — jerk, in this case. Note that the string variable is not listed in quotes. gets takes whatever you type and stuffs it into the jerk variable. It stops stuffing when you press Enter.

The final printf function is similar to the one in the WHORU.C program. The %s placeholder is used as a fill-in-the-blank for the jerk variable. Notice that the string ends with the \n (newline) escape sequence.

The compiler creates INSULT1.EXE, which you can run and play with. The output looks something like this:

```
Name some jerk you know:Sean
Yeah, I think Sean is a jerk, too.
```

- ✔ gets reads a variable just like scanf does. Yet no matter what reads it, the printf statement can display it.

- ✔ gets(var) is the same as scanf("%s",var).

- ✔ Oh, you Borland integrated environment people! Press Alt+F5 to see the program's output. Press Enter to return to the integrated environment.

- ✔ You can pronounce gets as "get-string" in your head. "Get a string of text from the keyboard." However, it probably stands for "get stdin," which means "get from standard input." "Get string" works for me, though.

On the virtues of puts

In a way, the puts function is a simplified version of the printf function. puts displays a string of text, but without all printf's formatting magic. puts is just a boneheaded, "Yup, I display this on the screen" command. The next function box shows you the format.

- ✔ One other major difference: puts always ends the string with the newline character — it "presses Enter" at the end of the string it displays. There's no way to avoid this side effect.

- ✔ puts can also be used to display the contents of string variables. In that case, the variable name replaces the string in double quotes — more on this in a few pages.

Function puts (display string)

The puts function displays text on the screen — a limited version of the printf function minus the fancy formatting stuff:

puts("*text*");

puts is followed by a left paren, and then comes the *text* you want to display in double quotes. That's followed by a right paren. The puts function is a complete C language statement, so it always ends with a semicolon.

Another silly DOS prompt program

To see how `puts` works, create the following program, STOP.C. Yeah, this is really silly, but we're learning here, so bear with me.

Name: STOP.C

```
#include <stdio.h>

void main()
{
    puts("Unable to stop: Bad mood error.");
}
```

Save the program to disk as STOP.C.

Compile it, link it, run it.

This program produces the following output when you type STOP at the DOS prompt:

```
Unable to stop: Bad mood error.
```

- ✔ Ha, ha.

- ✔ `puts` is not pronounced "putz."

- ✔ You don't have to put a \n at the end of a `puts` text string. `puts` always displays the newline character at the end of its output. (There is no way around this other than to use `printf` rather than `puts` for output.)

- ✔ Like `printf`, `puts` slaps a string of text up on the screen. The text is hugged by double quotes and is nestled between two parentheses.

- ✔ Like `printf`, you have to use \" if you want to display a string with a double quote in it. All the other \ characters work as well.

- ✔ Don't bother with the % characters, though. `puts` does not stick variables in the middle of its output. It's a display-string-only function.

Supplemental notes for this silly little program

The `puts` function contains a string in double quotes. There is no need for the `\n` (newline) character at the end because `puts` automatically displays it.

`puts` *and variables*

`puts` can display a variable, but only on a line by itself. Why a line by itself? Because no matter what, `puts` always tacks on that pesky newline character. There is no way to blend a variable into another string of text by using the `puts` function.

As an example, suppose that you want to display the contents of the `jerk` string variable on a line by itself. The following command comes to the rescue:

```
puts(jerk);
```

- ✔ Do not use `puts` with a nonstring variable. The output will be weird. (See Chapter 3 for the lowdown on variables.)

- ✔ You must first "declare" a string variable in your program by using the `char` keyword. Then you must stick something in the variable, which can be done by using the `scanf` or `gets` functions you've already seen. Only then does displaying the variable's contents by using `puts` make any sense.

Function `puts` (display string)

The `puts` function displays the contents of text variables, just like `printf` can, though `puts` displays only the variable's contents and no other text:

```
puts(var);
```

`puts` is followed by a left paren, and then comes *var*, which must be a string variable. That's followed by a right paren. The `puts` function always ends with a semicolon.

---

puts *and* gets *in action*

The following program is a subtle modification to INSULT1.C. This time, the last remaining printf statement has been removed and replaced with puts.

Name: INSULT2.C

```
#include <stdio.h>

void main()
{
    char jerk[20];

    puts("Name some jerk you know:");
    gets(jerk);
    puts("Yeah, I think %s is a jerk, too.",jerk);
}
```

Go ahead and make the modifications in the box to your INSULT1.C program by using your editor. However, save the source code file to disk as INSULT2.C. In the integrated environment, that's accomplished by using the Save As command from the File menu; other editors use different commands, so refer to your documentation.

Going from INSULT1.C to INSULT2.C

The only change required here is replacing the printfs in the program with puts. Change printf in lines 5 and 7 to puts, or use your editor's search-and-replace function to do it.

You can also remove the \n at the end of the text string in line 7; puts automatically sticks one in

there, so there's no reason for it. You aren't penalized if you forget to do this, however.

Nothing else in the program changes, though you need to save it under a new name; use your editor's Save As command.

After saving the file as INSULT2.C, compile it. If you're lucky and it runs, here is what you may see as output:

```
Name some jerk you know:
David
Yeah, I think %s is a jerk, too.
```

Ack! Who is this %s person who is such a jerk?

Fortunately, your compiler may just choke up and error on you, claiming that there's some extra garbage tossed into the puts function that doesn't belong there — the ,jerk part, to be specific.

puts is just not a simpler printf. The %s doesn't work, and the compiler can just deal with the ,jerk variable dangling at the end of the puts function.

Rather than replace printf with puts, you have to rethink your program's strategy. For one, puts automatically sticks a newline on the end of a string it displays. No more strings ending in \n! Second, puts can display only one string variable at a time, all by itself, on its own line. And last, the next bit of code shows the program the way it should be written by using only puts and gets.

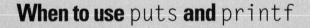

When to use puts **and** printf

- ✔ Use puts to display a single line of text — nothing fancy.

- ✔ Use puts to display the contents of a string variable on a line by itself.

- ✔ Use printf to display the contents of a variable nestled in the middle of another string.

- ✔ Use printf to display the contents of more than one variable at a time.

- ✔ Use printf when you don't want the newline (Enter) character to be displayed after every line, such as when you're prompting for input.

- ✔ Use printf when fancy formatted output is required.

Name: INSULT2.C

```
#include <stdio.h>

void main()
{
    char jerk[20];

    puts("Name some jerk you know:");
    gets(jerk);
    puts("Yeah, I think");
    puts(jerk);
    puts("is a jerk, too.");
}
```

Feel free to make the preceding modifications to your INSULT2.C program in your editor. Save the changes. Compile. Run.

The output looks funky, like one of those "you may be the first person on your block" sweepstakes junk mailers. But the program works the way it was intended:

```
Name some jerk you know:
David
Yeah, I think
David
is a jerk, too.
```

Lesson 2-4 Quiz

1. gets is to scanf as puts is to:

   A. Yiddish.

   B. prints.

   C. The keyboard.

   D. printf.

2. Which `gets` statement carries out the same function as the following `scanf` statement?

```
scanf("%s",firstname);
```

A. `gets(.firstname);`

B. `gets("%s",firstname);`

C. `gets("firstname");`

D. `getsf("firstname")`

3. Write a program using only one `puts` statement that displays the following output:

```
This is the first line
This is the last line
```

4. Match up the `puts` statement with the corresponding `printf` statement:

A. `puts(jerk);`   A. `printf("%s\n",jerk);`

B. `puts("Bletch!")`   B. `printf("Bletch!\n");`

5. Take the old MADLIB1.C program from Lesson 2-3 and rewrite it, substituting its lame `scanf` statements with `gets` statements.

Here we are at the end of another lesson. Please move away from your computer, take off your shoes, and relax.

Lesson 2-5: More Fun with `printf`

The lessons in this chapter have just begun to show you how the `printf` function can be used in your C programs. This lesson provides you with a review of how this powerful function works, plus a preview of things to come with the `printf` function.

So far, you should know three tricks:

✔ `printf` displays the text you put inside the double quotes. (If you don't yet know this trick, please return to Lesson 1-2.)

✔ `printf` requires the backslash character — an escape sequence — to display some special characters. (If you don't remember this one, please return to Lesson 2-1.)

✔ `printf` can display variables by using the % conversion character. (Refer back to Lesson 2-1 for a review of how this character works.)

The old displaying-text-with-`printf` routine

`printf`'s main purpose in life is to display text on the screen. Here is its most basic format:

```
printf("text");
```

The *text* is the text you want to display on the screen. It's enclosed in double quotes. The double quotes are enclosed in parentheses, and the entire statement must end with a semicolon.

✔ Special characters, such as a double quote, tab, backspace, and Enter (a new line), can be included in the text `printf` displays. These characters require the `printf` escape sequences, as described in the next section.

✔ `printf` can display two or more lines of text by using the \n (newline) escape sequence.

✔ To specify a double quote in your text string, use the \ " escape sequence.

The `printf` escape sequences

Table 2-1 lists all the `printf` escape sequences. Most of these you know from using them. Others are very specific and are introduced in later lessons, or maybe not, depending on my schedule.

Table 2-1	`printf` Escape Sequences
Sequence	*Represents*
\a	The speaker beeping
\b	Backspace (move the cursor back, no erase)
\f	Form feed (eject printer page; ankh character on the screen)
\n	Newline, like pressing the Enter key
\r	Carriage return (moves the cursor to the beginning of the line)
\t	Tab
\v	Vertical tab (moves the cursor down a line)
\\	The backslash character
\'	The apostrophe
\"	The double-quote character

(continued)

Table 2-1 *(continued)*

Sequence	Represents
\?	The question mark
\0	The "null" byte (backslash-zero)
\0	A character value in octal (base 8)
\xH	A character value in hexadecimal (base 16)
\XH	A character value in hexadecimal (base 16)

The blank space at the end of the table is included to allow you to add escape sequences that are particular to your compiler.

✔ You may want to flag this page with a Post-It note or dog-ear the corner. This is stuff no one remembers, so you'll wind up referring to Table 2-1 often.

The `printf` *escape sequence testing program deluxe*

To see how some of these characters work, create the PRINTFUN.C program, listed next. You will modify the `printf` statement at the core of the program to demonstrate how the various escape sequences affect text.

Name: PRINTFUN.C

```
/*
printf escape sequence demonstration program
*/

#include <stdio.h>
#include <conio.h>

void main()
{
    printf("Here is the \\a sequence: \a");
    getch();
}
```

Necessary notes

The first three lines are a comment — which I thought I'd add because it's appropriate for this chameleon program. Notice how /* and */ act like bookends to enclose the comment.

Also new: the line #include <conio.h> following the #include <stdio.h> line you're already familiar with. Type a pound sign and **include**, and then a left angle bracket, **conio**, period, little **h**, and a right angle bracket. Press Enter to end the line. It should be identical to the one above it, save for the conio versus stdio. (They both rhyme if you can pronounce them in your head.)

The bulk of the program consists of two statements: printf, which is used to test the escape sequences, and then getch, which is new.

The text string in printf contains two escape sequences. The first is \\, a double backslash that displays the backslash character. In this example, \\a displays \a — the escape sequence being tested. The second escape sequence is at the end of the string, \a.

Notice that the string in printf does not end in \n. The newline character would goof up the display for some of the fancier escape sequences (\r, \t, and \b).

The tenth line is the getch function, from the ch family, get variety. Like gets, this function reads the keyboard. However, where s in gets means string, the ch in getch means character; the getch function reads a single character from the keyboard. There is nothing between the parentheses, and the line ends in a semicolon.

In this program, the getch function acts as a "press any key" command.

Enter this program into your text editor. Save it to disk as PRINTFUN.C. Use the necessary notes if you have questions about what you're typing.

Compile and run PRINTFUN.C. The purpose here is to see how the \a sequence "appears" in the text that is displayed. Here is a sample of the program's output:

```
Here is the \a sequence: BEEP!
```

The speaker beeps. How ghastly! Pray that you're not testing this in the wee hours or you'll wake up the dog. Press Enter to "quit" the program.

✔ When the program runs, getch waits for you to press a key at the keyboard. This allows you to view the output before the program quits to DOS. getch is followed by empty parentheses ( ) and then a semicolon.

✔ Refer to Lesson 3-6 for more information about getch.

✔ The getch( ) function is available on only DOS computers, and I know that it works with both Borland and Microsoft compilers. It does not, however, work with UNIX systems and possibly some other compilers out there. For those systems, you have to make the following modifications to the PRINTFUN.C program:

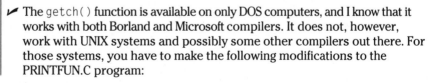

First, there is no need for the #include <conio.h> directive. In fact, it may generate an "unknown library" type of error.

Second, change getch() to getchar(), which is almost the same function but with char rather than ch before the parentheses.

The program runs the same, but you can't really "press any key"; you must press the Enter key to get the program moving.

✔ The Microsoft C++ compiler doesn't let you use the getch() function in a QuickWin window (those programs it creates and runs for you in Windows). My advice: Move to the DOS prompt and run the CL program, as described in this book's Lesson 1-3. Oh, you can use the getchar() function in a QuickWin window, but it just isn't the same.

Putting PRINTFUN to the test

The true test of the PRINTFUN program is to reedit it and replace the \\a and \a with another escape sequence. This way, you can test all the sequences to get a feel for what each of them does.

Begin by replacing line 9 in the program with the following:

```
printf("Here is the \\b backspace sequence:\b\b\b\b");
```

This line tests the \b, backspace, escape sequence. Save the changes to the program, compile it, and run it.

You see the cursor sitting below the *n* in sequence when the program runs. That's because \b backs up the cursor but does not erase. There are four \bs, which backs up the cursor four places from the end of the line. (If the cursor isn't right there, you have a rogue space in the program or you specified more or fewer \bs.)

The \n character you're familiar with, but what does \r do? How is a carriage return different from a new line? Edit line 10 in PRINTFUN.C to look like this and find out:

```
printf("Here is the \\r sequence:\r");
```

Save the change to disk, compile, and run.

In the output, you see the cursor flashing under the *h* at the beginning of the line. The carriage return resembles the carriage return on a typewriter: It moves you to the beginning of the line. It was only by whacking the line-feed bar on a typewriter that the page was advanced.

The \t character produces a tab, like pressing the Tab key. The cursor moves a predefined number of characters to the left. This is good for producing a table in which text has to be lined up. Edit line 7 in the program to read as follows:

```
printf("Able\tBaker\tCharlie\n");
```

Then insert the following lines immediately after the preceding printf statement:

```
printf("1\t2\t3\n");
printf("Alpha\tBeta\tGamma\n");
```

There are no spaces in this printf text string. The words Able, Baker, and Charlie are separated by \t (tab) escape sequences. The line ends with \n, the newline. The same holds true for the two new lines; \ts separate the numbers and words.

Double-check your source code! Ensure that you have \t twice in each printf statement and that \n ends each quoted string of text. Beware of rogue backslashes, which you'll have a tendency to type as you enter each line. When everything looks OK, save the PRINTFUN.C source code file to disk. Compile it. Run it. Here is some sample output:

```
Able    Baker   Charlie
1       2       3
Alpha   Beta    Gamma
```

Though the \ts in the printf statements look sloppy, the output is definitely organized. Tabular, dude!

✔ The "tab stops" are preset to every eighth column in C's output. Using a \t inserts a given number of space characters in the output, lining up the next bit of text at the next tab stop. I mention this because some people assume that the tab just moves over eight (or however many) characters. This is not the case.

✔ The \f and \v characters display special symbols under DOS; a form feed and vertical tab are not displayed.

✔ The remaining escape sequences should not be messed with at this point. In the future, you learn how they're used. Maybe.

Once again with the complex `printf` *format*

The `printf` function can also be used to display the contents of variables, which you've been seeing throughout this lesson with string variables and the `%s` placeholder. (The whole wacky world of variables is introduced in the next chapter.) To make this happen, `printf` uses the following format:

```
printf("format_string"[,var[,...]]);
```

Text still appears in double quotes, but it's followed by one or more variables, *var*. The variables are plugged in to appropriate spots in the `format_string` according to special percent-sign things. Those percent-sign things are called *conversion characters.* For example:

```
printf("Yeah, I think %s is a jerk, too.\n",jerk);
```

Here, the format string is text that `printf` displays on the screen: `Yeah, I think ____ is a jerk, too.` The `%s` is a conversion character — a blank — that must be filled by a string of text. (I call them placeholders, but the lords of C claim that they're conversion characters.)

After the format string is a comma and then `jerk`. The `jerk` is a string variable, whose contents replace the `%s` in `printf`'s output.

- ✔ You can specify any number of conversion characters in `printf`'s format string. For each conversion character, however, there must be a corresponding variable; three `%s` characters would require three string variables.

- ✔ Yeah, this works like fill-in-the-blanks, though % conversion characters are the blanks.

- ✔ You can specify both strings of text and numbers by using the proper conversion characters, described in the next section.

- ✔ Refer back to Figure 2-2 for an illustration of how the conversion characters work with variables in a `printf` statement.

The `printf` *conversion characters*

Table 2-2 lists all the `printf` conversion characters. So far, you've seen only `%s`. Some of the others are introduced in Chapter 3, which covers numbers and — ugh — math.

Table 2-2   The `printf` Conversion Characters

Conversion Character	Displays Argument (Variable's Contents) As
%c	Single character
%d	Signed decimal integer (int)
%e	Signed floating-point value in E notation
%f	Signed floating-point value (float)
%g	Signed value in %e or %f format, whichever is shorter
%i	Signed decimal integer (int)
%o	Unsigned octal (base 8) integer (int)
%s	String of text
%u	Unsigned decimal integer (int)
%x	Unsigned hexadecimal (base 16) integer (int)

The blank space at the end of the table is included to allow you to add conversion characters that are particular to your compiler.

✔ As with the escape sequences, the conversion characters are something you use often but never remember. I advise tacking a Post-It note to this page for future reference.

✔ "Argument" refers to the variable that will fill in this placeholder. Because a `printf` statement can have more than one variable and because C programmers are a belligerent bunch anyway, they're called arguments.

✔ For an example of using %c, refer to Lesson 3-6 and the SILLY.C program.

✔ Other programs in this book use %d, %e, %i, %u, and other placeholders. Then again, maybe they don't.

Additional formatting stuff

Your C manual contains a list of additional formatting information, bonus characters that can be used in conjunction with the `printf` conversion characters to additionally format `printf`'s output. That information is too complex and detailed to list here for every compiler. Instead, look up `printf` in your C reference manual and earmark the following formatting sections:

✔ Flags

✔ Width specifiers

✔ Precision specifiers

✔ Input-size modifiers

This is information you don't need at this point in learning the C programming language. However, it comes in handy as you begin working with numbers or require a little fancier output than what you've done with `printf` so far.

Lesson 2-5 Quiz

1. Which C language command would you use to display the message "My shoulder is out and I can't reach the coffee"?

   A. `printf("My shoulder is out and I can't reach the coffee");`

   B. `printf("%s","My shoulder is out and I can't reach the coffee");`

   C. `puts("My shoulder is out and I can't reach the coffee");`

   D. All of the above (though A is best).

2. Conversion character:

   A. A male Judy Garland impersonator.

   B. Them thar null modem adapters.

   C. `%s` or the whole parade of % characters.

   D. A politician who switches parties when the tide turns that way.

3. Escape sequence:

   A. The scene in a James Cameron film right after they assemble their weapons.

   B. \ followed by a character, used to insert secret codes and stuff in a text string displayed by `printf`.

   C. `sS`

   D. `←[2H`

4. Which of the following characters requires an escape sequence if you're to include it in text that `printf` will display?

   A. "

   B. n

   C. &

   D. {

Bonus question — worth 27.5 points!

What is the biggest disadvantage to nude cooking?

   A. No place to wipe hands.

   B. Dad takes longer to carve turkey.

   C. Hot grease splattering leads to new though easily hidden scars.

   D. Meals at Grandma's are less appealing.

The 5th Wave   By Rich Tennant

"THEY'RE REALLY TRYING TO MAKE THIS A 'SOMETHING FOR EVERYONE' CONVENTION THIS YEAR."

Chapter 2 Final Exam

1. Oh, no! That crazy Earl is knocking on your door again. His C program keeps "bombing" for some reason. He thinks that it has something to do with backslashes in his `printf` statement. Can you help Earl stick the backslashes into his `printf` statement?

```
printf("Please enter "your name," last name first:");
```

2. Being a wise guy, Earl sees your backslash solution and then poses the following query: "Then how can you put a backslash character into a `printf` string?" You answer with which of the following:

   A. The `//` escape sequence.

   B. The `\\` escape sequence.

   C. The é ➑ ➑ escape sequence.

   D. The `:-)` escape sequence.

3. Write a C program using `printf` and `scanf` that asks for your zodiac sign and then displays that answer back to you as a pickup line some lounge lizard would use. Name the program HEYBABE.C. (**Hint:** It is similar to the WHORU.C program.)

4. Rewrite the HEYBABE.C program, but substitute the `gets` command for `scanf`.

5. How big is the universe?

   A. Really big.

   B. Hugely big.

   C. Almost as big as the media's ego.

   D. Bigger than the media's ego.

6. Which two sets of characters mark the beginning and ending points for a comment in the C language?

   A. `;` and Enter

   B. `{` and `}`

   C. `/*` and `*/`

   D. `REM` and `MARK`

7. Which comment boo-boo is displayed in the following lines of code?

```
/*
pods*=1000; /* inflate number for alien bureaucracy */
printf("Total pods delivered to San Francisco: %d",pods);
*/
```

   A. Assume that the alien bureaucracy will be satisfied with an inflation of only 1,000 times more pods than you were contracted to deliver.

   B. It's the evil nested-comment faux pas!

   C. The comment is a fragment.

   D. San Francisco is already fully populated with pod people.

8. How can you compensate for atmospheric friction when you're piloting a UFO at 0.2C over Chicago?

   A. Ease off on the gluon drive.

   B. Invisibility.

   C. Power-on the anti-lamination at the expense of the backup batteries.

   D. Pull up the landing pods.

9. The following `printf` statement can be replaced by what?

```
printf("Cough up the money for this program or I'll erase your
        data.\n");
```

   A. `puts("Cough up the money for this program or I'll erase your data.\n");`

   B. `puts("Cough up the money for this program or I'll erase your data.");`

   C. `puts("Cough up the money for this program or I'll erase your data.")`

   D. `puts("Oh, heck, I'll just erase your data anyway.");`

10. The following `scanf` statement can be replaced by what?

```
scanf("%s",city);
```

   A. `gets("%s",city);`

   B. `gets("city");`

   C. `gets(city);`

   D. `gets(stty);`

11. What's one thing you should remember about the `puts` function?

    A. It's an output function.

    B. Say "put-ess" in front of Mom.

    C. It always sticks a newline character after its output.

    D. It was once married to the `gets` function, but they broke up when `gets` found `printf` more attractive.

12. To reduce the U.S. deficit, the government should:

    A. Soak the rich (which means you, by the way).

    B. Start a national sales tax or VAT tax.

    C. Hold more meetings, hire more government employees, and fuel the bureaucracy.

    D. Cut spending.

13. Which of the following `printf` statements would make noise?

    A. `printf("Clang! Bang! Crash!.\n");`

    B. `printf("Geraldo Rivera\n");`

    C. `printf("Ka BOOM!\n");`

    D. `printf("\arghghgh!\n");`

14. Which of the following is not an escape character?

    A. `\a`

    B. `\b`

    C. `\\`

    D. Steve McQueen in *The Great Escape* and *Papillon*.

15. Which of the following is not a conversion character?

    A. `%c`

    B. `%i`

    C. `%s`

    D. The emperor Constantine.

Chapter 3
Weeping Bitterly over Variables and (Gulp!) Math

• •

Lessons In This Chapter

▶ The ever-changing variable

▶ More numeric variables and a wee bit o' math

▶ Cussing, discussing, and declaring variables

▶ Constants and variables

▶ Numbers and numb-ers

▶ The other kind of variable type, the char

▶ The first dreaded math lesson

▶ The sacred order of precedence

Programs In This Chapter

KITTY.C	METHUS1.C	METHUS2.C	METHUS3.C
METHUS4.C	METHUS5.C	ICKYGU.C	SPEED.C
JUPITER.C	SILLY.C	WHICH.C	HEIGHT.C
LARDO.C	ASSESSED.C	DENTIST.C	PELLETS.C

Vocabulary Introduced In This Chapter

int	=	atoi	+
-	*	/	#define
float	char	getch	getche

• •

*I*t's time to confirm your worst fears. Yes, computers have something to do with math. But it's more of a passing fancy than the infatuation you're now dreading. Unless you're some hard-core type of engineer (the engi*nerd*), mathematics will play only a casual role in your programs. You'll add, subtract, divide, multiply, and maybe do a few other things. Nothing gets beyond the skills of anyone who can handle a calculator. It's really fourth-grade stuff, but because we work with variables — which is more like eighth-grade algebra stuff — this material may require a little squeezing of the brain juices. I'll try to make it as enjoyable as possible for you.

Lesson 3-1: The Ever-Changing Variable

A *variable* is a storage place. The C compiler creates the storage place and sets aside room for you to store strings of text or values — depending on the type of storage place you create. This is done by using a smattering of C language keywords you'll soon become intimate with.

What's in the storage place? Could be anything. That's why it's called a variable. Its contents may depend on what's typed at the keyboard, the result of some mathematical operation, a campaign promise, or a psychic prediction. And the contents can change too — just like the psychic prediction or campaign promise.

It's by juggling these variables that work gets done in most programs. When you play PacMan, for example, his position on the screen is kept in a variable because, after all, he moves (his position changes). The number of points PacMan racks up are stored in a variable. And when you win the game, you enter your name and that too is stored in a variable. The value of these things — PacMan's location, points, your name — are changing or can change, which is why they're stored in variables.

- ✔ Variables are information storage places in a program. They can contain numbers, strings of text, and other items too complex to get into right now.

- ✔ The contents of a variable? It depends. Variables are defined as being able to store strings of text or numbers. Their contents depend on what happens when the program runs, what the user types, the computer's mood, and so on. Variables can change.

- ✔ Where are variables stored? In your computer's memory. This isn't important right now; the computer makes room for them as long as you follow proper variable-creating procedures in your C programs.

Strings change

The following program is brought to you by the keyword char and by the printf and gets functions. In this program, a string variable, kitty, is created, and it's used twice as the user decides what to name her cat. The changing contents of kitty show you the gist of what a variable is.

Name: KITTY.C

```
#include <stdio.h>

void main()
{
     char kitty[20];

     printf("What would you like to name your cat?");
     gets(kitty);
     printf("%s is a nice name..What else do you have in
          mind?",kitty);
     gets(kitty);
     printf("%s is nice, too.\n",kitty);
}
```

Enter KITTY.C into your editor. If you're using an integrated environment, choose New from the File menu to start off with a blank editing window. Use the Cheat sidebar called "Extra soothing words on entering KITTY.C" if you need help typing the program. Save the file to disk as KITTY.C.

Compile KITTY.C into the final program, KITTY.EXE. If you get any errors, re-edit your source code. Check for missing semicolons, misplaced commas, and so on. Then recompile.

Extra soothing words on entering KITTY.C

The fifth line creates the kitty variable by using the char keyword. Space is set aside for 20 characters in kitty's name. The line ends with a semicolon.

The gets function in line 8 reads the keyboard, storing what you type in the kitty variable. Note that kitty is not enclosed in quotes; it's a variable, not a string of text. A semicolon ends the line.

The ninth line is a printf function that displays the contents of the kitty variable. The string in quotes begins with the %s placeholder. After the final double quote comes a comma and then the kitty variable, a right paren, and a semicolon.

There is no \n (newline) character at the end of the string in double quotes.

The tenth line is another gets function. It reads text typed at the keyboard and again stores it in the kitty variable.

Line 11 contains the final printf function. The string in quotes begins with the %s placeholder, which displays the new contents of the kitty variable. The string ends with a \n (newline) character after the period. Then comes the final double quote, a comma, the kitty variable, right paren, and semicolon.

Run the final program. The output looks something like this:

```
What would you like to name your cat?Rufus
Rufus is a nice name. What else do you have in mind?Fuzzball
Fuzzball is nice, too.
```

- ✔ The char keyword is used to create the variable and set aside storage for it.

- ✔ The kitty variable is assigned one value by using the first gets function. Then it's assigned a second value by the second gets function. Though the same variable is used, its value changes. This is the idea behind variables.

- ✔ It's the contents of the string variable that are displayed — not the variable name. In the KITTY.C program, the variable is named kitty. That's for your reference as a programmer. What's stored in the variable is what's important.

- ✔ For information about how the %s placeholder works to display a string variable's contents with printf, refer to Lesson 2-1.

- ✔ In the integrated environment, you have to press Alt+F5 to see the complete program output. Press Enter to return to the integrated environment.

- ✔ You can change and otherwise manipulate the contents of a string variable, but that requires work. The second volume of this book offers lessons on tweaking string variables and scrutinizing their contents.

Welcome to the world of numeric variables

Just as strings of text are stored in string variables, numbers are stored in numeric variables. This allows you to work with values in your program and to do the ever-dreaded math.

To create a numeric variable and set aside storage space for a number, you use a special C language keyword — just like char creates string variables. There are different keywords, however, depending on how big or weird the number is.

For now, you deal with the simplest form of number, the *integer*. Just say "IN-tuh-jur." Integer.

An integer is a whole number — meaning no fractions, decimal parts, or funny stuff — between 0 and 32,767. Negative numbers, from -32,768 up to 0, are also allowed. Any values larger than that require a different, noninteger type of number, and fractions or values with a decimal point (such as 1.5) are dealt with in a later lesson.

To use an integer variable in a program, you have to set aside space for it. This is done with the int keyword at the beginning of the program. The following keyword box lists the format.

Keyword `int`

The `int` keyword is used to set aside storage space for an integer variable. Integers can hold values from -32,768 through 32,767:

`int var;`

The keyword `int` is followed by a space (or a press of the Tab key) and then the name of the variable, *var*. This is a complete statement in the C language, and it ends with a semicolon.

Information about naming variables is in Lesson 3-3.

Information about declaring other types of numeric variables is in Lesson 3-5.

- ✔ Setting aside storage space for a variable is referred to as declaring the variable. This subject is hammered on in Lesson 3-3.

- ✔ An integer is a whole number, no fractions or dot-this or that. It can be any value from -32,768 up to 0 and then up to 32,767. For larger numbers, you have to use a different type of variable.

- ✔ The `int` keyword is used to set aside storage for an integer variable in your programs.

- ✔ Information about the different types of numbers and numeric variables in the C language is covered in Lesson 3-3. Also look into Lesson 3-5, which covers numeric variables specifically.

- ✔ Computer geeks worldwide want you to know that an integer ranges from -32,768 up to 0 and then up to 32,767 only on personal computers. Should you perchance ever program on a large, antique computer — doomed to ever dwindling possibilities of employment like those losers who program them — you may discover that the range for integers on those computers is somewhat different. Yeah, this is completely optional information; no need cluttering your head with it. But they'd whine if I didn't put it in here.

Using an integer variable in the Methuselah program

If you need only small, whole-number values in a C program, you should use an integer variable. As an example, the following program uses the variable age to keep track of someone's age. Other examples of using integer variables are to store the number of times something happens (as long as it doesn't happen more than 32,000-odd times), planets in the solar system (still 9), corrupt congressmen (always less than 524), and number of people who've seen Lenin in person (getting smaller every day). Think "whole numbers, not big."

The following program displays the age of the Biblical character Methuselah, an ancestor of Noah, who supposedly lived to be 969 years old — well beyond geezerhood. The program is METHUS1.C, from Methus, which was his nickname.

Name: METHUS1.C

```
#include <stdio.h>

void main()
{
    int age;

    age=969;
    printf("Methuselah was %i years old.\n",age);
}
```

Enter the text from METHUS1.C into your editor. Double-check everything and use the Cheat sidebar called "Supplemental scribblings for METHUS1.C" if you need extra help typing it in. Save the file to disk as METHUS1.C.

Compile the program. If you get any errors, reedit the source code and make sure that everything matches the preceding listing. Recompile.

Run the program and you'll see the following:

```
Methuselah was 969 years old.
```

Supplemental scribblings for METHUS1.C

The fifth line creates the age variable, used to store an integer value. It's indented and then comes the age keyword, a space (or tab), and the name of the integer variable, age. The line ends with a semicolon.

The sixth line is blank, separating the variable (or variables) from the rest of the main function.

The seventh line assigns the value 969 to the age variable by using the equal sign (=). age comes first, then the equal sign, and then the value (969) to be placed in the age variable. The line ends with a semicolon.

In the eighth line, the printf function is used to display the value of the age variable. printf comes first, then the left paren, and then a double quote to start the string printf displays. In the string is the %i conversion character — a place-holder for an integer value, just as %s is a place-holder for a string.

printf's formatting string ends with the \n (newline) character. Then comes the double quote, a comma, and the age variable. The statement ends with the right paren and a semicolon.

The variable age was assigned the value 969. Then the printf statement was used, along with the %i placeholder, to display that value in a string.

Assigning values to numeric variables

One thing worth noting in the METHUS1 program is that numeric variables are assigned values by using the equal sign (see the nearby Format box). The variable goes on the left, then the equal sign, and then the "thing" that produces the value on the right. This is the way it is, was, and shall be in the C language:

```
age=969;
```

Lo, the value 969 is safely stuffed into the age variable.

✔ It's worth noting that string variables cannot be defined in this way, by using an equal sign. You cannot say the following:

```
kitty="Koshka";
```

This just doesn't work! Strings can be read into variables from the keyboard by using the scanf, gets, or other C functions that do that. They can also be preset, which is shown in Lesson 3-3, and they can be manipulated in other ways, as described in *C For Dummies,* Volume II. But you cannot use an equal sign with them, like you can with numeric variables!

✔ Refer to Lesson 2-1 for more information about how printf uses placeholders like %i to display variables. Figure 2-2, back in Chapter 2, illustrated how it works.

✔ Table 2-2, also in Chapter 2, listed all the conversion characters (the %i thing) that can be used with the printf function.

Assigning a value to a numeric variable

To assign a value to an integer variable — or just about any numeric variable — the equal sign (=) is used. Here is the format:

```
var=value;
```

var is the name of the numeric variable. value is the value assigned to that variable. Read it as "The value of the variable var is equal to the value value." (I know, too many "values" in that sentence. So shoot me.)

And what could value be? It can be a number, a mathematical equation, a C language function that generates a value, or another variable, in which case var has that variable's same value. Anything that pops out a value — an integer value, in this case — is acceptable.

> ✔ The equal sign is used to assign a value to a variable. The variable goes on the left side of the equal sign and gets its value from whatever's on the right side.

Entering numeric values from the keyboard

Keep the METHUS1.C program warm in your editor's oven for a few seconds. What does it really do? Nothing. Because the value 969 is already in the program, there's no surprise. The real fun with numbers comes when they're entered from the keyboard. Who knows what wacky value the user will enter? (Yet another reason for a variable.)

There is a small problem with reading a value from the keyboard: Only strings are read from the keyboard. This was shown throughout Chapter 2. The scanf and gets functions read string variables. And there is a difference between the characters "969" and the number 969. One is a value, and the other is a string. (I'll leave it up to you to figure out which is which.) So the object is to covertly transform the string "969" into a value — nay, an *integer* value — of 969. The secret command to do this is atoi, the A-to-I function.

Function atoi

The atoi (pronounced "A-to-I") function converts numbers at the beginning of a string into an integer value. The *A* comes from the acronym ASCII, which is a coding scheme that assigns secret code numbers to characters. So atoi means "convert an ASCII (text) string into an integer value." This is how you can read integers from the keyboard. Here's the format:

var=atoi(*string*);

var is the name of a numeric variable, an integer variable created by the int keyword. That's followed by an equal sign, which is how you assign a value to a variable.

The atoi function follows the equal sign. Then comes the *string* to convert in parentheses. The string can be a string variable or a string "constant" enclosed in double quotes. Most often, the *string* to convert is the name of a string variable, one created by the char keyword and read from the keyboard by using gets or scanf or some other keyboard-reading function.

The line ends in a semicolon because this is a complete C language statement.

If the *string* does not begin with a number or if the number is too large or weird to be an integer, atoi spits back the value 0 (zero).

The atoi function also requires a second number-sign thingy at the beginning of your source code:

#include <stdlib.h>

This character is usually placed below the traditional #include <stdio.h> thing — both of them look the same, in fact, but it's stdlib.h in the angle pinchers that's required here. The line does not end with a semicolon.

The purpose of #include <stdlib.h> is to tell the compiler about the atoi function. Without that line, you may see some warning or "no prototype" errors, which typically ruin your day.

On the difference between numbers and strings, if you dare to care

It's important to know when a number is a value and when it's a string in C. A numeric value is what you find lurking in a numeric variable. This book calls those things *values* and not *numbers*. A value is 5 apples, 3.141 (etc.), "20,000 Leagues Under the Sea," and the number of pounds you can lose on celebrity diets featured in this week's *Star*. Those are values.

Numbers are what appear in strings of text. When you type 255, for example, you're entering a string. Those are the characters 2, 5, and 5 as found on your keyboard. The string "255" is not a value. I call it a number. By using the atoi function in the

C language, you can translate it into a value, suitable for storage in a numeric variable.

There are numbers and there are values. Which is which? It depends on how you're going to use it. Obviously, if someone is entering a phone number, house number, or ZIP code, it's probably a string. (My ZIP code is 94402, but that doesn't mean that it's the 94-thousandth-something post office in the U.S.) If someone enters a dollar amount, percentage, size, or measurement — anything you work with mathematically — it's probably a value.

- ✔ atoi is not pronounced "a toy." It's "A-to-I," like what you see on the spine of Volume I of a three-volume encyclopedia.
- ✔ Numbers are values; strings are composed of characters. Lesson 3-5 provides a wee bit of insight into how this works.
- ✔ Other C language functions are available for converting strings into non-integer numbers. This is how you translate input from the keyboard into a numeric value; you must squeeze a string by using a special function (atoi) and extract a number.

So how old is this Methuselah guy, anyway?

The following program is METHUS2.C, a gradual, creeping improvement over METHUS1.C. In this version of the program, you read a string the user types at the keyboard. That string — and it is a string, by the way — is then magically transformed into a numeric value by the atoi function. Then that value is displayed by using the printf function. This is a miracle happening here, something the ancients would be truly dazzled by, probably to the point of offering you food and tossing fragrant posies your way.

Name: METHUS2.C

```c
#include <stdio.h>
#include <stdlib.h>

void main()
{
    int age;
    char years[8];

    printf("How old was Methuselah?");
    gets(years);
    age=atoi(years);
    printf("Methuselah was %i years old.\n",age);
}
```

Hunt and peck the METHUS2.C program into your editor. Refer to the nearby blow-by-blow sidebar called "Slugging it out, line-by-line" for the details if you need extra help. Save the file to disk as METHUS2.C.

Compile the program. Repair any errors you may have encountered.

Run the program. The output you see may look something like this:

```
How old was Methuselah?26
Methuselah was 26 years old.
```

The user typed *26* for the age. That was entered as a string, transformed by `atoi` into an integer value, and finally displayed by `printf`. This is how you can read in numbers from the keyboard and then fling them about in your program as numeric values. Other lessons in this chapter, as well as the rest of this book, continue to drive home this message.

- ✔ OK, legend has it that the old man was 969 when he finally (and probably happily) entered into the hereafter. But by using this program, you can really twist history (though Methuselah probably had lots of contemporaries who lived as long as you and I do).

- ✔ If you forget the `#include <stdlib.h>` thing or you misspell it, a few errors may spew forth from your compiler. Normally these are tame "warning" errors, and the program works just the same. Regardless, get in the habit of including the `stdlib` thing when you use the `atoi` function.

- ✔ STDLIB.H is the standard library header file, in case you're curious. It's where the secret C language instructions for coping with the `atoi` function lurk. Hop forward to Lesson 6-1 for the full details.

✔ The `age=atoi(years)` function is how the string `years` is translated into a numeric value. The `atoi` function examines the string and spits up a number. That number is then placed in the `age` variable as a numeric value.

✔ Why not just print the string `years`? Well, you can. By replacing `age` with `years` and `%i` with `%s` in the final `printf` function, the program displays the same message. To wit:

```
printf("Methuselah was %s years old.\n",years);
```

The output is the same. However, only with a numeric variable can you perform mathematical operations. Strings and math? Give up now and keep your sanity!

Slugging it out, line-by-line, with METHUS2.C

Dispensing with the traditional aspects of the C program (the same #include <stdio.h>, the new #include <stdlib.h> thing, and void main() things you've been using for several hours now), the meat of this program begins when the variables are "declared." First comes the integer variable age at line 5:

```
int age;
```

This line tells the C compiler to set aside storage for one integer variable in the program.

In the sixth line, a string variable, years, is created:

```
char years[8];
```

char is followed by a space, then years, and then the size of the variable — the number of characters — in square brackets. There's room enough for eight characters in this string variable. That's more than enough for Methuselah's age, with room to be goofy.

Line 7 is blank, which is traditional; it separates the variable declarations from the rest of the program. (Refer to Lesson 3-3 for information about "declaring" a variable.)

Line 8 uses the printf function to display a prompt, asking the user to enter Methuselah's age. The line doesn't end with \n, the newline character, because it's a prompt:

```
printf("How old was Methuselah?");
```

The ninth line uses the gets function to read the keyboard. What's typed is stored in the string variable, years:

```
gets(years);
```

Line 10 contains the meat:

```
age=atoi(years);
```

The age variable is assigned a value, which is generated by using the atoi function. The way it works is that age just sits there with its mouth open, waiting for a numeric value. The value slides through the equal sign and into age's mouth.

atoi calculates the value based on what it finds in the text string, years. Hopefully, that string contains a value. If not, atoi shoots zero (0) through the equal sign. Otherwise, atoi slides over a number, which fits snugly in the age variable.

(continued)

(continued)

Line 11 finishes the program with a `printf` statement to display the numeric variable's value:

```
printf("Methuselah was %i years
   old.\n",age);
```

The `%i` in `printf`'s output is a blank to be filled in by the `age` variable. `%i` displays an integer value; `age` is an integer variable. The `\n` at the end of the formatting string displays the newline character — like pressing Enter.

TECHNICAL STUFF

No, you don't have to experiment with METHUS2.C, but I encourage you to try this

Thank goodness this isn't *Surgery For Dummies*. Unlike that sober tome, you're allowed to freely fiddle, poke, pull, experiment, and have fun here. Trying that with a cadaver is OK, but in Chapter 14 of *Surgery For Dummies*, "Finding That Pesky Appendix on Your Nephew," it's frowned on.

Run the METHUS2.C program again, either from the integrated environment or from the DOS prompt. When the program asks you for Methuselah's age, type the following value:

`1000000`

That's one million — a one with six zeroes and no commas. Press Enter and the output tells you that the old guy was 16,960 years old. The reason is that you entered a value greater than an integer — higher than 32,767. The value returned is the remainder of 1,000,000 divided by the size of an integer. (With your compiler, the number may be different from 16,960.)

How about typing the following value:

`-100`

Yes, Mr. M. could never be negative 100 years old, but the program accepts it. The reason is that integer values include negative numbers from -32,768 on up to 0.

Here is one you need to try:

`4.5`

Is the oldest human really four-and-a-half? Probably at one time. Still, the program insists that he was only four. That's because the point-5 part is a fraction. Integers don't include fractions, so all the `atoi` function reads is the 4.

Finally, the big experiment. Type the following as Methus' age:

`old`

Yes, he was old. But when you input "old" into the program, it claims that he was only zero. The reason is that the `atoi` function didn't see a number in your response. Therefore, it generates a value of zero.

Lesson 3-1 Quiz

1. They're called variables because:

    A. Their contents can change.

    B. They contain no meat, and young children despise them.

    C. They're very able to do many things.

    D. What are called variables?

2. Variables are:

    A. Diamonds, jewelry, watches, coins, etc.

    B. Strings of text or numbers.

    C. Changing constantly.

    D. A '50s recording group.

3. Match the keyword with the type of variable it creates:

    A. char   String or text variables

    B. int   Numeric variables

4. An integer is:

    A. Someone who cannot take care of himself.

    B. A number without a fraction or decimal part.

    C. A number between -32,000-something and 32,000-something.

    D. Probably B and C.

5. Values are assigned to numeric variables by using:

    A. A secret ballot.

    B. An equal sign.

    C. Eenie, meenie, miney, moe.

    D. PowerBall 6.

6. Why won't this line work?

```
kitty="kitty";
```

    A. You can't assign a string variable by using the equal sign; it works only with numbers.

    B. You can't name a string variable the same as its contents.

    C. It's just plain stupid to name your cat "kitty."

    D. There needs to be a backslash or some parentheses in there somewhere.

7. Write a C language program that asks for your age and then displays your age along with some snide comment.

8. Saint Redundancy, the father of all modern programming, stands atop Mount Recursion and proclaims "atoi, atoi!" What is he saying?

   A. Give me something small and cheesy, like I'd find in a Happy Meal!

   B. ASCII to integer! ASCII to integer!

   C. I've had enough, and I'm going back to Philadelphia to become an accountant!

   D. O sweet joy! For I have tasted the earth, and it tastes like dirt!

This is a long chapter. Please go do something fun, and come back later, when you're ready for more.

Lesson 3-2: More Numeric Variables and a Wee Bit o' Math

There's this school in Ohio where they teach all the budding computer-book authors how to write programming books. It's a hard course. Still, most of it is predictable. For example, the first C program is always "Hello, world." And the first traditional math program is usually some silly formula to convert the temperature from Celsius to Fahrenheit. Like we care. I mean, if it's cold out, it's cold. What everyone in Montana is really dying to know is, "Is it blowing?"

I'll dispense with tradition here, primarily because I've never been to Ohio (though I hear that the buzzard's return to Hinkley is truly a sight to behold). Instead, let's keep haranguing my dear old friend Methuselah, who was really a nice guy but not one to remember birthdays of his offspring.

You and Mr. Wrinkles

Time to modify the old Methuselah program again. This time, you create the METHUS3.C source code listed here. As with METHUS2.C, only subtle modifications are made to the original program. Nothing new, though we're building up to something later in the lesson.

Name: METHUS3.C

```
#include <stdio.h>
#include <stdlib.h>

void main()
{
    int methus;
    int you;
    char years[8];

    printf("How old are you?");
    gets(years);
    you=atoi(years);

    printf("How old was Methuselah?");
    gets(years);
    methus=atoi(years);

    printf("You are %i years old.\n",you);
    printf("Methuselah was %i years old.\n",methus);
}
```

Refer to the Blow-by-blow box nearby if you want help typing this in or understanding what it does. Double-check your source code carefully and save the file to disk as METHUS3.C.

Compile METHUS3.C. Fix any errors that sneak into the picture.

Run the program. You are asked two questions, and then METHUS3.EXE displays two strings of text — something like the following:

```
How old are you?29
How old was Methuselah?969
You are 29 years old.
Methuselah was 969 years old.
```

✔ You're not really 29.

✔ Yes, the `years` string variable is used twice. First, it reads in your age, and then the `atoi` function converts it and saves the value in the `you` variable. Then `years` is used again for input. This works because the original value was saved in another variable — a cool trick.

METHUS3.C under the microscrutinoscope

The METHUS3.C program has been divided up into four sections. This is more of a visual organization than anything particular to the C programming language. The idea is to write the program in paragraphs — or thoughts — similar to the way most people try to write English.

The first paragraph defines the three variables used in the program. Two integer variables are created, methus and you. A string variable, years, is created and made wide enough to store eight characters — more than enough for typing in your age:

```
int methus;

int you;

char years[8];
```

The next section, or paragraph, gets the user's age. The printf statement supplies the prompt, gets reads the input into the years string variable, and then the atoi function squeezes a value from the string and it's stored in the you integer variable:

```
printf("How old are you?");
```

```
gets(years);

you=atoi(years);
```

The third section does the same thing as the second section does, though the prompt is for Methuselah's age, and the value is placed in the methus integer variable:

```
printf("How old was Methuselah?");

gets(years);

methus=atoi(years);
```

The final paragraph uses two printf statements to display the results. In both statements, the %i placeholder is used to display the value of the numeric variable appearing at the end of the printf statement: you in the first one, methus in the second. Both strings end in \n (newline) characters to ensure that each is displayed on a line by itself:

```
printf("You are %i years
    old.\n",you);

printf("Methuselah was %i years
    old.\n",methus);
```

A wee bit o' math

Now is the time for all good programmers to do some math. No, wait! Please don't leave. This is cinchy stuff. The first *real* math lesson is still several pages away.

When you do math in the C programming language, it helps to know two things: First, know which symbols — or, to be technical, unique doodads — are used to add, subtract, multiply, and divide numbers. Second, you have to know what to do with the results. Of course, you never have to do the math. That's what the computer is for.

The basic mathematical symbols are neatly tucked into the following format box. There are more symbols than this, which I may or may not show you later, depending on my mood. Incidentally, the official C language term for these dingbats is *operators*. These are mathematical (or arithmetic — I never know which to use) operators.

Unlike in the real world, you have to keep in mind that the calculation is always done on the right, with the answer squirted out the equal sign to the left. For example, this line is OK:

```
diff=969-29;
```

The result of 969 minus 29 is calculated first — even though it doesn't come first in the statement. Then the result is scooped into the diff variable:

```
969-29=diff;
```

✔ Warning! Warning! The preceding line does not work. It tells the C compiler to take the value of the diff variable and put it into some numbers. Huh? And that's the kind of error you see when you try it: Huh? (Actually it's called an Lvalue error, and they're shamefully popular.)

✔ The calculation always goes on the *right* side of the equal sign. That's done first. Then the result is placed in the variable on the left side of the equal sign.

✔ Addition symbol: +

✔ Subtraction symbol: -

✔ Multiplication symbol: *

✔ Division symbol: /

✔ Having trouble remembering the math operators? Look at your keyboard's numeric keypad! The slash, asterisk, minus, and plus symbols are right there, cornering the number keys.

✔ You don't always have to work with two values in your mathematical functions. You can work with a variable and a value, two variables, functions — lots of things. C is flexible, but at this stage it's just important to remember that * means "multiply."

How much more do you have to go to break the Methuselah record?

The following METHUS4.C source code uses a bit of math to figure out how many more years you have to go before you can hold the unofficial title of the oldest human ever to live (or at least tie with him).

Before you do this, I want you to think about it. What are the advantages of being the oldest person ever to live? What else do we know about Methuselah? He died before the flood. He was a good man, well-received by The Man Upstairs. But what else? I mean, like, did he eat weird or something? Did he avoid the grape? The Bible offers no hints.

Operators for basic math

The addition operator is the plus sign, +. This sign is so basic that I can't really think of anything else you would use to add two numbers:

```
var=value1+value2;
```

Here, the result of adding value1 to value2 is calculated by the computer and stored in the numeric variable var.

The subtraction operator is the minus sign, –:

```
var=value1-value2;
```

Here, the result of subtracting value1 from value2 is calculated and gently stuffed into the numeric variable var.

Here's where we get weird. The multiplication operator is the asterisk — not the × character:

```
var=value1*value2;
```

In this line, the result of multiplying value1 by value2 is figured out by the computer, and the result is stored in the variable var.

For division, the slash, /, is used; the primary reason is that the ÷ symbol is not on your keyboard:

```
var=value1/value2;
```

Here, the result of dividing value1 into value2 is calculated by the computer and stored in the variable var.

TECHNICAL STUFF

Why the multiplication symbol is an asterisk (if you care to know)

In school you probably learned that the X symbol means "multiply." More properly, it's the × symbol, not the character X (or even little x). It's pronounced "times," as in "four times nine" for 4×9. In higher math, meaning that it was harder for you to get an "easy A," the dot was also used for multiplication: 4•9 for "four times nine." I've even seen that expressed as 4(9) or (4)(9), though I fell right back asleep.

Why can't computers use the X? Primarily because they're stupid. The computer doesn't know when you mean X as in "ecks" and × as in "times." So the asterisk (*) was accepted as a substitute. (There is no dot • character on the keyboard either.)

Using the * for multiplication takes some getting used to. The slash is kind of common — 3/$1 for "three for a dollar" or 33¢ each — so that's not a problem. But the * takes some chanting and bead counting.

Name: METHUS4.C

```c
#include <stdio.h>
#include <stdlib.h>

void main()
{
    int diff;
    int methus;
    int you;
    char years[8];

    printf("How old are you?");
    gets(years);
    you=atoi(years);

    methus=969;      /* Methuselah was 969 years old */

    diff=methus-you;

    printf("You are %i years younger than Methuselah.\n",diff);
}
```

The METHUS4.C program is eerily similar to METHUS3.C. There are only a few deviations, which you can read about in the Blow-by-blow description box toward the end of this section.

Enter METHUS4.C into your editor, or just make the necessary modifications to METHUS3.C. Cross-check your work with the preceding source code listing. Save the file to disk as METHUS4.C.

Compile the program. Fix any errors that may crop up. Then run the final product. Your output may look something like the following:

```
How old are you?29
You are 940 years younger than Methuselah.
```

Try entering a different age to see how that compares with Methuselah's.

- ✔ It does math! It does math!

- ✔ This program uses four — four! — variables: diff, methus, and you are all integer variables. years is a string variable.

- ✔ What happens if you enter a negative age — or an age greater than 969?

A closer look at METHUS4.C

This program's four variables are defined right up front. Each of them is a statement on a line by itself and ending with a semicolon. The variables can be created in any order, but all of them have to be created before they're used in the program. Notice that storage space for eight characters is set aside for the `years` string variable:

```
int diff;
int methus;
int you;
char years[8];
```

The next section of the program reads in the user's age from the keyboard. This section is identical to the three statements used in the METHUS3.C program for the same purpose (refer to that Blow-by-blow box for the details):

```
printf("How old are you?");
gets(years);
you=atoi(years);
```

The following line stuffs the value 969 into the `methus` variable. No messing around here — the value is placed directly there by the equal sign. Notice how a comment follows this statement and see how it's cleverly enclosed in the proper `/*` and `*/` character combinations:

```
methus=969;     /* Methuselah was
   969 years old */
```

Finally comes the math. To figure out how much longer you have to live to match Methuselah's record, you subtract your age from his. Pay special attention to the order of events in the following statement:

```
diff=methus-you;
```

The math part always goes on the right side of the equal sign. Your age, stored in the `you` numeric variable, is subtracted from Methuselah's and stored in the `methus` numeric variable. The result then slides through the equal sign and into the `diff` numeric variable.

Math always works from left to right in the C language: `methus` minus `you` means 969-29, or whatever your age may be. Do it backward and you get a negative number: 29-969 is negative something-or-other.

The final line prints the result by using the `printf` function:

```
printf("You are %i years younger
   than Methuselah.\n",diff);
```

The `%i` acts as a placeholder for an integer variable. The variable in this case is `diff`. This statement displays the difference in age between you and old Mr. M.

Bonus modification on the final Methuselah program!

Methuselah works hard until he's 65, and then he retires. Because he got his first job at 19, he's been contributing to Social Security. So as soon as he hits 65, he starts drawing his money out. And out. And out. And out some more.

How about writing a program that can do what no bureaucrat in Washington can do: Figure out how much money Methuselah is drawing from the system?

(We leave the "whether he earned it all" question up to future generations because, of course, if you ask Methuselah himself, he says that he did.)

Name: METHUS5.C

```
#include <stdio.h>
#include <stdlib.h>

void main()
{
        int contributed;
        int received;

        contributed=65-19;
        received=969-65;

        printf("Methuselah contributed to Social Security for %i
                years.\n",contributed);
        printf("Methuselah collected from Social Security for %i
                years.\n",received);
}
```

Type into your editor the source code for METHUS5.C — which I promise will be the last of the Methuselah suite of programs. Double-check your typing and all that stuff. Your fine sense of logic will want you to type *i* before *e* in *received*, though the illogic of English dictates otherwise. There is a Blow-by-blow box you can refer to for additional help and a description of how the program works. Save the file as METHUS5.C.

Compile it! Check for any errors or small pieces of meat the compiler may choke on. Dislodge them (reedit the source code) and compile again if you need to.

Run the program! Here is a sample of the output:

```
Methuselah contributed to Social Security for 46 years.
Methuselah collected from Social Security for 904 years.
```

✔ It seems fair to him.

✔ When math is used in a program with numbers rather than variables, the numbers are called *constants*.

✔ You can find more information on the subject of constants in Lesson 3-4.

BLOW BY BLOW

The lowdown on METHUS5.C

This program is divided into three parts. The first part declares the variables, the second part does the math, and the final part displays the results.

```
int contributed;

int received;
```

Two integer variables are created by using the two `int` keywords in the preceding lines. The first is `contributed`, which holds the number of years Methuselah contributed to Social Security. The second is `received`, which holds the number of years Methuselah was paid Social Security.

Math happens in the second part of the program. Values are thrust into the two integer variables by using some math with *constant* numbers.

```
contributed=65-19;

received=969-65;
```

The first statement calculates how many years Methuselah contributed to Social Security. He retired at 65. He started work (flipping burgers) at 19. The difference is calculated and slides into the `contributed` variable.

The second statement calculates how long Methuselah has been receiving Social Security. If he died at 969 and began receiving checks at 65, the difference is the value you want. That's stored in the `received` variable.

Notice how the smaller value is subtracted from the larger. C works from left to right with math: 65 minus 19; 969 minus 65. Still, the math part of the equation must be on the right. The variable that holds the result is on the left.

Finally, two `printf` statements display the results:

```
printf("Methuselah contributed to
    Social Security for %i
    years.\n",contributed);
```

```
printf("Methuselah collected from
    Social Security for %i
    years.\n",received);
```

In both `printf` statements, the `%i` placeholder is filled in by an integer variable's value. First comes the `contributed` variable and then `received`.

The direct result

Are variables necessary? Yes, when the value isn't known. In the last few Methuselah programs, the values were known for the most part. Only when you input your own age was there truly a need for a variable. Otherwise, *constant* values could have been used.

For example, the following program is another version of METHUS5. You don't have to type this program in, but look at the only two statements in the program. Gone are the variables and the statements that assigned them values:

```
#include <stdio.h>
#include <stdlib.h>

void main()
```

```
{
    printf("Methuselah contributed to Social Security for %i
        years.\n",65-19);
    printf("Methuselah collected from Social Security for %i
        years.\n",969-65);
}
```

The %i in the first printf function looks for an integer value to "fill in the blank." The printf function expects to find that value after the comma — and it does! The value is calculated by the C compiler as 65-19, which is 46. So the printf statement plugs the value 46 into the %i's placeholder. The same holds true for the second printf function.

It's possible to do the same thing without the math. You could figure out 65–19 and 969–65 in your head and then plug in the values directly:

```
printf("Methuselah contributed to Social Security for %i
    years.\n",46);
printf("Methuselah collected from Social Security for %i
    years.\n",904);
```

Again, the end result is the same. The %i looks for an integer value, finds it, and plugs it in to the displayed string. It doesn't matter to printf whether the value is a constant, a mathematical equation, or a variable. It must, however, be an integer value.

Lesson 3-2 Quiz

1. The unique little symbols you use to add, subtract, multiply, and divide numbers, values, variables, and stuff in the C language are called:

    A. Doodads.

    B. Dingbats.

    C. Operators.

    D. Fiddle Faddle.

2. Match the appropriate symbol with its mathematical operation:

    A. +   Addition

    B. -   Subtraction

    C. *   Multiplication

    D. /   Division

3. Which of the following C language statements places a value in the `attempts` variable?

   A. `attempts=tries+1;`

   B. `attempts=6+1;`

   C. `attempts=tries+attempts;`

   D. `They all do.`

4. Which of the following is a constant?

   A. The value 969.

   B. The letter *W* and sometimes *Y.*

   C. Room temperature.

   D. Getting the tune to "I'm Just a Girl Who Can't Say No" stuck in your head for an immeasurably long period of time.

5. What's one good thing to remember with the `atoi` function?

   A. That it's pronounced "A-to-I" and not "atoy!"

   B. That it's not spelled a-t-i-o.

   C. That you need the `#include <stdlib.h>` thing at the beginning of the program to make it work.

   D. It really enhances the flavor of beef.

Lesson 3-3: Cussing, Discussing, and Declaring Variables

Variables are what make your programs zoom. Programming just can't get done without them. So far you've just dabbled with variables but haven't been formally introduced. So along comes Valerie Variable.

Valerie is a numeric variable. She loves to hold numbers — any number — it doesn't matter. Whenever she sees an equal sign, she takes to a value and holds it tight. But see another equal sign, and she takes on a new value. In that way, Valerie is a little flaky. You could say that Valerie's values vary, which is why she's a variable.

Victor is a string variable. He contains bits of text — everything from one character to several of them in a row. As long as it's a character, Victor doesn't mind. But which character? Victor doesn't care — because he's a variable, he can hold anything.

- ✔ Yes, there is a point here. There are two main types of variables in C: numeric variables that hold only numbers or values, and string variables that hold text, from one to several characters long.

- ✔ There are several different types of numeric variables, depending on the *size* and *precision* of the number. The details are in Lesson 3-4.

- ✔ Before you use a variable, it must be declared. This is — oh, just read the next section.

"Why must I declare a variable?"

You are required to announce your variables to the C compiler before you use them. You do this by providing a list of variables near the beginning of the program. That way, the compiler knows what the variables are called and what type of variables they are (what values they can contain). Officially, this process is known as *declaring* your variables.

For example:

```
int count;
char key;
char lastname[30];
```

Three variables are declared here: an integer variable, `count`; a character variable, `key`; and a character variable, `lastname`, which is a string that can be as many as 30 characters long.

Doing this at the beginning of the program tells the compiler several things. First, it says, "These things are variables!" That way, when the compiler sees `lastname` in a program, it knows that it's a string variable.

Second, the declarations tell the compiler which type of variable is being used. The compiler knows that integer values fit into the `count` variable, for example.

Third, the compiler knows how much storage space to set aside for the variables. This can't be done "on the fly" as the program runs. The space must be set aside as the program is created by the compiler.

- ✔ Declare your variables near the beginning of your program, just after the line with the initial curly bracket. Cluster them all up right there.

- ✔ Obviously, you won't know all the variables a program requires before you write it. (Though they teach otherwise at the universities, such mental overhead isn't required by you and me.) So if you need a new variable, use your editor to declare it in the program. Rogue variables generate syntax or linker errors (depending on how they're used).

✔ If you don't declare a variable, your program does not compile. A suitable complaint message is issued by the proper authorities.

✔ Most C programmers put a blank line between the variable declarations and the rest of the program.

✔ There's nothing wrong with commenting a variable to describe what it contains. For example:

```
int count; /* busy signals from tech support. */
```

✔ However, cleverly named variables may avoid this situation:

```
int busysignals;
```

Variable names verboten and not

What you can name your variables depends on your compiler. There are a few rules, plus some names you cannot use for variables. When you break the rules, the compiler lets you know by flinging an error at you. To avoid that, try to keep the following guidelines in the back of your head when you create new variables:

✔ The shortest variable name is a letter of the alphabet.

✔ Use variable names that mean something. Single-letter variables are just hunky-dory. But `index` is better than `i`, `count` is better than `c`, and `name` is better than `n`. Short, descriptive variable names are best.

✔ Variables are typically in lowercase. (All of C is lowercase for the most part.) They can contain letters and numbers.

✔ Uppercase letters can be used in your variables, but most compilers tend to ignore the differences between upper- and lowercase letters. (You can tell the compiler to be case-sensitive by setting one of its options; refer to your programmer's manual.)

✔ You should not begin a variable name with a number. They can contain numbers, but you begin it with a letter.

✔ C lords use the underline, or "underscore," character in their variable names: `first_name`, `zip_code`, and so on. This technique is fine, though it's not recommended to begin a variable name with an underline.

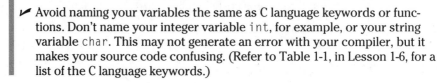

✔ Avoid naming your variables the same as C language keywords or functions. Don't name your integer variable `int`, for example, or your string variable `char`. This may not generate an error with your compiler, but it makes your source code confusing. (Refer to Table 1-1, in Lesson 1-6, for a list of the C language keywords.)

✔ Also avoid using the single letters *l* (lowercase L) and *o* (lowercase O) to name variables. Little L looks too much like a 1 (one), and O looks too much like a 0 (zero).

✔ Don't give similar names to your variables. For example, the compiler may assume that `forgiveme` and `forgivemenot` are the same variable. If so, an ugly situation can occur.

✔ Buried somewhere in one of the massive tomes that came with your compiler are the official rules for naming variables. These rules are unique to each compiler, which is why I'm not mentioning them all here. After all, I'm not paid by the hour. And it's not part of my contract.

Predefining variables

Say that Methuselah is 969 years old. If you were going to use that in a program, you could create the variable `methus` and then shove the value 969 into it. This requires two steps. First comes the declaration:

```
int methus;
```

This line tells the compiler that `methus` is capable of holding an integer-size value in its mouth and all that. Then comes the assignment, when 969 is put into the variable `methus`:

```
methus=969;
```

In C, it's possible to combine both steps into one. For example:

```
int methus=969;
```

This statement creates the integer variable `methus` and assigns it the value 969 — all at once. This is your first peek at C language abbreviation. (C is full of shortcuts and alternatives, enough to make you kooky.)

You can do the same thing with string variables — but this is a little weird. Normally, string variables are created and given a size. For example:

```
char prompt[22];
```

Here, a character string variable, `prompt`, is created and given room for 22 characters. Then you use `gets` or `scanf` to stick text into that variable. (You cannot use an equal sign!) When you create the variable and assign it a string, however, it's given this format:

```
char prompt[] = "So how fat are you, anyway?"
```

This command creates a string variable, `prompt`. That string variable already contains the text "So how fat are you, anyway?" Notice that there is no number in the brackets. The reason is that the compiler is smart enough to figure out how long the string is and use that value automatically. No guesswork — what joy!

- Numeric variables can be assigned a value when they're declared. Just follow the variable name with an equal sign and its value. Remember to end the line with a semicolon.

- You can even assign the variable a value concocted by using math. For example:

```
int screen=80*24;
```

This statement creates the integer variable `screen` and sets its value equal to 80 × 24, or 1,920. (Remember that * is used for multiplication in C.)

- String variables can be preassigned as well. Remember to leave the square brackets empty because the compiler automatically figures out the string's length.

- Even though a variable may still be assigned a value, that value can change. If you create the integer variable `methus` and assign it the value 969, there's nothing wrong with changing that value later in the program. After all, it is still a variable.

- Here's a trick that's also possible, but not necessary, to remember:

```
int start = begin = first = count = 0;
```

This statement declares four integer variables: `start`, `begin`, `first`, and `count`. Each of them is set equal to zero. `start` is equal to `begin`, which is equal to `first`, equal to `count`, which is equal to zero. You'll probably see this used more often than you end up using it yourself.

The old random-sampler variable program

To demonstrate how variables can be defined with specific values, the ICKYGU.C program was concocted. It works like those old Chinese all-you-can-eat places, where steaming trays of yummy glop lie waiting under grease-smeared panes of sneeze-protecting glass. Ah . . . reminds me of my college days and that bowel infection I had. Here's the source code:

Name: ICKYGU.C

```
#include <stdio.h>

void main()
{
    char menuitem[] = "Slimey Orange Stuff \"Icky Woka Gu\"";
    int pints=1;
    float price = 1.45;

    printf("Today special - %s\n",menuitem);
    printf("You want %i pint.\n",pints);
    printf("That be $%.2f, please.\n",price.);
}
```

Type this program into your editor. Double-check everything, and use the blow-by-blow sidebar if you want extra help or want to know what's going on. Save the program as ICKYGU.C.

Compile the program. Repair any unexpected errors — as well as those you may have been expecting — and recompile if need be.

Run the final program. You see something like the following displayed:

```
Today special - Slimey Orange Stuff "Icky Woka Gu"
You want 1 pint.
That be $1.45, please.
```

✔ This program contains three types of variables: a string, menuitem; an integer value, pints; and a floating-point value, price.

✔ If your output has the price as $1.450000, then you used the %f placeholder wrong in your printf statement. It's percent, dot, two, little *f*: %.2f. The dollar sign preceding all that is part of the output, not some crazy formatting thingamagoo.

✔ The price is a floating-point value because it contains a decimal part. See Lesson 3-5 (the section "How to make a number float"), where you are formally introduced to floating-point numbers and such.

✔ Table 2-2 in Lesson 2-5 contains a list of the printf function's placeholders. There you find that %f is used to display a floating-point number, such as the one that appears in ICKYGU.C.

BLOW BY BLOW

Up-to-date information about ICKYGU.C

This program has two parts. First comes the variable declarations and then a raft of `printf` statements that display the contents of the variables. In keeping with the lesson theme, the variables are all declared and assigned values at the same time. The first variable is `menuitem`, which is assigned to a string of text:

```
char menuitem[] = "Slimey Orange
    Stuff \"Icky Woka Gu\"";
```

The `char` keyword defines a character or string variable. The variable name is `menuitem`, and its length, normally enclosed in the square brackets, is blank. The compiler figures out the length based on the size of the string — which follows the brackets and an equal sign. Note how the string uses the escape sequence `\"` twice. This sequence inserts two double quotes into the string. The string still ends with a double quote (though `\""` looks kind of dorky), and a semicolon ends the statement.

The next two variable declarations define an integer variable and a floating-point, or decimal, variable:

```
int pints=1;
float price = 1.45;
```

The integer variable, `pints`, is set equal to 1. The floating-point variable, `price`, is set equal to 1.45. That decimal part is what forces you to use a floating-point value. (In fact, the "floating point" is that dot in the middle of the number — which is technically incorrect, but the way I remember it.)

The first `printf` statement displays the string value of the `menuitem` variable:

```
printf("Today special -
    %s\n",menuitem);
```

This is done by using the `%s` placeholder in `printf`'s formatting string. The `\n` escape sequence in the formatting string ends the output with a newline character.

The second `printf` statement displays the value of the `pints` integer variable:

```
printf("You want %i
    pint.\n",pints);
```

The `%i` placeholder is used to display the value, and the formatting string ends with the `\n`, newline, character.

The final `printf` statement is used to display the value of the floating-point price variable:

```
printf("That be $%.2f,
    please.\n",price.)
```

To do that, the `%f` (f for float) placeholder is used. However, `%f` requires some extra formatting power to display the value as a monetary amount. To meet this end, a dot-2 is inserted between the `%` and little f. That formats the output to only two decimal places. So rather than `%f`, the formatting string uses `%.2f`. (Without it, the dollar amount would be displayed with extra zeroes and just look funky.)

The dollar sign before the `%.2f` is part of the output string. Though it looks like some odd character you expect from the C programming language, it's just text to be displayed on the screen.

So maybe you want to chance two pints (though I wouldn't bother)

You can easily twist ICKYGU.C into doing some math for you. Suppose that you want to figure out how much two pints of the orange stuff is? First, you change the `pints` variable in the sixth line to read as follows:

```
int pints=2;
```

That fills the `pints` variable with 2. Then you have to stick some math into the final `printf` function, which calculates how much two pints of the sticky stuff would be. Make the following alterations:

```
printf("That be $%.2f,
    please.\n",pints*price.)
```

The only true change is in the last part of the line. Before, there was only the `price` variable. Now you have `pints*price`, which multiplies the value in `price` by the value in `pints`. Because `price` is a floating-point, or decimal, value, the result still is floating-point. This is the reason that the `%f` placeholder is still used in the formatting string.

Save these changes and recompile the program. You have to pay more, but — *mmmm* — your tummy will thank you.

Multiple declarations

C is full of abbreviations and shortcuts. This is one reason that no two C programs look alike: Programmers always take advantage of the different ways of doing things. One such trick is to declare several variables in one statement. I know, this used to be illegal in parts of the South, but it's now done aboveboard everywhere in the Union.

The following three `int` statements create three integer variables: `methus`, `you`, and `diff`:

```
int methus;
int you;
int diff;
```

The following single-line statement does the same thing:

```
int methus,you,diff;
```

Each of the variables is specified after the `int` keyword and a space. Each is followed by a comma, with the final variable followed by a semicolon to end the statement.

This shortcut is primarily a space-saving technique. It just takes up less screen space to declare all variables of one type on a single line than to have individual, itsy-bitsy int statements lining up at the beginning of a program.

> ✔ You can declare variables of only the same type in a multiple declaration. For example:

```
int top,bottom,right,left;
float national_debt,pi;
```

The integer variables are declared on one line, and the floating-point (noninteger) variables on another.

> ✔ Keep variables that are defined with a value on a line by themselves. To wit:

```
int first=1;
int the_rest;
```

Lesson 3-3 Quiz

1. Declaring your variables is almost as important as:

   A. Flossing.

   B. Looking under the hood for the cat on a cold morning.

   C. Checking for toilet paper stuck to your shoe before you walk onstage to accept that humanitarian award.

   D. Finding the perfect hat.

2. Which of the following is a good variable name?

   A. 8ball.

   B. _low_cal_.

   C. naughty.

   D. char.

3. Which of the following is an improper way to declare a variable?

   A. int methus=969;

   B. char question33[] = "What is that smell?";

   C. int gold,silver,copper,molybdenum;

   D. "Hi, my name is Todd, and I'll be your waiter-variable this evening."

4. As happens so often, Captain Kirk suddenly finds himself facing an evil twin double. How can you tell which is which?

    A. The "evil" Captain Kirk is the strong one, and his shirt isn't torn.

    B. The "evil" Captain Kirk is mentally thwarted and breaks down sobbing.

    C. The "evil" Captain Kirk doesn't eat food and loathes Mr. Spock.

    D. The "evil" Captain Kirk wears eyeliner.

Lesson 3-4: Constants and Variables

In addition to the variable, the C language has something called a `constant`. It's used like a variable, though its value never changes.

As an example, suppose that one day someone dupes you into writing a trigonometry program. In such a program, you have to use the dreaded value π (pi). That's equal to 3.1415926 (and on and on). Because it never changes, you can create a constant named `pi` that is equal to that value.

Another example of a constant is a quoted string of text:

```
printf("%s","This is a string of text");
```

The text `"This is a string of text"` is a constant used with this `printf` function. A variable can go there, though a string constant — a literal, quoted string — is used instead.

> ✔ A constant is used just like a variable, though its value never changes.
>
> ✔ A numeric constant is a number value, like π, that remains the same throughout your program.
>
> ✔ π is pronounced "pie." It's the Greek letter *P*. We pronounce the English letter *P* as "pee."
>
> ✔ A string constant is a bit of text that never changes, though that's really true of most text in a C language program. This chapter, therefore, concentrates primarily on numeric constants.

Dreaming up and defining constants

All this constant nonsense can seem silly. Then one day you are faced with a program like SPEED.C — only the program is much longer — and you truly come to realize the value of a C language constant and the nifty `#define` directive you learn about later in this lesson:

Name: SPEED.C

```c
#include <stdio.h>

void main()
{
    printf("Now, the speed limit here is %i.\n",55);
    printf("But I clocked you doin' %i.\n",55+15);
    printf("Didn't you see that %i MPH sign?\n",55);
}
```

Start over with a new slate in your integrated C language environment or on a new screen in your editor. Carefully type the preceding source code. There's nothing new or repulsive in it. Save the file to disk as SPEED.C.

Compile it! Fix it (if you have to)! Run it!

The output is pretty plain; something like the following is displayed:

```
Now, the speed limit here is 55.
But I clocked you doin' 70.
Didn't you see that 55 MPH sign?
```

So far, no big deal. But what if the speed limit were really 45? That would mean that you would have to edit the program and replace 55 with 45 all over. Better still, what if the program were 800 lines long and you had to do that? Not only that, but you had to change several other instances in which constants were used, and using your editor to hunt down each one and replace it properly would take months or years. Fortunately, the C language has a handy way around this dilemma.

✔ It's easy to argue that this isn't a problem. After all, most editors have a search-and-replace command. Unfortunately, searching and replacing numbers in a computer program is a dangerous thing to do. Suppose that the number were 1. Searching and replacing it would change other values as well: 100, 512, 3.141 — all those would be goofed up by a search-and-replace.

✔ For all you Mensa people out there, it's true that the nature of the program changes if the speed limit is lowered to 45. After all, was the scofflaw doing 70 or 60? To me, it doesn't matter. If you're wasting your excess IQ points on the problem, you can remedy it on your own.

✔ Refer to Lesson 2-5 for more information about how `printf` displays numbers.

The handy shortcut

The idea here is to come up with a handy shortcut for using number constants in C. There are two solutions.

The first solution is to use a variable to hold the constant value:

```
int speed=55;
```

This line works because the compiler sticks the value 55 into the speed integer variable, and you can then use speed rather than 55 all over your program. To change the speed, you have to make only one edit:

```
int speed=45;
```

Although this line works, it's silly because a variable is designed to hold a value that changes. The compiler goes to all that work, fluffing up the pillows and making things comfy for the variable, and then you misuse it as a constant. No, the true solution is to define the constant value as a *symbolic constant*. This is really cinchy, as the updated SPEED.C program shows:

Name: SPEED.C

```
#include <stdio.h>

#define SPEED 55

void main()
{
    printf("Now, the speed limit here is %i.\n",SPEED);
    printf("But I clocked you doin' %i.\n",SPEED+15);
    printf("Didn't you see that %i MPH sign?\n",SPEED);
}
```

Several changes are made here, each of which is discussed in the nearby blow-by-blow box.

Carefully edit your SPEED.C source code so that it matches what you see listed here. Save the file to disk again and then recompile. It has the same output because your only change was to make the value 55 a real, live constant rather than a value inside the program.

▌ ✔ The #define thingy is discussed in the next section.

- Again, the key here is that it takes only one, quick edit to change the speed limit. If you edit line 3 to read as follows:

```
#define SPEED 45
```

you've effectively changed the constant value 45 in three other places in the program. This change saves some time for the SPEED.C program — but it saves you even more time for longer, more complex programs that also use constant values.

- By the way, none of my C language documentation points out this attribute of the #define directive. But in my many years of being frustrated by the C language, I've found that this is the best way to put it to work.

- *Symbolic constant* is C technospeak for a constant value created by the #define directive.

The #define *directive*

Whenever your programs work with constants, you can use the #define directive to set them up. You do this at the beginning of the program, before the void main() function, up there with all the other pound-sign dealies. The format box nearby contains all the details.

How the #define thing
keeps the SPEED.C program sane

The program's new, third line is another one of those doohickeys that begins with a pound sign (#). This one, #define, sets up a numeric constant that can be used throughout the program:

```
#define SPEED 55
```

Begin the line with a pound sign and then type define in lowercase letters. That's followed by a space and then the shortcut abbreviation for the constant, SPEED, in this case. That's followed by another space (not an equal sign!) and then the value, 55. As with the #include thing, a semicolon does not end the line. In fact, two big boo-boos are using an equal sign and ending the line

with a semicolon. The compiler will surely hurl error-message chunks your way if you do that.

The shortcut word SPEED is then used in the program's printf statements to represent the value 55. There it appears just like a number or variable in the printf statement.

Secretly, what happens is that the compiler sees the #define thing and all by itself does a search-and-replace. So when the program is glued together, the value 55 is actually stuck into the printf statements. The advantage here is that you can easily update the constant values by simply editing the #define directive.

Construction #define

The #define construction (which is its official name, though I prefer calling it a directive) is used to set up what the C lords call a *symbolic constant* — a shortcut name for a value that appears over and over in your source code. Here is the format:

#define SHORTCUT value

Type #define, a space, the shortcut word, another space, and then the constant value. There is no semicolon at the end of the line, but notice that the line absolutely must begin with a pound sign. This line appears at the beginning of your source code, before the main() function.

It's also a good idea to tack on a comment to remind you of what the value represents, as in this example:

```
#define SPEED 55   /* the speed
   limit */
```

Here, SPEED is defined to be the value 55. You can then use SPEED anywhere else in your program to represent 55.

String constants can be created in the same way, though it's not as popular:

```
#define GIRLFRIEND "Mary"   /* This
   week's babe */
```

The only difference here is that the string is enclosed in double quotes, which is a traditional C-string thing.

- The shortcut word is usually written in ALL CAPS so as not to confuse it with a variable name. Other than that, the rules that apply to variable names typically apply to the shortcut words. Keep 'em short and simple is my recommendation.

- You have to keep track of which types of constants you've defined and then use them accordingly, as shown in this example:

```
printf("The speed limit is %i.\n",SPEED);
```

- And in this one:

```
puts(GIRLFRIEND);
```

- This line may look strange, but it's legit because the compiler knows what SPEED and GIRLFRIEND are shortcuts for.

- #define always begins with a pound sign and is written in lowercase.

- Keep the shortcut words brief and in ALL CAPS.

- There is no equal sign after the shortcut word!

- The line does not end with a semicolon (it's not a C language statement)!

- You can also use escape sequence, backslash-character things in a defined string constant. Refer to Lesson 2-5 for a list of 'em.

✔ String constants set up with #define are rare. Only if the string appears many times over and over in your program is it necessary to make it a constant. Otherwise, most programs use printf or puts to display text to the screen.

✔ You can also use math and other strangeness in a defined numeric constant. This book doesn't go into that subject, but something as obnoxious as the following is entirely possible:

```
#define SIZE 40*35
```

Here, the shortcut word SIZE is set up to be equal to 40×35, whatever that figures out to be.

✔ Using the #define thing isn't required, and you're not penalized if you don't use it. Sure, you can stick the numbers in there directly. And you can use variables to hold your constants. I won't pout about it. You won't go to C prison.

✔ Other pound-sign dealies may be covered elsewhere in this book. See Lesson 6-1 if you're lucky.

Lesson 3-4 Quiz

1. The value π is:

   A. A constant.

   B. A variable.

   C. A Greek letter that means *P*.

   D. Something I hope I never have to deal with in any program.

2. Throughout the course of your program, a constant would:

   A. Never change its value.

   B. Change its value only after being elected.

   C. Change its value under severe pressure or the promise of money or booze.

   D. Complain.

3. The advantage of the #define thing is that:

   A. You can set up a constant value once and then use a shortcut word to represent the value elsewhere in your program.

   B. Changing a constant value is as easy as editing the #define thing.

   C. It makes your programs look more cool.

   D. Probably A and B.

4. What does the following line do?

```
#define IQ 620   /* The author's IQ */
```

    A. Overstates the author's intelligence.

    B. Nothing, because there is no equal sign in the command.

    C. Sets everyone's IQ equal to 650.

    D. Creates a constant IQ that has the value 620.

5. A commotion occurs in the kitchen of a Chinese restaurant. Understanding a bit of Chinese, you decide to tell your fellow diners the following:

    A. The cook lost the recipe for the antidote.

    B. The new guy thought that the automatic vegetable slicer was the garbage chute.

    C. A cook says that the Band-Aid on his finger before he began making the chow mein is no longer there.

    D. They can't find their cat.

Lesson 3-5: Numbers and Numb-ers

Welcome to what will soon be one of many new, frustrating aspects of the C programming language. It's known as the C Numeric Data Type Puzzle. Unlike in real life, where we can just pull any number out of the ethers and be joyously happy with it, in C you must pull numbers from specific parts of the ethers based on which type of number it is. This makes the frustration factor begin rising, with the logical question, "What's a number type?"

OK. It isn't a "number type." It's a *numeric data type,* which is how you say "number type" if you work at the Pentagon. You have to tell the C compiler which type of number you're using, because it thinks about numbers differently from the way humans do. For example, you have to know the following things about the number:

? Will it be a whole number — without a fraction or decimal part?

? How big will the number be (as in value-large, not big-on-the-page-large)?

? If the number does have a fractional part, how precise must the number be? (Like to the thousandths, millionths, or gazillionths decimal place. Scientists have to know the precision when they send missiles to countries with opposing ideologies.)

I know that this is all alien to you. What most programmers want to do is say, "I need a number variable — just give me one, quick — before this value slips out the back of the computer and becomes a government statistic!" But you have to think a little more before you do that.

- The most common numeric data type is the integer.
- If you're going to work with decimal numbers, such as a dollar amount, you need the *floating-point* number.
- Keep reading.

Numbers in C

A number of different types of numbers are used in C — different numeric data types, so to speak. Table 3-1 lists them all, along with other statistical information. Flag the table with a Post-It note. This table is something you'll refer to now and again because only the truly insane would memorize it all.

Keyword	Variable Type	Range	Storage Required
char	character (or string)	−128 to 127	1 byte
int	integer	−32768 to 32,767	2 bytes
short			
short int	short integer	−32768 to 32,767	2 bytes
long	long integer	−2,147,483,648 to 2,147,483,647	4 bytes
unsigned char	unsigned character	0 to 255	1 byte
unsigned int	unsigned integer	0 to 65,535	2 bytes
unsigned short	unsigned short integer	0 to 65,535	2 bytes
unsigned long	unsigned long integer	0 to 4,294,967,295	4 bytes
float	single-precision floating point (accurate to 7 digits)	3.4×10^{38} to 3.4×10^{-38}	4 bytes
double	double-precision floating point (accurate to 15 digits)	1.7×10^{-308} to 1.7×10^{308}	8 bytes

Table 3-1   C Numeric Data Types

- The *keyword* is the C language keyword used to declare the variable type. You've been using int and char already in this book.

✔ The *variable type* tells you which type of variable the keyword defines. For example, char defines a character (or string) variable; int does integers; and so on. There are many variable types, each of which depends on the type of number or value being described.

✔ The *range* tells you how big of a number will fit into the variable type. For example, integers range from –32,768 up to 0 and up again to 32,767. Other types of variables handle larger values.

✔ Consider putting a Post-It note on this page and the preceding one to use for reference.

✔ The Storage Required column tells you how many bytes of storage each variable type requires. This is advanced stuff, not really necessary to know. Some computer scientists can look at the bytes required and proclaim, "Goodness! An integer on a PC occupies 16 bits of storage. That must explain the 32K range. Indeed. Hmmm. Pass the nachos."

Why use integers?

Obviously, if you have a double-precision floating-point number that can handle, essentially, numbers up to 1 gazillion, why bother with the puny little integer? Heck, make everything a double-whammy floating point and be done with it! Sounds good. Is bad.

Integers are truly the most common and handy types of numeric variables. Oftentimes you need only small, whole-number values when you're programming. Floating-point numbers are OK, but they require more overhead from the computer and take longer to work with. By comparison, integers are far quicker. And for this reason God saw fit to create integers (which He did on the third day, by the way).

You have to concern yourself with only two types of integers: the normal integer — the int — and the long integer — the long. (The "signed" and "unsigned" aspects are chewed over slowly later in this chapter.)

The int is a whole-number value, ranging from –32,768 to 32,767. It's ideally put to use for small numbers without a fractional part. In some versions of C, you may see this value referred to as a short or short int. In all DOS C compilers, it's just called int. (It rhymes with bent, not pint.)

The long is a whole-number value, ranging from –2,147,483,648 to 2,147,483,647 — a big range, but not big enough to encompass the national debt or Madonna's ego. This type of numeric variable is referred to as a long, or long int in some versions of C. With DOS C compilers, you can freely mince about, calling it just long.

In continuance with mankind's obsession with size, it would seem obvious — nay, greedy — to always want to use the `long` over the `int`. After all, bigger is better. Although that may be true, and I'll leave it up to psychologists to debate why we feel that way, the truth is that the smaller the variable type you can get away with, the quicker your program runs. The `int` variables are tiny and tidy, easy for the computer to figure on its two thumbs. `long` variables require a little more time to compute, and it wastes the computer's memory and processing power to use them when you're better off with `int`s. (You'll see why this is so as you continue to program in C.)

- ✔ You use the `int` and `long` keywords to declare integer variables. `int` is for smaller values; `long` is for larger values.

- ✔ The `%i` placeholder is used in the `printf` function to display `int` variables. (You can also use the `%d` placeholder; refer to Table 2-2.)

- ✔ `int` = `short` = `short int`

- ✔ Integer variables (`int`) are shorter, faster, and easier for the computer to deal with. If `Soup for One` were a variable, it would be an `int`. Use `int`s whenever you need a small, whole numeric value.

- ✔ Negative numbers — why bother? Sometimes you need them, but most of the time you don't. See the next section.

- ✔ The `char` variable type can also be used as a type of integer, though it has an extremely small range. These variables are used mostly to store single characters (or strings), which is discussed somewhere else. (Give me a second to look.) Oh, it's near the end of this very lesson.

Signed or unsigned, or "Would you like a minus sign with that, sir?"

Personally, I have this thing against negative numbers. They're good only when you play Hearts. Even so, that's justification because you may someday write a program that plays Hearts on the computer, in which case you will be in dire need of negative numbers (because you can write the program so that you always win).

When you declare a numeric variable in C, you have two choices: signed and unsigned. Everything is going to be signed unless you specifically type **unsigned** before the variable type.

A signed type of number means that a variable can hold a negative value. The standard `int` variable can hold values from –32,768 up to 32,767. That's half negative numbers, from –32,786 to –1, and then half positive numbers, from 0 up to 32,767. (Zero is considered positive in some cults.)

An unsigned number means that the variable holds only positive values. This unsigned number moves the number range all up to the positive side — no negatives (the C language equivalent of Prozac). Your typical `unsigned int` has a range from 0 up to 65,535. Negative numbers aren't allowed.

Table 3-2 illustrates the differences between the variable types as far as the values they can hold are concerned.

Table 3-2   What Signed and Unsigned Variables Can Hold

Signed	*Range*	*Unsigned*	*Range*
char	−128 to 127	unsigned char	0 to 255
int	−32768 to 32,767	unsigned int	0 to 65,535
long	−2,147,483,648 to 2,147,483,647	unsigned long	0 to 4,294,967,295

✔ Floating-point numbers (numbers with a decimal part or fractions) can be positive or negative without regard to any signed or unsigned nonsense.

✔ Floating-point numbers are covered later in this lesson.

✔ Normally, the differences between signed and unsigned values shouldn't bother you. And if they don't, hop over to Lesson 6-5 for a few programs that demonstrate how they can bother you.

✔ Lesson 4-6 uses an unsigned `char` variable in a C language "loop." This type of variable is required because otherwise the loop would run amok. (See Lesson 4-4 for more information about loops; see Chapter 7 also.)

✔ Signed variables can be maddening and the source of frustration as far as creepy errors are concerned. It works like this: Suppose that you add 1 to a signed integer variable. If that variable already holds the value 32,767, its new value (after you add 1) is −32,768. Yes, even though you *add* a number, the result is very negative. In that instance, you should be using an `unsigned int` variable type to avoid the problem.

✔ To use an unsigned variable and skirt around the negative-number issue, you must declare your variables by using the `unsigned int` or `unsigned long` keywords. Your C compiler may have a secret switch that allows you to always create programs by using unsigned variables; refer to your documentation to see what it is.

How to make a number float

Two scoops of ice cream . . . .

Integer variables are the workhorses in your programs, handling most of the numeric tasks. However, when you have to deal with fractions, numbers that have a decimal part, or very large values, you need a different type of numeric variable. That variable is the *float*.

The whole painful spiel on why we have signed integers

The signed/unsigned business all has to do with how numbers are stored inside a computer. The secret is that everything, no matter how it looks on the screen or in your program, is stored in the binary tongue inside the computer. That's counting in base 2 (ones and zeroes).

Binary numbers are composed of *bits,* or binary digits. The typical C language integer requires two bytes of storage inside the PC (see Table 3-1). Those two bytes contain 16 binary digits, or bits. (There are 8 bits in a byte.) For example:

```
0111 0010 1100 0100
```

This value is written as 29,380 in decimal (the human counting system). In binary, the ones and zeroes represent various multiples of two, which can get quite complex before your eyes, but is like eating ice cream to the computer.

Now look at this number:

```
0111 1111 1111 1111
```

This is the value 32,767 — almost a solid bank of ones. If you add one to this value, you get the following amazing figure:

```
1000 0000 0000 0000
```

How the computer interprets this binary value depends on how you define your variable. For a signed value, a 1 in the far left position of the number isn't a 1 at all. *It's a minus sign.* The preceding number becomes –32,768 in binary math. If the variable is an unsigned value, it's interpreted as positive 32,768.

So the deal with signed and unsigned numbers all depends on that pesky first bit in the computer's binary counting tongue. If you're working with a signed number, the first bit is the minus sign. Otherwise, the first bit is just another droll bit in the computer, happy to be a value and not a minus sign.

Keyword float (declare a floating-point numeric variable)

The float keyword is used to set aside space for a variable designed to contain a floating-point, or noninteger, value. Here is the format:

```
float var;
```

The keyword float is followed by a space or a tab, and then comes the variable name, *var.* The line ends in a semicolon.

```
float var=value;
```

In this format, the variable *var* is followed by an equal sign and then a *value* to be assigned to it.

Rules for naming variables are in Lesson 3-3.

Float is short for floating point. That somehow refers to the decimal point in the number. For example, the following number is a floating-point value:

```
123.4567
```

An integer wouldn't cut this number. It could be only 123 or 124. When you have a decimal, you need a floating-point number.

The range for floating-point numbers is quite large. With most DOS C compilers, you can store any number in the range 3.4×10^{-38} to 3.4×10^{38}. In English, that's a value between negative 340 undecillion and positive 340 undecillion. An undecillion is a 1 with 36 zeroes after it. That's a true, Carl Sagan-size value, though most numbers you use as floats are far less.

- ✔ Noninteger values are stored in `float` variables.

- ✔ Even though 123 is an integer value, you can still store it in a `float` variable. However . . .

- ✔ `float` variables should be used only when you need them. They require more internal storage and more PC processing time and power than integers do. If you can get by with an integer, use that type of variable instead.

"Hey Carl, let's write a floating-point number program!"

Suppose that you and I are these huge, bulbous-headed creatures all slimy and green and from the planet Redmond. We fly our UFO all over the galaxy, drink blue beer, and program in C on our computers. I'm Dan. Your name is Carl.

One day, while assaulting cows in Indiana, we get into this debate:

Dan: A light-year is 5,878,000,000,000 miles long! That's 5 trillion, 878 billion, plus change! I'm not walking that!

Carl: Nay, but it's only a scant 483,400,000 miles from the sun to Jupiter. That is but a fraction of a light-year.

Dan: How much of a fraction?

Carl: Well, why don't you type in the following C program and have your computer calculate the distance for you?

Dan: Wait. I'm the author of this book. *You* type in the program, JUPITER.C, and *you* figure it out. Sheesh.

Name: JUPITER.C

```
#include <stdio.h>

void main()
{
    float lightyear=5.878E12;
    float jupiter=483400000;
    float distance;

    distance=jupiter/lightyear;

    printf("Jupiter is %f lightyears from the sun.\n",distance);
}
```

Enter this program into your text editor. Be careful! Use the blow-by-blow description box if you need help. Check spelling, odd characters, other stuff. Save the file to disk as JUPITER.C.

Compile the program. If you see any errors, fix 'em up and recompile.

Run the program. The output looks something like the following:

```
Jupiter is 0.000082 lightyears from the sun.
```

Carl: A mere stumble!

Dan: I'm still not walking it.

- ✔ You use the float keyword to declare a floating-point variable.
- ✔ The %f placeholder is used in the printf function to display floating-point values.
- ✔ The float variables were used in this program for two reasons: The first was the humongous size of the numbers involved, and the second was that division usually produces a noninteger result — a number with a decimal part.

The E notation stuff

When you deal with very large and very small numbers, the old scientific E notation stuff crops up. I assume that it's OK to discuss this subject, because if you're interested in programs that deal with these types of numbers, you probably already have one foot in the test tube. (If this type of stuff bores you, just flip ahead to the quiz and be prepared to miss questions 7 and 8.)

BLOW BY BLOW

The gruesome details on the JUPITER.C program.

The first of three float (floating-point) variables defined in the program is `lightyear`, which contains the distance light travels (nonstop) in a year. The value is 5 trillion, 878 billion miles. That's 5,878,000,000,000 written out long ways.

In scientific notation, which is how scientists sneak around the requirement of typing zeroes and commas, the distance is written as 5.878E12. That means that the decimal in 5.878 should be shifted to the right 12 times. (The first time would be 58.78; the second time, 587.8; and on up to the Hulkian-size number that it is.)

In the program, the `float` keyword defines the variable `lightyear` as a floating-point number. It also assigns the value 5 trillion, 878 billion to that variable, using scientific notation:

```
float lightyear=5.878E12;
```

The number is written as 5.878E12. Yes, there is a big E in there. It's required for the scientific-notation thing. It's also required because the compiler cannot eat the literal value 5878000000000. This is the reason that the scientific notation is used.

The `float` keyword is next used to define the variable `jupiter`:

```
float jupiter=483400000;
```

`jupiter` is set equal to the mean distance between Jupiter and the sun, which is 484 million miles. Here, that's 4834 followed by 5 zeroes.

There's no need to mess with scientific notation here because the compiler can eat this relatively small-size number. (Anything over 100 billion usually requires the scientific "E" notation; you have to refer to your compiler's manual to check the size of its mouth.)

In the following line, the final floating-point variable, `distance`, is declared by using the `float` keyword:

```
float distance;
```

This variable contains the result of dividing the distance between the sun and Jupiter by the length of a light-year — to find out how many light-years Jupiter is from the sun. It is an extremely small number. The calculation is made with the following line:

```
distance=jupiter/lightyear;
```

The result of dividing the value in the `jupiter` variable by the value in the `lightyear` variable is calculated by the computer and then placed in the `distance` variable. The final `printf` statement displays the result:

```
printf("Jupiter is %f lightyears
    from the sun.\n",distance);
```

In `printf`'s formatting string, you'll find the %f placeholder. This character handles floating-point values. The float variable `distance` appears after the formatting string, and it's that value which is displayed in the output.

E notation is required in C when some numbers get incredibly huge. Those numbers are floating-point numbers — the floats, as you've come to know them. Integers don't count.

When you get a number over about eight or nine digits long, it must be expressed in E notation or else the compiler won't eat it. For example, take the length of a light-year in miles:

```
5,878,000,000,000
```

That's 5 trillion, 878 billion. In C, you don't specify the commas, so the number should be written as follows:

```
5878000000000
```

That's 5878 followed by nine zeroes. The value is still the same; only the commas — conveniently added to break up large numbers for your human eyeballs — have been removed. And though this number is within the range of a float, the compiler claims that it's too large. It's not the value that bugs the compiler, it's the length of the number (the number of digits).

To make the compiler understand the value, you have to express it by using fewer digits, which is where scientific notation comes in handy. Here's the same value in E notation, as you specified it in the JUPITER.C program:

```
5.878E12
```

Scientific, or E, notation uses a number in the following format:

    x.xxxxEnn

The *x.xxxx* is a value; it's one digit followed by a decimal point and then more digits. Then comes big E and then another value (*nn* in the preceding line. To find out the number's true size, you have to take the decimal point in the `x.xxxx` value and hop it to the right *nn* places. Figure 3-1 illustrates how this concept works with the light-year value.

When you enter E numbers in the compiler, use the proper E format. To display the numbers in E format with `printf`, you can use the `%e` placeholder. To see how this works, replace the `%f` in the JUPITER.C program with `%e`, save the change to disk, recompile, and run the result. The output is in E notation, something like the following:

```
Jupiter is 8.223886e-05 lightyears from the sun.
```

If the E has a negative number in front of it, as shown here, you hop the decimal point to the left *nn* places. This indicates very small numbers. You would translate the preceding value into the following:

```
.00008223886
```

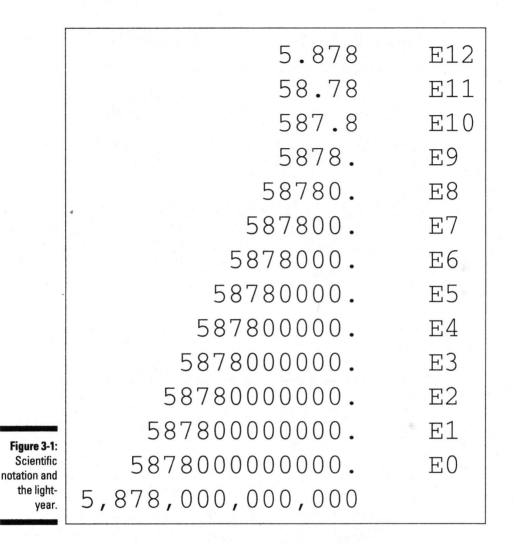

5.878	E12
58.78	E11
587.8	E10
5878.	E9
58780.	E8
587800.	E7
5878000.	E6
58780000.	E5
587800000.	E4
5878000000.	E3
58780000000.	E2
587800000000.	E1
5878000000000.	E0
5,878,000,000,000	

Figure 3-1:
Scientific
notation and
the light-
year.

✔ Scientific, or E, notation is required when numbers contain too many digits for the C compiler to eat.

✔ A negative E number means that the value is very small. Remember to move the decimal point to the left rather than to the right when you see this type of number.

✔ Some compilers allow you to use the %E (big E) placeholder in printf to output scientific-notation numbers with a big E in them.

Bigger than the float, it's a double!

For handling really huge numbers, C has its largest data type, the `double`. These types of variables can contain absolutely huge values and should be used only when you must work with those outer-space-size values or when you require a mathematical operation that must be very precise.

Double variables are declared by using the `double` keyword. "Double" comes from the term "double precision," which means that the numbers are twice as accurate as floats, which are also known as single-precision numbers.

What's "precision"? It deals with how decimal numbers, fractions, and very small and huge numbers are stored in a computer. Keep in mind that the computer uses only ones and zeroes to store information. For integers, that's great. For nonintegers, it means that some tomfoolery must take place. That tomfoolery works, but it tends to get inaccurate or "fuzzy" after a time, especially on the details.

As an example, gawk at the following number:

```
123.4567891234
```

That's a float if I ever saw one. But if you define that value as a `float` variable in C, the computer can store it only as a single-precision value. It can accurately hold only, say, the first eight digits. The rest — it makes them up! To wit:

```
123.45678422231
```

The first eight digits are precise. The rest — eh? This is single precision in action. Double precision can be accurate down to maybe 12 or 16 decimal places, but after that, it begins acting goofy as well.

The moral of this story is twofold: First, if you have to make float calculations with your computer, remember that the number can be only so accurate. After about eight digits or so, the rest of the output is meaningless. Second, if you need very precise calculations, use the `double` type of variable. It still has its problems, but it is more precise than the `float`.

- ✔ You use the `double` keyword to declare a double-precision floating-point variable in your C programs.

- ✔ If you ever print a value, say 123.456, yet the output you see is something like 123.456001, that extra "001" is the lack of precision the computer has when it's dealing with floating-point numbers. For the most part, any extra value added is insignificant, so don't let it bug you.

- ✔ Being accurate to eight digits is more than enough for most noninteger calculations. For sending people to Mars, however, I recommend the `double`. (I know that NASA reads these books intently.)

✔ Some compilers may offer quadruple-precision numbers with their own unique keywords and other rules and regulations.

✔ The greater the precision, the longer it takes the computer to deal with the numbers. Don't use more precision than you have to.

✔ Single, double, float, long — sounds a lot like craps to me!

Formatting your zeroes and decimal places

Float values can sure look gross when they're displayed by using the `%f` in the `printf` function. Ugh. This is where you have to plug your nose and plunge a little deeper into the murky waters of `printf` formatting. Fortunately, this is about the only time you really have to do this.

Between the `%` and the `f`, you can insert some special formatting characters. They control the `printf` function's output and may help you get rid of some excess zeroes or trim up the number that is displayed.

The whole happy parade of formatting characters appears in your C language reference guide, which is one of those books that came with your compiler. The following are just a few examples that show you how to trim up your numbers and avoid the cavalcade of zeroes that appears sometimes when you're dealing with floats and doubles.

```
%.2f
```

This placeholder displays the float number by using only two decimal places. This would be ideal for displaying dollar amounts. Without it, you may have $199.9500 displayed as a price — which won't appease your customer's sense of thrift any.

If you need to display more decimal places, specify that number after the dot:

```
%.4f
```

This placeholder formats floating-point numbers to display four digits after the decimal point. If the value isn't that small, zeroes pad out the four decimal places.

```
%6f
```

This format information tells `printf` to display the number by using six digits — which includes the decimal point. No matter how big the number is, it always is displayed by using six digits. Rather than leading zeroes, the number is padded on the left with spaces. So the number 123 is displayed as:

```
  123.
```

This line begins with two spaces, or is indented two spaces, depending on how you look at it.

Sometimes the %f may display a number that looks like this:

```
145000.000000
```

In that case, you can trim up the number by using either %.2f, which displays only two zeroes after the decimal point, or something like %6f, which limits the output to only six digits.

- ✔ An alternative to messing with numbers and other characters between the % and little *f* is to use the %e placeholder. It displays numbers in scientific format, which is usually shorter than the %f placeholder's output.

- ✔ Then there's the %g placeholder. That thing displays a floating-point number in either the %f or %e (scientific) format, depending on which is shorter.

- ✔ Yes, I know that this chapter was short on examples. But numbers are boring. So there.

Lesson 3-5 Quiz

1. There are different types of numbers in C because:

   A. If there weren't, it would be too easy.

   B. The compiler deals with numbers differently.

   C. Mildred set her heating pad on too high and it melted her wig to the pillow.

   D. Variety is the spice of life.

2. The two basic types of numbers in the C language are:

   A. The Ints and the Floats.

   B. The Warms and the Fuzzies.

   C. The AFC and the NFC.

   D. The Montagues and the Capulets.

3. Integers are best used for:

   A. Small values.

   B. Values without a decimal part.

    C. Speed.

    D. All of the above.

4. Floats are best used for:

    A. Terribly huge or embarrassingly tiny values.

    B. Values with a decimal part.

    C. Root beer.

    D. A and B.

5. "Float" is short for:

    A. Floating-point number.

    B. Flotissima.

    C. Flotsam.

    D. A buoyant, happy number.

6. If you did not — no — never wanted to use a negative integer variable, you would declare it:

    A. Unsigned.

    B. Minus-minus signed.

    C. Resigned.

    D. Consigned.

7. Match the following values to their corresponding scientific notations:

    A. 98.6   9.86E1

    B. 2001 A Space Odyssey   2.001E3

    C. 1,500,000,000,000*   1.5E12

    D. 0.000001 (one millionth)   1E-6

    *1995 budget of the United States federal government

8. What's the difference between single precision (`float`) and double precision (`double`)?

    A. A double can hold much huger values than a float can.

    B. A double is more precise.

    C. Double-precision values slow down the computer like four flat tires.

    D. All of the above.

SNACK BREAK

Now that you have all this information about numbers floating around in your head, go flop down somewhere (away from this book), and let it settle. Then come back, ready to learn about the important stuff in the next part of this chapter.

Lesson 3-6: The Other Kind of Variable Type, the char

Too many C language books seem to fixate on numbers and avoid completely the other type of variable — the character, or string, variable. These are definitely more fun. Rather than hold values — values, bah! — they hold individual characters or letters of the alphabet and complete strings of text. This certainly opens the floodgates of creativity over pounding the sand with numbers.

Though I talk about both single-character and string variables, there is really only one variable type, the char, which is defined by the keyword char. And I think, though I'm not certain, that it's pronounced "car" and not "char," as in "charred beyond all recognition."

Single-character variables

Like strings of text, the single-character variable is declared by using the char keyword. Unlike strings, the single-character variable holds only one character, no more. In a way, the character variable is like a padded cell. The string variable is merely several padded cells one after the other — like an asylum.

Keyword char (declare a single-character variable)

The char keyword is used to set aside storage space for a single-character variable. Here is the format:

```
char var;
```

char is written in lowercase, followed by a space and then var, the name of the variable to be created. (Refer to Lesson 3-3 for rules on variable names.) var is not followed by square brackets, as is done when you're creating a string variable. It's assumed that the value is one, as in char var[1];.

In the following format, you can predefine a single character value:

```
char var='c';
```

char is followed by a space. The name of the variable you're creating, var, is followed by an equal sign and then a character in *single* quotes. The statement ends in a semicolon.

Inside the single quotes is a single character, which is assigned to the variable var. You can specify any single character or use one of the escape sequences, as listed in Table 2-1, as single characters.

The single-character variable is ideal for reading one character (obviously) from the keyboard. The variable holds that one character. Then, by using miracles of the C language not yet known, you can compare that character with other characters and make your programs do wondrous things. This is how a menu system works, how you can type single-key commands without having to press Enter, and how you can write your own keyboard-reading programs. Oh, it can be fun.

The following statement creates the character variable ch for use in the program (you can also predefine the variable if need be):

```
char ch;
```

This next statement creates the character variable x and assigns to it the character value 'X' (big X):

```
char x='X';
```

When you assign a character to a single-character variable, you use single quotes. This is a must!

Some characters you can't really type at the keyboard. For example, to predefine a variable and stick the Tab key into it, you use an *escape sequence:*

```
char tab='\t';
```

This statement creates the character variable tab and places in that variable the tab character, represented by the \t escape sequence. (Refer to Table 2-1 for a list of all the escape sequences.)

- ✔ Single-character variables are created by using the char keyword.

- ✔ Do not use the square brackets when you're declaring single-character variables.

- ✔ If you predefine the variable's value with a character, enclose that character in single quotes. Don't use double quotes.

- ✔ You can assign almost any character value to the character variable. Special, weird, and other characters can be assigned by using the escape sequences discussed back in Chapter 2. Refer to Table 2-1 for a list; see the Techy box nearby for a description of how it's done.

- ✔ Information about creating string variables is presented in Lesson 2-2. This lesson deals primarily with single-character variables. *C For Dummies,* Volume II has more information about strings and the nonnumeric side of variables.

Typing those hard-to-reach characters

Some characters can't be typed at the keyboard or entered by using escape sequences. For example, the "extended ASCII" characters used on most PCs — which includes the line-drawing characters, math symbols, and some foreign characters — requires some extra effort to stuff into character variables. It's possible — just a little technical. Follow these steps:

1. The first step is to look up the character's secret code value — its ASCII or extended ASCII code number.

2. Convert that code number into base 16, the hexadecimal "hex" system. (This is why the hexadecimal values are usually shown in the ASCII tables and charts.)

3. Specify that hex value, which is two digits long, after the \x escape sequence.

4. Remember to enclose the entire escape sequence — four characters long — in single quotes.

Suppose that you want to use the British pound symbol, £, in your program. That character's secret code number is 156. Look it up in Appendix B. You can see that the hexadecimal value is 9C. (Hex numbers contain letters; see Lesson 6-7 if you're baffled.) So you would specify the following escape sequence in your program:

`'\x9C'`

Notice that it's enclosed in single quotes. The C, or any other hexadecimal letter, can be upper- or lowercase. When the escape sequence is assigned to a character variable, the C compiler takes the preceding number and converts it into a character—the £—which sits snug until needed.

Stuffing characters into character variables

You can assign a character variable a value in one of several ways. The first way is to just stuff a character in there, similar to the way you stuff a value into a numeric variable or your foot into a sock. If key is a character variable, for example, you can place the character 'T' in it with the following statement:

```
key='T';
```

The T, which must be in single quotes, ladies and gentlemen, slides through the equal sign and into the key variable's single-character holding bin. The statement ends in a semicolon. (I'll assume that key was defined as a character variable by using the char key; statement earlier in the program.)

In addition to single characters, you can also specify various escape sequences (the \-character things), values, and whatnot. As long as it's only one character long, you're hunky-dory.

The second way to stick a character into a single-character variable is to slide one from another character variable. Suppose that both old and new are character variables. The following is acceptable:

```
old=new;
```

The character in new is squirted through the equal sign and lands in the character variable old. After the preceding statement, both variables hold the same character. (It's a copy operation, not a move.)

Finally, several C language functions produce, or spit up, character values. One of the most popular is the getch function, which waits for a single key to be typed at the keyboard:

```
c=getch();
```

This statement causes the program to pause and wait for a key to be typed at the keyboard. getch sits and waits. Sits and waits. Sit. Wait. Sit. Wait. When a key is typed, its character "value" is slid across the equal sign and stored in the character variable, c.

- ✔ The getch function is conveniently covered in the next section.
- ✔ You can assign single characters to single-character variables. But . . .
- ✔ You still cannot use the equal sign to put a string of text into a string variable. Sorry. It just can't be done.

An extremely silly character-reading program

A useful program that takes advantage of single-character variables is still a few chapters off. Until then, you can get by with something short and silly, like the SILLY.C program presented in this section. But first, a word from our sponsors about the interesting getch function — which will soon be one of your favorites.

The SILLY.C program asks you to type one character from the keyboard. It's read by the getch function and then displayed by the printf function by using the %c placeholder.

Name: SILLY.C

```
#include <stdio.h>
#include <conio.h>

void main()
{
    char key;

    printf("Press a key:");
```

```
        key=getch();
        printf("Ouch!\nYou pressed the '%c' key.\n",key);
}
```

See the nearby Blow-by-blow box for some pointers on typing this program in. It has a few twists and turns in it, so be careful. Save the completed source code to disk as SILLY.C.

Compile the program. Any serious errors require reediting of your source code file. Check your spelling and the placement of the program's doodads and thingamabobs. Recompile.

Run the final result, the SILLY program. Here's a sample of the output:

```
Press a key:Ouch!
You pressed the 'q' key.
```

- ✔ No, the key you press isn't displayed. See the following section to display it.
- ✔ Single-character variables are declared by using the char keyword.
- ✔ The getch function is used to read the keyboard and return a character based on which key is pressed.

Function getch (read a character from the keyboard)

The getch function is used to read single characters from the keyboard. There's no need to press Enter; touching any letter, number, or symbol key does the trick. The format:

```
var=getch();
```

var is the character variable that holds the keyboard character that is typed. It's followed by an equal sign and then getch and two parentheses hugging nothing. This function is a complete statement and ends with a semicolon.

The var part of this function is optional. If you omit the var= from the statement and use only getch() by itself, you get the "press any key" function:

```
getch();
```

This statement in a C program waits for a key to be pressed. This statement can be used to pause a program while the user reads the screen or just sits around and drools in front of the monitor. (This was demonstrated in the PRINTFUN.C program, back in Lesson 2-5.)

Also required for getch() to work is the following line, near the beginning of your source code:

```
#include <conio.h>
```

This tells the compiler to locate the secret instructions for using the getch() function, and it can follow the #include <stdio.h> line already in your programs. Without that line, you would get various errors describing how getch() is not a function and, lordy, you must be out of your gourd. The line does not end with a semicolon.

One final note: The character typed is not displayed on the screen.

✔ Go peek at Lesson 6-1 for an explanation of what the #include <conio.h> command does and why it's necessary.

✔ Some compilers may lack the getch() function. If you get a slew of errors about it, your compiler is probably one of these. Refer to Lesson 2-5 for information about replacing the getch function with the getchar function. The program runs differently, but it still works.

✔ You can use the getch() function with only the DOS-prompt version of Microsoft C++. It just doesn't work in the QuickWin windows.

✔ I suppose that you pronounce getch just like it's written (rhymes with "wretch"), though I've heard C nerds call it "get character" out loud. That's more descriptive because it gets a character from the keyboard.

✔ To display the value of a single-character variable by using printf, the %c placeholder is used.

✔ Refer to Table 2-2 in Lesson 2-5 for a list of all the placeholders used with the printf function.

✔ Function keys and some other strange keys don't display any characters. You typically see a blank (a space) between the single quotes — and then some weird character at the next DOS prompt. The reason is that the getch function cannot read in the function keys in a sane manner. See Lesson 7-5 for more details.

The naughty details on the SILLY.C program.

After the traditional, initial parade of C stuff (including the new conio line), the program begins with a variable declaration:

```
char key;
```

The single-character variable key is defined by using the char keyword. char is followed by a space and then key, and then a semicolon ends the statement. This line sets aside storage space in the program for a single character — one that is read from the keyboard later by using the getch function.

```
printf("Press a key:");
```

This printf function prompts the user to type a key. The line doesn't end with a newline character (the \n thingy) because this is a prompt. The next statement waits for the key to be pressed:

```
key=getch();
```

First comes the key variable, where the character will be stored. That's followed by an equal sign and then the getch function. Because getch is a function, it must be followed by a set of parentheses, though there's nothing between them. The line ends with a semicolon.

getch waits and waits for a key to be pressed. When one is pressed, it's piped through the equal sign and stored in the key character variable. The program's final printf statement displays the result:

```
printf("Ouch!\nYou pressed the '%c'
    key.\n",key);
```

(continued)

(continued)

The printf function displays Ouch! and then a newline character, \n.. This has the comic effect of displaying Ouch! after the Press a key prompt. Ha. Ha.

The %c is the placeholder for single-character variables. It's enclosed in single quotes to make it stand out from the rest of the text. The formatting string ends with the \n, newline, character and a final double quote. Then comes a comma, and the key character variable is specified. printf uses the "value" of the key variable to fill in the blank made by the %c character.

Do I hear an echo hear an echo?

The getch function has a counterpart, getche. The extra e at the end of getche stands for "echo." It means, "Get a character from the keyboard and display that character on the screen after the user types it."

To see how the getche function works, change the SILLY.C program from the preceding section. You have to change lines 9 and 10 as follows:

In line 9, change the getch function to getche. Just insert a little *e* between the getch and its parentheses:

```
key=getche();
```

Function getche (read a character from the keyboard with echo)

The getche function works just like the getch function, though the character that is typed is also displayed on the screen. Here is the format:

```
var=getche();
```

var is the character variable that holds the keyboard character that is typed. That's followed by an equal sign, then getche, and then a right parenthesis and a left parenthesis with nothing between them. The line ends with a semicolon.

getche does not display a newline character after displaying the character that is typed.

Like you did with the getch() function, you need the following line at the beginning of your source code for the compiler to be agreeable with the getche() function:

```
#include <conio.h>
```

This line usually follows the common #include <stdio.h> line already in your programs. Remember that the line does not end with a semicolon.

Because getch is pronounced "get character," I suppose that getche is pronounced "get character echo" (though I'm not completely certain about these things).

In line 10, delete the `Ouch!` — but not the first `\n`:

```
printf("\nYou pressed the '%c' key.\n",key);
```

This change is necessary because the character they type is displayed at the prompt, thanks to `getche`. The `Ouch!` would be distracting. The initial `\n` is still needed because you have to begin this line on a new line; `getche` displays the character you type but does not follow it with a newline.

Run the program again and you see the character you type after you type it:

```
Press a key:q
You pressed the 'q' key.
```

> ✔ The `getche` function works just like `getch`, though the character typed is displayed on the screen after it is typed.
>
> ✔ There are times when you need `getch` and times when you need `getche`. It all depends on whether you want the user to see the output after the character is typed.
>
> ✔ See Lesson 6-1 for more information about the `#include` directive and what it does.

Character variables as values

If you want, you can live your life secure in the knowledge that the `char` keyword sets aside storage space for single-character variables and strings. That's all well and good, and it will get you an A on the quiz. You can stop reading now if you want.

The horrible truth is that a single-character variable is really a type of integer. It's a tiny integer, but an integer nonetheless. The reason that this isn't too obvious is that treating a `char` as an integer is really a secondary function of the single-character variable. The primary purpose of single-character variables is to store characters. But they can be used as integers. It's twisted, so allow me to explain in detail.

The basic unit of storage in a PC is the byte. Your computer has so many bytes (or megabytes) of memory, the hard drive stores so many megabytes, and so on. Each one of those bytes can be looked on as storing a single character of information. A *byte* is a character.

Without boring you with the details, know that a byte is capable of storing 256 values, from 0 up to 255. That's the range of an unsigned `char` integer: from 0 to 255 (see Table 3-1). Because a character is a byte, the `char` can also be used to store those tiny integer values.

When the computer deals with characters, it doesn't really know an A from a B. It does, however, know the difference between 65 and 66. Internally, the computer uses the number 65 as a code representing the letter *A.* The letter *B* is code 66. In fact, all letters of the alphabet, number characters, symbols, and other assorted jots and tittles each have their own character codes. The coding scheme is referred to as *ASCII,* and a list of the codes and characters is in Appendix B.

Essentially, when you store the character "A" in a char variable, you place the value 65 into that variable. Internally, the computer sees only the 65 and, lo, it's happy. Externally, when the character is "displayed," an A shows up. That satisfies you and me, supposing that an "A" is what we want.

This is how char variables can be both integers and characters. The truth is, they *are* integers. However, we treat them like characters. The following program, WHICH.C, reads a character from the keyboard and displays it by using the printf function. It's almost the same as SILLY.C, covered early in this lesson. The trick with WHICH.C is that the character is displayed as both a character and a numeric, integer value. Such duality! Can you cope?

Name: WHICH.C

```
#include <stdio.h>
#include <conio.h>

void main()
{
    char key;

    printf("Press a key on your keyboard:");
    key=getche();
    printf("\nYou pressed the '%c' key.\n",key);
    printf("Its ASCII value is %i.\n",key);
}
```

To create this source code, use your text editor to load the source code for the file SILLY.C. Then insert the final printf statement shown here.

Save the file to disk by using your editor's Save As command. Name the file WHICH.C and save it.

Compile WHICH.C and create the final program, WHICH.EXE. If you get any errors, double-check the source code, fix it up, and recompile.

Run the final program. If you press the A key, the output on your screen looks something like this:

```
Press a key on your keyboard:A
You pressed the 'A' key.
Its ASCII value is 65
```

The second `printf` statement displays the key variable by using the `%c` placeholder. This placeholder tells `printf` to display the variable as a character. In the third `printf` statement, the variable is displayed by using the `%i` placeholder. That one tells `printf` to display the variable as an integer value — which it does.

✔ All letters of the alphabet, symbols, and number keys on the keyboard have ASCII codes.

✔ ASCII code values range from 0 up to 127.

✔ Code values higher than 127 — from 128 up to 255 — are called *extended* ASCII codes. Those characters are standard for the PC, but not on other computers. This is just a technical snit. Please feel free to call all 255 characters and their codes ASCII.

✔ Appendix B in this book lists all the ASCII characters and their values.

✔ A later lesson shows you how to "compare" one letter or ASCII character with another. What's being compared is really the character's code value, not its aesthetics.

Lesson 3-6 Quiz

1. The `char` keyword is used to create which type of variables?

    A. Single-character variables.

    B. Tiny fishes.

    C. Briquettes.

    D. Variables with third-degree burns.

2. Which of the following C language statements does not put a single character into the `key` variable?

    A. `key='X';`

    B. `key=getch();`

    C. `key=francis_scott;`

    D. `char key;`

3. If the average helium balloon can hoist 2 1/2 ounces of weight, how many balloons would it take to float the cat?

    A. 38.

B. 47.

C. Actually, it would take too many balloons to make this practical.

D. As a cat lover, I find this question revolting.

4. What's the difference between the `getch()` and `getche()` functions?

A. One is pronounced with a Spanish accent.

B. The letter *e*.

C. Both read a character from the keyboard, but one displays the character and the other does not (I don't know which).

D. The *e* one must echo the character. Yeah. That's it.

Lesson 3-7: The First Dreaded Math Lesson

Actually, this isn't the first dreaded math lesson, but it's the first lesson that dwells on math almost long enough to give you a headache. But don't panic! It's the computer that does all the work. You're only required to assemble the math in the proper order for the answers to come out right. And if you do it wrong, the C compiler tells you and you can start over. No embarrassment. No recriminations. No snickering from the way-too-smart girl exchange student from Transylvania.

An all-too-brief review of the basic C mathematical operators

Table 3-3 shows the basic C mathematical operators (or it could be arithmetic operators — whatever). These are the symbols and scribbles that make basic math happen in a C program.

Table 3-3	C's Mathematical Doodads		
Operator or Symbol	**What You Expected**	**As Pronounced By Sixth Graders**	**Task**
+	+	"Plus"	Addition
-	−	"Minus"	Subtraction
*	×	"Times"	Multiplication
/	÷	"Divided by"	Division

You use the symbols to do the following types of math operations:

- Work with values directly:

```
total = 6 + 194;
```

The integer variable `total` contains the result of adding 6 and 194.

In the next line, the variable `result` (which can be either an integer or a float variable) contains the result of multiplying 67 by 8:

```
result = 67 * 8;
```

The float variable `odds` contains the result of dividing 45 by 122:

```
odds = 45/122;
```

In all cases, the math operation to the left of the equal sign is performed first. The math is worked from left to right by the C compiler. The value that results is placed in the numeric variable.

- It works with values and variables:

```
score = points*10;
```

Here, the variable `score` is set equal to the value of the variable `points` times 10.

- It works with just about anything; functions, values, variables, or any combination:

```
height_in_cm = atoi(height_in_inches)*2.54;
```

Here, the variable `height_in_cm` is set equal to the value returned by the `atoi` function times 2.54. The `atoi` function manipulates the variable `height_in_inches` (which is probably a string input from the keyboard).

- The math part of the equation is calculated first and is worked from left to right. The result is then transferred to the variable sitting on the left side of the equal sign.

- This book first touched on the mathematical operators in Lesson 3-2.

The old "how tall are you" program

You can use "the power of the computer" to do some simple yet annoying math. As an example, I present the HEIGHT.C program, source code shown next. This program asks you to enter your height in inches and then spits back the result in centimeters. Granted, this is a typically dull C language program. But bear with me for a few pages and you'll have some fun with it.

Name: HEIGHT.C

```
#include <stdio.h>
#include <stdlib.h>

void main()
{
    float height_in_cm;
    char height_in_inches[4];

    printf("Enter your height in inches:");
    gets(height_in_inches);
    height_in_cm = atoi(height_in_inches)*2.54;
    printf("You are %.2f centimeters tall.\n",height_in_cm);
}
```

Enter this trivial program into your C compiler's editor. Be careful with what you type; some long variable names are in there. Use the Blow-by-blow box if you need help deciphering what's going on. Also, it's "height" and not "hieght." (I mention this because I tried to compile the program with that spelling mistake — not once, but twice!) Save the file to disk as HEIGHT.C.

Compile the program. Watch for any syntax or other serious errors. Fix them if they crop up.

Run the HEIGHT program. Your output looks something like this:

```
Enter your height in inches:60
You are 152.40 centimeters tall.
```

If you're 60 inches tall (5 feet exactly), that's equal to 152.40 centimeters — a bigger number, but you're still hovering at the same altitude. The program is good at converting almost any length in inches to its corresponding length in centimeters.

- ✔ Height. It has *e* before *i*. Yet another example of why English is the worst-spelled language on the planet. (This will be your number-one typo if you get a syntax error in the program.)

- ✔ The atoi function reaches into the string you input and pulls out an integer value. And it's atoi, not atio (yet another reason, though invalid, to hate English spelling). Refer to Lesson 3-1 for additional information about atoi.

✔ There are 2.54 centimeters in one inch. It's not that this knowledge will get you anywhere, at least not in the United States. However, should you be on "Jeopardy" and the Final Jeopardy answer is 2.54, you'll know the question. (By the way, an easy mnemonic for remembering how many centimeters are in an inch is to scream "two-point-five-four centimeters per inch" at the top of your lungs 30 times.)

✔ There are 0.39 inches in a centimeter. Actually, a centimeter is about as long as your thumbnail is wide — providing, of course, that you don't have colossal thumbs.

BLOW BY BLOW

Revised and extended remarks on HEIGHT.C

The program requires two variables. One is needed to hold the result of the mathematical calculation — which must be a float. The second is needed to hold the value entered from the keyboard. First the float, height_in_cm, is created:

```
float height_in_cm;
```

The second character variable created is height_in_inches:

```
char height_in_inches[4];
```

The 4 in square brackets tells the compiler to reserve space for four characters to be entered.

In both cases, the variable names are highly descriptive. Underlines are used to separate the words, which is allowable in a variable name.

In the next two lines, the printf function displays a message prompt, and then the gets function retrieves any text typed at the keyboard:

```
printf("Enter your height in
   inches:");
gets(height_in_inches);
```

The text is stored in the height_in_inches string variable. Notice that the printf formatting string doesn't contain the newline character, \n, at the end. The reason is that it's a prompt. Also, the gets function displays the newline when Enter is pressed to end input.

In the following statement, the atoi function translates the value held in the string variable, height_in_inches, into an integer. Then that value is multiplied by 2.54. (The asterisk is used for multiplication.) The result is then slid through the equal sign and stored in the float variable, height_in_cm:

```
height_in_cm =
   atoi(height_in_inches)*2.54;
```

Both the value 2.54 and the height_in_cm variable are floats. The value is obviously a float because it contains a decimal part. height_in_inches is an integer because that's the type of value the atoi function returns. When you multiply an integer by a float, however, the result is a float. This is why the height_in_cm variable is a float.

The final printf function displays the result:

```
printf("You are %.2f centimeters
   tall.\n",height_in_cm);
```

The %.2f placeholder in the printf function's formatting string is what displays the value of the float variable, height_in_cm. It's really %f. But in that format, too many zeroes are displayed. By inserting .2 in there, only two digits are displayed after the decimal point—good enough for this program.

Unethical alterations to the old "how tall are you" program

Though I'm not standing behind you, I can clearly see the HEIGHT.C program source code still sitting in your editor. Good. Change line 10 as follows:

```
height_in_cm = atoi(height_in_inches)*2.54*1.05;
```

After the 2.54 and before the semicolon, insert ***1.05** (times one point-oh-five). This increases your height by five-hundredths of a centimeter for each inch you have in height. The end result? Wait! Save the file and recompile it. Then run it again:

```
Enter your height in inches:60
You are 160.02 centimeters tall.
```

That may not mean much to you. But suppose that you're corresponding to some French person who's romantically interested in you. If so, you can tell him or her that, according to a program run on your computer, you're 160.02 centimeters tall. That means nothing to an American, but it means that you're three whole inches taller in France. If you were 5'10" (70 inches), the program would produce the following:

```
Enter your height in inches:70
You are 186.69 centimeters tall.
```

Now you're 186.69 centimeters tall — or 6'1½" tall! They'll be swooning!

And now, the confession:

The purpose of this is not to tell you how to cheat when you're programming a computer, nor is there any value in deceiving the French. For the most part, people who run programs want accurate results. However, it does show you the following:

```
height_in_cm = atoi(height_in_inches)*2.54*1.05;
```

The variable `height_in_cm` is equal to the result of three mathematical operations: First, an integer is produced based on the value of the string variable `height_in_inches`. That's multiplied by 2.54, and the result is multiplied again by 1.05.

Having a long mathematical formula is perfectly OK in C. You can add, multiply, divide, and whatnot all the time. To ensure that you always get the result you want, however, you must pay special attention to something called the order of precedence. That's the topic of the next lesson.

✔ An equation in C can have more than two items. In fact, it can have a whole chorus line of items in it.

✔ To increase the height value by .05 (five-hundredths or 5 percent), it's necessary to multiply the number by 1.05. If you just multiply it by .05, you decrease it by 95 percent. Instead, you want to increase it by 5 percent, so you multiply it by 105 percent, 1.05. I stumbled on this accidentally, by the way.

The delicate art of incrementation (or "Just add one to it")

The mathematical concept of "just add 1 to it" is called *incrementation*. You move something up a notch by incrementing it — for example, shifting from first to second, racking up another point in Gackle Blaster, or increasing your compensation by a dollar an hour. These are examples of incrementation.

Increasing the value of a variable in C happens all the time. It involves using the following funky equation:

```
i=i+1;
```

This math problem serves one purpose: It adds 1 to the value of the variable i. Looks funny, but it works.

Suppose that i equals 3. Then $i+1$ (which is 3 + 1) would equal 4. Because the right side of the equal sign is worked out first in C, that means that the value 4 would be slid over and put into the i variable. The preceding statement *increments* the value of the i variable by 1.

You can also use the equation to add more than 1 to a value. For example:

```
i=i+6;
```

This equation increments the value of the i variable by 6. (Though purists will argue that the word *increment* means strictly to "add one to." Then again, true purists wouldn't put any dressing on their salad, so what do they know anyway?)

✔ To add 1 to a variable — i, in this instance — you use the following C language mathematical statement thing:

```
i=i+1;
```

This is known as incrementation.

✔ No, that's not *incrimination*. Different subject.

✔ Examples of incrementing values include: altitude as a plane (or space-ship) climbs; miles on an odometer; your age before and after your birthday; number of fish the cat has eaten; your weight over the holidays; and so on.

✔ Incrementation — $i=i+1$ — works because C figures out what's on the right side of the equal sign first. $i+1$ is done first. Then it replaces the original value of the i variable. It's when you look at the whole thing all at once (from left to right) that it messes with your brain.

Unhappily incrementing your weight

The following program is LARDO.C, a rather rude, interactive program that uses math to increment your weight; you input what you weigh and then LARDO calculates your newfound bulk as you consume your holiday feast.

Name: LARDO.C

```
#include <stdio.h>
#include <stdlib.h>

void main()
{
    char weight[4];
    int w;

    printf("Enter your weight:");
    gets(weight);
    w=atoi(weight);

    printf("Here is what you weigh now: %i\n",w);
    w=w+1;
    printf("Your weight after the potatoes: %i\n",w);
    w=w+1;
    printf("Here you are after the mutton: %i\n",w);
    w=w+8;
    printf("And your weight after dessert: %i pounds!\n",w);
    printf("Lardo!\n");
}
```

Type the preceding source code into your text editor. The only truly new material here is the w=w+1 equation, which increments the value of the w variable by one. The final equation, w=w+8, adds eight to the value of the w variable.

Check your typing and be mindful of semicolons and double quotes. Save the file to disk as LARDO.C.

Compile LARDO.C. Fix any errors, if need be.

The following sample of the program's final run uses 175 as the user's weight:

```
Enter your weight:175
Here is what you weigh now: 175
Your weight after the potatoes: 176
Here you are after the mutton: 177
And your weight after dessert: 185 pounds!
Lardo!
```

✔ This program doesn't need to be insultive — but what the hey! The idea here is to show how the w=w+1 equation is used to add 1 to the value of a variable. This is called *incrementation*. (This is what God does to your weight every morning that you lug your pudgy legs onto the scale.)

✔ Yeah, 175 pounds! I'm sure that you typed in an equally modest value rather than something more representative of your true girth.

✔ There's more to come on this incrementation nonsense! (See Lesson 4-7.)

Bonus program! (One that may actually have a purpose in life)

Monopoly is perhaps one of the greatest board games ever invented, and it can be terrific fun — especially when you own rows of hotels and your pitiful opponents land on them like flies on a discarded all-day sucker. The only problem at that point is drawing the Community Chest card that proclaims the following:

> You are assessed for street repairs. $40 per house, $115 per hotel.

So you count up all your houses and multiply that number by $40, and then all the hotels by $115 (which is a strange number), and then you add the two values. It's a terrible thing to do to one's brain in the middle of a Monopoly game. But the mental drudgery can be easily abated by a simple computer program, one such as ASSESSED.C:

Name: ASSESSED.C

```
#include <stdio.h>
#include <stdlib.h>
```

```
void main()
{
     int houses, hotels, total;
     char temp[4];

     printf("Enter the number of houses:");
     gets(temp);
     houses=atoi(temp);

     printf("Enter the number of hotels:");
     gets(temp);
     hotels=atoi(temp);

     total=houses*40+hotels*115;

     printf("You owe the bank $%i.\n",total);
}
```

Carefully type this program into your editor on a new screen. Double-check your semicolons, parentheses, and quotes. Then save it to disk as ASSESSED.C.

Compile! Fix any errors, if need be. Then run the program. Suppose that you have nine houses and three hotels. Here is what your output would look like:

```
Enter the number of houses:9
Enter the number of hotels:3
You owe the bank $705.
```

Amazing how easy the computer could figure that out! Of course, at this point in the game, you can easily afford the $705 in funny money. All you need is some poor sap to land on St. Charles Place with its hotel, and you've made the money back jiffy pronto.

- ✔ Notice how the `temp` variable is used to hold and help convert two different strings into numbers? This example illustrates how variables can change and, well, be variable (see Lesson 3-1).

- ✔ The mathematical computation in line 17 works because of something called the Sacred Order of Precedence, which is covered in the very next lesson.

- ✔ You might think, and rightly so, that the total displayed by the program should be a float variable. After all, dollar amounts usually have a decimal part; $705.00 rather than $705. But in this case, because all the values will be integers, it just makes more sense to stick with a `total` integer variable. Keep in mind that integers are faster, which is especially apparent in larger programs.

BLOW BY BLOW

The lowdown on ASSESSED.C

The program uses four variables: three integer variables to hold the number of houses, hotels, and the total amount owed, plus a character variable required to read input from the keyboard. These variables are defined up front:

```
int houses, hotels, total;
char temp[4];
```

The next chunk of the program is used to read in the number of houses that are owned. A `printf` statement displays the prompt, and the `gets` function reads the keyboard and stores whatever was typed into the `temp` variable. Finally, the `atoi` function converts what was typed at the keyboard (and stored in the `temp` variable) into an integer value, which is then stored in the `houses` variable:

```
printf("Enter the number of
    houses:");
gets(temp);
houses=atoi(temp);
```

The same three statements are used similarly in the next chunk of the program to read in the number of hotels that are owned. The `temp` variable again is used with `gets` to read the keyboard (because the old value of `temp` has already been converted into a value and stored in the `houses` variable). But in line 15, the new text typed at the keyboard is converted into the `hotels` variable:

```
printf("Enter the number of ho-
    tels:");
gets(temp);
hotels=atoi(temp);
```

Line 17 makes the calculation of the amount owed. The formula is the number of houses, stored in the `houses` variable, times $40, plus the number of hotels, stored in the `hotels` variable, times $115. That amount is calculated and stored in the `total` variable:

```
total=houses*40+hotels*115;
```

The final `printf` statement displays the result by using the `%i` placeholder. The dollar sign before the `%i` makes the value read as a dollar amount:

```
printf("You owe the bank
    $%i.\n",total);
```

Lesson 3-7 Quiz

1. Please match the C language mathematical operator with its proper task:

   A. +   Addition

   B. -   Subtraction

   C. *   Multiplication

   D. /   Division

   E. ≅   Confusion

2. Adding one to a number is referred to as:

    A. Incrimination.

    B. Incrementation.

    C. Incrustration.

    D. Incineration.

3. To add one to the variable `incme`, the following C language statement is used:

    A. `incme=incme+1;`

    B. `incme=1+1;`

    C. `incme+1;`

    D. `incme! incme! incme!;`

4. Understanding the art of incrementation, if Hazel were to quit working for Mr. B, who would her next employer be?

    A. Mr. C.

    B. Mr. B+1.

    C. Mr. B=B+1;

    D. Mr. Welfare.

Nerdy math bonus question — worth 400 points!

Write a program to solve the following equation:

Given that a person with size 12 shoes has a foot about 30.5 centimeters long and that the span from Reggio di Calabria to San Cataldo on the Strait of Otranto is about 340 kilometers (34,000,000 centimeters) wide, approximately what size shoe would Italy wear?

Lesson 3-8: The Sacred Order of Precedence

Precedence refers to what comes first. The fact that the theater is on fire, for example, takes precedence over the fact that we'll miss the second act if we leave in a hurry.

The *order of precedence* is a double redundancy (which in itself is redundant several times over). It refers to which of the mathematical operators has priority over the others. For example, a plus sign just can't march into the middle of a group of numbers and expect to add things the way it wants to. In C, other mathematical operations are done before addition. It's just proper.

A problem from the pages of the dentistry final exam

Witness with your own eyes the following long and complex mathematical equation that may one day slink into one of your C programs:

```
answer = 100 + 5 * 2 - 60 / 3;
```

This is one of those tough math questions from the dentistry final exam. Yes, most of the dentists would rather be pulling teeth — even their own. The preceding problem isn't really a problem for you, though. The computer figures the answer. But what is it?

Is the answer 50? One hundred plus 5 is 105, times 2 is 210, minus 60 is 150, divided by 3 is 50. Will the compiler force the computer to do that for you automatically? Or will the value 90 be placed into the answer variable?

Ninety? Yes, the value of the answer variable is 90. This all has to do with My Dear Aunt Sally and the order of precedence. Before getting into that, the following is DENTIST.C, a program you can type in to prove that the answer is 90 and not 50:

Name: DENTIST.C

```
#include <stdio.h>

void main()
{
    printf("%i",100+5*2-60/3);
}
```

Enter this short and sweet program into your editor. Compile it. Run it. It's a sole printf statement, with only %i in double quotes. That's followed by a comma and then the math question from the dentistry final.

Run the program. The result will shock you:

```
90
```

> ✔ The order of your mathematical equations is important. Not knowing how the C compiler works out its math means that you may not get the answer you want. This is why you have to know the order of precedence and, more importantly, My Dear Aunt Sally.

✔ When the DENTIST.C program runs, the computer works on the equation 100+5*2-60/3 first in the printf function. The result is then passed over to the fill-in-the-blanks %i and is displayed on the screen.

✔ I could have expanded DENTIST.C to declare the answer integer variable, assign the value to that variable, and then use printf to display the variable's contents. But, naaah. That would be too long of a program. The C language is full of short ways to do things. The solo printf statement in DENTIST.C is just one example of a scrunched-up C program.

What's up, Sally?

My Dear Aunt Sally is a mnemonic, or "a silly thing we say to remember something we would forget otherwise, which isn't saying much because we nearly always forget our own phone number and family birthdays." In this case, My Dear Aunt Sally is a mnemonic for Multiplication, Division, Addition, and Subtraction. That's the order in which math is done in a long C language mathematical equation — the order of precedence.

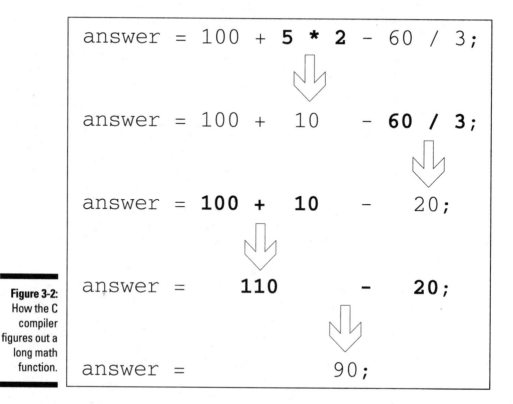

Figure 3-2: How the C compiler figures out a long math function.

The compiler actually scopes out an entire equation — the whole line — and does the multiplication first, and then the division, and then the addition and subtraction. Things just aren't from left to right anymore. Figure 3-2 illustrates how the mathematical example in the preceding section figures out to be 90.

Here's another puzzle:

```
answer = 10 + 20 * 30 / 40;
```

In this statement, the multiplication happens first, then the division, and then the addition. When the multiplication and division are next to each other, as in the preceding line, it goes from left to right.

When the computer is finished counting its thumbs and the preceding statement is "resolved," the answer variable contains the value 25. You can prove this by editing the DENTIST.C program and replacing the math already there in the preceding math equation. Recompile and run the program to confirm that the answer is 25. Or just trust me and let it go at that.

- ✔ My Dear Aunt Sally. *M*ultiplication (*), *d*ivision (/), *a*ddition (+), and *s*ubtraction (–) are done in that order in the C language's long mathematical equations.

- ✔ The reason that the order of precedence is important is that you must organize your mathematical equations if you expect the proper answer to appear.

- ✔ The ASSESSED.C program from the preceding lesson also took advantage of the order of precedence:

```
total=houses*40+hotels*115;
```

  The number of houses times 40 is worked out first, and then hotels times 115 is done second. The last step is to add the two together.

- ✔ A way to control the order of precedence is by using the parentheses, as discussed in the obviously named section "Using parentheses to mess up the order of precedence," later in this chapter.

The confounding magic-pellets problem

I hated those math-class story problems when I was a kid. In fact, I still do. In any event, here I am in my adulthood, making up something like the following:

> Suppose that you have 100 of these magic pellets. They double in quantity every 24 hours. So after a day, you have 200. But first you have to give 25 to the butcher in exchange for three dozen lamb's eyeballs for a casserole you want to surprise your spouse with. If so, how many magic pellets would you have the next day?

Don't bother stewing over the problem. The equation is as follows:

```
100 - 25 * 2;
```

That's 100 magic pellets, minus 25 for the eyeballs and then times 2 (doubled) the next day. In your head, you can figure that 100 minus 25 is 75. Multiply 75 by 2 and you have 150 magic pellets the next day. But in C, this just wouldn't work; the order of precedence (that Sally person) would multiply 25 by 2 first. That would calculate to 50 magic pellets the next day. What a gyp!

The following C program, PELLETS.C, illustrates how the magic-pellet problem is confounded by C's order of precedence. This is a somewhat more complex version of the basic DENTIST.C program, presented earlier in this lesson:

Name: PELLETS.C

```
#include <stdio.h>

void main()
{
    int total;

    total=100-25*2;
    printf("Tomorrow you will have %i magic pellets.\n",total);
}
```

Enter this program into your editor. There's really nothing new here, so a Blow-by-blow box isn't necessary. Still, double-check everything you type with the preceding source code. Save the file to disk as PELLETS.C.

Compile PELLETS.C. Fix any errors.

Run the PELLETS program. Your output looks like this:

```
Tomorrow you will have 50 magic pellets.
```

Uh-huh. Try explaining that to the IRS. Your computer program, diligently entered, tells you that there are 50 pellets, when tomorrow you will actually have 150. The extra 100? They were lost to the order of precedence. In the PELLETS.C program, addition must come first. The way that works is by using parentheses.

Using parentheses to mess up the order of precedence

My Dear Aunt Sally can be quite overbearing. She's insistent. Still, even though she means well, she goofs up sometimes. In the PELLETS.C program, for example, she tells the C compiler to multiply 25 by 2 first and then subtract the result from 100. Anyone who reads the problem knows that you must subtract 25 from 100 first and then multiply what's left by 2. The problem is convincing the C compiler — and Aunt Sally — how to do that.

✔ The order of precedence can be circumvented by using parentheses. When the C compiler sees parentheses, it quickly darts between them, figures out the math, and then continues with multiplication, division, addition, and subtraction in that order, from left to right, outside the parentheses.

To fix the PELLETS.C program, you have to change the seventh line to read as follows:

```
total=(100-25)*2;
```

The C compiler does the math in the parentheses first. So, at once, 25 is subtracted by 100 to equal 75. Then the rest of the math is done: 75 times 2 is 150 — the correct number of magic pellets.

I beg of you to make the preceding change to line 7 in your PELLETS.C program. Stick the left parenthesis before 100, and insert the right one after 25. Save the changes to disk, recompile, and then run the program. The result will please you:

```
Tomorrow you will have 150 magic pellets.
```

✔ The math that appears in the parentheses is always done first. It doesn't matter whether it's addition, subtraction, whatever — it's always done first in the equation.

✔ Inside the parentheses, the math is still worked from left to right. Also, multiplication and division still have priority inside the parentheses. It's just that whatever is in the parentheses is done before whatever is outside. Here's a summary for you:

1. Work inside the parentheses first.

2. Multiplication and division first, addition and subtraction second.

3. Work from left to right.

✔ If you've ever worked with complex spreadsheet equations, you're familiar with the way parentheses can be used to force some math operations to be done before others. And if you don't use spreadsheets, then, hey, you learned something in a C book you can apply to your spreadsheeting. Such value.

✔ Yeah, you can even put parentheses inside parentheses. Just make sure that they match up; rogue parentheses produce syntax errors just like missing double quotes and absent curly brackets do.

✔ It doesn't matter where the parentheses are in the math equation; what's in them is always done first. For example:

```
total=2*(100-25);
```

In this statement, 100 minus 25 is calculated first. The result, 75, is then multiplied by 2. This holds true no matter how complex the equation gets — though I'm afraid that you'll run away or faint if I show you a more complex example.

Lesson 3-8 Quiz

1. The order of precedence refers to:

    A. The pecking order for sneeze marks in a C math problem.

    B. The way math is done in a C language program.

    C. Washington, Jefferson, Adams, Monroe, etc.

    D. Who gets dibbies on the front seat.

2. In the sacred order of precedence, who is My Dear Aunt Sally?

    A. She is the head nun.

    B. She's the grand poobah's live-in aunt, who usually bakes the after-meeting cookies.

    C. She's a mnemonic for multiplication, division, addition and subtraction, the order in which long math problems are done in C programs.

    D. Some old bat.

3. What's the one surefire way to defeat My Dear Aunt Sally and foil the sacred order of precedence?

    A. Bond. James Bond.

    B. Tactical nukes.

    C. Carefully placed parentheses.

    D. A lethal cheese grater.

4. The fourth question.

    A. 42.

    B. Magic pellets are illegal in France.

    C. "So, how's the family?"

    D. Hey! No more stuffy head.

5. How is math done in C?

    A. Work inside the parentheses first; multiplication and division first, and then the addition and subtraction section; work from left to right.

    B. The computer does the math.

    C. No, underpaid and overworked Oompa-Loompas do the math.

    D. Any ol' which way.

Chapter 3 Final Exam

1. Variables are used in C to store what?

    A. Items that must be kept cold.

    B. Items that must be kept warm.

    C. Numbers and text that can change.

    D. Numbers and text that must be kept either warm or cold.

2. What must be done before a variable can be used in a C program?

    A. The variable must be declared.

    B. The variable must be announced.

    C. The variable must be introduced.

    D. The variable must be conjured.

3. Numeric variables can hold what?

    A. Numerics.

    B. Numbers.

    C. Only tiny numbers.

    D. Only numbers that can be typed from the keyboard.

4. What is the `int` type of variable?

    A. A variable that can hold only integer values, which is just about any number that doesn't have a fraction or decimal part — a whole number, if you will.

    B. Any itty-bitty variable.

    C. A variable that goes into something.

    D. An interior variable.

5. What is the `float` type of variable?

    A. A variable whose value is so small that it can literally float around the program.

    B. A large, bulbous, balloon-size value.

    C. A number that contains a fraction or a decimal part; also very large and very small values.

    D. Answer C isn't goofy, so I'll choose it.

6. Write a program that declares an `int` variable representing your age and a `float` variable representing your hat size. The program then multiplies the two values to produce an estimate of your IQ. The result should be displayed by a `printf` statement. (Refer to the `HEIGHT.C` program, earlier in this chapter, for an example.)

7. What kind of values does a `char` variable hold?

   A. Single characters, such as L or K but not M.

   B. Colors found only in nature.

   C. Characters and strings of text.

   D. Values created by anyone named Charlie.

8. Soylent Green is made out of:

   A. Plankton.

   B. Chlorophyll (with a drop of Retsin).

   C. Chiggers.

   D. People! It's people!

9. What's wrong with the following C language directive?

   ```
   #define WEATHER=15;
   ```

   A. There is no equal sign in a constant definition.

   B. There is no semicolon at the end of a `#define` directive.

   C. The weather is not a constant.

   D. Both A and B.

10. Your user types a string at the keyboard. How do you convert it into a numeric value — nay, an integer?

   A. You use the `atoi` function.

   B. You use the `atio` function.

   C. You use the `convertointty` function.

   D. There is no need to convert the value.

11. Match the mathematical operation with its C language symbol:

   A. Multiplication   *

   B. Division   /

   C. Addition   +

   D. Subtraction   –

12. Incrementation is which of the following?

    A. The snail crawling up the well three inches during the day but slipping back two inches at night.

    B. Adding one to a variable's value.

    C. Adding anything to a variable's value.

    D. Adding one to a snail's value.

13. Which of the following have not been pseudonyms for the *Starship Enterprise* in a *MAD* magazine "Star Trek" parody?

    A. *Boobyprize.*

    B. *Improvise.*

    C. *Yentaprise.*

    D. *Compromise.*

14. What does the getch function do?

    A. Reads a single character typed at the keyboard.

    B. Displays a single character on the keyboard.

    C. Forces the computer to belch uncontrollably.

    D. Causes the computer to wait.

15. Write a program that uses getche to read two characters from the keyboard. The program prompts the user for each character and then displays them both by using a printf function.

16. How does the order of precedence affect math done in a C program?

    A. It subtly influences the outcome to favor the Mob.

    B. The answer is always wrong unless My Dear Aunt Sally types it.

    C. Multiplication and division are done first and then addition and subtraction — no matter how the math problem is typed out.

    D. Answers always appear numerically sorted.

Bonus question — worth 25 IQ points!

17. Which of the follwing is not a book of the Bible?

    A. Obidiah

    B. Zachariah

    C. Jeremiah

    D. Jumboliah

Chapter 4

Decision Making
(or "I'll Have What She's Having")

● ●

Lessons In This Chapter

▶ The mighty `if` command

▶ OK, `if` it isn't true, what `else`?

▶ `if` with characters and strings

▶ Formatting your C source code, first lesson

▶ `for` going loopy

▶ Loop busting

▶ Shortcuts and the art of incrementation (or another dreaded math lesson)

▶ More incrementation, more madness

Programs In This Chapter

GENIE1.C	TAXES.C	GENIE2.C	GENIE3.C
GREATER.C	OUCH.C	100.C	ASCII.C
FOREVER.C	TYPER1.C	OLLYOLLY.C	CHANT.C
1000.C			

Vocabulary Introduced In This Chapter

`if`	`else`	`for`	`break`
`++`	`—`	`+=`	`-=`
`*=`	`/=`		

● ●

*N*o one can rightly accuse computers of making decisions. No, they make *comparisons* based on what you tell them to do. The idea is to have the computer handle some predictable yet unknown event: A choice is made from a menu; the little man opens the door with the hydra behind it in some game; the user types something goofy; and so on. These are all things that happen, which the computer must deal with.

The comparisons the computer makes — the options it has — are dictated to it by the programmer. That's you. What you can do is say, "OK, I'm having the user type in a choice, from A to Q. For each of those choices, I have to tell the computer to do something." You don't know which choice the user will make, yet you write your program so that it can handle each one: If they type A, do this; if they type B, do that; if they type C, do something else; and on down the list.

Keep in mind that the computer doesn't decide what to do. Instead, it follows a careful path you set down for it. It's kind of like instructing small children to do something, though with the computer it always does exactly what you tell it to and never pauses eternally in front of the TV set or wedges a Big Hunk into the sofa. That's what's covered in this chapter's lessons.

Lesson 4-1: The Mighty if Command

OK, if isn't a command. It's yet another keyword in the C programming language. The if keyword allows your programs to make decisions. The decisions are based on a comparison. For example:

❐ If the contents of variable *X* are greater than variable *Y*, then scream like they're twisting your nipples.

❐ If the contents of the variable *calories* are very high, then it must taste very good.

❐ If it ain't broke, don't fix it.

❐ If Greg Studmuffin doesn't ask me out to the prom, then I'll have to go with Melvin Faysazits.

All of these are examples of important decisions, similar to those you can make in your C programs by using the if keyword. However, in the C programming language, the if keyword's comparisons are kind of, sort of — dare I say it? — mathematical in nature. Here are more accurate examples:

❐ If the value of variable A is equal to the value of variable B.

❐ If the contents of variable ch are less than 132.

❐ If the value of variable zed is greater than 1,000,000.

These are really simple, scales-of-justice evaluations of variables and values. The if keyword makes the comparison, and if the comparison is true, your program does a particular set of things.

❐ if is a keyword in the C programming language. It allows your programs to make decisions.

❐ if decides what to do based on a comparison of (usually) two items.

❐ The comparison if makes is mathematical in nature: Are two items equal to, greater than, less than — and so on — to each other. If they are, then a certain part of your program will run. If not, then that part of the program does not run.

❐ The if keyword creates what is known as a "selection statement" in the C language. I have this down in my notes, probably because it's in some other C reference I've read at some time or another. *Selection statement.* Impress your friends with that if you can remember it. Just throw your nose in the air if they ask what it means. (That's what I do.)

The computer-genie program example

The following program is GENIE1.C, one of many silly computer "guess the number" programs you write when you learn to program. Computer scientists used to play these games for hours in the early days of the computer. They'd probably drop dead if we could beam back a Nintendo through time.

What GENIE1.C does is to ask for a number, 0 through 9. You type that at the keyboard. Then, using the magic of the if statement, the computer tells you whether the number you entered is less than 5. This was a major thigh-slapper when it was first written in the early 1950s.

Name: GENIE1.C

```
#include <stdio.h>

void main()
{
    char num[2];
    int number;

    printf("I am your computer genie!\n");

    printf("Enter a number from 0 to 9:");
    gets(num);
    number=atoi(num);

    if(number<5)
    {
        printf("That number is less than 5!\n");
    }

    printf("The genie knows all, sees all!\n");
}
```

Enter this source code into your text editor. The only new stuff comes with the if statement cluster near the end of the program. Use the Blow-by-blow description box to help you type that in; this is radical new stuff — curly brackets in the middle of a program — which you've never seen before. Better double-double-check your typing.

Save the file to disk as GENIE1.C.

Compile GENIE1.C. If you see any errors, run back to your editor and fix them. Then recompile.

Run the final program; type **GENIE1** at the DOS prompt or run the program from your integrated environment. You see the following lines displayed:

```
I am your computer genie!
Enter a number from 0 to 9:
```

Type a number, somewhere in the range of 0 to 9. For example, you can type 3. Press Enter and you see:

```
That number is less than 5!
The genie knows all, sees all!
```

- ✔ If you see only the line The genie knows all, sees all!, you probably typed a number greater than 4 (which includes 5 and up). This is because the if statement tests only for values *less than* 5. If the value is less than 5, then That number is less than 5! is displayed. The next section elaborates on how this works.

- ✔ Yes, the computer genie doesn't know all and see all if you type a number 5 or greater.

- ✔ Did you notice the extra set of curly brackets in the middle of this program? That's part of how the if statement works. Also notice how they're indented.

- ✔ Information on working with curly brackets in the middle of the main function as well as on indenting and formatting your C source code is in Lesson 4-4.

BLOW BY BLOW

How that genie is so darn smart

The program begins with two variable declarations: a string variable, num, and an integer, number:

```
char num[2];

int number;
```

The num string variable is given space for two characters. That's the number key 0 through 9 plus the Enter keypress that ends input. A blank line follows the variable declarations, separating them from the rest of the program.

```
printf("I am your computer
    genie!\n");
```

The first printf statement displays the program's "title" (so to speak). This is followed by a blank line. Then comes the part of the program that prompts for a number to be typed, reads that number into a string variable, and then translates the number into a numeric value:

```
printf("Enter a number from 0 to
    9:");

gets(num);

number=atoi(num);
```

These three lines should be familiar to you. (If not, review Lesson 2-4 on gets and Lesson 3-1 on atoi.) The printf statement displays a prompt. The gets statement reads the keyboard and stuffs what's typed into the num string variable. Then the atoi function is used to translate the number in the string variable, num, and slide it through the equal sign into the number integer variable. This is how input from the keyboard is translated into a value.

The preceding three statements are followed by a blank line, and then comes the mighty if statement:

```
if(number<5)
```

if is followed by parentheses, which contains the comparison that the if keyword tests. In this case, the comparison is the number integer variable and the value 5. The < symbol between them means "less than." The test reads "if the value of the variable number is less than 5." If this is true, then the cluster of statements following the if keyword is executed. If the test proves false, the cluster of statements is skipped.

Notice that the if test is not followed by a semicolon! Instead, it's followed by a statement enclosed in curly brackets:

```
{

    printf("That number is less
        than 5!\n");

}
```

The statements the if keyword executes if the test passes are enclosed in curly brackets. The first, left curly bracket is in the same column as if. Then comes a new line that's indented one tab stop in from the curly bracket. It's a printf statement — the message that's displayed if the value entered is less than 5. This line ends in a semicolon.

The third line is unindented (press Shift+Tab to unindent in your editor). The right curly bracket is in the same column as the left curly bracket two lines up. Press Enter to end this line — no semicolon — and then press Enter to separate this group of statements from the final printf statement:

```
printf("The genie knows all, sees
    all!\n");
```

Then comes the final curly bracket to end the main function.

Keyword if

The if keyword is used to make decisions in your programs. It makes a comparison. If the result is true, then the rest of the if statement is executed. If the comparison isn't true, then the program skips over the rest of the if statement (see Figure 4-1 a little later).

The if statement is actually a statement "block" that can look like this:

```
if(comparison)
{
        statement(s);
}
```

if is followed by a set of parentheses in which a *comparison* is made. The comparison is mathematical in nature, using the symbols shown in Table 4-1. What's being compared is usually the value of a variable against a constant value. (See the table for examples.)

If the result of the comparison is true, then the statements between the curly brackets that follow the if are executed. If the result is false, the statements are conveniently skipped over — ignored like a geeky young lad at his first high school dance but with a zit the size of Houston on his chin.

Yes, there can be more than one statement. And each of the statements ends with a semicolon. All are enclosed in the curly brackets. This is technically referred to as a *code block.*

The curly brackets are how you know which statements "belong" to if. Actually, the whole darn thing is part of the if statement.

The if *keyword, up close and impersonal*

It's unlike any other C language word you've seen so far. The if keyword has a unique format, with plenty of options and room for goofing things up. Yet it's a handy and powerful thing you can put in your programs — something you'll use a lot. The nearby format box describes in detail the if keyword's format.

Figure 4-1 illustrates how the if keyword affects a program. if causes the computer to pause and make a comparison. If the comparison statement is true, then the statements belonging to the if keyword are processed by the computer. But if the comparison is false, then the statements are casually skipped over — completely ignored by the computer just as you or I ignore the calorie count on a vat of ice cream if we're hungry enough.

So far, all your programs have run from the top down, where the first lines in your source code are obeyed by the computer before the last lines are. In the program snippet shown in Figure 4-1, the program *execution* (a fancy word for "to kill" but also meaning "the computer obeys these instructions in this order") is changed by the if keyword. This is how if affects programs, allowing them to make decisions and change the way the program runs based on those decisions.

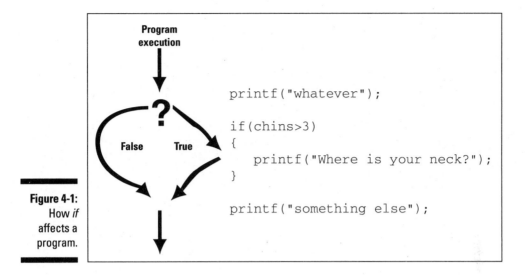

```
          Program
          execution
             |
             v

    ?          printf("whatever");

False    True   if(chins>3)
                {
                    printf("Where is your neck?");
                }

                printf("something else");
```

Figure 4-1:
How *if*
affects a
program.

Table 4-1 Symbols Used in if Statement Comparisons

Comparison	Meaning or Pronunciation	"True" Examples
<	Less than	1 < 5
		8 < 9
==	Equal to	5 == 5
		0 == 0
>	Greater than	8 > 5
		10 > 0
<=	Less than or equal to	4 <= 5
		8 <= 8
>=	Greater than or equal to	9 >= 5
		2 >= 2
!=	Not equal to	1 != 0
		4 != 3.99

The GENIE1 program from the preceding section used the following if statement:

```
if(number<5)
{
    printf("That number is less than 5!\n");
}
```

The first line is the i f keyword and its comparison in parentheses. What's being compared is the value of the numeric variable number and the constant value 5. The comparison is "less than." Is number less than 5? If so, then the statement in curly brackets is executed. If not, then the whole deal is skipped over.

Consider the following modifications:

```
if(number==5)
{
    printf("That number is 5!\n");
}
```

Now the comparison is number==5 (is the number typed in equal to five)? If it is, then the printf statement displays That number is 5!

```
if(number>=5)
{
    printf("That number is more than 4!\n");
}
```

These changes compare the value of number with 5 again. This time the test is greater than *or* equal; is the number typed in 5 or more than 5? If the number is greater than or equal to 5, it must be more than 4, and the printf statement goes on to display that important info on the screen.

The following modification to the GENIE1.C program doesn't change the i f comparison, as in the previous examples. Instead, it shows you that there can be more than one statement belonging to i f:

```
if(number<5)
{
    printf("That number is less than 5!\n");
    printf("By goodness, aren't I smart?\n");
}
```

Everything between the curly brackets is executed when the comparison is true. Advanced C programs may have lots of stuff in there; as long as it's between the curly brackets, it's executed only i f the comparison is true. (This is why it's indented — so that you know that it all belongs to the i f statement.)

- The comparison if makes is usually between a variable and a value. It can be a numeric or single-character variable. It cannot, however, be a string. Lesson 3-3 covers comparing single-character variables. The second volume of this book has more information about comparing strings of text.

- In comparing a variable to a value, the variable should always come first. (It may work the other way around. Then again, it may not, so always put your variable first, as shown in this book.)

- Less than, greater than, and their ilk should be familiar to you from basic math. If not, then you read the symbols from left to right: The > symbol is *greater than* because the big side comes first; the < is *less than* because the lesser side comes first.

- The symbols for less than or equal to and greater than or equal to always appear that way: <= and >=. Switching them the other way generates an error.

- The symbol for "not" in C is the exclamation point. So != means "not equal." What is !TRUE (not-true) is FALSE. If you think that it's butter, but it's !. No, I do ! want to eat those soggy zucchini chips.

- When you're making a comparison to see whether two things are equal, you use *two* equal signs. I think of it this way: When you build an if statement to see whether two things are equal, you think in your head "is equal" rather than "equals." For example:

```
if(x==5)
```

Read this statement as "if the value of the x variable *is equal* to 5, then . . . ." If you think "equals," you have a tendency to use only one equal sign — which is very wrong.

- If you use one equal sign instead of two, you don't get an error; however, the program will be wrong. The nearby Techy box attempts to explain why this is so.

- If you've programmed in other computer languages, keep in mind that there is no "end-if" word in the C language. The final curly bracket is what signals to the compiler that the if statement has ended.

- Also, no then word is used with if, as in the if-then thing they have in the BASIC programming language.

Clutter not thy head with this comparison nonsense

The comparison in the if statement doesn't have to use any symbols at all! Strange but true. What the C compiler does is to figure out what you've put between the parentheses. Then it weighs whether it's true or false.

For a comparison using <, >, ==, or any of the horde in Table 4-1, the compiler figures out whether the comparison is true or false. However, you can really stick just about anything between the parentheses — any valid C statement — and the compiler will determine whether it works out to true or false. For example:

```
if(input=1)
```

This if statement doesn't figure out whether the value of the input variable is equal to 1. No, you need *two* equal signs for that. Instead, what happens between these parentheses is that the numeric variable input is given the value 1. It's the same as this:

```
input=1;
```

The C compiler obeys this instruction, stuffing 1 into the input variable. Then it sits back and strokes its beard and thinks, "Now does that work out to be true or false?" Not knowing any better, it figures that the statement must be true. So it tells the if keyword that, and the cluster of statements that belong to the if statement are then executed.

A question of formatting the if *statement*

The if statement is your first "complex" C language statement. There are many more, but if is the first and possibly the most popular, though I doubt that a popularity contest for programming language words has ever been held (and, then again, if would be great as Miss Congeniality but definitely come up a little thin in the swimsuit competition).

Though you've only seen the if statement used with curly brackets, it can also be displayed as a traditional C language statement. For example, consider the following — one of the modifications from the GENIE1 program:

```
if(number==5)
{
    printf("That number is 5!\n");
}
```

In C, it's perfectly legitimate to write this as a more traditional type of statement. To wit:

```
if(number==5) printf("That number is 5!\n");
```

This looks more like a C language statement. It ends in a semicolon. Everything still works the same; if the value of the number variable is equal to 5, the printf statement is executed. If number doesn't equal 5, the rest of the statement is skipped.

Although this is all legal and you won't be shunned in the C programming community for using it, many negatives are associated with this format:

❐ It looks like an error — like two statements on the same line or something heinous along those lines.

❐ It's harder to read. The curly braces and the extra "air" they add to the source code make deciphering the program easier.

❐ You cannot specify multiple statements in this format. If more than one C language statement needs to belong to the if, they must appear in curly brackets.

✔ This is really technical stuff and you're not required to remember this variation of the if statement. I bring it up in case you ever see it used and wonder why it doesn't error. (This book continues to use curly brackets with the if keyword for a time.)

✔ Other keywords in C share this "should I use curly brackets or put everything on one line?" conundrum. The for keyword, covered in Lesson 4-5, and the while keyword, found in Chapter 7, are two other instances in the C language when curly brackets become optional.

The final solution to the income-tax problem

I've devised what I think is the most fair and obviously good-intentioned way to decide who must pay the most in income taxes. You should pay more taxes if you're taller and more taxes if it's warmer outside. Yessir, it would be hard to dodge this one.

This is an ideal problem for the if keyword to solve. You pay taxes based on either your height or the temperature outside, multiplied by your favorite number and then ten. Whichever number is higher is the amount of tax you pay. To figure out which number is higher, the program TAXES.C uses the if keyword with the greater-than symbol. This is done twice — once for the height value and again for the temperature outside.

Name: TAXES.C

```
#include <stdio.h>
#include <stdlib.h>

void main()
{
    int tax1,tax2;
    char height[4],temp[4],favnum[5];

    printf("Enter your height in inches:");
    gets(height);
    printf("What temperature is it outside?");
    gets(temp);
    printf("Enter your favorite number:");
    gets(favnum);

    tax1 = atoi(height) * atoi(favnum);
    tax2 = atoi(temp) * atoi(favnum);

    if(tax1>tax2)
    {
        printf("You owe $%i in taxes.\n",tax1*10);
    }
    if(tax2>=tax1)
    {
        printf("You owe $%i in taxes.\n",tax2*10);
    }
}
```

This is the most involved program so far in this book. You have to be extra careful when you're typing it in. There's nothing new in it, but it covers almost all the information presented in the past few chapters. Double-check each line as you type it into your editor.

Save the file to disk as TAXES.C.

Compile TAXES.C. Fix any errors you may see.

Run the program. If you're at the DOS prompt, type **TAXES** and press Enter:

```
Enter your height in inches:
```

Type your height in inches. Five feet is 60 inches; six feet is 72 inches. The average person is 5'7" or so tall — 67 inches. Press Enter.

```
What temperature is it outside?
```

Right now, at midnight near Seattle after a sullen spring day, it's 42 degrees. That's Fahrenheit, by the way. Don't you dare enter the smaller Celsius number. If you do, the IRS will hunt you down like a delinquent country-music star and make you pay, pay, pay.

```
Enter your favorite number:
```

Type your favorite number. Mine is 16. Press Enter.

So if I type 71 (my height), 42, and 16, I see the following result, due April 15:

```
You owe $11360 in taxes.
```

Sheesh! And I thought the old system was bad. I guess I need a smaller favorite number.

- ✔ More information about using the `gets` function is in Lesson 2-4.
- ✔ Information about using the `atoi` function is in Lesson 3-1.
- ✔ The second `if` comparison is "greater than or equal to." This catches the case when your height is equal to the temperature. If both values are equal, then the values of both the `tax1` and `tax2` variables will be equal. The first `if` comparison, "`tax1` is greater than `tax2`," fails because both are equal. The second comparison, "`tax1` is greater than or equal to `tax2`," passes when `tax1` is greater than `tax2` or when both values are equal.

- ✔ If you enter zero as your favorite number, the program doesn't say that you owe any tax. Unfortunately, the IRS does not allow you to have zero — or any negative numbers — as your favorite number. Sad, but true.

BLOW BY BLOW

Detailed and potentially knowledge-boosting information about TAXES.C

The TAXES.C program is divided into four sections: variable declaration; prompts and input; calculation; and the final decision making with the two if statements.

```
int tax1,tax2;
char height[4],temp[4],favnum[5];
```

First comes the variable declarations. This program uses five variables: two numeric integer variables, tax1 and tax2, and then three string variables, height, temp, and favnum. The first two string variables have room to hold four characters, and the favnum variable can hold five (just in case someone has a large favorite number — which is highly taxing but possible). Notice how these are all declared on two lines. Commas separate the variable names. A semicolon ends each line.

In the prompts and input section, three printf functions display three different prompts, and three corresponding gets functions read in the three different string variables:

```
printf("Enter your height in
    inches:");
gets(height);
printf("What temperature is it
    outside?");
gets(temp);
printf("Enter your favorite num-
    ber:");
gets(favnum);
```

The \n, newline escape sequence, isn't required in any of these strings because the gets function "displays" the Enter key when you press it.

```
tax1 = atoi(height) * atoi(favnum);
tax2 = atoi(temp) * atoi(favnum);
```

The calculation part of the program performs two mathematical operations. The atoi function is used to generate an integer value based on a number stored in a string. The value is generated first. So with the first statement in the preceding lines, an integer value is created from the height variable and then from the favnum variable, and then the two are multiplied. The result — an integer value — is stored in the tax1 variable. The same thing happens in the second line, though the value is based on the temp string variable and is stored in the tax2 integer variable.

This approach is used to make the program shorter. The other approach is to create integer variables for the height, favnum, and temp string variables, convert each one over, and then do the math. The two preceding code lines combine those two steps.

The first of the if decisions compares the value of the tax1 variable with the value of the tax2 variable. If the value of tax1 is greater, then the printf statement is executed. printf uses the %i placeholder to display the value of the tax1 variable, multiplied by 10:

```
if(tax1>tax2)
{
    printf("You owe $%i in
    taxes.\n",tax1*10);
}
```

In the second if decision, the value of tax2 is compared with tax1, this time to see whether tax2 is greater or whether both the values are equal. The >= means "greater than or equal to." If the tax2 value is greater or if both values are equal, then the result is displayed by the printf statement belonging to the if:

```
if(tax2>=tax1)
{
    printf("You owe $%i in
    taxes.\n",tax2*10);
}
```

Lesson 4-1 Quiz

1. The `if` keyword helps you to do what in your programs?

    A. Make decisions.

    B. Compare values.

    C. Add more curly brackets and indentation.

    D. All of the above.

2. When the thing `if` compares is true:

    A. Bells ring, birds sing, the sun shines . . . ah! Spring is here.

    B. The statements belonging to the `if` keyword are executed.

    C. The compiler gets very happy and ignores any errors.

    D. The computer beeps.

3. To see whether two values are equal, the following comparison is made:

    A. `(var1=var2)`

    B. `(var1~var2)`

    C. `(var1;var2)`

    D. `(var1==var2)`

4. Match up the comparison symbol with how it's pronounced:

    A. `<`   Less than

    B. `==`   Equal to

    C. `>`   Greater than

    D. `<=`   Less than or equal to

    E. `>=`   Greater than or equal to

    F. `!=`   Not equal to

5. True or false: The comparison the `if!` keyword makes is either true or false.

Bonus question (only for those reading and absorbing everything!) — worth 2 points!

What is a "code block"?

    A. A baggie tied over your PC's modem port to prevent communications.

    B. Writer's block for programmers.!

    C. When Kent McCord says, "One-Adam-12 Roger. Will respond code . . . uh, um . . . responding at code . . . er . . . ahh . . . ."

    D. A section of a C program set off and hugged by its own set of curly brackets.

Lesson 4-2: If It Isn't True, What Else?

Hold on to that tax problem!

No, not the one the government created. Instead, hold on to the TAXES.C source code introduced from the last lesson. If it's already in your text editor, great. Otherwise, load it into your editor for editing. (Use the Load or Open command from the File menu and find the file TAXES.C on disk.)

The last part of that program consists of two if statements. The second if statement, which should be near line 23 in your editor, is really not necessary. Rather than use if in that manner, you can take advantage of another word in the C language, else.

Change line 23 in the TAXES.C program. It looks like this right now:

```
if(tax2>=tax1)
```

Edit that line: Delete the if keyword and the comparison in parentheses and replace it with the following:

```
else
```

That's it — just else by itself. No comparison, no semicolon, and make sure that you type it in lowercase.

Save the file back to disk.

Compile TAXES.C. Run the final result. The output is the same because the program hasn't changed. What you've done is to create an if-else "structure," which is yet another way to handle the decision-making process in your C programs.

- ✔ The else keyword is actually a second, optional part of an if cluster of statements. It groups together statements that are to be executed when the condition if tests for isn't true.

- ✔ Or else what?

- ✔ Alas, if you input the same values as in the old program, you still owe the same bundle to Uncle Sam.

Covering all the possibilities with else

The if-else keyword combination allows you to write a program that can make either-or decisions. By itself, the if keyword can handle minor decisions and execute special instructions if the conditions are just so. But when if is coupled with else, your program takes one of two directions, depending on the comparison if makes (see Figure 4-2).

If the comparison is true, then the statements belonging to the if are executed. But if the comparison is false, then the statements belonging to the else are executed. The program goes one way or the other, as illustrated in Figure 4-2. Then after going its own way, the statement following the else's final curly bracket is executed. Like: "You guys go around the left side of the barn, we'll go around the right, and we'll meet you on the other side."

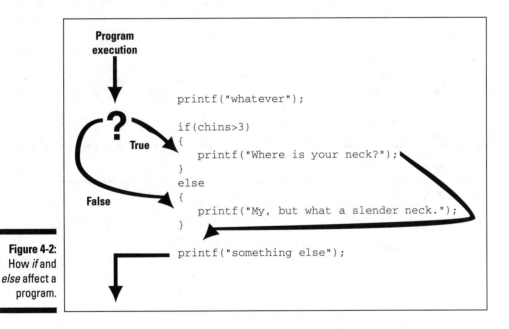

Figure 4-2:
How *if* and
else affect a
program.

Keyword else

The else keyword is used in an if statement. It holds its own group of statements that will be executed (OK, "obeyed") when the if comparison isn't true. Here is the format:

```
if(comparison)
{
        statement(s);
}
else
{
        statement(s);
}
```

The if keyword tests the comparison in parentheses. If it's a true comparison — no foolin' — then the *statements* that appear in curly brackets right after the if are executed. But if the comparison is false, then those *statements* following the else keyword and enclosed in curly brackets are executed. One way or another, one group of statements is executed, and the other isn't.

The else keyword, like all words in the C language, is in lowercase. It is not followed by a semicolon. Instead, a set of curly brackets follows the else. The curly brackets enclose one or more *statements* to be run when the comparison if makes isn't true. Notice that those statements each must end in a semicolon, obeying the laws of C first etched in stone by the ancient Palo Altoites.

The statements belonging to the else keyword are executed when the condition the if keyword evaluates is false. Table 4-2 illustrates how this works, showing you the opposite conditions for the comparisons an if keyword would make.

Table 4-2: if comparisons and their opposites

If Comparison	Else Statement Executed By This Condition
<	>= (Greater than or equal to)
==	!= (Not equal to)
>	<= (Less than or equal to)
<=	> (Greater than)
>=	< (Less than)
!=	== (Equal to)

✔ I don't know about you, but all those symbols in Table 4-2 would certainly make an interesting rug pattern.

✔ The else keyword is always used with if.

✔ Both if and else can have more than one statement enclosed in their curly brackets. if's statements are executed when the comparison is true; else's statements are executed when the comparison is false.

- ✔ "Executed" means to run. C programs execute, or run, statements from the top of the source code (the first line) down to the bottom. Each line is executed one after the other unless statements like if and else are encountered. In that case, the program executes different statements depending on the comparison if makes.

- ✔ When your program doesn't require an either-or decision, you don't have to use else. For example, the TAXES program has an either-or decision. But suppose that you're writing a program which displays an error message when something doesn't work. In that case, you don't need else; if there isn't an error, the program should continue as normal. (This makes sense when it's introduced in a later chapter; see Lesson 6-3 and its MOON.C program to sneak-peek an example.)

- ✔ If you're the speaker of another programming "tongue," notice that the C language has no "end-else" word in it. This isn't smelly old Pascal, for goodness' sake. The final curly bracket signals the end of the else statement, just as it does with if.

Silly formatting trivia

The if-else structure need not be heavy-laden with curly brackets. Just as you can abbreviate an if statement to one line, you can also abbreviate if-else. I don't recommend this, which is why I'm being terribly brief and won't ever show a program that illustrates examples this crudely:

```
if(tax1>tax2)
{
    printf("You owe $%i in taxes.\n",tax1*10);
}
else
{
    printf("You owe $%i in taxes.\n",tax2*10);
}
```

Here you see the meat-and-potatoes of the TAXES.C program, the if-else structure. Because if and else both have only one statement belonging to them, you can abbreviate this as follows:

```
if(tax1>tax2)
    printf("You owe $%i in taxes.\n",tax1*10);
else
    printf("You owe $%i in taxes.\n",tax2*10);
```

This format keeps the indenting intact, which is one way to see what belongs to what (and also to easily identify the if-else structure). The following format is also possible, though it makes the program hard to read:

```
if(tax1>tax2) printf("You owe $%i in taxes.\n",tax1*10);
else printf("You owe $%i in taxes.\n",tax2*10);
```

Everything is scrunched up on two lines; the if statement has its own line, and the else its own line. Both lines end with a semicolon, which is how this works as two statements in the C language. But look-it. It's gross! Please don't write your programs this way.

You can do this trick — eliminating the curly brackets — whenever only one statement appears with an if or else keyword. If multiple statements must be executed, you're required by law to use the curly brackets. This is why I recommend them all the time: no sense risking prison over brevity. To wit:

```
if(tax1>tax2)
    printf("You owe $%i in taxes.\n",tax1*10);
else
{
    printf("You owe $%i in taxes.\n",tax2*10);
    printf("It pays to live where it's cold!\n");
}
```

Because two printf statements belong to the preceding else, the curly brackets are required.

Fastidious scriveners of the C language will appreciate the source-code formatting information offered in Lesson 4-4.

The strange case of else-if and even more decisions

The C language is rich with decision making. The if keyword helps if you need to test for only one condition. True or false, if handles it. And if it is true, a group of statements is executed. Otherwise, it's skipped over. (And after the if's group of statements is executed, the program continues as before.)

Either-or conditions are the daily bread of the if-else duo. Either way, one set of statements is executed and not the other, depending on the comparison made by if.

Now what about "one, two, or the third" types of decisions? For them, you need the miraculous and overly versatile else-if combination. This really drives you batty, but it's handy.

The following program is a modification of the GENIE1.C source code, shown in the preceding lesson. This time the `else-if` combination is used to allow the computer genie to accurately report whether the number is less than 5, equal to 5, or greater than 5.

Name: GENIE2.C

```
#include <stdio.h>
#include <stdlib.h>

void main()
{
    char num[2];
    int number;

    printf("I am your computer genie!\n");

    printf("Enter a number from 0 to 9:");
    gets(num);
    number=atoi(num);

    if(number<5)
    {
        printf("That number is less than 5!\n");
    }
    else if(number==5)
    {
        printf("You typed in 5!\n");
    }
    else
    {
        printf("That number is more than 5!\n");
    }

    printf("The genie knows all, sees all!\n");
}
```

Start working on this source code by loading the GENIE1.C source code you created in the preceding lesson. Use your editor's Load command to stick the GENIE1.C source code into its own editing window. Make modifications so that the latter part of the program looks like the new, GENIE2.C source code just listed.

Watch your indenting. Pay attention to everything; there are two equal signs in the `else-if` comparison. Pay attention to where semicolons go and where they don't go.

After inserting the new lines, save the file to disk as GENIE2.C. Use the Save As command in your editor to give the file a new name as it's saved to disk. (This way, the GENIE1.C source code remains intact on disk — though there's really no special reason for you to keep it around. Sentimentality, maybe.)

Compile GENIE2.C. If the error monster rears its ugly head, reedit the source code and then recompile.

Run the final result and see how much more clairvoyant the computer genie has become. Type a 3 and you see `That number is less than 5!` Type a 9 and you see `That number is more than 5!` Type 5 and the genie knows, `You typed in 5!`

- ✔ The `else-if` comparison resembles combined `else` and `if` statements. The second `if` comes right after `else` and a space. Then it has its own comparison statement, which is judged either true or false.

- ✔ In GENIE2.C, the `else-if` comparison is `number==5`, testing to see whether the value of the `number` variable is five. Two equal signs are used for this comparison.

- ✔ You can do `else-if`, `else-if`, `else-if` all day long if you want. However, the C language has a better solution. See Lesson 7-5 for information about the `switch-case` keywords.

Bonus program! The really, really smart genie

There is always a solution. If you wanted to, you could write a program that would `if`-compare any value, from zero up to infinity and back again, and the "computer genie" would accurately guess it. But why bother with `if` at all?

OK, the `if` keyword is the subject of this lesson, along with `if-else` and `else-if` and so on. But the following source code for GENIE3.C doesn't use `if` at all. It cheats so that the genie always guesses correctly.

Name: GENIE3.C

```
#include <stdio.h>
#include <conio.h>

void main()
{
```

```
    char num;

    printf("I am your computer genie!\n");

    printf("Enter a number from 0 to 9:");
    num=getche();

    printf("\nYou typed in %c!\n",num);

    printf("The genie knows all, sees all!\n");
}
```

You can create this source code by editing either GENIE1.C or GENIE2.C. Make the necessary modifications, and then save the source code to disk as GENIE3.C by using the Save As command in your editor.

Compile the program. Fix any errors that you hopefully don't get. Run the result.

```
Enter a number from 0 to 9:8
You typed in 8!
The genie knows all, sees all!
```

Run the program again and again with different numbers. Hey! That genie knows exactly what you typed! Wonder how that happened? Must be your deftness with the C language. Tame that computer!

✔ The problem with GENIE3.C? It doesn't make a decision. The genie isn't smart at all — it's just repeating what you already know. The purpose behind if, else, and so on is that they allow you to make a decision in your program.

✔ Refer to Lesson 3-6 for more information about the getche function.

Lesson 4-2 Quiz

1. When you want to make an either-or decision in the C language, what type of structure do you use?

    A. An either-or structure.

    B. A large, brick structure.

    C. A true-false structure.

    D. An if-else structure.

2. Consider the following snippet of C language source code:

```
if(var<3)
{
        printf("Boy, that var is sure less than 3.");
}
else
{
        printf("Aunt Vera said she never smelled such a smell.")
}
```

In this source-code snippet, when is the second `printf` statement executed?

A. When the value of variable `var` is not less than 3.

B. When the value of variable `var` is 3.

C. When the `if` condition is false.

D. All of the above.

3. When an `if-else` type of deal (see preceding code) appears in a program, when does the program not execute one or the other set of statements?

A. The program always executes one or the other.

B. The program skips over the whole deal when the `if` condition is false.

C. The program executes the `else` part of the statement only when the computer is on.

D. The program, unable to make up its mind, stands idly in front of the refrigerator, waiting for the appropriate snack to appear before its eyes.

4. When you have several conditions you want to test for, you can use:

A. `if, if, if, if, if` until your typing fingers are sore.

B. The `if, else-if, else-if, else-if, else` type of thing.

C. `if, only-if, if-if, of,` and the `retch` function.

D. Pascal.

5. To teach incorruptible moral values to our youth, it's important to:

A. Instill a fine sense of religion and family.

B. Apply for an obscenely huge government grant.

C. Beat them until they get it.

D. Give up.

Time for another well-deserved break. Try not to soak up all this stuff at one time.

Lesson 4-3: Iffy Characters and Strings

Apologies are in order for the past two lessons. Yes, I definitely drifted into Number Land for a while. Computer programs aren't all about numbers, and the judgment the if keyword makes isn't limited to comparing dollar amounts, ecliptic orbits, subatomic particle masses, or calories in various fudgy cookie snacks. No, you can also compare letters of the alphabet in an if statement. This should finally answer the mystery of whether the T is "greater than" the S and explain why the dollar sign is less than the minus sign.

The world of if without values

I ask you: How can one compare two letters of the alphabet? Truly, this subject is right up there with "How many angels can dance on the head of a pin?" and "Would it be a traditional dance, gavotte, rock, or perhaps heavenly hokey-pokey?"

Yet comparing letters is a necessary task. If you write a menu program, you have to see whether the user selected option A, B, or C. That's done by using the handy if keyword. For example:

```
if(key=='A')
```

Here, key is a single-character variable holding input from the keyboard. The comparison if makes is to see whether the contents of that variable are equal to the letter A, which is enclosed in single quotes. This is a legitimate comparison. Did they type an *A?*

Computers and math (do I even have to remind you to skip this stuff?)

Sad to say, too much about computers does deal with math. The computer evolved from the calculator, which has its roots in the abacus, which is somehow related to fingers and thumbs. After all, working with numbers is called "computing," which comes from the ancient Latin term *computare.* That literally means "hire a few more accountants and we'll never truly know what's going on."

Another word for "compute" is *reckon,* which is popular in the South as "I reckon." Yet another word for "compute" is *figure,* which is popular in the !South (not-South) as "I figure." Computers reckon. Go figure.

✔ When if tests to see whether two things are equal, two equal signs are used. Think "is equal to" rather than "equals."

✔ To compare a single-character variable with a character — letter, number, or symbol — you must enclose that character in single quotes. Single character, single quotes.

✔ When you compare a variable — numeric or single character — to a constant, the variable always comes first in the comparison.

✔ The getch and getche functions can be used to read single characters from the keyboard. These were covered in Lesson 3-6.

✔ On a good day, 4.9E3 angels can dance on the head of a pin, given the relative size of the pin, the size of the angels, and whether they all are doing it at once or taking turns.

✔ When you "compare" two letters or numbers, what you're really comparing are their ASCII code values. This is one of those weird instances when the single-character variable acts more like an integer than a letter, number, or symbol.

Which is greater: S or T, $ or — . . . ?

Is the T greater than the S? Alphabetically speaking, yes. T comes after S. But what about the dollar sign and the minus? Which of those is greater? And why should Q be lesser than U, since everyone knows that U always follows Q. Hmmm.

To solve this great mystery of life, the source code for a program, GREATER.C, is listed next. This program asks you to enter two single characters. These characters are compared by an if statement, as well as by if-else. The greater of the two is then displayed. Although this program doesn't lay to rest the angels-on-the-head-of-a-pin problem, it will soothe your frayed nerves over some minor alphabetic conundrums.

Name: GREATER.C

```
#include <stdio.h>
#include <conio.h>

void main()
{
    char a,b;
```

```
printf("Which character is greater?");
printf("\nType a single character:");
a=getche();
printf("\nType another character:");
b=getche();

if(a > b)
{
    printf("\n'%c' is greater than '%c'!\n",a,b);
}
else if (b > a)
{
    printf("\n'%c' is greater than '%c'!\n",b,a);
}
else
{
    printf("\nNext time, don't type the same character
        twice.");
}
}
```

Enter the source code for GREATER.C into your editor. Make sure that you enter all the proper curly brackets, confirm the locations of semicolons, watch your double quotes, and pay attention to the other minor nuances (or nuisances) of the C language.

Save the file to disk as GREATER.C.

Compile GREATER.C.

Run the final program. You are asked the following question:

```
Which character is greater?
Type a single character:
```

Type a character, such as the $ (dollar sign). There's no need to press Enter after typing the character; the `getche` function just waits for one character to be typed:

```
Type another character:"
```

Type another character, such as – (minus sign or hyphen). You see the results:

```
'-' is greater than '$'!
```

- ✔ The ASCII code value for the minus sign is 45. The code value for the dollar sign is 36. Because 36 is less than 45, the computer thinks that the '-' is greater than the '$'. This also holds true for letters of the alphabet and their ASCII code values.

- ✔ See Appendix B for a gander at ASCII values.

- ✔ Run the program again and try typing these two letters: **a** (little *a*) and **Z**. The big Z is less than the little A, even though A comes before Z in the alphabet. The reason is that there are two alphabets in the ASCII code; one for uppercase letters and the other for lowercase. The uppercase letters have smaller values than the lowercase letters do, so "a-z" always is greater than "A-Z."

- ✔ For more information about the getche function, refer to Lesson 3-6.

Severely boring trivia on the nature of "alphabetical order"

So why is it A, B, C first and why does the Z come last? The answer is buried in the bosom of trivia, which most computer junkies are also fond of memorizing. Since I was curious, I thought I'd look it up. And lo, here is what I found.

Our alphabet is based on ancient alphabets, which in turn are based on even older, dinosaur-age alphabets. Back in those days, the letters they used were based on symbols for various things they encountered in everyday life, and the symbols were often named after those things as well: The letter *A* was named after and shaped like the ox, an important beast. B was named after a house and shaped like a door. And so on for all the letters. This is how it was for most of the early Semitic languages, which used phonics rather than pictographs or ideographs.

The Greeks borrowed their alphabet from the Semites. The Romans stole their alphabet from the Greeks (the Romans stole just about everything). But the Romans didn't really steal all of Greek. They left out a few sounds they didn't think they needed: (theta), U, V, X, Y, and Z. Eventually, they realized that the sounds were important, so they added them to the end of their alphabet in the order they were accepted. (The theta was never added by the Romans, though some middle English scripts used a Y symbol to represent it.)

That sort of explains how the alphabet got to be in alphabetical order. The ASCII numbering scheme came about from the early teletype days as a way to encode numbers, common symbols, and secret codes. There's probably a story to tell there, but at this stage in the book, I'm just too lazy to look it up.

BLOW BY BLOW

Musings on how the GREATER.C program works

The program requires two character variables to hold the two keys that are pressed. They are declared as a and b:

```
char a,b;
```

The first printf statement is the program's "title." The next one prompts for input. Note how the \n was used at the beginning of the line to separate it from the preceding printf statement's output. This is to be consistent with the other printf statements, which each start with \n, the newline. Why? Because getche reads in a character and displays it but does not display the newline character. Without the new line character at the beginning of the printf statements, the program's output would look weird. (Feel free to edit the source code and move the \ns to the end of the printf format string to drive home this point.)

```
printf("Which character is
    greater?");
printf("\nType a single charac-
    ter:");
a=getche();
printf("\nType another charac-
    ter:");
b=getche();
```

The getche function is used to read the keyboard and assign character values to the a and b variables. getche echoes the character that is typed. The next few lines evaluate the input:

```
if(a > b)
{
```

```
    printf("\n'%c' is greater than
    '%c'!\n",a,b);
}
```

The first if statement evaluates if the character stored in variable a is greater than variable b. If so, then its printf statement displays that. Note how %c is used in printf and how it's enclosed in single quotes. Each printf statement begins with a newline character.

```
else if (b > a)
{
    printf("\n'%c' is greater than
    '%c'!\n",b,a);
}
```

After a is tested to be greater than b, the opposite test is made by using the else-if statement. The printf statement there looks identical; however, the a and b variables have been reversed to reflect that the contents of variable b are greater than a.

```
else
{
    printf("\nNext time, don't type
    the same character twice.");
}
```

Finally, an else statement ends the decision structure, handling the only possible remaining condition: The a and b variables contain the same character. When that happens, an appropriately rude message is displayed.

Using the `if` *keyword to compare two strings*

The `if` keyword cannot be used to compare strings. It can be used only to compare single-character variables.

- ✔ If you try to use `if` to compare two strings, the result is, as they say, "unpredictable." The program compiles without any errors (maybe), but it definitely doesn't run the way you anticipated.
- ✔ *C For Dummies*, Volume II has more information about comparing strings.

Lesson 4-3 Quiz

1. The `if` statement doesn't really compare two character values; instead, it:

   A. Compares their secret ASCII codes.

   B. Compares the way they're shaped.

   C. Just guesses.

   D. Tests to see which letter represents a more important animal.

2. When comparing two character values, you should enclose each of them inside what?

   A. A bun.

   B. Earmuffs.

   C. Single quotes.

   D. Parentheses.

3. If A>B and B>A are not true, then what could be true?

   A. Math was just not my thing.

   B. A and B are equal: A==B.

   C. It's obvious that A and B cannot be friends, so the government should just throw some money their way.

   D. There is a large bee hovering near your armpit.

4. In the event of a water landing, you should do which of the following:

   A. Put your seat backs and tray tables into the upright and locked position.

   B. Put on — but do not inflate — the life preserver stowed under your seat.

   C. Use your seat bottom as a flotation device.

   D. "Water landing." Yeah, right.

Lesson 4-4: Formatting Your C Source Code

You're venturing closer to the nirvana all C programmers hope one day to attain: a program rich with indentation and curly brackets. Forget what the program does — how it looks is what impresses some people.

Of course, I'm kidding. Formatting your C code with indentation and curly brackets is done for only one reason: to add some sense of readability to your programs. This process can be rough. It's not enough just to know what int, char, atoi, and other freakish words mean. You also have to be able to weed out the programmer's intent and figure out which statements belong to which if and which else and whatnot and whereforeto and hereafter. Also, C source code can look really neat and impressive if it's formatted properly.

Overall, C programs do have a specific look to them. You should note and be mindful of the following list of points. These are all important and required, but how they look is something you're free to play with, which is the topic of this lesson.

- ✔ C programs make use of the curly brackets or braces. These clutch various parts of the program (which you see more of shortly).

- ✔ C programs are in lowercase. All the C keywords and functions are in lowercase, though uppercase does appear from time to time.

- ✔ Functions in C programs make use of parentheses.

- ✔ Semicolons.

The old top-down once-over

Formatting is trivial. What's important to remember is that a C program works its way through your source code from the top down, from left to right — just like you read text on a page.

The program begins with the main() function.

The program ends with the last curly bracket holding the main function together. After that, control of your computer returns to DOS or Windows or your compiler's integrated environment or whatever.

- ✔ Of course, not everything is top-down straight. An if statement can cause your program to hop and jump around some statements. Refer to the TAXES.C program from Lesson 4-1 for an example.

- ✔ Later lessons disclose other statements, similar to if, which cause your program's flow to be not quite top-down. Forget that I told you that until you come to those lessons (in Chapters 5 and 7, mostly).

Formatting your source code

C source code usually appears in the following format:

```
#include <stuff.h>

function()
{
    statement;
    statement;
}
```

Up top are various pound-sign things. #include is the most popular, though you were also introduced to #define, in Lesson 3-4. There are others as well. The whole lot is chewed on in Lesson 6-1.

The function comes next in C source code, up against the left margin (column 0) in your editor. Functions have parentheses that belong to them — even when nothing is inside. This has been the case with the void main() function throughout this book so far. Nothing alarming here.

The next line is the first curly bracket, which marks the beginning of the group of statements that belong to the function. All the statements are indented one tab stop, which helps you to identify them as belonging to the function.

The last curly bracket appears on a line by itself, in the first column position. This bracket should line up with the first curly bracket, so if you took a ruler on your screen and drew a line between the curly brackets, you would have a straight, vertical line that you would later have to work off using some cleanser and a damp washcloth.

- ✔ It doesn't matter how "deep" your tab stops are. The typical tab stop is eight characters (or "spaces") indented. I prefer a four-character tab stop. The amount of indent that is made can usually be adjusted somewhere in your editor (typically under the "Options" menu).
- ✔ There must always be a starting (left) and ending (right) curly bracket. The way this book formats source code, these brackets line up at the same tab stop.

Indenting, phase two

When you have if statements, any statements belonging to them are also indented. For example:

```
    statement;
    if(compare)
    {
```

```
        statement;
        statement;
    }
    statement;
```

The `if` statement appears even with the other statements, indented at one tab stop. Its first curly bracket appears in the same column as well. But any statements belonging to `if` are indented another tab stop.

The final curly bracket belonging to the `if` statement lines up with other statements at the first tab stop.

- Other C language words similar to `if` have their own "structures." They usually appear indented along with the `if` statement and its curly brackets.

- Sometimes you have to indent your source code a third or even fourth time. As with the `if` statement, this is done to line up all the statements that belong to various keywords and such in the C language.

Not formatting your C source code

I'm bringing up the formatting issue in this lesson because there aren't any draconian rules about how you format your C source code. It's all up to you. Eventually you'll find a method that works best with the erratic and haphazard way you program, something you like, or you'll just get into the habit of indenting your source code and not have a sane reason for it.

As far as the C compiler is concerned, it really doesn't care how the source code is formatted. Seriously, the compiler only cares about curly brackets, semicolons, parentheses, and quote marks matching up. Everything else is referred to as "white space" and is ignored.

To prove this, gander at the following source code:

Name: STOP.C

```
void main(){puts("Unable to stop: Bad mood error.");}
```

Here, you find the program STOP.C, which I stole from an earlier chapter. Of course, this doesn't look like the STOP.C you typed in and compiled. That's because I've removed all the white space: the Enter keypress at the end of each line; the tab to indent the statement; and any other stray spaces. The result is this single-line source code.

If you like, you can edit your STOP.C source code file by using your text editor. Use the Delete key and make it look like the source code just listed. Compile the program, and the final results will be the same. The compiler doesn't complain because the source code "looks funny." Everything that counts is in there.

✔ White space is what you pad your C source code with. You press Enter to separate one line from the next, keep the curly brackets by themselves, and so on. You press Tab to indent various portions of the source code, and you probably press the spacebar a few times to "air out" the math. Although this makes the source code readable, it's all ignored by the compiler.

✔ White space is optional.

✔ Though the white space is optional, I highly recommend that you keep it in there and continue to format your C source code as shown in this book. It's too easy to miss a semicolon or foul up a string of text by trying to be cute. (And besides, a one-line program will show only that line number in any error messages you may get.)

✔ The reason that no one formats source code on one line is that it makes it highly cryptic. Some advanced C geeks actually pride themselves in writing such indecipherable source code. Of course, if we had brains the size of beach balls or were from the planet Vulcan, we could understand this type of source code — and enjoy writing it as well.

Other alternatives

Since the compiler isn't fussy about what your source code looks like, how you format it is up to you. Here is a common variation to what's been shown in this book:

```
function()
{
    statement;
    if(compare)
        {
        statement;
        statement;
        }
    statement;
}
```

Here, the curly brackets are indented along with the rest of the statements belonging to if. The outside curly brackets are still at column 1, however. (This is usually consistent with all C programmers, no matter what their minor formatting fetish.)

```
function()
{
    statement;
    if(compare) {
        statement;
        statement;
    }
    statement;
}
```

Here you see the classic "K&R" formatting, from the venerable C language tome *The C Programming Language,* by Brian W. Kernighan and Dennis M. Ritchie (yes, *the* Dennis Ritchie who concocted the C language oh so long ago). The initial curly bracket for the if statement appears at the end of the if line. This saves a little on white space, though since there isn't a white-space drought currently happening, it's merely a matter of taste.

```
function()
{
    statement;
    if(compare) {
        statement;
        statement;
        }
    statement;
}
```

This is the way I prefer to format my C code. The initial curly bracket after if doesn't become an "orphan" on a line by itself. And the final curly bracket lines up with the other statements in the if. This is a scary deviation because you can't do the "ruler trick" to see whether your curly brackets line up. But hey, I'm insane and do what I like because the compiler lets me get away with it.

Lesson 4-4 Quiz

1. Formatting your C code is primarily:

    A. For morons.

    B. Optional.

    C. Designed to make the program more readable.

    D. Copying what's written down in the book.

2. You're in a Chinese restaurant and want to order a beverage that will impress your friends. You order:

   A. Tea.

   B. Tsing Tao beer.

   C. Nestle's Quick.

   D. Alka-Seltzer water.

3. What is "white space?"

   A. What space looks like in reverse.

   B. The maximum volume to which you can inflate a nurse.

   C. Tabs, spaces, blank lines, and other "airy" aspects of C language source code.

   D. What lives in the middle of a Twinkie.

4. Which of the following is not a part of C language source code:

   A. Curly brackets

   B. Lowercase.

   C. Semicolons.

   D. Body lice.

Lesson 4-5: For Going Loopy

One thing computers enjoy doing more than anything else is repeating themselves. Humans? We think that it's punishment to tell a kid to write "*National Geographic* films are not to be giggled at" 100 times on a chalkboard. Computers? They wouldn't mind a bit. They'd *enjoy* it, in fact.

Doing things over and over is referred to as *looping*. When a computer programmer writes a program that counts to 1 zillion, she writes a "loop." The *loop* is called such because it's a chunk of programming instructions — code — that is executed a given number of times. Over and over.

As an example of a loop, consider the common shampoo program. I lifted these instructions off a bottle of shampoo sitting right here in my shower:

> Wet hair. Gently massage lather through hair. Rinse thoroughly.
> Repeat, if desired.

This primitive program contains a loop. The loop is based on "Repeat, if desired," which is a sort-of if statement (if you can believe it).

The shampoo instructions are rather erratic and don't make much sense if you set out to follow them literally. I'm positive that if shampooing hair were a new concept, everyone would be clamoring for a *Shampooing For Dummies* book. Here's the new, clarified shampoo program:

1. Wet hair (stick head under shower nozzle — and I'm assuming that they mean head hair here).

2. Pour shampoo on palm of hand (I'm shocked that they left this step out — shocked!).

3. Gently massage lather through hair (using hand with shampoo glop on it).

4. Rinse thoroughly (re-stick head under shower nozzle; remove hand when convenient).

5. Repeat steps 2 through 4, if desired.

The loop here is that instructions 2 through 4 are repeated. They're done over, based on the if-desired condition in step 5. If you assume that "if desired" is true, based on the fact that you've just crawled under your car and used your head as a grease mop until your hair is almost toxic. In that case, you "loop through" instructions 2 through 4, shampooing your hair twice.

In conclusion, loops always have three parts:

❏ A start

❏ The middle part (the part that is repeated)

❏ An end

This is what makes up a loop. The start is where the loop is set up, usually some programming-language instruction that says "I'm going to do a loop here — stand by to repeat something." The middle part are those instructions that repeat over and over. And finally, the end marks the end of the repeating part or a condition on which the loop ends ("until desired" in the shampoo example).

✔ The C language has several different types of loops. It has `for` loops, which you read about in this lesson; `while` loops and `do-while` loops, covered in Chapter 7; and the ugly `goto` keyword, also covered in Chapter 7.

✔ The instructions held within a loop are executed a specific number of times, or they can be executed until a certain condition is met. For example, you can tell the computer to "do this a gazillion times" or "do this until your thumb gets tired." Either way, several instructions are executed over and over.

✔ After the loop has finished going its rounds, the program continues. But while the loop is, well, "looping," the same part of the program is run over and over.

Repetitive redundancy, I don't mind

The following source code is for OUCH.C, a program which proves that computers don't mind doing things over and over again. No, not at their expense. Not while you sit back, watch them sweat, and laugh while you snarf popcorn and feast on carbonated beverages.

What this program does is to use the `for` keyword, one of the most basic looping commands in the C language. The `for` keyword creates a small loop that repeats a single `printf` command five times.

Name: OUCH.C

```c
#include <stdio.h>

void main()
{
    int i;

    for(i=0 ; i<5 ; i=i+1)
        printf("Ouch! Please, stop!\n");
}
```

Enter this source code into your editor. The new deal here is the `for` keyword, at line 7. Type what happens in there carefully. Notice that the line which begins with `for` doesn't end with a semicolon, but the line that follows it does.

Here's a text-editing tip: Press the Home key to move the cursor to the start of the line (column 1) to type the last curly bracket. Some editors continue to indent the lines in anticipation of your typing more indented statements. The Home key quickly zips you over to the start of the line, where you can type the right curly bracket that ends the `main` function.

Save the file as OUCH.C.

Compile OUCH.C by using your compiler. Be on the lookout for errors here. There may be a missing semicolon in `for`'s parentheses.

Run the final program. You see the following displayed:

```
Ouch! Please, stop!
Ouch! Please, stop!
Ouch! Please, stop!
Ouch! Please, stop!
Ouch! Please, stop!
```

BLOW BY BLOW

Taking the verbal backhoe to OUCH.C

The OUCH.C program is really quite simple, yet it has a great deal of output for such a short program. This is thanks to the repetition induced by the `for` statement.

```
int i;
```

The program uses one variable, the integer variable `i`. This is declared right up front by using the `int` keyword. A blank line follows.

The next two lines set up a `for` loop that repeats a total of five times. The idea is to display the text `Ouch! Please stop!` five times in a row:

```
for(i=0 ; i<5 ; i=i+1)
```

The `for` loop is defined by using the `for` keyword, followed by three items in parentheses. The first item is `i=0`, which *initializes* (sets up) the `i` variable at the start of the loop. This could be a statement by itself (and is, in fact). A semicolon separates the first item from the second.

The second item is a comparison, similar to one you would find in a `if` statement. What's compared is the value of the `i` variable against the value 5. The loop continues to execute as long as this statement — `i<5` — is true. A semicolon separates this item from the last item.

The final item tells the compiler what to do each time the loop executes. In this case, it adds 1 to the value of the variable `i`, `i=i+1`. The idea here is to increment the variable `i` from 0 to 4 — which satisfies the `i<5` condition. That means that the loop will work through five times.

```
    printf("Ouch! Please, stop!\n");
```

The `printf` statement is what the for loop executes five times. It's indented one tab stop to show that it belongs to the `for` loop. The text that's displayed is `Ouch! Please, stop!`, ending in a newline character. This line ends in a semicolon (because it's really the "end" of the `for` statement).

See? Repetition doesn't hurt the PC. Not one bit.

✔ The `for` loop has a start, middle, and an end. The middle part is the `printf` statement — the part that gets repeated. The rest of the loop, the start and end, are nestled within the `for` keyword's parentheses. (The next section deciphers how this stuff works.)

✔ The `printf` statement is indented, which shows that it "belongs" to the `for` loop. Another way to show this is by using curly brackets — just as you did with the `if`-structure:

```
    for(i=0 ; i<5 ; i=i+1)
    {
        printf("Ouch! Please, stop!\n");
    }
```

The curly brackets aren't required when you have only one statement that's repeated. But if you have more than one, they're a must. (Samples of this are sprinkled throughout the rest of this book.)

✔ Buried in the `for` loop is the following statement:

```
i=i+1
```

This is how you add 1 to a variable in the C language. It looks weird, but it works. Refer back to Lesson 3-6 for explanations on why this is so.

✔ Don't worry if you can't understand the `for` keyword just yet. Read through this whole chapter, constantly muttering "I *will* understand this stuff" over and over. Then go back and reread it if you need to. But read it all straight through first.

For doing things over and over, there's the `for` *keyword*

The word *for* is one of those words that gets weirder and weirder the more you say it: for, for, fore, four, foyer .... For he's a jolly good fellow. These are for your brother. For why did you bring me here? An eye for an eye. For the better to eat you with, my dear. Three for a dollar. And on and on. For it can be maddening.

Keyword `for` (looping and looping)

The `for` keyword sets up a for-loop. It defines a starting condition, an ending condition, and the stuff that goes on while the loop is executing over and over. The format can get a little deep, so take this one step at a time:

```
for(starting;while_true;do_this)
    statement;
```

After the keyword `for` comes a set of parentheses. Inside the parentheses are three items, separated by two semicolons. A semicolon does not end this line.

The first item is `starting`, which sets up the starting condition for the loop. The second item is `while_true`, which tells `for` to keep looping as long as a certain condition is true. The final item, `do_this`, tells the `for` keyword what to do each time the loop executes once.

The `statement` is a statement that follows and belongs to the `for` keyword. The `statement` is repeated a given number of times as the `for` keyword works through its loops. This `statement` must end with a semicolon.

If more than one `statement` belongs to the `for` structure, curly brackets must be used to corral them:

```
for(starting;while_true;do_this)
    {
    statement;
    statement;
    /* etc. */
    }
```

In the C language, `for` is used as a simple looping command. In the parentheses belonging to `for` are placed the start, ending, and "as it's happening" conditions that control the loop. Any statements to be repeated follow the parentheses on the next line. The nearby format box has the full `for` format.

One of the most confusing aspects of the `for` keyword is what happens to the three items inside its parentheses. But take heart: It confuses both beginners and the C lords alike (though they won't admit to it).

I'll use the following `for` statement from OUCH.C as an example, which will help you understand how `for`'s three parentheses' pieces' parts make the loop go 'round:

```
for(i=0 ; i<5 ; i=i+1)
```

The first item tells the `for` loop where to begin. In this line, that's done by setting the integer variable `i` equal to 0. This is just a plain old C language statement that fills a variable with a value:

```
i=0
```

The value 0 slides through the parentheses into the integer variable `i`. No big deal.

The `for` keyword uses the variable `i` to count the number of times it repeats its statements.

The second item is a condition — like you would find in an `if` statement — that tells the `for` loop how long to keep going; to keep repeating itself over and over as long as the condition specified is true. In the preceding code line, as long as the statement `i<5` (the value of the variable `i` is less than 5) is true, the loop continues repeating. This is the same as the following `if` statement:

```
if (i<5)
```

So if the value of variable `i` is less than 5, keep going.

The final item tells the `for` loop what to do each time it repeats. So far, the loop would repeat forever: `i` is equal to 0, and the loop repeats as long as `i<5` (the value of `i` is less than 5). That condition is true, so `for` would go on endlessly, like a federal farm subsidy. However, the last item tells `for` to increment the value of the `i` variable each time it loops:

```
i=i+1
```

The compiler takes the value of the variable `i` and adds 1 to it each time the `for` loop is run through once. (Refer to Lesson 4-7 for more info on the art of incrementation.)

Altogether, the `for` loop works out to repeat itself — and any statements that belong to it — a total of five times. Table 4-3 shows how it works.

Table 4-3 How the Variable i Works Its Way Through the for Loop

Value of i	Is i<5 true?	Statement	Do This
i=0	Yes, keep looping→	`printf`...(1)	i=0+1
i=1	Yes, keep looping→	`printf`...(2)	i=1+1
i=2	Yes, keep looping→	`printf`...(3)	i=2+1
i=3	Yes, keep looping→	`printf`...(4)	i=3+1
i=4	Yes, keep looping→	`printf`...(5)	i=4+1
i=5	No — stop now!		

In Table 4-2, the value of the variable i starts out equal to zero, as set up in the `for` statement. Then the second item — the comparison — is tested. Is i<5 true? If so, then the loop marches on.

As the loop works, the third part of the `for` statement is calculated and the value of i is incremented. Along with that, any statements belonging to the `for` command are executed. When those statements are done, the comparison i<5 is made again and the loop either repeats or stops based on the results of that comparison.

- ✔ The `for` loop can be cumbersome to understand because it has so many parts. However, it's the best way in your C programs to repeat a group of statements a given number of times.

- ✔ The third item in the `for` statement's parentheses — do_this — is executed only once for each loop. This is true whether `for` has one or several statements belonging to it.

- ✔ Where most people screw up with the `for` loop is the second item. They remember that the first item means "start here," but they think that the second item is "end here." It's not! The second item means "keep looping while this condition is true." It works like an if comparison. The compiler won't pick up and flag this as a boo-boo, but your program does not run properly when you make this mistake.

- ✔ Don't forget to declare the variable used in `for`'s parentheses. This is a another common mistake made by just about everyone. Refer to Lesson 3-3 for more information about declaring variables.

✔ Here's a handy plug-in for loops you can use. Just substitute the big *X* in the following line for the number of times you want the loop to work:

```
for(i=1 ; i<=X ; i=i+1)
```

You must declare i to be an integer variable. It starts out equal to 1 and ends up equal to the value of *X*. So to do a loop 100 times, you use the following command:

```
for(i=1 ; i<=100 ; i=i+1)
```

Having fun whilst counting to 100

This section has the source code for a program called 100.C. This program uses a for loop to count to 100 and display each number on the screen. Indeed, this is a major achievement: Early computers could only count up to 50 before they began making wild and often inaccurate guesses about what number came next. (Refer to your phone bill to see what I mean.)

Trivial fodder on for's lack of a semicolon

The for statement looks like it lacks a semicolon, but that's only because it has a second part. Here's the format again:

```
for(starting;while_true;do_this)
    statement;
```

The second part, statement on the second line, is followed by a semicolon, and, in fact, that semicolon is what ends the for statement. So the format should really look like this:

```
for(starting;while_true;do_this)
    statement;
```

Most programmers split the statement on two lines for readability's sake.

The point here is that if you ever decide to use a for loop without any statements attached (which is possible though uncommon), you have to format it like this:

```
for(starting;while_true;do_this);
```

That semicolon must be there. If you forget it, the program may not error (depending on what follows the for statement), but it will definitely not work the way you hoped. To remember, most programmers format it this way:

```
for(starting;while_true;do_this)
    ;
```

The core of 100.C is similar to OUCH.C. In fact, the only reason I've tossed it in here is that for loops are so odd to some folks that you need two program examples to drive home the point.

Name: 100.C

```
#include <stdio.h>

void main()
{
    int i;

    for(i=1 ; i<=100 ; i=i+1)
        printf("%i\t",i);
}
```

Type this source code into your editor. Watch your indentations.

In the for statement, the i variable starts out equal to 1. The while_true condition is i<=100 — which means that the loop works, although the value of variable i is less than or equal to 100. The final part of the statement increments the value of i by 1 each time the loop works.

The printf statement displays the value of the integer variable i by using the %i placeholder. (i? %i? Coincidence?) The \t escape sequence inserts a tab into the output, lining up everything by nice, neat columns.

Save the file to disk as 100.C. (This is a chess-club joke; C in Roman numerals is 100. *Hardy-har-har.*)

Compile the program and run it. You see 10 rows of 10 columns and numbers 1 through 100 neatly displayed. Amazing how fast the computer can do that.

- ✔ The output actually shows you the value of the variable i as the for loop works, repeating the printf statement 100 times and incrementing the value of the i variable 100 times as well.

- ✔ Change the for statement in line 5 of your 100.C source code to make the loop go up to 10,000. Use your editor to make it read as follows:

```
for(i=1 ; i<=10000 ; i=i+1)
```

Just insert 2 extra zeroes after the 100 that are already there. Save the change to disk and recompile. It will take the computer longer to count to 10,000 when you rerun the program, but it still works. Diligent, ain't it?

✔ Actually, it doesn't take the computer long to count to 10,000 at all. What takes it time is *displaying* the numbers on the screen. If the computer didn't have to display the numbers, it could count from 1 to 10,000 in less than the blink of an eye — or faster.

✔ Yes, both numbers and letters can be used to name a program: 100 is as legitimate a program name as, say, 123 (which is 123.EXE and was written in Microsoft C, by the way).

Lesson 4-5 Quiz

1. All loops have three parts:

   A. Start. Middle. End.

   B. The setup. The hook. The sting.

   C. Act I. Intermission. Act II.

   D. The engagement ring. The wedding ring. Suffering.

2. The `for` keyword in the C language does what?

   A. Tells the reader who the program is dedicated to.

   B. Sets up a simple loop, a structure with repeating statements.

   C. It's the dative case.

   D. Confuses the heck out of everyone.

3. How many times will the following `for` statement loop 'round?

   ```
   for(i=0 ; i<10 ; i=i+1)
       printf("Ouch! Please, stop!\n");
   ```

   A. 9

   B. 10

   C. 11

   D. The statement will not loop because I know more about C than you do.

4. Combine techniques from both OUCH.C and 100.C to write a program that displays `Ouch!` on the screen followed by a number, 1 through 99. Make the program have two `printf` statements, clutched by curly brackets after the `for` statement. I'm serious. Do this.

Time for a break. Step away from the book, please. The loopiness continues on the next page.

Lesson 4-6: Bustin' Outta Here!

Loops are one of the handiest things you can toss into a program — like rich, creamy, high-fat dressing on top of dull (yet cold and crisp) lettuce. It's only by using loops that programs become useful. Just about anything useful a computer can do for you is accomplished by using a loop: sorting, searching, listing, getting "hung" up. This is all thanks to loops.

The completely loopy lessons are saved for Chapter 7. The task here is to round out coverage of the lovely yet foreboding `for` keyword as well as show you some interesting anti-loop devices designed to let you foil the attempts of even the most (over)diligent computer program.

At last — the handy ASCII program

This section has the source code for ASCII.C — which I proudly proclaim as the first really useful program in this book. What ASCII.C does is to display the ASCII characters and their corresponding codes, from code 32 on up to code 127. This proves handy because it's easier to type ASCII at the DOS prompt to see the codes than it is to keep looking them up in appendixes. (And if you program for any length of time, you look up ASCII codes almost hourly.)

Name: ASCII.C

```
#include <stdio.h>

void main()
{
    unsigned char a;

    for(a=32;a<128;a=a+1)
        printf("%3i = '%c'\t",a,a);
}
```

Enter this source code into your editor. It contains a basic `for`-loop that repeats a `printf` statement several dozen times. The nearby Blow-by-blow box explains how everything works and offers some typing tips if you need them.

After double-checking your work, save the source code to disk as ASCII.C.

Compile the program by using your compiler.

When you run the final result, you see a five-column display on your screen, illustrating the ASCII characters and their codes, from code 32 (the "space" character) on up to code 127, which looks like a little house but is really supposed to be the Greek letter Delta (as in Δ Burke).

- ✔ I use this program all the time to quickly scope out ASCII code values.

- ✔ The `for` loop in the ASCII.C program starts with the value 32, `a=32`. It increments (by 1) on up to the value 127, which is the last stop before `a<128`. The incrementation is done by the handy `a=a+1` equation in the `for` keyword's parentheses.

- ✔ Notice how the `printf` function uses the character variable `a` twice, once as an integer and again as a character. This works by using both the `%i` and `%c` placeholders in `printf`'s format string.

- ✔ The number 3 in `printf`'s `%3i` placeholder directs `printf` to always display three characters when it prints the integer value. This ensures that all the code values line up right-justified (there is a space before the two-digit numbers).

- ✔ Here's a secret: The `a` variable in ASCII.C could be either an integer or character variable. Whichever way you declare it, the program will work. This is because in the `for` loop `a` is used as a value, and in the `printf` function it's used as both a character and a value. This works for both `int`s and `char`s, as long as the value never rises higher than 255 (the largest "value" you can store in a `char` variable).

- ✔ Here's another secret: The variable `a` must be declared as an unsigned character. This has to do with negative numbers and other screwy computer values. If variable `a` were just a `char` variable, the loop would repeat endlessly; adding 1 to `a` when it equals 127 gives a value of –127 and the loop just repeats forever. (To prove this, edit out the word *unsigned* in the ASCII.C source code, recompile, and step on the Break key to stop the madness.)

Beware of infinite loops!

Some things are eternal. Love, they say. Diamonds, of course. Death and taxes, yup. And some loops can be eternal as well, though you don't really want them to be. Actually, eternal is too endearing a term. Moody programmers prefer the term *infinite,* as in "it goes on forever and never stops." Yes, kind of like the Energizer Bunny.

The infinite loop is a repeating section of your program that repeats without end. I can think of no practical application for this. In fact, the infinite loop is usually an accident — a bug — that pops up in a well-meaning program. You don't really know it's there until you run the program. Then when the program just sits there and doesn't do anything or when something is splashed on the screen again and again with no hint of stopping, you realize that you've created an infinite loop. Everybody does this.

The hows, whys, and whats of ASCII.C

The program uses a single variable, both in the `for` loop to keep count as well as for display as an ASCII character and code. Because the main purpose of this variable is as a character, the `char` type is used. `char`s have it in their nature to also be used as numbers, so you can get away with using them in the `for` loop. Furthermore, the variable is declared unsigned so that you can get away with using the value 128 in that variable (otherwise, you would get a compiler "warning" error about the number being out of range):

```
unsigned char a;
```

The number of times the `for` loop repeats itself depends on the ASCII code values the program displays. The codes from 0 up to 31 are "control characters," which you can't really display by using the `printf` function. Therefore, the ASCII.C program displays only the codes and

characters from 32 on up to 127. Those two values, 32 and 127, provide the basis of the `for` loop:

```
for(a=32;a<128;a=a+1)
```

The loop starts with the variable a equal to 32, the code for the first ASCII character to display. The loop increments (a=a+1) as long as the value of a is less than 128 (a<128). This takes care of all the ASCII codes from 32 to 127.

```
printf("%3i = '%c'\t",a,a);
```

Each time the `for` loop works, the `printf` statement is executed. It uses the a variable to display the ASCII code value and then the character represented by that code value. This works with the same variable because you can display a `char` as either an integer value, done with the %i, or as a character, done with the %c.

The following program is FOREVER.C, an on-purpose infinite loop you can type in and try out. Using a misguided `for` command, the program repeats the `printf` statement *ad infinitum*.

Name: FOREVER.C

```c
#include <stdio.h>

void main()
{
    int i;

    for(i=1;i=5;i=i+1)
        printf("The computer has run amok!\n");
}
```

Type this source code into your text editor. It's very similar to your first for-loop program, OUCH.C. The difference here is in the for loop's "while true" part and the message that is repeated. Save the source code to disk with the name FOREVER.C.

Compile the program. Even though the for statement contains a deliberate infinite loop, no error message is displayed (unless you goofed up and typed in something else). After all, the compiler may think that you're attempting to do something forever as part of your master plan. How would it know otherwise?

When you run the program, forever, you see the following messages scrolling madly up your screen:

```
The computer has run amok!
```

Indeed, it has! Press Ctrl-Break to stop the madness.

- Infinite loops aren't shameful — they're more like embarrassing. You definitely won't detect them until the program runs, which is a great argument for testing every program you create.

- Ctrl+Break works here because the program is displaying a message on the screen. DOS can stop that with Ctrl+Break. But DOS cannot stop other types of infinite loops — especially those that may not have any output. In that case, your computer will be "hung," and you may have to press the Reset button or Ctrl+Alt+Delete to regain control. Isn't programming fun?

- The program loops forever because of a flaw in the for loop's "while true" part — the second item in the parentheses:

```
for(i=1;i=5;i=i+1)
```

The C compiler sees i=5 and figures, "OK, I'll put 5 into the i variable." It isn't a true-false comparison (like something you would find with an if statement), which was expected, so the compiler guesses that it's true and keeps looping — no matter what. Note that the variable i is always equal to 5 because of this; even after it's incremented with i=i+1, the i=5 statement resets it back to 5.

- What the for statement should probably look like is the following:

```
for(i=1;i<=5;i=i+1)
```

This line repeats the loop five times.

- Some compilers may detect the "forever" condition in the for statement and flag it as an infinite loop. If so, you're lucky.

- You're lucky! The infinite loop is flagged as a `Possibly incorrect assignment` warning error. The compiler still makes the finished (and flawed) program, though.

Breaking out of a loop

Infinite loops can be done on purpose, but only if there's a way out. For example, you wouldn't hesitate to ride a really scary-looking carnival ride with a really creepy guy at the controls if you knew that you could stop the ride at any time by using a tiny button you're clutching near your chest. This concept is applied to computer programs all the time.

As an example, most word processors work with an infinite loop hidden inside their programs. The loop sits and scans the keyboard, over and over, waiting for you to type a command. Only when you type the proper "I want to quit" command does the thing stop and you return to DOS. This is like a controlled infinite loop — not really infinite because there's a way out.

The following program is TYPER1.C, a first stab at a word processor, though there's nothing you can do in the program except type and see what you type on the screen. The program is set up with an on-purpose infinite `for` loop. However, the new `break` keyword is used with the `if` command to bust out of the loop when you press the ~ (tilde) key.

Name: TYPER1.C

```c
#include <stdio.h>
#include <conio.h>

void main()
{
    char ch;

    printf("Press the ~ key to stop\n");

    for(;;)
    {
        ch=getche();
        if(ch=='~')
        {
            break;
        }
    }
    printf("\nDone!\n");
}
```

This program wins the award for having the most indentation and curly brackets so far in this book. Be careful as you type it into your editor. Save the file to disk as TYPER1.C.

Compile TYPER1.C. The for(;;) statement won't error. This is because the semicolons are required, but what's between them is not (a peculiarity of the for keyword). Fix any syntax errors or other "fatal" errors you may encounter while compiling. Common errors include missing a curly bracket or using the wrong one (right versus left), forgetting the single quotes around the tilde (~) in the if comparison, and the placement of semicolons at the end of some lines but not others.

Run the resulting program. TYPER works somewhat like a typewriter. You can type away and fill the screen with text. And like a typewriter, the Backspace key doesn't backspace and erase (it just backspaces). Tab and other "control" keys display funny characters on the screen. And Enter acts like the carriage return without the line feed. (Press Ctrl+J to line-feed.)

When you're done typing, press the tilde (~) key. (This is TYPER's only "command.")

- ✔ The for loop in TYPER1.C is infinite because its "while true" condition is missing. Gone! Because of this, the compiler assumes that the condition is true all the time and the program loops infinitely. The first and last part of the for statement's items aren't included either, though the semicolons inside the parentheses are still required to meet the demands of C etiquette.

- ✔ Belonging to the for loop are several statements. Because of this, they're enclosed in curly brackets.

- ✔ The getche function waits for a key to be pressed on the keyboard and displays that character. The character is then saved in the ch variable. (Refer to Lesson 3-6 for more information about the getche function.)

- ✔ The if statement tests the ch variable to see whether it's equal to the ~ (tilde) character. Note that two equal signs are used. If the comparison is true, meaning that the user typed the ~ key, then the break command is executed. Otherwise, break is skipped and the loop repeats, reading another character from the keyboard.

- ✔ Refer to Lesson 4-3 for more information on using single characters in an if comparison.

The break *keyword*

To stop a loop, you use the break keyword. This applies to the for loop demonstrated in this lesson and all the other loops demonstrated later in Chapter 7. The official formatting stuff is shown in the nearby format box.

Keyword break

The break keyword gets you out of a loop. No matter what the loop's ending condition, break immediately issues a "parachute out of this plane" command. The program continues with the next statement after the loop or quits if there are no more statements.

```
break;
```

The break keyword is a C language statement unto itself and must end properly with a semicolon.

You must use break within a loop. If you don't, the compiler generates an error. After all, if there is no loop to break out of, what good is the break statement?

break stops only the loop it's in. It does not break out of a "nested loop" (a loop within a loop).

The loop that break breaks you out of doesn't have to be an endless loop. break can stop any loop, at any time. It's often used with an if statement to test some condition. Based on the results of the test, the loop is stopped by using break (just as was done with TYPER1.C in this lesson).

- ✔ If you use break outside of a loop — when there's nothing to break out of — the compiler goes berserk and generates an error.

- ✔ The most common use of the break keyword is in while loops, which are covered in Lesson 7-1.

- ✔ Nested loops are covered in Lesson 7-4 — if you're interested.

- ✔ Funny how the word is break and not "brake." The same twisted logic applies to the Break key on your keyboard.

Lesson 4-6 Quiz

1. Why must the char variable a be unsigned in ASCII.C?

   A. The post office won't deliver it otherwise.

   B. That's how char variables are declared when they're used in a loop.

   C. If the variable were signed, through mathematical buffoonery the program would loop incessantly.

   D. Bad people will find the program and forge a signature otherwise.

2. What is an "infinite loop?"

   A. What Einstein taught his cat to jump through.

   B. The driving pattern you must attempt in order to make a left turn in San Francisco.

   C. What happens to the Christmas tree lights when they're improperly stored.

   D. A slice of code in a program that repeats over and over without ever stopping, not even to giggle.

3. What causes infinite loops?

   A. Two stellar bodies of similar mass influenced by a black hole.

   B. A computer program that doesn't provide a way for a loop to stop.

   C. Ethereal bureaucracy.

   D. The same thing that causes hiccups.

4. To stop a potential infinite loop, you can:

   A. Use the break keyword.

   B. Use the stop keyword.

   C. Threaten the computer with a small child.

   D. Pound on the keyboard! Stomp on the Reset button! Tear the plug from the wall! Cut down the power lines! Toss yourself into the core of a local nuclear reactor! That should stop it.

Lesson 4-7: Shortcuts and the Art of Incrementation (or Another Dreaded Math Lesson)

Loops in a program are closely tied to the art of incrementation (which was introduced briefly in Lesson 3-7, if you care to go back for a review). When a for loop repeats something seven times, a variable somewhere gets incremented seven times. For example:

```
for(i=0;i<7;i=i+1)
```

This for statement sets up a loop that repeats seven times, from i=0 and up by 1 seven times as long as the value of i is less than 7 (i<7).

If you find the concept of starting the loop at 0 strange, the following `for` statement performs the same trick, working itself out over and over seven times:

```
for(i=1;i<=7;i=i+1)
```

Here, `i` actually increments from 1 up to 7. The C lords prefer to start loops with the counting variable at 0, for reasons that were clear to me once and possibly will be clear to both of us before the book is done. Whatever the case, incrementing is central to the idea of looping.

- ✔ Refer to Lesson 4-4 for more information about the `for` loop. (Is it just a coincidence that it's in Lesson 4-4?)

- ✔ Oh, and Table 4-3 illustrates exactly how a variable gets incremented in a `for` loop.

- ✔ Keep in mind that the `for` statement is merely a skeleton for a loop. It repeats a group of statements a given number of times. The `for` statement itself only controls the looping.

Cryptic C operator symbols Volume I: The `inc` operator (++)

The art of incrementation is taking a variable and adding 1 to its value. So no matter what the original value of the variable `count`, it is 1 greater after the following equation:

```
count=count+1;
```

Face it: This is an awkward thing to look at. Yet no loop happens without it, which means that incrementing happens frequently in C programs. Even so, few C programmers will use the preceding statement. Instead, they resort to a shortcut, the incrementation operator, which is two plus signs holding hands:

```
count++;
```

The incrementation operator, ++, works like other mathematical operators you've seen in other horrid math lessons: the +, −, *, and / for addition, subtraction, multiplication, and division, respectively. The difference here is that ++ works without an equal sign. It just tells the compiler, "Yo! Add one to the value of this variable. Thank you. Thank you very much." It's quick and tidy but a bit cryptic (which is why I didn't throw it at you right away).

Operator ++

The increment operator is ++, two plus signs together. What it does is to increase by 1 the value of the variable it's attached to.

```
var++;
```

After this statement, the value of the variable var is increased by 1. This is the same as the following equation:

```
var=var+1;
```

The incrementation operator is used all over in the C language. It may appear as a statement by itself or as part of a looping statement, such as the for keyword.

✔ Yes, you can say "plus plus" in your head when you see ++ in a program.

✔ You do not need an equal sign when you use ++. Just stick it at the end of a variable, and that variable will be incremented by 1.

✔ The equation i++ is the same as $i = i+1$.

✔ So here we go:

```
var=3;          /* the variable var equals three */
var++;          /* Oops! var is incremented here */
                /* From here on, var equals four */
```

✔ The ++ operator would be used as follows in a for statement:

```
for(i=0;i<7;i++)
```

The i++ replaces the $i = i+1$, as has been demonstrated in the past few lessons.

✔ This is where the C language begins to get truly cryptic. Given the separate pieces of a for loop, most knowledgeable humans can detect that $i = 1$ means "i equals 1" and that $i < 7$ means "i is less than 7," and even that $i = i+1$ is "i equals i plus 1." But toss i++ at them and they think "i plus plus? Weird."

✔ Now can anyone possibly guess why they call the new version of the C programming language C++? Anyone?

Another look at the LARDO.C program

Lesson 3-7 first touched on the idea of incrementing a variable in a program. That program was LARDO.C, which I'm certain is near and dear to your heart and has impressed many a friend and family member. Unfortunately, now that you know the ++ thing, the program would really be an embarrassment if you showed it to a C guru. Seriously, all those gauche w=w+1 things need to be properly changed to w++ commands. Short. Sweet. Cryptic. It's what computers are all about!

The following program is an update to the LARDO.C source code, which is probably still sitting on your hard drive somewhere. Load that old file into your editor and make the necessary changes so that the program looks like the new LARDO.C source code listed here.

Name: LARDO.C

```
#include <stdio.h>
#include <stdlib.h>

void main()
{
    char weight[4];
    int w;

    printf("Enter your weight:");
    gets(weight);
    w=atoi(weight);

    printf("Here is what you weigh now: %i\n",w);
    w++;
    printf("Your weight after the potatoes: %i\n",w);
    w++;
    printf("Here you are after the mutton: %i\n",w);
    w=w+8;
    printf("And your weight after dessert: %i pounds!\n",w);
    printf("Lardo!\n");
}
```

Edit your source code (use the Cheat box to help you sort through the minor changes). Save the file to disk again, using the same name, because this program is so much more superior to the original. Then compile.

The only changes you need to make to LARDO.C

This is cinchy: Change line 13 from w=w+1 to w++. Then change line 15 the same way. Remember that the w++ thing is a full-on C language statement, requiring a semicolon, just as it did before.

Those two lines are the only ones you have to change.

Fix any errors if you got 'em. Otherwise, the program runs the same as it did before. The only true difference? You took advantage of the incrementation operator, ++, and earned the clever wink of sophisticated C language programmers worldwide.

✔ Notice that the w=w+8 statement was not modified. This is because the variable w is increased by 8, not just 1. Yes, there is a shortcut for that, but you won't be exposed to it until the next lesson.

Ready or not, here I come!

Loops don't necessarily have to go forward. They can also count down, which is definitely more dramatic and required in some occupations — such as launching spacecraft and other things you find yourself doing every day.

Consider OLLYOLLY.C, a program that counts backward. And that's about all it's good for.

Name: OLLYOLLY.C

```
#include <stdio.h>

void main()
{
    int count;

    for(count=10;count>0;count=count-1)
                printf("%i\n",count);

    printf("Ready or not, here I come!\n");
}
```

Start off your editor with a new slate and carefully type in the source code for OLLYOLLY.H. The only strange stuff you encounter is in the `for` loop's parentheses, which may look a little funky — but it's counting backward! Will the loop work? Will the computer explode? How can this be happening?

Quit pondering and type.

Save the file to disk as OLLYOLLY.C. Compile it. Run it.

The results on your screen will look like this:

```
10
9
8
7
6
5
4
3
2
1
Ready or not, here I come!
```

Yes indeed, the computer can count backward. And it did it in a `for` loop with what looks like a minimum of fuss — but still a little techy. The following section discusses the details.

- ✔ To prove that you're not going crazy, refer to Lesson 4-5's 100.C program. That counted from 1 to 100 using a `for` loop. The only difference here, aside from the `printf` statements, is that the loop worked itself backward.

- ✔ Backward-counting loops in C are possible but rare. Most of the time when you have to do something 10 times, you do it forward, from 0 through 9 or from 1 through 10 or however you set up your `for` loop.

0, to count backward

Counting backward or forward makes no difference to the computer. You just have to tell the C language in which direction you want to go.

To count forward, you increment a variable's value. So if you have the variable `f`, you do the following:

```
f=f+1;
```

Or even this:

```
f++;
```

Either way, the value of variable f is one greater than it was before; it's been incremented.

To count backward, you subtract 1 from a variable's value, which is exactly the way you do it in your head: 10, 9, 8, 7, and so on. This looks identical to the incrementing statement, save for the minus sign:

```
b=b-1;
```

Here, the value of variable b is 1 less than it was before. So if b came in with a value of 5, this statement sets b's value to 4. This process is known as *decrementing* a variable's value.

- ✔ Decrementing, or subtracting 1 (or any number) from a variable's value is just common subtraction. The only big deal here is that decrementing is done in a loop, which makes the loop count backward.
- ✔ Incrementing = adding (one) to a variable's value.
- ✔ Decrementing = subtracting (one) from a variable's value.
- ✔ Decrementing works because C first figures out what's on the right side of the equal sign:

  ```
  b=b-1;
  ```

  First comes b-1, so the computer subtracts 1 from the value of variable b. Then that value is slid through the equal signs back into the variable b. The variable is decremented.

How counting backward fits into the for loop

Take another look at line 7 from the OLLYOLLY.C program:

```
for(count=10;count>0;count=count-1)
```

This is basic for loop stuff. The loop has a starting place, a while-true condition and a do-this thing. (Refer to Lesson 4-5 for more information about the guts of the for loop.) The parts are listed in Table 4-4.

Table 4-4	How the for Loop Counts Backward
Loop Part	*Condition*
Starting	count=10
While-true	count>0
Do-this	count=count-1

Everything in the backward-counting for loop works per specifications. The loop begins by setting the value of the count variable equal to 10. And it loops as long as the value of the count variable is greater than 0 (count>0). But each time the loop repeats, the value of the count variable is decremented. So it works backward.

Again, there is no reason to loop backward . . . except that the printf statement belonging to the loop displays the numbers 10 through 1 in a countdown manner. Normally (which means about 99 percent of the time), you loop forward only. This is not only easier to do in your head, but it's also less likely to be a source for programming boo-boos than when you try to loop backward.

- Most loops count forward. The backward-counting loop in C is possible but rarely used.

- You can't do a backward loop without decrementing the loop's variable.

- Other than decrementing the loop's variable, the only other difference is in the loop's while-true condition (the one in the middle). That requires a little more mental overhead to figure out than with normal for loops. Yet another reason why this type of loop is rare.

- OK. So the question arises, "Why bother?" Because you have to know about decrementing and the cryptic - - operator, covered in the next section.

Cryptic C operator symbols Volume II: The dec operator (- -)

Just as there is a shortcut for incrementing a variable's value, there is also a shortcut for decrementing a variable's value. (You saw this coming from a mile back, most likely.) As a quick review, you can add 1 to a variable's value — *increment* it — by using the following C language statement:

```
i=i+1;
```

Or if you're cool and remember the shortcut, you can use the cryptic ++ operator to do the same thing:

```
i++;
```

Operator - -

The decrement (from the Latin for "subtract one from this number") operator is - -, which is two minus signs glued together. What it does is decrease the value of its companion variable by one.

After this statement, the value of the variable *var* is decreased by one:

```
var--;
```

This is the same as the following C language statement:

```
var=var-1;
```

The - - operator can be used as a statement by itself or occasionally (though not commonly) as part of a looping statement, such as the for keyword.

Both examples add 1 to the value of variable i.

Now consider the following:

```
d=d-1
```

This statement subtracts one from the value of variable d, decrementing it. Here's the whiz-bang, cryptomic shortcut:

```
d--;
```

The - - is the decrement operator, which subtracts one from a variable's value. The nearby sidebar explains all the details.

Just like the incrementation operator, ++, the decrementing operator, - -, works like other mathematical operators in the C language. In keeping with the theme of being cryptic, however, there is no equal sign. The - - tells the compiler to subtract one from the associated variable's value and — *poof!* — it's done.

- ✔ Oh, I would pronounce this one "minus-minus," though I've never heard anyone do it aloud.

- ✔ The equation d-- is the same as d=d-1.

- ✔ There is no penalty for using d=d-1 if you forget about the - - thing.

- ✔ Don't bother with an equal sign when you use the decrementing operator, - -. Glue it to the end of the variable you want to decrement and you're done.

- ✔ So here we go (again):

```
var=3;              /* the value of variable var is three */
var--;              /* Whoa! var is decremented here */
                    /* Now the value of var equals two */
```

✔ The -- operator is used as follows in a for looping statement:

```
for(d=7;d<0;d--)
```

The d-- replaces the d=d-1, as has been demonstrated in the past few lessons.

A final improvement to OLLYOLLY.C

Now that you know about --, you can improve the awkward and potentially embarrassing OLLYOLLY.C program by spiffing it up with the decrementation operator.

Load OLLYOLLY.C into your editor again (if it's not there right now) and clickety-clack the down-arrow key to line 7. Edit the for statement there, replacing the count=count-1 part with the cryptic, though proper, count-- thing. Here's how that line should look when you're done editing:

```
for(count=10;count>0;count--)
```

Save the source code file back to disk and then recompile it.

The program runs the same, but your C programming buddies will nod their heads in amazement at your deft use of the decrementation operator.

Lesson 4-7 Quiz

1. Which of the following C language operators increases the value of a variable by one?

    A. =1

    B. ++

    C. +1

    D. 11

2. Loops in the C language can go:

   A. Forward and backward.

   B. Left and right.

   C. Up and down.

   D. Around the lady hovering before the magician.

3. Counting backward in C is achieved by:

   A. Subtracting or decrementing in a loop.

   B. Reversing the polarity on your computer's power supply.

   C. Compiling using the Australian model.

   D. Sheer luck.

4. The art of decreasing a variable's value is referred to as:

   A. Decrementing.

   B. Desecration.

   C. Dementia.

   D. Deflation.

5. Rewrite the program 100.C (from Lesson 4-5) so that it counts backward from 100 to 1. If you don't want to cheat, don't look at the following hint:

   ```
   for(i=100 ; i>0 ; i=i-1)
   ```

   Or:

   ```
   for(i=100 ; i>0 ; i--)
   ```

6. How can you tell whether the exotic woman you picked up in a strange bar is really a man?

   A. She sings bass in a barbershop quartet.

   B. She has feet the size of snowshoes.

   C. She didn't get the plot twist in *The Crying Game*.

   D. She missed a few whiskers around her Adam's apple.

Lesson 4-8: More Incrementation, More Madness

Incrementation and looping go hand in hand like (this week's) Hollywood's hottest couple.

Looping is an important part of programming — doing things over and over like a famous actor rehearses his lines. In C, that can be done only with the `for` loop if you increment (or decrement) a variable's value.

Tied in with looping are the ++ and -- operators, which can also be used independently from looping to increase or decrease a variable's value — like some actresses increase or decrease their size through various surgical techniques.

Given that, you should still keep in mind that incrementing and decrementing doesn't have to be done one tick at a time. For example, the LARDO.C program boosts the w variable's value by eight by using the following statement in line 17:

```
w=w+8;
```

Here, the value of the variable w is increased by 8. The following statement decreases it by 3:

```
w=w-3;
```

This is still a form of incrementing and decrementing, though values larger than 1 are used. Perfectly legit. And — as a bonus — you can use these types of incrementing or decrementing in loops. An example is coming forthwith.

> ✔ Although you can increment a variable by a value larger than 1, the ++ operator increases a variable's value by only 1. The same holds true for --, which always decreases a variable's value by 1.

> ✔ Yes, there are handy shortcuts for increasing or decreasing a variable's value by an amount greater than 1. The latter part of this lesson introduces you to that technique — yet another cryptic aspect of programming in C.

Leaping loops!

After losing or wining an American Little League game, either team takes turns in the following chant:

2, 4, 6, 8, who do we appreciate?

This is followed by the other team's name. It's a nice, polite, all-American athletic chant, meaning either "You sad sacks were easy to beat and, if we were unsupervised, we'd be vandalizing your bicycles by now" or "You defeated us through treachery and deceit and, if we were unsupervised, we'd be pummeling your heads with our aluminum bats."

Anyway, the following program uses a `for` loop to generate the 2, 4, 6, 8 part of the chant. It's a `for` loop that, yes, skips a bit as it counts. This is what I call a leaping loop.

Name: CHANT.C

```
#include <stdio.h>

void main()
{
    int i;

    for(i=2;i<10;i=i+2)
                    printf("%i ",i);
    printf("who do we appreciate? Borland!\n");
}
```

Choose New in your editor and type in the preceding source code. In the `printf` statement in the `for` loop, note the space after the `%i`. So it goes "double quote, percent, little *i*, space, double quote." Save the file to disk as CHANT.C.

Compile and run the program. Here is what your output should look like:

```
2 4 6 8 who do we appreciate? Borland!
```

✔ The loop starts at 2 and increments up to 10 by using the `i=i+2` formula. So the loop reads like this: "Start with `i` equal to 2, and while the value of `i` is less than 10, repeat the following, adding 2 to variable `i` each time you loop."

✔ If you changed line 7 of the program, you could have the loop count by even numbers up to any value. For example:

```
for(i=2;i<1000;i=i+2)
```

This modification makes the computer count by twos from 2 to 998. This doesn't do much for the chant, but it works. (Indeed, it would take forever to get to The Pizza Place if that were the case.)

✔ Feel free to change `Borland` in the program to `Lotus`, `Novell`, or even `Microsoft` if you feel in a cheery way toward any of them.

✔ Leaping loops are possible, but like the counting-backward loop, they're rare. Most programmers just want a loop to repeat a given number of times. The mental overhead to figure that out for a leaping loop isn't worth the bother. So only when you need a loop that counts even numbers, by threes or fives or whatever, should you bother with a leaping loop.

Counting to 1,000 by fives

The following program is an update to the old 100.C program from back in Lesson 4-5. In this case, the program counts to 1,000 by fives — a task that would literally take days without a computer.

Name: 1000.C

```
#include <stdio.h>

void main()
{
        int i;

        for(i=5;i<=1000;i=i+5)
                        printf("%i\t",i);
}
```

Start off with a new, clean slate in your editor. Type in the preceding source code. It's nothing fancy. Indeed, it's just a take-off from the old 100.C program. Save the file to disk as 1000.C.

Compile 1000.C and run the result. Your screen will fill with values from 5 to 1000, all lined up in rows and columns.

✔ This leaping loop counts by fives because of the i=i+5 part of the for statement. The i=i+5 operation keeps increasing the value of the i variable by 5.

✔ The loop begins counting at 5 because of the i=5 part of the for loop. It stops counting at 1,000 because of the i<=1000 part of the loop. That's "less than or equal to 1000," which is how you get to 1,000.

Cryptic C operator symbols
Volume III: The madness continues

C is full of shortcuts, and mathematical operations are where you find most of them clustered like bees over a stray Zagnut bar. So far, the two most cryptic shortcuts are for changing a variable's value by 1: ++ to increment and -- to decrement. But there are more!

To add 5 to a variable's value, for example, such as in the 1000.C program, you used the following:

```
i=i+5
```

The cryptic C language shortcut for this operation is:

```
i+=5
```

This means, "Increase the value of variable i by five." Unfortunately, it just doesn't *look* like that's what it means. Although I can swallow ++ to increment and -- to decrement, the += thing seriously looks like a typo. Sad news: It's not. Even sadder: There are more of them, one each for adding, subtracting, multiplying, or dividing a variable's value by a certain amount (or by another variable). Table 4-5 lists them.

Table 4-5   Cryptic Shortcuts for Common Math Operations

Long, Boring Way	Cryptic Shortcut
var=var+5	var+=5
x=x+y	x+=y
var=var-5	var-=5
x=x-y	x-=y
var=var*5	var*=5
x=x*y	x*=y
var=var/5	var/=5
x=x/y	x/=y

In the table you see two examples for each cryptic shortcut. The first uses the variable var, which is modified by a constant value, 5. The second uses two variables; the first one, x, is modified by another variable, y.

Yes, the shortcuts for incrementing, decrementing, or changing a variable are cryptic. You don't have to use them. There is no penalty for forgetting about them. I refer to them here for two reasons: It can be done, and C gurus love tossing this stuff into programs; so don't let the shortcuts scare you when you see them.

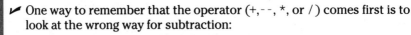

✔ Technically, these things are referred to as *assignment operators*. Don't memorize that term. Even I had to look that up.

✔ Hey: Good idea to stick a Post-It note on the preceding page or flag it by dog-earing the corner. These cryptic shortcuts aren't easy to remember.

✔ One way to remember that the operator (+,--, *, or /) comes first is to look at the wrong way for subtraction:

```
var=-5
```

This is not a shortcut for var=var-5. Instead, it sets the value of variable var equal to negative five. Ipso fasto, var-=5 must be the proper way to do it.

✔ Remember that these mathematical-shortcut cryptic operators aren't necessarily limited to use in for loops. Each of them can be a C language statement unto itself, a mathematical operation to somehow pervert a variable's value. To wit:

```
term+=4;
```

This statement increases the value of the variable term by 4.

Lesson 4-8 Quiz

1. Which of the following for statements makes a loop that counts by twos?

   A. for(i=2;i<2;i=2)

   B. for(two;too;to);

   C. for(i=0;i<100;i=i+2)

   D. for(all the animals; Noah counts them; two-by-two)

2. Lo, it's daylight savings time. But which part of Indiana refuses to go along?

   A. The part Dan Quayle is from.

   B. The part that contains IDG Books.

   C. The eastern part.

   D. The silly part.

3. Modify the program 1000.C so that it uses a shortcut rather than `i=i+5` in its `for` loop.

4. Which of the following cryptic statements multiplies the value of the variable `wambooli` by 34?

   A. `wambooli*34=;`

   B. `wambooli**34;`

   C. `wambooli=*34;`

   D. `wambooli*=34;`

Chapter 4 Final Exam

1. How does the `if` keyword make a decision?

    A. It examines your PC's entrails.

    B. Bones.

    C. Chickens.

    D. It makes a comparison.

2. Which symbol would be used to see whether the value of variable `a` is greater than or equal to the value of variable `b`?

    A. a >= b

    B. a => b

    C. a ≥ b

    D. Both A and B.

3. What are the signs that someone is choking?

    A. Victim cannot sing.

    B. Victim cannot laugh.

    C. Victim cannot whistle.

    D. All of the above.

4. To handle an either-or type of decision, you use which famous pair of C language statements?

    A. `printf` and `scanf`

    B. `eitherf` and `orf`

    C. `thisaway` and `thataway`

    D. `if` and `else`

5. When you use `if` to compare to characters, what is really being compared?

    A. The character's ASCII values.

    B. The character's moral values.

    C. The character's aesthetic values.

    D. The character's character.

    The next few questions refer to the following bit of code:

```
if(a<b)
    {
    printf("Blorf!");
    }
else if(a>b)
    {
    printf("Wambooli!");
    }
else
    {
    printf("Fragus!");
    }
```

6. If the a variable equals 10 and b equals 7, what message is displayed?

    A. Blorf!

    B. Wambooli!

    C. Fragus!

    D. I'm sorry, but life just isn't fair.

7. If the a variable equals 1 and the b variable equals 100, what message is displayed?

    A. Blorf!

    B. Wambooli!

    C. Fragus!

    D. We'll see.

8. If both a and b equal the same value, what message is displayed?

    A. Blorf!

    B. Wambooli!

    C. Fragus!

    D. What is it about "no" that you just don't understand?

9. Men have one less rib than women do. True or false?

10. How many times will the following statement loop?

```
for(i=0;i<10;i++)
```

    A. Nine times.

    B. Ten times.

    C. Eleven times.

    D. *New York Times.*

11. Which of the following C language statements will stop a loop dead in its tracks?

   A. `Boo!`

   B. `Hello, I'm from the IRS.`

   C. `Immigration!`

   D. `break;`

12. The incrementation operator is:

   A. `++`

   B. `+1`

   C. `inc`

   D. `upsie-daisy`

13. The decrementing operator is:

   A. `--`

   B. `-1`

   C. `dec`

   D. `babyfalldown`

14. Which of the following is the correct way to greet the Pope at the top of a letter?

   A. Yo, Pope.

   B. Most Holy Father.

   C. Your Holiness.

   D. You in the Hat.

15. Which of the following `for` loops will count backward by fives?

   A. `for(i=100;i>0;i=i-5)`

   B. `for(i=5;i>0;i+=5)`

   C. `for(i=100;i>5;i++5)`

   D. `for(5=i;ii;aye;eye)`

16. Match the following statements with their shortcuts:

   A. `x=x+1;`   `x++;`

   B. `x=x*5;`   `x+=5;`

   C. `x=x-5;`   `x-=5;`

   D. `x=x-1;`   `x-;!`

   E. `x=x/5;`   `x/=5;`

"OH SURE, IT'S NICE WORKING AT HOME. EXCEPT MY BOSS DRIVES BY EVERY MORNING AND BLASTS HIS HORN TO MAKE SURE I'M AWAKE."

Chapter 5
Your Very Own Functions

Functions are where you "roll your own" in the C language. They're nifty little procedures, or series of commands, that tell the computer to do something. All that's bundled into one package, which your program can then use repeatedly and conveniently. In a way, writing a function is like adding your own commands to the C language.

If you're familiar with computer programming languages, then functions are similar to subroutines or procedures. If you're not familiar with computer programming (and *bless you*), think of a function as a shortcut. It's a black box that does something wonderful or mysterious. After you construct the function, the rest of your program can use it — just like any other C language function or keyword. This chapter definitely puts the *fun* into function.

Lesson 5-1: Writing That First Function

Are functions necessary? No. Not at all. But without them, two ugly and inappropriate things happen: Your source code gets unwieldy because you would have to stuff everything into the sole main() function. Second, and most important, your programs would contain a great deal of duplicate instructions. Unwieldy happens. But redundancy should always be avoided.

Suppose that you write a program which plays "Alexander's Rag Time Band" every time the user does something pleasing. Because the programming required to play the song is odd and unique, you decide to write a function to conduct the PC's orchestra. For giggles, say that it looks like this:

```
playAlex()
{
     sound(466); delay(125);
     sound(494); delay(375);
     sound(466); delay(125);
     sound(494); delay(1000);
     /* and there would be more... */
}
```

With all that neatly tucked into a function, your program can then "call" the function every time it wants to play the song. So rather than repeat a vast chorus line of commands (as shown here), you merely stick the following in your code:

```
playAlex();
```

That's a C language "command" that says "Go off yonder to said playAlex function, do what you must while you're there, and then return to this here very spot to continue a-workin'." Lo, the function has made writing the program easier.

✔ You create a function by writing it in your source code. The function has a name, optional doodads, plus its own C language code that carries out the function's task. More on this later.

✔ To use a function, you *call* it. Yoo-hoo! This is done by typing the function's name in your program, followed by the empty parentheses:

```
playAlex();
```

This command "calls" the playAlex() function, and the computer goes off and does whatever it's instructed to do in that function.

✔ Yes, that's right. Calling (or using) a function is as easy as sticking its name in your source code, just like any other C language statement.

✔ Some functions require information in their parentheses. For example, `puts`:

```
puts("Oh, what a great way to start the day.");
```

✔ Some functions *return* a value. That is, they produce something your program can use, examine, compare, whatever. The `getch` function returns a character typed at the keyboard, which is typically stored in a character variable, `thus`:

```
thus=getch();
```

✔ Some functions both require parentheses stuff and return a value.

✔ Other functions (such as `playAlex`) do neither.

✔ Functions are nothing new. Your programs so far have been full of them, such as `printf`, `getche`, `atoi`, and others. Unlike your own, these functions are part of the compiler — almost part of the C language itself. Even so, the functions you write work just like those others do.

✔ Creating a function doesn't really add a new word to the C language. However, you can use the function just like any other function in your programs; `printf`, `getche`, etc.

A potentially redundant program in need of a function

I like to think of functions as removing the redundancy from programs. If there's anything done more than once, shuffle it off into a function. That makes writing the program so much easier. And it also breaks up the `main` function in your source code (which can get tediously long).

The following sample program is BIGJERK1.C, a litany of sorts devoted to someone named Bill, who is a jerk.

Name: BIGJERK1.C

```
#include <stdio.h>

void main()
{
```

```
        printf("He calls me on the phone with nothing say\n");
        printf("Not once, or twice, but three times a day!\n");
        printf("Bill is a jerk!\n");
        printf("He insulted my wife, my cat, my mother\n");
        printf("He irritates and grates, like no other!\n");
        printf("Bill is a jerk!\n");
        printf("He chuckles it off, his big belly a-heavin'\n");
        printf("But he won't be laughing when I get even!\n");
        printf("Bill is a jerk!\n");
}
```

Type this program into your editor. Double-check all the parentheses and double quotes. They're maddening. Maddening!

Compile and run BIGJERK1.C. It displays the litany on the screen. Ho-hum. Nothing big. Yet notice that one chunk of the program is repeated three times. Smells like a good opportunity for a function.

- ✔ Most of the redundancy a function removes is much more complex than a simple printf statement. Ah, but this is a demo.

- ✔ None of the Bills I personally know is a jerk. Therefore, read into this program what you will.

- ✔ In the olden days (and I'm really showing my age here), every byte in a program was vital. A message such as Bill is a jerk repeated over and over meant that precious bytes of data were being wasted on a silly text string. Ancient programmers such as myself honed their skills by removing excess bytes from programs like this. Shaving a program's size from 4,096 bytes down to 3,788 bytes was considered a worthy accomplishment. Of course, with today's multimegabyte hummers, saving space like that is considered trivial.

The noble jerk() *function*

Time to add your first new word to the C language, the jerk() function. OK, jerk isn't a C language word. It's a function. But you use it in a program just as you would use any other C language word or function. The compiler doesn't know the difference — provided you set everything up properly.

Next is the new, improved "Bill is a jerk" program. It contains the noble jerk() function, right in there living next to the primary main() function. This is a major step in your programming skills. A moment to be savored. Pause to enjoy a beverage after typing this.

Name: BIGJERK2.C

```c
#include <stdio.h>

void main()
{
    printf("He calls me on the phone with nothing say\n");
    printf("Not once, or twice, but three times a day!\n");
    jerk();
    printf("He insulted my wife, my cat, my mother\n");
    printf("He irritates and grates, like no other!\n");
    jerk();
    printf("He chuckles it off, his big belly a-heavin'\n");
    printf("But he won't be laughing when I get even!\n");
    jerk();
}


/* This is the jerk() function */

jerk()
{
    printf("Bill is a jerk\n");
}
```

Type the source code for BIGJERK2.C in your editor. Pay special attention to the formatting and such. Save the file to disk as BIGJERK2.C. Compile and run. The output from this program is the same as the first BIGJERK program.

- ✔ You should see a slew of warning errors with this one: there are `no proto-type` errors and one `Function should return a value`. These messages are cured in the section "About all them darn prototyping errors."

- ✔ Two warning errors should rear their ugly heads here: A `'jerk'` unde-`fined` error and a `no return value` error. The Borland compiler really has it right here; these are `no prototyping` errors, and they're discussed in the section "About all them darn prototyping errors," later in this chapter.

- ✔ Even if you got the preceding `no prototyping` errors, the program runs. This type of error is a warning and usually doesn't affect the program's output. Usually.

How the `jerk()` function works in BIGJERK2.C

A function works like a magic box. It produces something. In the case of the `jerk` function in BIGJERK2.C, it produces a string of text displayed on the screen. Bill is a jerk. Like that.

In the BIGJERK2.C program, the computer ambles along, executing C language instructions as normal, from top to bottom. Then it encounters the following:

```
jerk();
```

That's not a C language keyword, and it's not a function known to the compiler. So the computer looks around and finds a jerk function defined in your source code. Contented, it jumps over there and executes those statements in that function. When it reaches the last curly bracket in the function, the computer figures that it must be done, so it returns to where it was in the main program. This happens three times in BIGJERK2.C.

Figure 5-1 illustrates what's happening in a graphic sense. Each time the computer sees the jerk() function, it executes the commands in that function. This works just as though those statements were right there in the code (as shown in the figure) — which, incidentally, is exactly how the BIGJERK1.C program worked.

✔ The computer still reads instructions in the source code from the top down in the main function. However, when it sees another function, such as jerk(), it temporarily sidesteps to run the instructions in that function. Then it returns back to where it was.

✔ Keep in mind that not all functions are as simplistic as jerk(). Most of them contain many lines of code — stuff that would be too complex and redundant to use all over the place in a program.

```
void main()
{
    printf("He calls me on the phone with nothing say\n");
    printf("Not once, or twice, but three times a day!\n");
        {
        printf("Bill is a jerk!\n");
        jerk();
        printf("He insulted my wife, my cat, my mother\n");
    printf("He irritates and grates, like no other!\n");
        {
        printf("Bill is a jerk!\n");
        jerk();
        printf("He chuckles it off, his big belly a-heavin'\n");
    printf("But he won't be laughing when I get even!\n");
        {
        printf("Bill is a jerk!\n");
        jerk();
}
```

Figure 5-1: How a function works in a program.

The Tao of functions

The C language allows you to put as many functions as you want in your source code. There really is no limit, though most programmers like to keep their source-code text files to a manageable size.

Traditionally, the main function comes first in your source code. Other functions you create come after it. This isn't a hard and fast rule, so don't be surprised if you stumble across some C language source code that lists the main function last. (Regardless of its position, main is always run first by the computer.)

Here's the format of a typical function:

```
type name(stuff)
```

The most basic part is name(). The type and stuff are optional. The name is the function's name, and the parentheses are required.

The type tells the compiler what the function does, what type of value it generates. This is something you read more about in Lesson 5-3. *Types* include: char for functions that return character values; int for functions that produce integers; void for functions that return nothing (like your cousin who's always borrowing money); and there are other types as well.

The stuff defines whatever value (or values) are sent off to the function for evaluation, manipulation, or mutilation. This subject is covered in Lesson 5-3.

The function also requires curly braces enclosing statements, the instructions that carry out what the function is supposed to do. Therefore, the full format for the function is shown here:

```
type name(stuff)
{
        statement(s);
}
```

✔ Call this *defining a function*. Call this *declaring a function*. Call it *doing a function*. (The official term is *defining a function*.)

✔ Naming rules for functions are covered in the next section.

✔ When programs get really huge, you'll probably break up your source code into various *modules*. Modules are basically other source-code files that contain various functions. This topic is covered in this book's second volume, *C For Dummies*, Volume II.

✔ The function's type and the stuff in the parentheses are optional for the most part. If your compiler is set up to be ANSI C compatible, however, the type and the stuff in parentheses must be defined. This is known as *prototyping* and may explain why you got some warning errors when you compiled BIGJERK2.C.

✔ Your C language library reference lists functions using the preceding format. For example:

```
int atoi(const char *s);
```

This format from the Borland C manual explains how the atoi function works. Its *type* is an int and its *stuff* is a character string, which is how you translate const char *s into English. (Also noted in the format is that the #include <stdlib.h> thing is required at the beginning of your source code when you use the atoi function.)

How to name your functions

Functions are like your children, so, for heaven's sake, don't give them a dorky name. You're free to give your functions just about any name, but keep in mind the following notes:

✔ Functions are named by using letters of the alphabet and numbers. Almost all compilers insist that your functions begin with a letter. Refer to your programmer's manual to see whether this is something your compiler is fussy about.

✔ Do not use spaces in your function names. Instead, use underlines. For example, this is not a function name:

```
get the time()
```

A nerdy aside you don't have to read

The original C language programming book, *The C Programming Language,* by Brian Kernighan and Dennis Ritchie, lists the following as "a minimal function:"

```
dummy() { }
```

Who would have known!

The preceding line is referred to as a do-nothing function. It works, but because its curly brackets are empty, it doesn't do much.

✔ But this is:

```
get_the_time()
```

✔ You can use upper- or lowercase when you're naming your functions. A common tactic is to capitalize key letters in the function's name:

```
getTheTime()
```

✔ Most compilers scoff at function-name capitalization. For example, they might think that `Jerk()` and `jerk()` are two different functions. (The only way to be certain is to try changing capitalization in a program, such as BIGJERK2.C, to see whether your compiler chokes.)

✔ If you end up using capital letters in your function names, make sure that you stay consistent with them.

✔ Keep your function names short and descriptive. A function named `f()` is permissible yet ambiguous — it's like saying "nothing" when someone asks you what you're thinking.

✔ Some compilers may forbid you to begin a function name with an underline. Sounds bizarre, I know, but the following may be verboten:

```
_whatever()
```

✔ Avoid naming your functions the same as other C language functions or keywords. Be unique! (The list of keywords is provided in Table 1-1 in Chapter 1.)

✔ The function name `main` is reserved for your program's first function.

About all them darn prototyping errors

Prototyping is something they added to the C language to help you avoid some nasty errors. The compiler wants you to tell it about your functions so that it's sure you're using them properly. I know, sounds a little like the compiler doesn't trust you. But you probably don't trust it much either, so the respect is mutual.

You have to do two things to appease the prototyping gods. First, you have to properly configure the `jerk` function itself. Change line 18 in the program to read as follows:

```
void jerk()
```

This line tells the compiler that the `jerk()` function returns no values. That takes care of the `function should return a value` error. (Functions that return values are covered in Lesson 5-4; functions that don't return a value are `void`. So there.)

Next, you have to tell the compiler about the `jerk` function way early in the program. Essentially, this is what prototyping is all about: You tell the compiler, "Hello? There is a `jerk` function later in this program and here's what you should expect to see." You do this by sticking a line up top that looks like the start of the `jerk` function — but ends with a semicolon:

```
void jerk(void);
```

Stick this line between the `#include <stdio.h>` and the `void main()` that starts the `main` function. So the first part of your program looks like this:

```
#include <stdio.h>

void jerk(void);

void main()
```

The `void jerk(void);` line is the prototype. It tells the compiler to expect a `jerk` function later on and that the function will be of the `void` type and have `void` stuff in its parentheses. Heavy-duty `void` material. Just follow along if you don't understand it.

Make the editing changes per the preceding instructions. A final rendition of the BIGJERK2.C program is shown in Figure 5-2.

```
#include <stdio.h>

void jerk(void);

void main()
{
        printf("He calls me on the phone with nothing say\n");
        printf("Not once, or twice, but three times a day!\n");
        jerk();
        printf("He insulted my wife, my cat, my mother\n");
        printf("He irritates and grates, like no other!\n");
        jerk();
        printf("He chuckles it off, his big belly a-heavin'\n");
        printf("But he won't be laughing when I get even!\n");
        jerk();
}
```

```
/* This is the jerk() function */

void jerk()
{
        printf("Bill is a jerk\n");
}
```

When you're done, resave BIGJERK2.C to disk. Recompile and you won't be bothered by the various warning errors again.

✔ The prototype is basically a rehash of a function that appears later in the program.

✔ The prototype must shout out what type of function the program is and describe what kind of stuff should be between the parentheses.

✔ The prototype must also end with a semicolon. This is *muy importanto*.

✔ I usually copy the first line of the function to the top of the program, paste it in there, and then add a semicolon. For example, with BIGJERK2.C, I copied line 18 (the start of the jerk function) to the top of the source code and pasted it in, adding the necessary voids and semicolon.

```
#include <stdio.h>

void jerk(void);

void main()
{
  printf("He calls me on the phone with nothing say\n");
  printf("Not once, or twice, but three times a day!\n");
  jerk();
  printf("He insulted my wife, my cat, my mother\n");
  printf("He irritates and grates, like no other!\n");
  jerk();
  printf("He chuckles it off, his big belly a-heavin'\n");
  printf("But he won't be laughing when I get even!\n");
  jerk();
}

/* This is the jerk() function */

void jerk()
{
  printf("Bill is a jerk\n");
}
```

Figure 5-2:
The final, complete BIGJERK.C source code.

✔ If you want to avoid prototyping errors — but only for this book — you can switch off your compiler's ANSI C compatibility. This should be in your compiler's Options menu or something similar. There is a way of selecting the compiler's level of fussiness, whether it's plain old C, K&R C (Kernighan and Ritchie), ANSI C, and so on. Just turn off ANSI C mode and the compiler forgets about prototyping — and so can you too.

Lesson 5-1 Quiz

1. Functions serve what purpose?

    A. They serve to unclutter the `main` function and help you avoid redundancy in your programs.

    B. They introduce more curly brackets and such into a C program, which makes it looks neater and impresses your friends.

    C. They work without your having to think about it, like Renuzit Solid.

    D. They're just cool.

2. What other name besides "functions" could they have called them?

    A. Procedures.

    B. Subroutines.

    C. Gizmos.

    D. What are "they"?

3. Define "tedium":

    A. Pretending to be interested in two full hours of unedited family video.

    B. A Bob Hope film festival.

    C. Watching complete "gavel-to-gavel" coverage of the Democratic National Convention.

    D. Spending seven hours with a C programming guru who never shuts up and refers to tea as "cha."

4. Functions you create are just like the `main` function, except that:

    A. They aren't named `main`.

    B. They require something called prototyping.

    C. They do something ingenious and specific.

    D. All of the above.

5. To use a function in a program, you:

    A. Call it.

    B. Hail it.

    C. Phone it.

    D. Lure it.

6. Which of the following C language statements properly calls the `eatPet` function?

    A. `call(eatPet);`

    B. `eatPet();`

    C. `gogo eatPet();`

    D. `gosub eatPet();`

7. Why do you prototype?

    A. It's necessary for testing and to show to the media.

    B. To avoid nasty errors that may happen later, especially in larger programs.

    C. Because the compiler pukes if you don't.

    D. Me? I don't prototype.

8. How would the following function be prototyped?

```
void jerk()
```

    A. `void jerk()`

    B. `void jerk();`

    C. `void jerk(void);`

    D. `{void}{jerk}{void}{;-:0)>!!)`

9. What is Van Wolverton's first name?

    A. Mister.

    B. Van.

    C. Ira.

    D. Van Wolverton is his first name.

It's break time. Run like mad to the refrigerator. Then come back.

Lesson 5-2: Contending with Variables in Functions

Each function you create can use its own, private set of variables. This is a must. Just like the main function, other functions require integer or character variables that help the function do its job. A few quirks are involved with this, of course — a few head-scratchers that must be properly mulled over so that you can understand the enter function/variable gestalt.

- ✔ Please refer to Lesson 5-1 for an introduction to functions if you haven't yet read it.

- ✔ Also refer to Lesson 5-1 for information about prototyping, which explains some of the strange nonsense you may not recognize in this lesson's programs.

Bombs away with the BOMBER program!

The following program, BOMBER.C, contains a function that has its very own, unique variable. The dropBomb() function uses the variable x in a for loop to simulate a bomb dropping. This could be an exciting element of a computer game you may yearn to write. (Indeed, the sounds you hear in any computer game are generated by functions similar to this program's dropBomb() function.)

By the way, this is one of those rare instances in which there are two programs, one for Borland C++ (which has nifty sound-making statements) and one for Microsoft C++ (which is brain-dead when it comes to making the PC talk). Each source code listing is flagged appropriately.

Name: BOMBER.C

```
#include <stdio.h>
#include <conio.h>
#include <dos.h>

void dropBomb(void);              //The devious prototype

void main()
{
    printf("Press any key to drop bomb:");
    getch();
    dropBomb();
    printf("\nYikes!\n");
}
```

```
void dropBomb()
{
    int x;

    for(x=880;x>440;x-=10)
    {
                    sound(x);
                    delay(100);
    }
    nosound();
}
```

Name: BOMBER.C

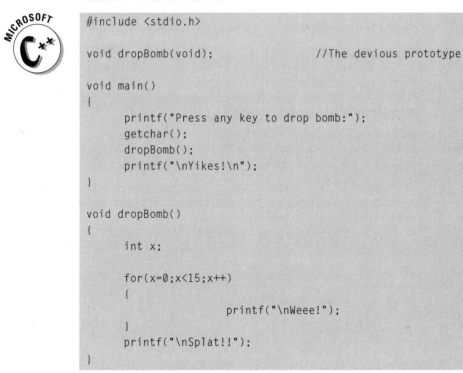

```
#include <stdio.h>

void dropBomb(void);                    //The devious prototype

void main()
{
    printf("Press any key to drop bomb:");
    getchar();
    dropBomb();
    printf("\nYikes!\n");
}

void dropBomb()
{
    int x;

    for(x=0;x<15;x++)
    {
                    printf("\nWeee!");
    }
    printf("\nSplat!!");
}
```

Type the source code as listed here, proper to your compiler. Save the file to disk as BOMBER.C. Compile and run.

The output is different for each program. The Borland version of BOMBER.C looks like this:

```
Press any key to drop bomb:
Yikes!
```

And it plays a lovely bomb-dropping sound over the PC's speaker after you press the any key (Enter).

The Microsoft version is mute because it lacks Borland's fancy sound commands. Its output looks like this:

```
Press any key to drop bomb:
Weee!
Weee!
```

(and so on)

```
Splat!!
Yikes!
```

In either program, the variable x is used in the dropBomb() function just fine. Nothing quirky. Nothing new. This is how variables are used in functions.

- ✔ If you receive some type of prototype or type mismatch errors when you're compiling, it might be due to the capitalization of your function name. There is a difference between dropbomb() and dropBomb() — especially when you're prototyping. Double-check to ensure that you didn't commit this heinous crime.

- ✔ See how the dropBomb() function declares the variable x:

```
int x;
```

This works just like it does in the main function: declare the variables right up front. Refer to Lesson 3-3 for more information about declaring variables.

- ✔ Check out that for loop in the Borland version of BOMBER.C:

```
for(x=880;x>440;x-=10)
```

This loop counts backward from 880 to 440 in steps of 10. It counts backward because x-=10 is a bizarre shortcut for x=x-10. See Lesson 4-7 for more information.

- ✔ Because the Microsoft C++ version is rather generic, it also compiles under Borland C++. Type it in and name it BOMBERM.C if you like. Compile and run it to see how depressing life can be with Microsoft C++.

- ✔ Don't fret too much about the sound functions used in BOMBER.C. You can play with them on your own (and it can be dreadfully fun), if you like. However, I'd wait to get *C For Dummies,* Volume II, which goes into gross detail about both graphics and sound with Borland C++.

```
void dropBomb()
{
    int x;

    for(x=880;x>440;x-=10)
    {
                    sound(x);
                    delay(100);
    }
    nosound();
}
```

Name: BOMBER.C

```
#include <stdio.h>

void dropBomb(void);                    //The devious prototype

void main()
{
    printf("Press any key to drop bomb:");
    getchar();
    dropBomb();
    printf("\nYikes!\n");
}

void dropBomb()
{
    int x;

    for(x=0;x<15;x++)
    {
                    printf("\nWeee!");
    }
    printf("\nSplat!!");
}
```

Type the source code as listed here, proper to your compiler. Save the file to disk as BOMBER.C. Compile and run.

The output is different for each program. The Borland version of BOMBER.C looks like this:

```
Press any key to drop bomb:
Yikes!
```

And it plays a lovely bomb-dropping sound over the PC's speaker after you press the any key (Enter).

The Microsoft version is mute because it lacks Borland's fancy sound commands. Its output looks like this:

```
Press any key to drop bomb:
Weee!
Weee!
```

(and so on)

```
Splat!!
Yikes!
```

In either program, the variable x is used in the dropBomb() function just fine. Nothing quirky. Nothing new. This is how variables are used in functions.

- ✔ If you receive some type of prototype or type mismatch errors when you're compiling, it might be due to the capitalization of your function name. There is a difference between dropbomb() and dropBomb() — especially when you're prototyping. Double-check to ensure that you didn't commit this heinous crime.

- ✔ See how the dropBomb() function declares the variable x:

```
int x;
```

This works just like it does in the main function: declare the variables right up front. Refer to Lesson 3-3 for more information about declaring variables.

- ✔ Check out that for loop in the Borland version of BOMBER.C:

```
for(x=880;x>440;x-=10)
```

This loop counts backward from 880 to 440 in steps of 10. It counts backward because x-=10 is a bizarre shortcut for x=x-10. See Lesson 4-7 for more information.

- ✔ Because the Microsoft C++ version is rather generic, it also compiles under Borland C++. Type it in and name it BOMBERM.C if you like. Compile and run it to see how depressing life can be with Microsoft C++.

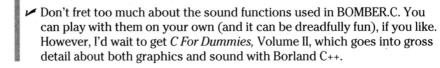

- ✔ Don't fret too much about the sound functions used in BOMBER.C. You can play with them on your own (and it can be dreadfully fun), if you like. However, I'd wait to get *C For Dummies*, Volume II, which goes into gross detail about both graphics and sound with Borland C++.

```
void dropBomb()
{
    int x;

    for(x=880;x>440;x-=10)
    {
                    sound(x);
                    delay(100);
    }
    nosound();
}
```

Name: BOMBER.C

```
#include <stdio.h>

void dropBomb(void);                        //The devious prototype

void main()
{
    printf("Press any key to drop bomb:");
    getchar();
    dropBomb();
    printf("\nYikes!\n");
}

void dropBomb()
{
    int x;

    for(x=0;x<15;x++)
    {
                    printf("\nWeee!");
    }
    printf("\nSplat!!");
}
```

Type the source code as listed here, proper to your compiler. Save the file to disk as BOMBER.C. Compile and run.

The output is different for each program. The Borland version of BOMBER.C looks like this:

```
Press any key to drop bomb:
Yikes!
```

And it plays a lovely bomb-dropping sound over the PC's speaker after you press the any key (Enter).

The Microsoft version is mute because it lacks Borland's fancy sound commands. Its output looks like this:

```
Press any key to drop bomb:
Weee!
Weee!
```

(and so on)

```
Splat!!
Yikes!
```

In either program, the variable x is used in the dropBomb() function just fine. Nothing quirky. Nothing new. This is how variables are used in functions.

- ✔ If you receive some type of prototype or type mismatch errors when you're compiling, it might be due to the capitalization of your function name. There is a difference between dropbomb() and dropBomb() — especially when you're prototyping. Double-check to ensure that you didn't commit this heinous crime.

- ✔ See how the dropBomb() function declares the variable x:

```
int x;
```

This works just like it does in the main function: declare the variables right up front. Refer to Lesson 3-3 for more information about declaring variables.

- ✔ Check out that for loop in the Borland version of BOMBER.C:

```
for(x=880;x>440;x-=10)
```

This loop counts backward from 880 to 440 in steps of 10. It counts backward because x-=10 is a bizarre shortcut for x=x-10. See Lesson 4-7 for more information.

- ✔ Because the Microsoft C++ version is rather generic, it also compiles under Borland C++. Type it in and name it BOMBERM.C if you like. Compile and run it to see how depressing life can be with Microsoft C++.

- ✔ Don't fret too much about the sound functions used in BOMBER.C. You can play with them on your own (and it can be dreadfully fun), if you like. However, I'd wait to get *C For Dummies*, Volume II, which goes into gross detail about both graphics and sound with Borland C++.

```
void dropBomb()
{
    int x;

    for(x=880;x>440;x-=10)
    {
                    sound(x);
                    delay(100);
    }
    nosound();
}
```

Name: BOMBER.C

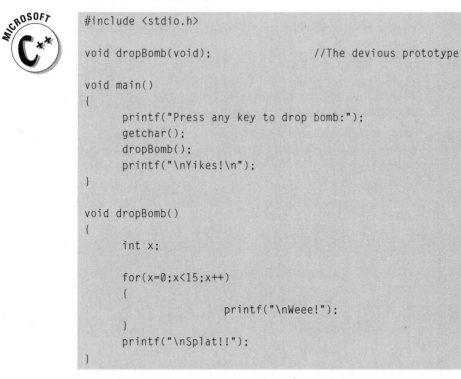

```
#include <stdio.h>

void dropBomb(void);                    //The devious prototype

void main()
{
    printf("Press any key to drop bomb:");
    getchar();
    dropBomb();
    printf("\nYikes!\n");
}

void dropBomb()
{
    int x;

    for(x=0;x<15;x++)
    {
                    printf("\nWeee!");
    }
    printf("\nSplat!!");
}
```

Type the source code as listed here, proper to your compiler. Save the file to disk as BOMBER.C. Compile and run.

The output is different for each program. The Borland version of BOMBER.C looks like this:

```
Press any key to drop bomb:
Yikes!
```

And it plays a lovely bomb-dropping sound over the PC's speaker after you press the any key (Enter).

The Microsoft version is mute because it lacks Borland's fancy sound commands. Its output looks like this:

```
Press any key to drop bomb:
Weee!
Weee!
```

(and so on)

```
Splat!!
Yikes!
```

In either program, the variable x is used in the dropBomb() function just fine. Nothing quirky. Nothing new. This is how variables are used in functions.

- ✔ If you receive some type of prototype or type mismatch errors when you're compiling, it might be due to the capitalization of your function name. There is a difference between dropbomb() and dropBomb() — especially when you're prototyping. Double-check to ensure that you didn't commit this heinous crime.

- ✔ See how the dropBomb() function declares the variable x:

  ```
  int x;
  ```

  This works just like it does in the main function: declare the variables right up front. Refer to Lesson 3-3 for more information about declaring variables.

- ✔ Check out that for loop in the Borland version of BOMBER.C:

  ```
  for(x=880;x>440;x-=10)
  ```

  This loop counts backward from 880 to 440 in steps of 10. It counts backward because x-=10 is a bizarre shortcut for x=x-10. See Lesson 4-7 for more information.

- ✔ Because the Microsoft C++ version is rather generic, it also compiles under Borland C++. Type it in and name it BOMBERM.C if you like. Compile and run it to see how depressing life can be with Microsoft C++.

- ✔ Don't fret too much about the sound functions used in BOMBER.C. You can play with them on your own (and it can be dreadfully fun), if you like. However, I'd wait to get *C For Dummies,* Volume II, which goes into gross detail about both graphics and sound with Borland C++.

✔ The BOMBER.C program for Borland C++ contains three `include` directives:

#include <stdio.h>	**Required to use** `printf()`
#include <conio.h>	**Required to use** `getch()`
#include <dos.h>	**Required to use** `sound()`, `nosound()`, and `delay()`

Will the dual variable BOMBER.C program bomb?

Modify the source code for BOMBER.C in your editor. Change the `main` function so that it reads as follows:

```
void main()
{
    char x;

    printf("Press any key to drop bomb:");
    x=getch();
    dropBomb();
    printf("\nYou pressed the '%c' key to kill all those
        people!\n",x);
}
```

Remember to use `x=getchar()` rather than `x=getch()` as shown here.

What you're doing here is creating another x variable for use in the `main` function. This variable operates independently of the x variable in the `dropBomb()` function. To prove it, save your changes to disk and then compile and run the program.

The output is the same for this modified version of the program; the two x variables didn't confuse the computer because each one works off by itself. The only new addition is the cheerful message that tells you which key you used to drop the bomb.

✔ Variables in different functions can share the same name.

✔ For example, you could have a dozen different functions in your program and each one uses the same variable names. No biggie. They're all independent of each other because they're nestled tightly in their own functions.

✔ Variable x not only is used in two different functions — independently of each other — but also represents two different types of variable: a character and an integer. Weird.

✔ If you press the Enter key to drop the bomb, the program displays it like this:

```
You pressed the '
' key to kill all those people!
```

Yeah, that's the Enter key — it starts a new line. Other keys that don't display characters produce equally puzzling results.

A more straightforward, dull math example

The following source code is for the program DULLMATH, which is really silly and unambitious. Of course, it does show you three functions: main, here, and there, which you haven't seen before.

What goes on with DULLMATH.C is that a variable v is declared in both the here() and there() functions. In here(), the variable v is given a value, which is displayed right in that function. In the there() function, the variable v's value is increased by five (v+=5) and displayed. If you're a skeptic, you would assume that the second value displayed would be the same as the first plus five. Because both variables are different, however, the second v does not have the same value as the first. Honest.

Name: DULLMATH.C

```
#include <stdio.h>

void here(void);              // silly prototype error
void there(void);             // avoiding technique

void main()
{
    here();
    there();
}

void here()
{
    int v;
```

```
        v=6*5;
        printf("The value of v here is %i\n",v);
}


void there()
{
        int v;

        v+=5
        printf("The value of v there is %i\n",v);
}
```

Type in this program, painful as it is, and save it to disk as DULLMATH.C. Compile. Run. You know the routine.

The results look something like this:

```
The value of v here is 30
The value of v there is 871
```

You probably won't see the value 871 displayed on the second line, but you definitely won't see 35 either. The truth is summarized as follows:

1. The v variables in each function are different.

2. The here() function creates the v variable and assigns it the value 30.

3. The there() function creates another variable, naming it v. That variable's value is increased by five. However, because the variable was never set to anything originally, the result is random. (See the Techy sidebar to learn why that's so.)

✔ Variables with the same names in different functions are different.

✔ So what's the point again? I think it's that you don't have to keep on thinking of new variable names in each of your functions. If you're fond of using the variable i in your for loops, for example, you can use i in all your functions. Just declare it and don't worry about it.

✔ There is a remote chance that the second value displayed could be 35. This doesn't mean that both variables are the same, however. It just means that, through sheer luck, the value 30 was already present in memory when the compiler created the v variable. (See the sidebar "Strange variable values of the undefined" for an explanation.)

Strange variable values of the undefined

When you declare a variable in C, the compiler sets aside storage space for it. This subject was covered way back in Lesson 3-3. That space is just a chunk of memory in your computer. Any old chunk. And who knows what may have been stored in that chunk of memory before? Well, whatever it is, that information is "assigned" to your variable before you assign it a value.

For example, from the DULLMATH.C program's `there()` function, take the following:

```
int v;
```

This tells the compiler to set aside storage space for an integer-size variable named v. The compiler does that, picking out a cozy spot somewhere close in memory. And lo, suppose that the chunk of memory contains the value 866. (Who knows why? It's just there. Sitting in memory.)

If you assigned the variable a number, it would replace whatever random information was already in memory. So the following line:

```
v=30;
```

would store the value 30 in the variable v's memory. Bye-bye 866. But if you did the following:

```
v+=5;
```

you would be adding 5 to the random value already in v's memory space. If that value were 866, v would equal 871 — or whatever random value was displayed when you ran the DULLMATH program.

All this explains the random number you see when you run the program. It also explains other strange numbers you may see when you accidentally forget to assign a variable a value.

How we can all share and love with global variables

There are times when you do have to share a variable between two or more functions. Most games, for example, store the score in a variable that's accessible to a number of functions: the function that displays the score on the screen; the function that increases the score's value; the function that decreases the value; functions that store the score on disk; and so on. All those functions have to access that one variable. That's done by creating a global variable.

A *global variable* is one that any function in the program can use. The main function can use it — any function. They can change, examine, modify, do whatever to the variable. No problem.

The opposite of a global variable is a *local variable*. This is what you've seen so far. A local variable exists inside only one function — like the variables x and v in this lesson's sample programs. Those are local variables, unique to the functions they're created in and ignored by other functions in the program.

✔ A global variable is available to all functions in your program.

✔ A local variable is available only to the function in which it's created.

✔ Global variables can be used in any function without having to redeclare them. If you have a global integer variable `score`, for example, you don't have to stick an `int score;` declaration in each function which uses that variable. The variable has already been declared and is ready for use in any function.

✔ There is a difference between a global variable and a variable sent off to a function for manipulation. Confused? Keep reading, especially Lesson 5-3, which discusses how variables are "passed" to functions for examination.

Making a global variable

Global variables differ from local variables in two ways. First, because they're global variables, any function in the program can use them. Second, they're declared outside of any function. Out there. In the void. Midst the chaos. Strange, but true.

For example:

```
#include <stdio.h>

int score;

void main()
{
```

Etc. . . .

Think of this source code as the beginning of some massive program, the details of which aren't important right now. Notice how the variable score is declared. It's done outside of any function, traditionally just before the `main` function and after the pound-sign dealies (and any prototyping nonsense). This is how global variables are made.

If more global variables are required, they would be created in the same spot, right there before the `main` function. Declaring them works as it normally does; the only thing different is that it's done outside of any function.

✔ Global variables are declared outside of any function. This typically is done right before the `main` function.

✔ Other than being declared outside a function, everything you know about creating a variable applies to creating global variables: You must specify the type of variable (`int`, `char`, `float`, and so on), the variable's name, and the semicolon.

✔ You can also declare a group of global variables at one time, such as:

```
int score,tanks,ammo;
```

✔ And you can preassign values to global variables if you want:

```
char prompt="What?";
```

✔ Global variable names must be unique! If you give your global variable a name already used by some local variable somewhere (or vice versa), mass hysteria will ensue.

An example of a global variable in a real, live program

For your pleasure, please refer to the final rendition of the BOMBER.C program, BOMBER2.C, listed next. This program builds on the original BOMBER.C program, adding a running total of the number of people you kill with the bombs. That total is kept in the global variable `killed`, defined right up front. Details of how this program works are held in the Blow-by-blow box nearby.

Name: BOMBER2.C

```
#include <stdio.h>
#include <conio.h>
#include <dos.h>

void dropBomb(void);              //The devious prototype

int killed;                       //A global variable

void main()
{
        char x;

        killed=0;

        for(;;)
        {
                printf("Press ~ to end your mission\n");
                printf("Press any key to drop bomb:");
                x=getchar();
                if(x=='~')
                {
                        break;
```

```
                                 }
                                 dropBomb();
                                 printf("\n%i people killed!\n",killed);
        }
}

void dropBomb()
{
      int x;

      for(x=880;x>440;x-=10)
      {
                        sound(x);
                        delay(100);
      }
      nosound();
      killed+=15;                               //rack up the dead
}
```

Name: BOMBER2.C

```
#include <stdio.h>

void dropBomb(void);                    //The devious prototype

int killed;                             //A global variable

void main()
{
      char x;

      killed=0;

      for(;;)
      {
                  printf("Press ~ to end your mission\n");
                  printf("Press any key to drop bomb:");
                  x=getchar();
                  if(x=='~')
                  {
                              break;
                  }
                  dropBomb();
                  printf("\n%i people killed!\n",killed);
```

```
        }
}

void dropBomb()
{
     int x;

     for(x=0;x<15;x++)
     {
                    printf("\nWeee!");
     }
     printf("\nSplat!!");
     killed+=15;                                    //rack up the dead
}
```

Type in the source code for BOMBER2.C as appropriate to your compiler;
Borland C++ users type in the Borland code, and everyone else can suffer with
the Microsoft C++ version. You can build on your original BOMBER.C program,
but remember to save this file to disk as BOMBER2.C.

Compile and run the program.

Here is the output for the Borland version of the program (minus the sound):

```
Press ~ to end your mission
Press any key to drop bomb: (click)
(Oooooooooooooooooooooooo)
15 People killed!
Press ~ to end your mission
Press any key to drop bomb: (click)
(Oooooooooooooooooooooooo)
30 People killed!
Press ~ to end your mission
Press any key to drop bomb:
```

The program effectively keeps a running tally of the dead by using the global
killed variable. The variable is manipulated (incremented, actually) in the
dropBomb() function and is displayed in the main function. Both functions
share that global variable.

✔ See how the global variable is declared right up front? The #includes usually come first, and then the prototyping stuff, and then the global variables. (A lot of junk can happen "up there." Lesson 6-1 goes into the details.)

✔ No, there is no challenge to this game.

✔ For more information about the endless for loop (for(; ;)), refer to Lesson 4-6.

✔ Understanding how the if keyword compares characters was covered in Lesson 4-3.

BLOW BY BLOW

Everything you wanted to know about BOMBER2.C

The program works because of an endless loop in the main function:

`for( ; ; )`

This loop causes the computer to forever obey the instructions between for's curly brackets. The loop stops when the tilde key (~) is pressed. You test for this by using the following if command:

`if(x=='~')`

If the value of the character variable x is equal to the tilde, if's statement is executed. In this case, it's a single break command, which halts the endless loop and quits the BOMBER2.C program.

The global variable killed is used to keep track of the dead. It's declared before the main function, which makes it a global variable. The second statement in the main function sets killed's value to zero. This is known as "initializing the variable."

It's the dropBomb() function that actually manipulates the value of the killed variable. After the special effects, the value of the killed variable is increased by 15 by using the following statement:

`killed+=15; //rack up the dead`

The killed variable is also used in the main function with a printf statement, which displays killed's current value.

Lesson 5-2 Quiz

1. Each function you create can use its own, private set of:

    A. Ginsu knives.

    B. Golf clubs.

    C. "Star Trek" commemorative collector plates.

    D. Variables.

2. Is there anything special you have to do when you're declaring a variable in your very own function?

    A. No, nothing special.

    B. Yes, but I forgot what it was.

    C. You must use the function declaration statements `fint`, `fchar`, and `ffloat`.

    D. It helps to wear a hat in the sun.

3. If you have two functions and each declares a variable with the same name, what will happen?

    A. The fabric of the universe will unravel!

    B. The compiler will erase your hard drive!

    C. Another Democrat will be elected president!

    D. Nothing will happen. The two variables are independent of each other.

4. What is a global variable?

    A. The weather.

    B. Peace.

    C. The world population.

    D. A variable defined outside a function.

5. What is the opposite of a global variable?

    A. A galactic variable.

    B. A hemispherical variable.

    C. A local variable.

    D. A continental variable.

6. Elvis Presley made 33 feature films in his lifetime. Which one is universally acclaimed as the best?

    A. *Jailhouse Rock*

    B. *Flaming Star*

    C. *Viva Las Vegas*

    D. *Change of Habit*

Lesson 5-3: Marching a Variable Off to a Function

Blindly type in the following program, a modification of the BIGJERK.C cycle of programs you worked with in Lesson 5-1:

Name: BIGJERK3.C

```
#include <stdio.h>

void jerk(int repeat);

void main()
{
    printf("He calls me on the phone with nothing say\n");
    printf("Not once, or twice, but three times a day!\n");
    jerk(1);
    printf("He insulted my wife, my cat, my mother\n");
    printf("He irritates and grates, like no other!\n");
    jerk(2);
    printf("He chuckles it off, his big belly a-heavin'\n");
    printf("But he won't be laughing when I get even!\n");
    jerk(3);
}

/* The jerk() function repeats the refrain for the
value of the repeat variable*/

void jerk(int repeat)
```

```
{
    int i;

    for(i=0;i<repeat;i++)
                printf("Bill is a jerk\n");
}
```

You can edit this source code from the original BIGJERK2.C file, but save this file to disk as BIGJERK3.C. There are some changes, mostly with the jerk() function and the statements that call that function. Don't miss anything or you'll get some nasty error messages.

Compile and run.

The program's output looks something like this:

```
He calls me on the phone with nothing say
Not once, or twice, but three times a day!
Bill is a jerk
He insulted my wife, my cat, my mother
He irritates and grates, like no other!
Bill is a jerk
Bill is a jerk
He chuckles it off, his big belly a-heavin'
But he won't be laughing when I get even!
Bill is a jerk
Bill is a jerk
Bill is a jerk
```

The jerk() function has done been modified! It can now display the litany's refrain any old number of times. Amazing. And look what it can do for your poetry.

The details of how this worked are hammered out in the rest of this lesson. The following check marks may clear up a few key issues.

✔ Notice how the jerk() function has been redefined:

```
void jerk(int repeat);
```

✔ This line tells the compiler that the function is hungry for an integer value, which it calls repeat.

✔ The new jerk() function repeats the phrase Bill is a jerk for whatever number you specify. For example:

```
jerk(500);
```

This statement calls the `jerk()` function, which then repeats the message 500 times.

✔ The C-geek vernacular for sending a value of a variable to a function is "passed." So you *pass* the value 3 to the `jerk()` function with the following statement:

```
jerk(3);
```

✔ The value you send along to a function is called a *parameter*. It can be said, in a nerdly way, that the `jerk()` function has one parameter; an integer variable (which is a number).

✔ The `jerk()` function is prototyped as follows:

```
void jerk(int repeat);
```

This means that the compiler is expecting an integer value each time you call the `jerk()` function. If you forget to put a value in there (suppose that you call the function with `jerk()` instead), a `Too few parameters` type of error occurs. This is one of the reasons you prototype functions. If you didn't, and you used `jerk()` to call the function, your program would invariably screw up.

✔ The variable `repeat` is not a global variable. Instead, it's a value that's passed to the `jerk` function, which that function then uses to do something wonderful.

Functions that actually funcQ

All functions should really do something. The primitive functions in Lessons 5-1 and 5-2 were fine, but they just didn't do much other than spit out a message on the screen. Ho-hum. Although that's OK and you won't go to C prison for writing functions like that, it just doesn't serve up the function motif. I mean, functions must chew on something and spit it out. Real meat-grinder stuff. Functions that func.

Generally speaking, you can write four types of functions:

❒ **Functions that work all by themselves, not requiring any extra input.** This describes the functions from Lessons 5-2 and 5-3. Ho-hum functions, but often necessary.

❒ **Functions that take input and use it somehow.** The `jerk()` function in BIGJERK3.C is an example. These functions are passed values, which they chew on and then do something useful.

❒ **Functions that take input and produce output.** These functions receive something and give you something back in kind (known as "generating a value"). For example, a function that computed your weight based on your shoe size would swallow your shoe size and cough up your weight. So to speak. Input and output.

❐ **Functions that produce only output.** These functions generate a value or string, returning it to the program — for example, a function that may tell you where the *Enterprise* is in the Klingon Empire. You call the whereEnt() function and it returns some galactic coordinates.

  ✔ Lesson 5-4 discusses how functions can return values.

  ✔ Any function can fall into any category. It all depends on what you want the function to do. After you know that, you build the function accordingly.

  ✔ Sending a value to a function or getting a value back isn't the same as using a global variable. Instead, think of a function like the atoi function. It takes a string and converts it into a value. The atoi function works like a machine; it examines one thing and produces some sort of result. Although you can use global variables with a function, the values the function produces or generates don't have to be global variables.

  ✔ Refer to Lesson 5-2 for information about global variables.

How to send a value to a function

Sending a value to a function is as easy as getting a sunburn. Just follow these steps:

1. **Know what kind of value you're going to send the function.**

   It can be any normal C variable type: int, float, char, and so on. However, don't mess with strings for the time being. Single characters are OK, but strings lead to a number of headaches that the second volume of this book deals with in person.

2. **Define the variable in the function's parentheses.**

   Say that you want an integer value. Go ahead and declare it in the parentheses following the function's name:

   ```
   void jerk(int repeat)
   ```

   Do not follow the variable name with a semicolon! This is one of those rare times. Otherwise, you declare the variable as you normally would. Here, the integer variable repeat is declared. This means that the jerk() function will require an integer variable, which it names repeat.

3. **Somehow use the variable in your function.**

   The compiler doesn't like it when you declare a function that eats a variable and then that variable isn't used in the function. The message reads something like jerk is passed a value that is not used or Parameter 'repeat' is never used in function jerk. It's a warning error, but a good point to make: Use your variables!

By the way, the variable passed along is used inside the function just like any other variable. It doesn't have to be redeclared because it's declared at the beginning of the function. Otherwise, use it as normal, such as:

```
for(i=0;i<repeat;i++)
```

This line tells the computer to loop around `repeat` times. (Note that the variable `i` was declared inside the function because it's just a normal variable, used only in the function and not passed from anywhere.)

4. **Properly prototype the function.**

   This must be done or you get a host of warning errors. My advice: Select the line that starts your function; mark it as a block. Then copy it to up above the `main` function. After pasting it in, add a semicolon:

```
void jerk(int repeat);
```

   No sweat.

5. **Remember to send the proper values when you're calling the function.**

   Because the function is required to eat values, you must send them along. No more are there empty parentheses! You must fill them and fill them with the proper type of value: integer, character, floater, whatever. Only by doing that can the function properly do its thing.

✔ The parameter is actually referred to as an *argument*. This gives you a tiny taste of C's combative nature.

✔ The name you give the function's parameter (its passed-along variable, argument, whatever) is used when you're defining and prototyping the function, and inside the function.

✔ You can treat the function's parameter as a local variable. Yeah, it's defined in the prototype. Yeah, it appears on the first line. But inside the function, it's just a local variable.

✔ By the way, the variable name used inside the function must match the variable name defined inside the function's parentheses. More on this in the next section.

Avoiding variable confusion (must reading)

You don't have to call a function by using the same variable name the function uses. Don't bother reading that twice. This is a confusing concept, but work with me here.

Suppose that you're in the `main` function where a variable named `count` is used. You want to pass along its value to the `jerk()` function. You would do so as follows:

```
jerk(count);
```

This tells the compiler to call the `jerk()` function, sending it along the value of the `count` variable. Because `count` is an integer variable, this works just fine. But keep in mind that it's the variable's *value* that is passed along. The name `count`? It's just a name in some function. Who cares! Only the value is important.

In the `jerk()` function, the value is referred to by using the variable name `repeat`. This is how the `jerk()` function was set up:

```
void jerk(int repeat)
```

Whatever value is sent, however it was sent, always is referred to as `repeat` inside the function.

- ✔ I bring this up because it's a confusing concept. You can call any function with any variable name. Only inside that function is the function's own variable name used.

- ✔ This is confusing because of the variable names used by the function. You can find this in your C manual as well. You'll see some function listed like this:

```
int putchar(int c);
```

This means that the `putchar()` function requires an integer value, which it refers to as `c`. However, you can call this function by using any value or variable name. It makes no difference. What's important, however, is that it be an integer variable.

How to send more than one value to a function

You can pass along any number of items to a function. All you have to do is declare them inside the function's parentheses. It's like announcing them at some fancy diplomatic function; each item has a type and a name and is followed by a lovely comma dressed in red taffeta with an appropriate hat. There is no semicolon at the end because this is a formal occasion.

For example:

```
void bloat(int calories, int weight, int fat)
```

This function is defined as requiring three integer values: calories, weight, and fat.

```
void jerk(int repeat, char c)
```

Here you see a modification of the jerk() function, which now requires two values: an integer and a character. These values are referred to as repeat and c inside the jerk() function. In fact, the following program, BIGJERK4.C, uses said function:

Name: BIGJERK4.C

```c
#include <stdio.h>

void jerk(int repeat, char c);

void main()
{
    printf("He calls me on the phone with nothing say\n");
    printf("Not once, or twice, but three times a day!\n");
    jerk(1,'?');
    printf("He insulted my wife, my cat, my mother\n");
    printf("He irritates and grates, like no other!\n");
    jerk(2,'?');
    printf("He chuckles it off, his big belly a-heavin'\n");
    printf("But he won't be laughing when I get even!\n");
    jerk(3,'!');
}

/* The jerk() function repeats the refrain for the
value of the repeat variable*/

void jerk(int repeat, char c)
{
    int i;

    for(i=0;i<repeat;i++)
                printf("Bill is a jerk%c\n",c);
}
```

Type in the preceding source code. You can start with the BIGJERK3.C source code as a base. You have to edit line 3 to modify the prototyping; edit lines 9, 12, and 15 to modify the way the jerk( ) function is called (remember to use single quotes); change line 20 to redefine the jerk( ) function itself; and change line 25 so that the printf statement displays the character variable c. Be sure to save the file to disk as BIGJERK4.C.

Compile and run the program. The output looks almost the same, but you see the effects of passing the single-character variable to the jerk( ) function in the way the question marks and exclamation points appear:

```
He calls me on the phone with nothing say
Not once, or twice, but three times a day!
Bill is a jerk?
He insulted my wife, my cat, my mother
He irritates and grates, like no other!
Bill is a jerk?
Bill is a jerk?
He chuckles it off, his big belly a-heavin'
But he won't be laughing when I get even!
Bill is a jerk!
Bill is a jerk!
Bill is a jerk!
```

✔ Yes, you can mix and match variables passed to a function. You could group an int, a char, and a float and send them all off for manipulation, no problem.

✔ In this example, a single-character variable was passed along to the function. This is cinchy to do. Strings? They're harder. Refer to the next section.

How to send strings to a function

Sending strings off to functions is tricky stuff. It encroaches on a C language topic called *pointers,* which everyone agrees is kind of scary (but primarily because it's never properly explained).

Rather than shy away from the topic or plant a seed that says "strings are taboo!," here is the source code for a program, LILJERK.C. This program uses a special jerk( ) function that accepts the name of a particular jerk you know — a string passed to a function. (This is a combination of both the BIGJERK cycle of programs as well as the INSULT2.C jewel you learned about in Lesson 2-4.)

Name: LILJERK.C

```
#include <stdio.h>

void jerk(char *name);

void main()
{
    char whoever[20];

    printf("Name some jerk you know:");
    gets(whoever);
    jerk(whoever);
}

void jerk(char *name)
{
    int i;

    for(i=0;i<3;i++)
                    printf("%s is a jerk\n",name);
}
```

Carefully type in the preceding program. Those asterisks before the name variable are required in the function's prototype and definition. Save the file to disk as LILJERK.C.

Compile and run.

```
Name some jerk you know:
```

Type in the person's name. For example, Lynn. Press Enter and you see:

```
Lynn is a jerk
```

The string was successfully passed to the function, thanks to the asterisk goobers.

> ✔ One thing that may goof you up here is how the function is called with the whoever variable, but the name variable is used inside the function itself. If this puzzles you, please read the section "Avoiding variable confusion," earlier in this lesson.

- The %s placeholder is used in the printf function to display a string value. Refer to Lesson 2-5 and Table 2-2 for a list of all the percent-thing conversion characters.

- To call a function with a string, you could just stick an asterisk in front of the variable name when you're setting up the function. To wit:

```
void jerk(char *name)
```

And you could also say that calling the function with a single character is done without the asterisk:

```
void jerk(char c)
```

This is correct, but it's akin to a young child saying "Red means stop, green means go, and yellow means go real fast." You really have to expose yourself (intellectually speaking) to a few rudiments of strings, as discussed in *C For Dummies,*Volume II, before you play with this one on your own.

- Technically speaking, char *name does not mean "the string variable name" to the compiler. Instead, it means, "this is a location in memory that tells me where a string starts." This is a wildly abstract and unusual concept that most people memorize over and over only to confuse themselves more. Rather than be confused, please wait until Volume II discusses strings. If you do otherwise, your strings will start behaving oddly.

The inner workings of the LILJERK.C program

The jerk() function in this program is prototyped and defined with a string variable, which is declared by using the syntax char *name. This means that a string variable will have to be passed to that function. This is what the first part of the main function does:

```
char whoever[20];
printf("Name some jerk you know:");
gets(whoever);
```

A string variable, whoever, is created, roomy enough for 20 characters. The printf statement displays a prompt, and then gets is used to read the keyboard and fill up the whoever variable with whatever was typed. Then the jerk() function is called with the whoever string variable as its parameter:

```
jerk(whoever);
```

The jerk() function expects a string variable, defined as name, which is used inside the function in a printf statement:

```
printf("%s is a jerk\n",name);
```

TECHNICAL STUFF

Another way to argue with a function

This book teaches you the modern, convenient way of declaring variables (or "arguments") shuffled off to a function. To wit:

```
void jerk(int repeat, char c);
```

You can also use the original format:

```
void jerk(repeat, c)
int repeat;
char c;
```

This declaration does the same thing, but it's a little more confusing because the variable name is introduced first and then the "what it is" comes on the following line (or lines). Otherwise, the two declarations are the same; the next line would contain the first curly bracket, and then comes the function's statements.

My advice is to stick with the format used in this book and try not to be alarmed if you see the other format used. Older C references may use the second format, and certain fogey C programmers may adhere to it. Beware!

Lesson 5-3 Quiz

1. You have to pass along a float to a function. Which of the following functions can eat it?

    A. `void hungry(root beer);`

    B. `void receiver(float football);`

    C. `void passie(gimme float);`

    D. `float hungry(variable);`

2. Suppose that a function named `gobble()` accepts a value. How would you send that function the value 5?

    A. You'd put five cents in an envelope and stuff it into drive A on your computer.

    B. You'd put 5 in the `chomp` variable and use the `gobble(chomp);` statement.

    C. You'd have to use the `gobble(5);` statement.

    D. Either B or C will do it.

3. Which were Frank Sinatra's best years?

    A. The early, crooner stage.

    B. The '50s.

    C. From the '60s to his "retirement."

    D. Postretirement '80s and '90s.

4. What would be the proper prototype for the following function?

```
void gravity(int fatness)
```

A. `void gravity(int fatness;);`

B. `int gravity(fatness);`

C. `gravity(fatness)`

D. `void gravity(int fatness);`

5. You've declared a function, such as the one shown here:

```
void taxes(int income)
```

6. What is a proper example of using the integer value in this function?

A. `i=income;`

B. `income*=1000;`

C. You have to declare `income` as an integer value.

D. Just use the `income` variable in the function.

Super Lotto bonus question — worth 16 points!

Associate the president with his favorite musical instrument:

A. Richard Nixon	Piano
B. Harry Truman	Ukulele
C. Bill Clinton	Saxophone
D. John F. Kennedy	Marilyn Monroe

Lesson 5-4: Something for Your Troubles (Functions that Return Something)

In order for some functions to properly func, they must return a value. You pass along your birthday, and the function magically tells you how old you are (and then the computer giggles at you). This process is known as returning a value, and a heck of a lot of functions do that.

To return a value, a function must obey these two rules:

Warning! Rules approaching.

❐ The function has to be *defined* as a certain type (int, char, float, etc. — just like a variable).

❐ The function has to return a value.

The function type tells you what type of value it returns. For example:

```
int birthday(int date);
```

The function birthday() is defined here. It's an integer function and will return an integer value. (It also requires an integer parameter, date, which it uses as input.)

The following function, nationalDebt(), returns the national debt of the United States as a double value:

```
double nationalDebt(void)
```

The void in parentheses means that the function doesn't require any input. Likewise, when a function doesn't produce any output, it's defined as a void:

```
void USGovernment(float tax_dollars)
```

The USGovernment() function requires very large numbers as input but produces nothing. Therefore, it's a function of type void. Easy to remember.

✔ Any value produced by a function is returned by using the return keyword. This is covered later in this lesson.

✔ Notice that C language functions, like atoi or getchar — functions that return values — are listed in your C language library reference by using this same format:

```
int atoi(char *s)
char getchar(void)
```

This means that the atoi function returns an integer value and that getchar returns a single-character value.

✔ Another reason functions should be prototyped: The compiler double-checks to confirm that the function is returning the proper value and that other parts of the program use that int, float, or char value as defined.

✔ You need a double-size variable to handle the national debt. Referring to Table 3-1 in Lesson 3-5, the float variable, although it's capable of handling a number in the trillions, is accurate to only 7 digits. The double is accurate to 15 digits. If the debt were calculated as a float, it would lose accuracy around the $100,000 mark.

✔ Although you can define a function as a type of void, you cannot declare a void variable. It just doesn't work that way.

✔ Functions can return only a single value. So unlike sending a value to a function, in which the function can receive any number of values, they can cough up only one thing in return. I know. Sounds like a gyp.

✔ Actually, the preceding check mark is untrue. Functions can return several values. They do this through the miracle of pointers and structures, two advanced subjects touched on in this book's sequel, *C For Dummies, Volume II.*

Finally, the computer tells you how smart it thinks you are

The following program calculates your IQ. Supposedly. What's more important is that it uses a function which has real meaning: For the past few chapters, you've used the following set of C language statements to get input from the keyboard:

```
input=gets();
x=atoi(input);
```

The gets function reads in text typed at the keyboard, and atoi translates it into an integer value. Well, ho-ho, the getval() function in the IQ.C program does that for you, returning the value happily to the main function.

Name: IQ.C

```
#include <stdio.h>
#include <stdlib.h>

int getval(void);

void main()
{
    int age,weight,area;
    float iq;

    printf("Program to calculate your IQ.\n");
    printf("Enter your age:");
    age=getval();
    printf("Enter your weight:");
```

```
        weight=getval();
        printf("Enter the your area code:");
        area=getval();

        iq=(age*weight)/area;
        printf("This computer estimates your IQ to be %f.\n",iq);
}

int getval(void)
{
        char input[20];
        int x;

        gets(input);
        x=atoi(input);
        return(x);
}
```

Type the source code for IQ.C into your editor. The new deal here is the
getval() function, which returns a value by using the never-before-seen
return keyword. Save the file to disk as IQ.C.

Compile. Run.

Here is what the sample output may look like, using fictitious figures for myself:

```
Enter your age:33
Enter your weight:175
Enter your area code:208
The computer estimates your IQ to be 27.000000.
```

Of course. I knew it was that high. I'm not boasting or anything. It's only an
estimate, after all.

- ✔ By using this formula, only old, fat people living in low-numbered area
  codes can get into Mensa.

- ✔ This program has some problems. For example, the final value needs to be
  a floating-point number, and it's not (unless your age, weight, and area
  code are very special). This problem is fixed in the next section.

- ✔ Note how getval() is defined as an integer function. Inside getval(), an
  integer value is produced by the atoi function. It's saved in the x variable,
  which is then returned to the main function by using the return(x);
  statement. Everything is an integer, so the function is of that type as well.

- ✔ In the main function, getval() is used three times. The values it produces (what it funcs) is saved in the age, weight, and height integer variables, respectively.

- ✔ Yeah, you probably lied too when you entered your weight. But don't! The more tumid you are, the smarter the program thinks you are.

Fixing IQ.C by using the old type-casting trick

The computer estimates your IQ based on the following formula:

```
iq=(age*weight)/area;
```

That is, your IQ is equal to your age multiplied by your weight, with that total divided by your area code. All those variables are integers, and, incidentally, this is the exact formula used by my kid's school district.

Alarm! Whenever you divide any two values, the result will probably be a float. No, count on it being a float. That's just the way math works. Decimals and fractions. Messy stuff.

To make this function work, the variable iq is declared as a float — right up at the beginning of the program, just as it should. But there's a problem: The value calculated by the equation still is stuffed into an integer. (Eh?) Even though the calculated result probably has a decimal part, all those variables are integers, and the result is an integer. (Hey, the compiler doesn't assume anything, remember?)

To fix the problem, you must do something known as *type casting.* This is where you tell the compiler to temporarily forget what type of variable is there and instead assume that it's something else.

Edit line 19 in the IQ.C source code to read as follows:

```
iq=(float)(age*weight)/area;
```

Insert the word float in parentheses right after the equal sign. Save the file back to disk. Compile and run. You'll notice that your IQ changes to a more floaty number in the output:

```
The computer estimates your IQ to be 27.764423.
```

Now the number is a true `float`.

- ✔ An easy way to solve the problem, of course, is to declare all the variables as floats. But then you couldn't use the `atoi` function because it converts only integers. (Actually, an `atof` function converts strings into floats, but I won't mention it here.)

- ✔ It helps to think of this trick as "balancing an equation." For example:

```
iq=(age*weight)/area;
```

Think of the statement as follows:

```
float=int*int/int;
```

To wring a `float` out of the right side, you have to force the compiler into making it a `float` value. Hence:

```
float=(float)int*int/int;
```

- ✔ You can type cast any variable. Often the `(float)` is used as shown here when you're manipulating integer values. Another common case is when you're dealing with C language functions that require specific types of values. For example, the `sin` function computes the sine of an angle (yawn), but it requires a `double` value. If you only passed it an integer variable x, you would have to use the following statement:

```
result=sin((double)x);
```

Here, the integer variable x is converted into a `double` for processing by the `sin` function. The result is saved in the `result` variable.

- ✔ Type casting is also known in some circles as *type conversion.*

- ✔ Actually, the parentheses in the function aren't necessary. Remember My Dear Aunt Sally, from Lesson 3-8? The equation figures out from left to right anyway, so `age` is multiplied by `weight` first, and then that total is divided by the `area` value. There's nothing wrong with sticking parentheses in there, however, to make it more readable.

- ✔ Lesson 6-5 has more information about type casting, though this section pretty much covered everything you need to know.

Return to sender with the return *keyword*

Functions that return values need some type of mechanism to send those values back. Unlike other functions, information just can't fall off the edge, with the compiler assuming that the last curly bracket means "Hey, I must return the variable, uh, x. Yeah. That's it. Send x back. Now I get it."

No. To properly return a value, you need the proper return keyword. The format is listed in a box nearby.

- ✔ Technically speaking, all functions can end with a single return; as their last statement. When return isn't there, the compiler automatically returns when it sees the function's last curly bracket. (Execution falls off the edge. Ahhh!)

- ✔ Functions defined as an int, char, or whatever must return that type of value.

- ✔ void functions can use return, but it must not return anything! Just use return(); or return; by itself in a void function. Otherwise, the compiler waggles its warning error finger at you.

- ✔ If your function is supposed to return something but has nothing to return, use the return(0); statement.

- ✔ The return keyword doesn't necessarily have to come at the end of a function. There are times when you have to use it in the middle of a function, such as in BONUS.C, shown next.

Keyword return

The return keyword is used to send a value back from a function, to return a value from the function. Here is the format:

```
return(something);
```

The *something* is a value the function must return. What kind of value? Depends on the type of function. It can be an integer, character, string (which is tricky), floater, whatever. And you can specify either a variable name or a constant value.

```
return(total);
```

Here, the value of the variable total is returned from the function.

```
return(0);
```

Here, the function returns a value of zero.

By the way, the something is optional. For the void type of functions, you can use the return(); statement by itself to cause the program to return, say, in the middle of something (see BONUS.C in this lesson for an example).

Give that human a bonus!

The following program, BONUS.C, contains a function that has three — count 'em, three — `return` statements. This program proves that you can stick a `return` plum-dab in the middle of a function and no one will snicker at you. In fact, often it's useful.

Name: BONUS.C

```
#include <stdio.h>

float bonus(char x);

void main()
{
        char name[20];
        char level;
        float b;

        printf("Enter employee name:");
        gets(name);
        printf("Enter bonus level (0, 1 or 2):");
        level=getchar();
        b=bonus(level);
        b*=100;
        printf("The bonus for %s will be $%.2f.\n",name,b);
}

/* Calculate the bonus */

float bonus(char x)
{
        if(x=='0') return(0.33);            //Bottom-level bonus
        if(x=='1') return(1.50);            //Second-level bonus
        return(3.10);                       //Best bonus
}
```

Type this source code into your editor. Save it to disk as BONUS.C. You'll notice that the `bonus()` function contains three `return` statements, each of which returns a different value to the `main` function. Also, the function is a `float` type, which you haven't seen before in this book.

Compile and run.

Here is a sample of the output:

```
Enter employee name:Bill
Enter bonus level (0, 1, or 2):0
The bonus for Bill will be $33.00
```

Run the program a few more times with some new names and values. Try not to be impressed by its flexibility.

- ✔ Poor Bill.

- ✔ The getchar function is used in line 14 of this function because it allows you to type a character and then press the Enter key. The character typed is saved in the char variable level.

- ✔ You may have a temptation to type cast the 100 in line 15: b*=100;. But you don't have to because there isn't a variable over there. If the 100 were saved in an int variable, say rate, type casting would be necessary:

```
b*=(float)rate;
```

- ✔ Notice how the floating-point value 0.33 is written out. Numbers should always begin with a number, not a decimal point. If the value .33 is specified, the compiler may choke. Always begin numbers with a number, 0 through 9.

- ✔ You may think of the statements in the bonus() function as being rather brief. Ha! What do you know . . . .

Actually, they are. They're scrunched up real tight, but that doesn't mean that you have to write your programs like that. In the Techy box "No need to bother with this C language trivia if you're in a hurry," you can see several alternative formats that get the same job done. This is something you should try with your C programs constantly (and the next chapter dwells on this issue): See whether you can write your programs with brevity and legibility.

No need to bother with this C language trivia if you're in a hurry

C is a flexible language that offers many ways to format a solution to a particular problem. Take the bonus() function in the BONUS.C program. Here are four different ways that function can be written and still carry out the same task:

The long, boring way:

```
float bonus(char x)
{
        int v;

        if(x=='0')
        {
                        v=0.33;
        }
        else if(x=='1')
        {
                        v=1.50;
        }
        else
        {
                        v=3.10;
        }
        return(v);
}
```

The long, boring way minus all the darn curly brackets:

```
float bonus(char x)
{
        int v;

        if(x=='0')
                        v=0.33;
```

```
//This works because only one
//statement follows 'if'
        else if(x=='1')
                        v=1.50;
        else
                        v=3.10;
        return(v);
}
```

And without the integer variable v:

```
float bonus(char x)
{
        if(x=='0')
                        return(0.33);
        else if(x=='1')
                        return(1.50);
        else
                        return(3.10);
}
```

Finally, without the else:

```
float bonus(char x)
{
        if(x=='0')
                        return(0.33);
        if(x=='1')
                        return(1.50);
        return(3.10);
}
```

You can substitute any of the preceding bonus() functions in your BONUS.C source code. Everything works just fine. Lesson 5-5 contains even more shortcut info, stuff that can potentially boggle your mind.

Lesson 5-4 Quiz

1. To return a value, a function must:

    A. Put its return address on the envelope.

    B. Be defined as a certain type: `int`, `char`, **whatever.**

    C. Have a good throwing arm.

    D. Get an RMA.

2. What kind of value does the following function return?

```
int dollars(int kopeks)
```

    A. Dollars.

    B. Kopeks.

    C. Integers.

    D. Monetary.

3. What does the `return` keyword do?

    A. It returns a value from a function.

    B. It can be used to end a function.

    C. It ends a line of text.

    D. Both A and B.

4. What is type casting?

    A. Forcing the outcome of a math problem or function to be a particular variable type.

    B. Setting the font for writing on a friend's broken leg.

    C. I don't know because I don't believe in watching people fish on TV.

    D. Ask Adam West.

5. Which of the following countries is not located in Africa?

    A. Suriname.

    B. Mauritania.

    C. Sierra Leone.

    D. Cameroon.

Lesson 5-5: C Functions Work from the Inside Out

The following program is cheap and dirty. Type it in quickly before anyone sees you:

Name: C&D.C

```
#include <stdio.h>

void main()
{
     printf("You typed the %c character.\n",getchar());
}
```

Don't puzzle yourself trying to figure it out — just type the preceding few lines into your editor and save it to disk as C&D.C (for cheap and dirty).

Compile and run the program. Here is a sample of the output:

The computer just waits. Press the **T** key and then press Enter. You see:

```
You typed the T character.
```

Strange! Bizarre!

Feeling a little out of sorts? That's because the getchar function is buried in the middle of a printf function.

Outrageous! Unheard of!

Yet it works. And what's even stranger is that the getchar function actually goes first. How and why that happens is the subject of this lesson. So open your mind and be prepared to absorb some new information about how C functions work from the inside out.

- ✔ C functions work from the inside out — like an infection!

- ✔ Actually, this lesson is optional reading. It's just shortcut stuff, which isn't required in order to know C but is necessary in order to recognize what some of your fellow programmers are doing (and what's possible).

✔ Because C works its statements from the inside out, the computer finds `getchar` first. It sits and waits for a character. When it has one, that character is immediately passed off to the `printf` function.

✔ The `getchar` function produces a variable, yet the Q&D.C program doesn't store the variable you typed at the keyboard. There's no need to store the character because `getchar`'s output is immediately absorbed by the `printf` function. (Keep reading and you'll understand how.)

✔ Here is the old, traditional way (which also works) for writing this program:

```
#include <stdio.h>

void main()
{
        char c;

        c=getchar();
        printf("You typed the %c character.\n",c);
}
```

The character variable c is created, and then used with `getchar` in a statement, and then used with `printf` in a statement.

The C language works from the inside out

There are lots of strange things that go in inside the C language. For example:

```
if(x==5)
{
     break;
}
```

You know that the preceding group of statements can be abbreviated as follows:

```
if(x==5)
     break;
```

And you can even put the two statements on one line:

```
if(x==5) break;
```

Another strange thing is that you can stick functions inside other functions. All you have to do is ensure that the function inside produces something the function outside needs. Figure 5-3 illustrates this concept.

Figure 5-3:
Using
functions as
variables.

The atoi function requires a string for input. The gets function produces a string. It's entirely possible (and legal, in most states) to stick a gets function *inside* an atoi function:

```
atoi(gets(name));
```

The gets function still needs its parentheses, and it still needs a place to store input, so a variable must be specified (such as name here). You may also notice a little parenthetical overdose in such a statement — but it works: Since gets produces the string atoi needs, nothing messes up. And this works out fine because the C language works itself from the inside out when it comes to functions in statements. Let me say that a little louder:

The C language works from the inside out. Functions inside other functions run first.

In the atoi/gets monster shown earlier, gets works first, getting input from the keyboard, which it then immediately passes off to atoi.

✔ Although sticking functions inside other functions is possible, it's not a required part of C programming. It does make things easier, and you will see others using it in their source code, which is why I bring it up here.

✔ The more you work together various functions, the higher the degree of sophistication it takes to decipher what it is you're doing. Therefore . . .

✔ If you're going to do this, you have to comment your source code carefully.

Modifying the IQ.C program from Lesson 5-4

Pull up the old IQ.C program from Lesson 5-4. Load it into your editor for a wee bit of modification.

Consider the three final statements in the getval() function inside IQ.C. I've commented them next so that you're reacquainted with what they do:

```
gets(input);        //Get input from the keyboard
x=atoi(input);      //Convert it to an integer value
return(x)           //Return that value to the program
```

There you see the gets/atoi problem mentioned in the preceding section (and in Figure 5-3). gets produces a string. atoi swallows that string. The two statements can be combined as follows:

```
x=atoi(gets(input));              //get input, make int.
```

Make this modification to your IQ.C source code. Edit the program so that one line is combined with the other, making one compound statement. Yeah, it's ugly. But it works.

Save IQ.C back to disk. Compile. Run. You notice no difference in the output. The program runs just as it did before. (Which bring up the "Big Deal!" point, but that isn't the issue here.)

You can make one additional modification to the getval() function. Since atoi produces an integer value and that's what the return statement returns, you can combine even more:

```
return(atoi(gets(input)));
```

Looks like gets was following too closely when return put on the brakes. Fortunately, there were no injuries (though rubberneckers got an eyeful).

Carefully edit your IQ.C source code to make the preceding modification. Remember to count your parentheses, making sure that they all match up; the statement ends with three of them (which looks odd).

Save the file to disk again. Compile and run. The program runs the same.

- ✔ You may get a warning error telling you that the variable x is never used in the getval() function. Oh, well. So it isn't used. It's not like it has feelings or anything.

- ✔ The following statement is monstrous, *monstrous!*

```
return(atoi(gets(input)));
```

Still, this is something you encounter (and can do yourself, if you like) in your C voyages.

- ✔ Remember that the functions work from the inside out. In the following statement, gets works first, and then atoi, and then return:

```
return(atoi(gets(input)));
```

You must think, "OK, gets reads in input, and then atoi converts it to an integer value, and then return sends it back. I think I may have that now."

- ✔ Even if you don't get it, it's OK. Just mark this lesson in the book and refer to it later when you encounter this phenomenon.

The common if *example*

A common use of the confounding compounding function phenomenon is in if statement comparisons. For example, quite a few programs have used the following statements:

```
ch=getch();
if(ch=='~')
```

The first statement reads a character from the keyboard and saves it in the ch variable. The second statement compares the character with the tilde. If the tilde was typed, the condition is true, and the statements belonging to if are executed. (This is all Lesson 4 stuff, if you need a review.)

Most C programmers write these two statements as one. To wit:

```
if(getch()=='~')
```

This means that both things happen at a time. First, because the statement works its functions from the inside out, the computer waits for a character to be typed at the keyboard. Then that character is immediately passed to the if statement for comparison.

To see how this works, load the old BOMBER2.C program into your editor. Combine lines 19 and 20 from the source code to read as follows:

```
if(getch()=='~')
```

(You can also go up and delete line 11, which declares the x variable, because that variable is no longer used in this program.)

Save your changes to disk. Compile and run. The program works the same, but when your C programming buddies scan it, they'll be impressed with your compound statement — and in an if comparison, no less.

✔ A drawback to using this technique is that the character getch fetches from the keyboard isn't saved in any variable. So if a later part of the program needs to use that character, it can't. In that instance, you have to use two statements (the old-fashioned way).

✔ The warning is of no concern in the BOMBER program, where getch is used only for a quick comparison.

Lesson 5-5 Quiz

1. If there were one lesson to draw from this chapter, it would be:

    A. C functions work from the inside out.

    B. C functions can sure look hairy.

    C. I thought I mastered C until this lesson.

    D. Now is a good time for a cool, refreshing beverage.

2. The following statement contains the `getchar` and `putchar` functions. Which one goes first?

    ```
    putchar(getchar());
    ```

    A. Holy cripes! Where did you dig up the `putchar` function?

    B. The `putchar` function runs first, displaying the character `getchar` reads from the keyboard.

    C. Because C works from the inside out, I suppose that `getchar` goes first.

    D. Because `getchar` comes before `putchar` alphabetically, it should go first.

3. Reassemble the following two statements into one:

    ```
    smelly=garlic();
    return(smelly);
    ```

4. The universal donor:

    A. O

    B. A

    C. B

    D. AB

5. The universal recipient:

    A. O

    B. A

    C. B

    D. AB

6. How many times is the phrase "inside out" used in this lesson?

Lesson 5-6: Creepy DOS and BIOS Functions

A phrase that's popular with computer programmers is called *reinventing the wheel.* Essentially, it means this:

> *Og*: Wow. What wonderful cart you make. Should hold lots of ox dung!

> *Gronk*: Ugh. But me must invent wheel to move cart around.

> *Og*: Silly Gronk. Wheel already invented! Just buy one from Shifty Thorg, the Wheel Dealer.

> *Gronk*: Ugh. Me silly. Why reinvent wheel? Ha. Ha.

> *Og*: Ha. Ha.

The computer can do a lot for you. In fact, much of the simple stuff has already been created — basic functions you'll use every day. These functions exist in your PC's BIOS. For example, functions to display text on the screen, clear all or part of the screen, move the cursor, change the video mode, and so on are all there, ready for you to use.

DOS also comes with its own set of functions. For example, opening a file, creating a file, making a subdirectory — these are all functions already written for you. All you have to know is how to access the functions. After that, the computer does the work.

✔ The BIOS contains functions that deal with computer basics: displaying a character on the screen, printing a character, reading a character from the keyboard. This is all basic input and output — basic I/O. In fact, that's what BIOS stands for: Basic Input/Output System.

✔ DOS contains functions that deal with the disk drives, directories, and files. It also deals with memory (somewhat), the computer's clock, dirty laundry, and a few other esoteric items.

✔ This chapter shows you a couple of common DOS and BIOS functions. Most C compilers contain their own functions, however, so that you never really have to use the DOS functions. (Which brings up the "Why bother?" issue, which I don't get into here.)

✔ Borland compilers contain various *bios*-this and *bios*-that functions that carry out simple BIOS functions, but without the clumsiness demonstrated in this chapter.

✔ Unfortunately, DOS and the BIOS aren't as complete as with other operating systems. Even though you can use these functions, most programmers prefer to write their own (faster) functions that do the same thing. No, this isn't reinventing the wheel. It's more like Gronk inventing the jet engine for his ox cart.

✔ The *BIOS* is a program that starts your computer and contains the functions that let programs you write (and DOS) communicate with the PC's hardware. The BIOS program lives on a ROM (Read-Only Memory) chip inside your PC. There are actually many BIOSs, but the one talked about here is the PC's BIOS. (Other BIOSs include the hard disk BIOS, video BIOS, network BIOS, and so on.)

✔ Using the BIOS or DOS functions with the C language is tricky. It involves some strange setup because what you're doing is communicating with the PC's microprocessor directly. This isn't scary or hard, and it doesn't make the computer blow up. But it is complex and ugly to look at.

✔ DOS and BIOS functions are categorized into things referred to as *interrupts*. Think of an interrupt as a phone line linking you with DOS or the BIOS. After you "dial up" or *call* an interrupt, you can then use one of the many functions the interrupt supervises. This is really strange lingo, so don't bother memorizing it.

Know thy DOS version

One of the cheesier DOS functions is one that returns the current DOS version, both major and minor release numbers. This was necessary beginning with DOS version 2.0 (major release 2, minor release 0) because it did things that DOS 1.0 couldn't. Ever since then, many programs check the DOS version to ensure that they can do what they're supposed to. If not, they display nasty `improper DOS version` error messages.

The program DOSVER.C calls on a DOS function that tells you the major and minor release numbers for whatever version of DOS you're running. Like typing the VER command at the DOS prompt, this program petitions DOS directly to see which version number it is. Better wear something nice for this.

Name: DOSVER.C

```
#include <stdio.h>
#include <dos.h>

void main()
{
        int major,minor;
        union REGS regs;           //required for making DOS calls

        regs.h.al=1;               //Get version number
        regs.h.ah=0x30;            //Get version function 30h
        int86(0x21,&regs,&regs);   //Call DOS
```

```
    major=regs.h.al;                    //get major version no.
    minor=regs.h.ah;                    //get minor version no.

    printf("This is DOS version %i, release %i\n",major,minor);
}
```

Carefully type the source code for DOSVER.C into your editor. The Cheat box nearby has some pointers for your typing. When you're done, double-check the items in that box, and then save the file to disk as DOSVER.C.

Compile DOSVER.C. Any errors you see are probably due to a typo, so compare the line with the error in it (or before or after that line) with the sample listed nearby. Resave and recompile after you've found your boo-boo.

Run the program. Here is a sample of the output for MS-DOS 6.2:

```
This is DOS version 6, release 20
```

All the mess of the DOSVER.C source code yielded some pretty smart results. Hopefully, it's true!

- ✔ Refer to the section "The lowdown on calling BIOS and DOS functions," later in this lesson, for information about all the strangeness in this program.

- ✔ Also see the section "A few brief, painless words about microprocessor registers," which tells you what the `regs.h.whatever` things are, mean, and do.

- ✔ A Blow-by-blow box nearby describes how the DOSVER.C program works. It may help if you read the entire chapter before going back to review the program as described in that box.

- ✔ Most DOS functions aren't used by C programmers; there are C functions that do the same thing without the mess witnessed in DOSVER.C. Even so, you may encounter a program that pulls this stunt, or you may one day have to access a DOS function your compiler doesn't know about.

- ✔ This program makes use of *hexadecimal* numbers, which are those values that begin with `0x` and sometimes contain the letters *A* through *F*. This is definitely *not* what they taught me in school. Wait until Lesson 6-6 for the full, boring details.

- ✔ The DOS interrupt is number 21h, which is a hexadecimal value. The Get Version function number is 30h, another hex value. Are you curious about the corresponding decimal values? Don't be! The number isn't a specific value here — it's just the "name" of the function according to DOS. As long as you copy it down properly, you will never have any problem.

✔ I couldn't get this program to work on my UNIX computer. I wonder why . . . .

✔ In Borland C (and Turbo C), you can use the variables _osmajor and _osminor to get the DOS version numbers. The following variation on DOSVER.C does the job:

```
#include <stdio.h>
#include <dos.h>

void main()
{
        printf("This is DOS version %i,\
        release %i\n",_osmajor,_osminor);
}
```

(The backslash is used in the printf statement here to split it between two lines.)

✔ You never have to use this function in any of your C programs to make sure that it will run. The compiler already includes a miniprogram in all your C programs that checks the DOS version for you. You can, however, use this function to display such information, proving how smart your programs are.

Some crazy things to watch for when you type in the DOSVER.C source code

Line 7: The second word, REGS, *must* be capitalized. This is the name of a *union,* which is a type of variable whose characteristics you shouldn't concern yourself with. The last regs on this line should be in lowercase.

Line 9: You type regs, period, h, period, al, equals one, semicolon. Everything is in lowercase, and you must use periods. A common goof here is to use commas or some other character that will annoy the compiler.

Line 10: Type regs, period, h, period, ah, and an equal sign. Then type a zero, little x, 30,

semicolon. What you're doing is entering a number in hexadecimal (base 16) format — which is really nerdy but required when you're poking around rudely with the microprocessor. Type zeroes and not capital letter *O*s.

Line 11: The int86 function has three items hugged in its parentheses. The first is 0, little x, 21. Then comes a comma. Then ampersand regs. Another comma. Another ampersand-regs.

Lines 13 and 14: Make sure that you type periods after regs and the little h in each line.

The finer points of calling the DOS Get Version function

The `major` and `minor` integer variables (line 6) are used to hold the major and minor DOS version numbers. In line 7, the `union` declaration sets up the microprocessor variables used to call and return values from the Get Version function.

```
int major,minor;
union REGS regs;
   //required for making DOS calls
```

To get the DOS version number, you first stick the value 1 into the microprocessor's AL register, which is done in line 9.

```
regs.h.al=1;//Get version number
```

To tell the DOS interrupt that you want function 30h (30-hexadecimal), that value is stuffed into the microprocessor's AH register in line 10 by using the proper C hexadecimal number format 0x30:

```
regs.h.ah=0x30;
   //Get version function 30h
```

Line 11 actually performs the DOS function call by using the `int86` function:

```
int86(0x21,&regs,&regs); //Call DOS
```

The interrupt number for DOS is 21h, which is specified in C as 0x21. Then comes the set of microprocessor registers used for input, &regs, and finally the set used for output, which is the same: &regs. All this is messy, but because what it's doing is controlling the computer's microprocessor directly, that can be accepted. (Maybe not understood, but accepted.)

```
major=regs.h.al;
   //get major version no.
minor=regs.h.ah;
   //get minor version no.
```

After the DOS function call, the version numbers are stored in the microprocessor's AL and AH registers. These values are read into the `major` and `minor` integer variables in lines 13 and 14. The result is displayed by `printf` in line 16:

```
printf("This is DOS version %i,
   release %i\n",major,minor);
```

A few brief, painless words about microprocessor registers

When you call a BIOS or DOS function (or interrupt), you must diddle with the microprocessor. This diddling is actually kind of nifty. For a fleeting moment, you have direct control over the computer's most vital gut. You place specific values into the microprocessor — deliberately — and then tell it to do your bidding. This is powerful stuff. And that explains why programs which use creepy DOS or BIOS functions are a little on the cryptic side.

No one expects a computer's microprocessor to jump out of its tiny wafer and say, "I'm Bud, and I wanna shake your hand!" Instead, the burden falls on you to shake the microprocessor's hand. To make that work, you have to place values into the microprocessor directly. The holding bins for those values are called the microprocessor's *registers*.

Oh, I could go into great detail here about microprocessor registers and all that, and I'd seriously bore you to tears. Essentially, there are two doohickeys you should know about:

```
union REGS regs;
```

This statement basically provides a function in your program with a whole smorgasbord of microprocessor registers to deal with as variables. So whenever you have a desire to fiddle with the microprocessor — which implies that you must either stick values inside its wee li'l registers or read values from those registers — you need the preceding line in your assortment of variable declarations. It's that simple.

The second doohickey is knowing the names of the registers themselves. Other documentation refers to the registers by their real names — the names you would use if you were sitting next to the microprocessor at a fine dining establishment and were asking it whether its goose liver pâté was also undercooked. But in your C program, you have to refer to the registers by special variable names. These names and their corresponding (true) microprocessor register names are listed in Table 5-1.

Table 5-1   Microprocessor Registers and Their C Language Variable Names

Register	Variable	Register	Variable
AX	regs.x.ax	CX	regs.x.cx
AH	regs.h.ah	CH	regs.h.ch
AL	regs.h.al	CL	regs.h.cl
BX	regs.x.bx	DX	regs.x.dx
BH	regs.h.bh	DH	regs.h.dh
BL	regs.h.bl	DL	regs.h.dl

✔ How do you know when to use a microprocessor register/C language variable doohickey? You are told. The instructions for getting the DOS version number, for example, are written out something like this:

```
Call with:
AL = 1        Get DOS version flag (whatever that means)
AH = 30h      Get Version Number Function
Return:
AL            Major version number
AH            Minor version number
```

✔ Your job is to translate the raw microprocessor registers into C language variables. So, as shown here (and from Table 5-1), you would use the `regs.h.al` and `regs.h.ah` variables both before and after the call to DOS.

✔ In order to use the microprocessor register variables, you must declare them by using the `union REGS regs;` statement. This is so important that I almost wrote this paragraph in Latin!

✔ An unfortunate aspect of using DOS and BIOS functions is that they're often written in hexadecimal. This shouldn't pose a problem, because all you have to do is copy down the same values. Lesson 6-6 is a good place to visit if this concept befuddles you.

✔ Another vital step is to actually make the phone call to DOS — to call the DOS interrupt by using the `int86` function. This information is covered in the section "The lowdown on calling BIOS and DOS functions," later in this chapter.

✔ Four microprocessor registers are known to DOS: A, B, C, and D. The full register has room for 16 bits and is described as AX, BC, CX, and DX. Half registers can also be used, each of which holds 8 bits. So the full 16-bit AX register is also two 6-bit registers, AH and AL, which stand for A-High and A-Low. You can conveniently forget this information in three minutes.

The almost-handy clear screen function

In my travels, I'd have to say that 90 percent of the BIOS function calls are to the video interrupt — the direct phone line to your PC's video- and screen-control center. There you can find an armada of video functions, from primitive graphics stuff to routines that display characters on the screen and scroll and clear the screen. Fun stuff — such as the ZAPSCRN1.C program you see listed next.

Name: ZAPSCRN1.C

```c
#include <stdio.h>
#include <dos.h>

#define VIDEO 0x10              //Video interrupt
#define COLS 80                 //Screen width
#define ROWS 25                 //Screen rows

void cls(void);

void main()
{
    printf("Press Enter to clear the screen");
    getchar();
    cls();
    printf("Ah, how refreshing...");
}

void cls(void)
{
    union REGS regs;

    regs.h.ah=0x06;             //func 6, scroll window
    regs.h.al=0x00;             //clear screen
    regs.h.bh=0x07;             //make screen "blank"
    regs.h.ch=0x00;             //Upper left row
    regs.h.cl=0x00;             //Upper left column
    regs.h.dh=ROWS-1;           //Lower right row
    regs.h.dl=COLS-1;           //Lower right column
    int86(VIDEO,&regs,&regs);
}
```

Carefully type the source code for ZAPSCRN1.C into your editor. The main
function is easy, but pay special attention to the cls() function. It contains all
the hieroglyphics required to call your PC's BIOS function that clears the
screen. Again, you're programming the PC's microprocessor directly with all
those dotty statements.

Save the file to disk as ZAPSCRN1.C.

Compile. You may get a warning error for the getchar function in line 13.
That's because getchar returns a value you don't do anything with; it's used as
a "press any key" function and, honestly, who cares which key was pressed?
That's a never-mind error, so the program works just fine. If you get other
errors, however, please fix them and recompile.

Run the program.

```
Press Enter to clear the screen
```

Do so; press the Enter key.

Zap! The screen is cleared. The following message is displayed:

```
Ah, how refreshing...
```

Minor problem: The cursor wasn't moved up to the left corner of the screen. A nerd would say, "You didn't *home* the cursor." Alas, it's true. The cls() function clears the screen but neglects to move the cursor. This problem is remedied in the section "CLS II," at the end of this chapter.

✔ Refer to Lesson 6-6 for more information about hexadecimal numbers, which appear in this program in the 0x00 format.

✔ The cls() function dials up the BIOS video interrupt, 10h (ten hexa-decimal).

✔ The video interrupt's function 6 is used to scroll the screen; the value 6 is put into the microprocessor's AH register in line 22. However, when the microprocessor's AL register is equal to zero (line 23), this function clears a swath of the screen instead of scrolling it. The remaining values set in the cls() function clear the entire screen.

✔ The microprocessor's CL and CH registers hold the values that indicate the upper left corner of the part of the screen to clear (lines 25 and 26). To clear the entire screen, values of 0x00 (zero) and 0x00 (zero) are used, which represent row 1 and column 1 on the screen.

✔ The microprocessor's DL and CH registers identify the lower right corner of the part of the screen to clear (lines 27 and 28). These registers are filled with the values ROWS and COLS, as defined earlier in the program. How-ever, one is subtracted from each value. That's because the BIOS thinks that the screen starts at row 0, column 0 and ends at row 24, column 79. In practice, humans count beginning at row 1, column 1 and end at row 25, column 80. So the "minus one" there is for the computer's benefit.

✔ The cls() function was written so that you can use it in your programs. To do so, just include the function as written here, along with its proto-type, in any C source code. Remember to #include <dos.h> and #define VIDEO, COLS, and ROWS at the beginning of the program for everything to work.

✔ The #define directives are used to identify the BIOS video interrupt line plus the screen dimensions. You can change these values to affect the rest of the program if you like. For example, change the value for ROWS to 12, and change COLS to 40. Recompile and run the program, and only a quarter of the screen will clear. (The #define directive makes it easy to modify a program without having to wade through its guts.)

✔ Refer to Lesson 3-4 for more information about the #define dealie.

✔ In Borland C++ and Turbo C, you can use the clrscr function to clear the screen. Just replace the cls() function and all its references in the ZAPSCRN1.C program, and stick the following line into the main function:

```
clrscr();   //clear the screen
```

✔ The upper left corner of the screen is known as "home" for the cursor. (Don't bother looking for the little house with a chimney and flower boxes.) *Homing* the cursor means moving the cursor to that home position. Computer trivia: Back in the early days of microcomputing, the old Apple II had a command that cleared the screen: HOME.

The lowdown on calling BIOS and DOS functions

The C language isn't that hard when you compare it to, say, Vulgar Latin. Most of the words are sort of like English. Things work fairly logically. And unless you've ventured off to do things on your own, you probably haven't encountered any truly boggling errors. (But wait — they're coming!)

The C compiler does much of the hard work for you, translating your desires into instructions for the microprocessor. But when you want to use DOS or BIOS functions, things get cryptic because it's now *you,* the programmer, not the compiler, dealing with the microprocessor.

To use the DOS and BIOS functions, you must program the PC's microprocessor. You do this in three steps:

1. Place values in the microprocessor's registers (storage areas inside the microprocessor itself).

2. Place a phone call to the DOS or BIOS interrupt.

3. Read any values returned by the interrupt, which are conveniently stored in the microprocessor's registers.

Placing values into the microprocessor's registers is done by using C language variable equivalents to the register names, as illustrated in Table 5-1. For example, if your instructions are to put the value 16h (16 hexadecimal) into the AL register, you do the following:

```
regs.h.al=0x16;                      //put 16 into AL
```

What does this mean? I dunno. But it's how you stick the 16h value into the AL register by using C. Just follow that formula, and you'll survive.

For step 2, you have to use the `int86` function, the format for which is shown here:

```
int86(interrupt,&regs,&regs);
```

This C language function dials up a DOS or BIOS interrupt, as specified by *interrupt*. The first `&regs` thing passes along the values to be stuck in the various microprocessor register storage places in step 1; the second `&regs` thing returns any values.

In the final step, you can use C to evaluate any information returned from the function. You do this by examining the proper registers according to the function. For example, one BIOS function returns the cursor's row and column position in two registers. You can examine those values by using the variable register names and the `if` keyword, if you're up to it.

✔ Which registers do you use? Which interrupt number? It depends on what you're doing. Most reference manuals list the interrupts and function numbers, and you will use them to help you call the various DOS and BIOS functions.

✔ Also refer to the box "Out-of-print book recommendations for additional study" for a list of suggested reading material.

✔ DOS and BIOS functions are called by using *interrupts*. Grouped inside the interrupts are the various functions that do interesting and amusing things.

✔ What's an *interrupt?* It's like a vast, overlord function that contains other functions. This is an extremely nontechnical description that would be laughed at in academic circles.

✔ The interrupt and function numbers are usually listed in hexadecimal format. The DOS interrupt is 21h, written as `0x21` in C. The BIOS video interrupt is 10h, written `0x10`.

✔ You typically call a DOS or BIOS interrupt by specifying a function number in the AH register. To call function 9, for example, you stick `0x09` in the AH register by using the following C language statement:

```
regs.h.ah=0x09;      //Stick 9 in the AH reg.
```

✔ One of the reasons that this is so weird is that you're bridging the gap here between C programming and assembly language — the tongue of the gods! Assembly language is about programming the micoprocessor itself, which is akin to building a wall in your garden molecule-by-molecule as opposed to using bricks. This may help to explain why things are so messy, but that's what you deal with when you program the microprocessor directly.

CLS II

The problem with the ZAPSCRN1.C program is that it clears the screen but doesn't move, or *home,* the cursor. To do that, you have to call another BIOS function, one of the video interrupts, that moves the cursor around on the screen.

The following program is ZAPSCRN2.C. It contains the `locate()` function, which moves the cursor to a specific column (going left to right) and row (going up and down) on the screen. This function is used at the end of the `cls()` function to home the cursor, making it behave like you would expect.

Name: ZAPSCRN2.C

```
#include <stdio.h>
#include <dos.h>

#define VIDEO 0x10                          //Video interrupt
#define COLS 80                             //Screen width
#define ROWS 25                             //Screen rows

void cls(void);
void locate(int col,int row);

void main()
{
    printf("Press Enter to clear the screen");
    getchar();
    cls();
    printf("Ah, how refreshing...");
}

void cls(void)
{
    union REGS regs;

    regs.h.ah=0x06;                         //func 6, scroll window
    regs.h.al=0x00;                         //clear screen
    regs.h.bh=0x07;                         //make screen "blank"
    regs.h.ch=0x00;                         //Upper left row
    regs.h.cl=0x00;                         //Upper left column
    regs.h.dh=ROWS-1;                       //Lower right row
    regs.h.dl=COLS-1;                       //Lower right column
    int86(VIDEO,&regs,&regs);
```

```
        locate(0,0);              //"Home" the cursor
}


/* LOCATE Function
Move the cursor to position col,row, where col
ranges from 0 to 79 and row from 0 to 24. Upper
left corner = 0,0; lower right corner = 79,24
*/


void locate(int col,int row)
{
    union REGS regs;

    regs.h.ah=0x02;               //Vid func 2, move cursor
    regs.h.bh=0x00;               //video screen (always 0)
    regs.h.dh=row;                //cursor's row pos
    regs.h.dl=col;                //cursor's col pos
    int86(VIDEO,&regs,&regs);
}
```

Create the source code for ZAPSCRN2.C by editing the ZAPSCRN1.C program already in your editor. First add the call to the locate() function at the end of the cls() function in the old program. Then add the locate() function. Remember to copy the prototype to the beginning of the program or else you get a whole hive full of errors.

Save your source code to disk as ZAPSCRN2.C. Use the Save As command to do this.

Compile. You'll probably get the same warning error you did for the first program; it's just the getchar function being goofy — no problem. Fix any other errors you may have typed, if necessary.

Run the program. It works the same as ZAPSCRN1.C, but after the screen is cleared, the cursor moves to the upper left corner — just like DOS's CLS command. By golly, you've rewritten it!

- ✔ As with the cls() function, feel free to use the locate() function in your programs to move the cursor around on the screen.

- ✔ By the way, later programs in this book use both the cls() and locate() functions. Bone up on how to copy and paste in your editor so that you don't have to do a bunch of retyping every time they're used.

✔ Both the cls() and locate() functions contain the union REGS regs; declaration. This is required because both functions use the micoprocessor register variables.

✔ The locate() function uses the BIOS video interrupt function 2 to move the cursor. This value is put into the microprocessor's AH register in line 45. The value 0 is put into the BH register in line 46. To move the cursor to a specific row and column, those values are put into the DH and DL registers in the following two lines.

✔ In Borland C++ and Turbo C, the gotoxy function is used to move the cursor around on the screen. For example:

```
gotoxy(1,1);                              //move to row 1, column 1
```

This statement "homes" the cursor to the first column, first row (upper left corner of the screen). The X (row) position comes first, and then the Y (column) position. This is easy to remember because the function is named gotoxy. (Both gotoxy and the locate() function in ZAPSCRN2.C work the same way.)

Out-of-print book recommendations for additional study

Writing BIOS or DOS function calls in C is pretty much a dead art, primarily because no one writes DOS programs anymore. Boo-hoo. Sniff, sniff. If you're curious, you'll have to obtain a source for the various interrupts and functions. Here are my favorite references:

Microsoft MS-DOS Programmer's Reference, available from Microsoft Press. This book is updated with each new version of DOS, and I don't have the latest one, so I can't cough up the ISBN number. On the plus side, it's never out of print, so

this will probably be the source you get if you can't find the others mentioned here.

Advanced MS-DOS, by Ray Duncan, formerly available from Microsoft Press. This book is out of print (shows you how popular BIOS and DOS interrupts are), so if you spy it at a used-computer-book store, buy it no matter what!

Peter Norton's IBM Programmer's Guide, which may not actually have that title and may or may not be available from Microsoft Press. As with everything else on this topic, books are fading away fast.

Lesson 5-6 Quiz

1. What is "reinventing the wheel?"

    A. Doing a lot of unnecessary work someone else has already done.

    B. Making any large, circular object that is then mounted on an axle and used for mobility.

    C. Any big, new government program designed to help the poor.

    D. All of the above.

2. Which of the following *is not* required for a DOS function to work in C?

    A. `union REGS regs;`

    B. `regs.h.ah=0x30;`

    C. `int86(0x21,&regs,&regs);`

    D. `onion REGGIE 0x23;`

3. Name a common interrupt.

    A. Anyone from Texas.

    B. The phone ringing.

    C. Religious strangers glad to stand outside your front door.

    D. The BIOS video interrupt.

4. Match the variable with its microprocessor register:

    A. `regs.h.al AL`

    B. `regs.x.cx CX`

    C. `regs.h.dh DH`

    D. `regs.h.dl DL`

5. Name a song you can never get out of your head:

    A. The Doublemint-gum song ("Double, double your refreshment.")

    B. "I'm Just a Girl Who Can't Say No" (from *Oklahoma!*)

    C. "Bibbidi-Bobbidi-Boo" (from Disney's *Cinderella*)

    D. "The Mexican Hat Dance" (from Mexico)

6. Where is *home?*

    A. The upper left corner of the screen.

    B. Where Mom lurks.

    C. Somewhere down south.

    D. Where the heart is.

Lesson 5-7: The Old Random-Number Function

Random numbers are a big deal when it comes to programming a computer. They come in handy, for example, with computer games. No computer game would ever be possible without a random number here or there. Without them, the game would be predictable: "Oh, I'm passing by the planet Bothar, and here is where the Omnivorous Space Slug tries to taunt me into a gavotte."

So what's random? The next card drawn from a well-shuffled deck. The roll of a dice. The spin of a roulette wheel. Whether Cindy will overlook your huge beer gut as you attempt your first date after the divorce. These are all random, maybe-this-or-that events. If you want to include this random aspect in your programs, you need a special function that produces random numbers. After that's done, no one can predict when the *Enterprise* will be attacked or when the tornado whips through your village or whether Door Number 2 leads to the treasure this time or to certain doom.

- ✔ The phone company is rumored to have this random-number program it routinely uses to foul up your bill.

- ✔ Random-number routines are the root of the most evil program ever devised for a budding programmer: The Guess the Number program. I spare you that torture in this book. (Well, maybe not.)

- ✔ In the C language, random numbers are produced by using the rand function. It is formally introduced later in this lesson.

- ✔ Random numbers must be *seeded* for them to be more unpredictable. This subject is also covered later in this lesson.

- ✔ Actually, random numbers generated by a computer aren't truly random at all. See the box called "You too can waste a few seconds reading this information about random numbers" for more information.

Using the rand function

Random numbers are generated in C by using the rand function. It spits back a random number depending on the whims of your PC's microprocessor carefully combined with the birthdate of the guy who wrote your C compiler plus his girlfriend's weight in drams. The box nearby carefully describes the rand function.

You too can waste a few seconds reading this information about random numbers

Are they random numbers? Only if they can't be predicted. Unfortunately, with computers the numbers can be predicted. They're still more or less jumbled, like street numbers in Seattle. But overall the random numbers a computer generates aren't truly random. Instead, they're *pseudo-random*.

A pseudo ("SOO-doh") random number is random enough for most purposes. But because the number is based on a computer algorithm, or set routine, its outcome isn't really random. Even if you base the random number on the time of day — *seed* the random number by using another, potentially random value — the results still aren't random enough to appease the mathematical purists. So we live with it.

Function rand

The rand function coughs up a random number. Here is the format:

```
int rand();
```

The rand function returns an integer value, somewhere in the range of 0 through 32,767. So if you want to save the random number into the r variable, you use the following statement:

```
r=rand();
```

Cinchy stuff.

To make the compiler understand the rand function, you must add the following line at the beginning of your source code:

```
#include <stdlib.h>
```

This line tells the compiler all about the rand function and makes everyone happy.

The following program shows the rand function in action. RANDOM1.C produces 100 random numbers, which it displays neatly on the screen. The random numbers are produced by the rand function inside this program's rnd() function. The reason that this was done, as you may be fearing, is that you modify the rnd() function to new levels of spiffiness as this lesson progresses.

Name: RANDOM1.C

```
#include <stdio.h>
#include <stdlib.h>
```

```
int rnd(void);

void main()
{
    int x;

                                //display 100 random numbers
    for(x=0;x<100;x++)
            printf("%i\t",rnd());
}

int rnd(void)
{
    int r;

    r=rand();                   //spit up random num.
    return(r);
}
```

Type the source code for RANDOM1.C into your editor. The tricky stuff here is the guts of the `for` loop and the hieroglyphics in the following `printf` statement. Double-check everything. Save the file to disk as RANDOM1.C.

Compile the program. Fix any errors, which are probably limited to missing semicolons or forgotten parentheses.

Run it! Here is a sample of the output:

346	130	10982	1090	11656	7117
17595	6415	22948	31126	9004	14558
3571	22879	18492	1360	5412	26721
22463	25047	27119	31441	7190	13985
31214	27509	30252	26571	14779	19816
21681	19651	17995	23593	3734	13310
3979	21995	15561	16092	18489	11288
28466	8664	5892	13863	22766	5364
17639	21151	20427	100	25795	8812
15108	12666	12347	19042	19774	9169
5589	26383	9666	10941	13390	7878
13565	1779	16190	32233	53	13429
2285	2422	8333	31937	11636	13268
6460	6458	6936	8160	24842	29142
29667	24115	15116	17418	1156	4279
15008	15859	19561	8297	3755	22981
21275	29040	28690	1401		

Prisoner roll call!

Seriously, notice how the numbers are different, nay, random. I mean, would you have thought of that many that quickly?

- ✔ The random numbers are probably in the range of 0 to 32,000-something — as promised. The numbers you see on your screen are probably different from those just shown (unless you're using a Borland compiler, like I did).

- ✔ In UNIX, the numbers produced by the RANDOM1.C function are most likely incredibly huge. The reason is probably the nature of the UNIX system's C compiler. Don't be shocked if it happens to you.

- ✔ The for loop in this program counts to 100 by using the integer variable x:

```
for(x=0;x<100;x++)
```

The value of x starts out at 0, and the loop continues as long as the value of x stays below 100. Each time the loop repeats, the value of x increases by 1. Refer to Lessons 4-5 and 4-7 for a review if anything in there confuses, confounds, or befuddles you.

- ✔ The printf function displays the random number by using the %i place-holder (for integers), followed by the tab character escape sequence, \t. This is how the numbers appear all lined up in columns.

- ✔ The printf function also uses the output from the rnd() function directly. This gobbling of one function inside another was dwelled on in Lesson 5-5.

- ✔ The range of random values may not be 0 to 32,767 for your compiler. You may want to check the rand function in the documentation to see whether your compiler coughs up the different values.

Planting a random-number seed

Ho! Before you get all happy about the new CASINO program you're about to write and sell for millions to Las Vegas, try rerunning the RANDOM1.C program again. Just choose Run from your compiler's integrated environment or type the RANDOM1 command again at the DOS prompt. Here is what I saw:

```
346    130    10982  1090   11656  7117   17595  6415   22948  31126
9004   14558  3571   22879  18492  1360   5412   26721  22463  25047
27119  31441  7190   13985  31214  27509  30252  26571  14779  19816
21681  19651  17995  23593  3734   13310  3979   21995  15561  16092
18489  11288  28466  8664   5892   13863  22766  5364   17639  21151
20427  100    25795  8812   15108  12666  12347  19042  19774  9169
5589   26383  9666   10941  13390  7878   13565  1779   16190  32233
53     13429  2285   2422   8333   31937  11636  13268  6460   6458
6936   8160   24842  29142  29667  24115  15116  17418  1156   4279
15008  15859  19561  8297   3755   22981  21275  29040  28690  1401
```

Yup, more random numbers. But wait a second. Aren't those the *same* numbers? Identically the same numbers? Did the compiler goof? Did you foul up?

Fortunately, that was no error. The computer generated the set of random numbers because that's all it knows. Sure, they're random all right, but they're the same numbers because, between then and now, the compiler's rand function remained unchanged.

Don't feel cheated! This is a common situation. The rand function is only quasirandom. To make it more random (more *pseudo*random) you have to plant a wee, tiny seed. This seed is a value the compiler uses to help make the random numbers more random. To plant the seed, you use the srand function, described in the next box .

Function srand

The srand function is used to help kick off the computer's random-number machine in a more random manner. Here is the format:

srand((unsigned)*seed*)

The seed value is an unsigned integer value or variable, ranging from 0 up to 65,000-something. It's that value the compiler uses to help seed the random-number-generation equipment located in the bowels of your PC.

You must include the following line at the beginning of your source code to make the srand function behave:

#include <stdlib.h>

Because the rand function already requires this line, there's no need to specify it twice. (Unless you're just seeding the random-number generator out of some perverse horticultural lust.)

✔ See Table 3-2 and the section "Signed or unsigned, or 'Would you like a minus sign with that, sir?' " in Lesson 3-5 for more information about unsigned integer variables.

✔ The (unsigned) deal is used to ensure that the number srand uses is of the unsigned type. This is known as *type casting*. Refer to Lesson 6-5 for the full details.

✔ Using the value 1 (one) to seed the random-number generator causes the compiler to start over by using the same, uninspirational numbers you witness when srand isn't used at all. Avoid doing this if possible.

Randoming up the RANDOM program

Now comes the time for some really random numbers. The following source code is for RANDOM2.C, a mild modification to the original program. This time a new function was added, seedrnd(), which lets you reset the random-number generator and produce more random numbers.

Name: RANDOM2.C

```
#include <stdio.h>
#include <stdlib.h>

int rnd(void);
void seedrnd(void);

void main()
{
     int x;
     seedrnd();                    //prepare random-number gen.
                                   //display 100 random numbers
     for(x=0;x<100;x++)
                     printf("%i\t",rnd());
}

int rnd(void)
{
     int r;

     r=rand();                     //spit up random num.
     return(r);
}

void seedrnd(void)                 //seed the random number
{
```

```
      int seed;
      char s[6];

      printf("Enter a random number seed:");
      seed=(unsigned)atoi(gets(s));

      srand(seed);
}
```

Type this program into your editor. You can start by editing the RANDOM1.C source code. Add the prototype for seedrnd( ) up front, and then insert the call to seedrnd( ) in the main function. Finally, tack the seedrnd( ) function itself to the end of the source code. Double-check the whole thing before you save to make sure that you didn't leave anything out.

Save the file to disk as RANDOM2.C by using your editor's Save As command.

Compile and run. You see the following:

```
Enter a random number seed:
```

Type a number, from 0 up to 32,000-something. Press Enter and you see a new and more random bunch of numbers displayed.

The true test that this worked is to run the program again. This time, type a different number as the seed. The next batch of random numbers will be completely different from the first.

✔ You have to seed the randomizer only once, as this program does up in the main function. Some purists insist on calling the seedrnd( ) function (or its equivalent) lots of times. Hey, random is random as random can be with a computer. No sense in wasting time.

✔ This program combines three C statements into one. The statement appears in line 30:

```
seed=(unsigned)atoi(gets(s));
```

This is actually a compilation of the following two statements:

```
gets(s);
seed=(unsigned)atoi(s);
```

First, gets( ) reads in a string variable. Second, it's converted into an integer variable by the atoi function, which is passed over to the seed variable in proper unsigned format. Refer to Lesson 5-5 for more information on how this works.

Streamlining the randomizer

Nothing annoys me like a klutzy program. I'm talking not about how it's written, but how it looks — its presentation. When a program must ask you to seed the randomizer, something is wrong. A computer should be smart enough to do that itself. And it can, as long as it finds a source of ever-changing numbers it can use to seed the randomizer.

One such source is the computer's clock. Most PCs keep time down to the hundredths of seconds. That means that every 1/100th of a second, a new number is available to seed the randomizing gears. Heck, even the current second would be good enough to seed the randomizer. It just needs to be a number that is different from one second to the next, that's all.

The following source code is for the RANDOM3.C program. This program is identical to RANDOM2.C except that the seedrnd() function has been streamlined to only one statement; it now uses the current time to seed the random-number generator.

Name: RANDOM3.C

```
#include <stdio.h>
#include <stdlib.h>
#include <time.h>                        //for seeding randomizer

int rnd(void);
void seedrnd(void);

void main()
{
    int x;
    seedrnd();
                                         //display 100 random numbers
    for(x=0;x<100;x++)
                printf("%i\t",rnd());
}

int rnd(void)
{
    int r;

    r=rand();                            //spit up random num.
    return(r);
}
```

```
void seedrnd(void)
{
    srand((unsigned)time(NULL));
}
```

Create the source code for RANDOM3.C in your editor. You can start with RANDOM2.C. Add the new third line, #include <time.h>, which lets you use the computer's clock to seed the random-number generator. Then modify the seedrnd() function as shown in this code. Save the file to disk as RANDOM3.C by using your editor's Save As command.

Compile and run the program. Notice that the output is similar and randomly different. What you don't notice is the program begging you to seed the randomizer. That's all handled automatically now.

✔ The time function in line 27 returns the time of day from the computer's internal clock. It's called by using the constant value NULL, which is essentially the value zero. (This constant is defined in the stdio.h "header file" — the #include <stdio.h> line sets it all up; see Lesson 6-1 for more information.)

✔ The value returned by the time function will be some number, which isn't important. What is important is that it is an unsigned integer value, which is what the (unsigned) type cast does. (Refer to Lesson 6-5 for more on that.)

✔ No matter what, know that the following statement in any of your C programs properly and somewhat randomly seeds the random-number-generating apparatus:

```
srand((unsigned)time(NULL));
```

✔ The time function (and therefore the preceding randomizing seeding statement) requires the following statement at the beginning of your source code:

```
#include <time.h>
```

✔ As well as:

```
#include <stdlib.h>
```

✔ Incidentally, Borland C's randomize function does exactly the same job as srand((unsigned)time(NULL));. It too requires the #include <time.h> definition at the beginning of your source code.

The diabolical Dr. Modulus

You may have noticed that the random numbers produced by the computer are wildly random and often unsuitable. For example:

```
Your turn, BOB.
You rolled a 23415 on the dice. This lands you on Boardwalk, but
          you've passed Go 585 times, which nets you a gross of
          $117,000!
```

That gets old after a while.

There needs to be a way to round down the numbers — a hacksaw to chop off excess values and just give you numbers in, say, a certain range.

Lo, there is such a way. It's a mathematical concept called *modulus*.

Ah-ooga! Ah-ooga! Mathematical concept alert! Ah-ooga!

Modulus — bah! This term is better known to you as "the remainder" as in, "When you divide 6 into 10, you get a remainder of 4." Well, 6 gazinta 10 is *modulo 4.* This is written in C as:

```
4 = 10 % 6;
```

I don't expect you to remember what a modulus is or does, nor do I expect you to know when to use *modulus,* or the ablative, *modulo.* The box nearby explains the format, which is the same for any of C's mathematical operators. What's important to know is that you can use the modulus doohickey to pare down larger numbers into smaller, more convenient chunks.

✔ The modulus operator is %, the percent sign. Pronounce it "mod."

✔ The big number comes first in a modulus equation.

✔ No math! The modulus is used here to help you pare down your random numbers. That's all! You can dwell on the mathematical aspects of the % in other C language books.

✔ *Gazinta* means "goes into." I point this out here because my managing editor loathes it when I use nondictionary words.

✔ Actually, if you want to pare down a large random number as a roll of the dice, you need the following equation:

```
dice1=(23415 % 6)+1;
```

First get 23,415 "mod" 6. This produces a number in the range of zero to five. (Zero to five as a remainder; you can't have a remainder of six when you divide by six.) After the mod calculation, you add one to the number and you get a value in the range of one to six, which are the true numbers on any given side of a die.

✔ In the My Dear Aunt Sally theme of things, a modulus operation comes just after division and before addition. See the Techy box called "Introducing My Dear Mother's Aunt Sally (Ugh!)."

✔ "Ah, yes, Dr. Modulus. I'm familiar with your work in astrogenetics. Is it true that you got kicked out of the academy for engineering a third sex in mice?" "You read too much, lad."

Operator % (modulus)

The modulus is the remainder when you divide `blah` by `ugh`, as in:

```
modulus = blah % ugh;
```

Read it this way: If you take the huge number `blah` and divide it by the smaller number `ugh`, you get a remainder, which is the `modulo` value.

Suppose that `blah` is a big number in the following statement:

```
m = blah % 5;
```

The values of variable `m` are in the range of zero through four, depending on the remainder of `blah` divided by five.

```
m = blah % 10;
```

The values of variable `m` for the preceding statement range from zero through nine.

```
m = blah % 2;
```

The values for `m` for this statement are either zero or one; zero for even-numbered values of `blah`, and one for the odd numbers.

When `ugh` is larger than `blah` (5 MOD 10), the result is always equal to `ugh`. Therefore, you want the larger value (`blah`) to come first.

You can take the value 23,415, for example, and pare it down to a multiple of 6, which is the number of sides on a die. This is written as follows:

```
dice1=23415 % 6;
```

The computer calculates how many times 6 gazinta 23,415. It then places that value in the `dice1` variable. The end result is the number 3, which is a more realistic roll of a die than 23,415. (Of course, you roll two dice in Monopoly, so this would have to be done again for the second die — and you have to add 1 to the value because you can't roll 0.)

Introducing My Dear Mother's Aunt Sally (Ugh!)

Remember My Dear Aunt Sally, from Lesson 3-8? It's a mnemonic (a thing that makes you remember something) for multiplication, division, addition, and subtraction, which is the order in which things get done in a long C math statement. Well, add to that the modulus operation, which takes precedence over addition and subtraction. So it goes like this:

My Dear Mother's Aunt Sally

*	Multiplication
/	Division
%	Modulus
+	Addition
–	Subtraction

Therefore, the following statement to get a roll of the dice:

```
dice1=(23415 % 6)+1;
```

does the same thing without the parentheses:

```
dice1=23415 % 6+1;
```

The modulus operation (`23415 % 6`) comes first regardless, and then one is added to the result. Of course, putting the parentheses in there for readability's sake is always forgivable.

Rolling the dice with yet another RANDOM program

You should have a whole pile of random numbers spewing forth from your computer, like New Yorkers fleeing their buildings during an August power outage. There's one more keen improvement left to be made to the rnd() function. It's time to add an automatic range-finder. The following program, RANDOM4.C (the last in the suite), has an rnd() function that coughs up random values only in the range of zero to whatever number you specify. This program should bring some order to your random numbers.

Name: RANDOM4.C

```
#include <stdio.h>
#include <stdlib.h>
#include <time.h>                           //for seeding randomizer

int rnd(int range);
void seedrnd(void);

void main()
```

```
{
        int x;
        seedrnd();
                                                //display 100 random numbers
        for(x=0;x<100;x++)
                        printf("%i\t",rnd(10));
}

int rnd(int range)
{
        int r;

        r=rand()%range;                         //spit up random num.
        return(r);
}

void seedrnd(void)
{
        srand((unsigned)time(NULL));
}
```

Create the source code for RANDOM4.C. Start with your RANDOM3.C program and make four modifications: Change the typecast of the rnd() function so that it requires an integer value, (int range), in line 5; change the printf function in line 14 so that the rnd() function is called with a value of 10; change the declaration of the rnd() function in line 17; and add the modulus math in line 21. Save the file to disk by using the name RANDOM4.C.

Compile and run the program. Here's a sample of the output you might see:

4	1	3	0	6	6	1	0	8	9
2	9	5	9	8	7	6	8	0	9
5	6	2	0	5	8	5	5	9	0
9	9	2	6	1	2	0	2	0	7
8	4	4	7	1	6	0	0	5	1
3	7	1	2	1	2	5	0	8	5
9	2	0	7	9	8	4	5	6	0
8	8	7	6	0	8	3	9	3	4
0	4	0	5	5	6	3	0	4	3
7	6	1	2	2	7	6	7	4	8

Everything is in the range of zero through nine, which is what the rnd(10) call does in line 14.

✔ The rnd() and seedrnd() functions become handy as you write your own C programs, specifically, games. Feel free to copy and paste these functions to other programs you may write. Remember that both require the #include <stdlib> directive, with seedrnd() also requiring #include <time.h>.

✔ Now, to generate a roll of the dice, you stick the rnd() function in your program and use the following statement:

```
dice=rnd(6)+1;                  //Roll dem bones!
```

✔ Take a peek at the program DIBBLE.C, located in Appendix D, for a silly example of using random numbers as well as the cls() and locate() functions from the preceding lesson. The program DRUNK.C, in Appendix D, also uses these functions.

✔ Using the ever-collapsing C language function ability, it's possible to rewrite the rnd() function down to only one statement:

```
return(rand()%range);
```

Refer to Lesson 5-5 for more information about how this works and why you would want to bother.

✔ The Borland compiler contains a random function that returns a random value in a specified range. For example:

```
random(7);
```

This function returns a random value in the range of zero to six. This works exactly the same as the rnd() function in RANDOM4.C.

✔ You're now only moments from writing your own Monopoly game . . . .

Lesson 5-7 Quiz

1. Why are random numbers important to your programming?

    A. They allow for an element of unpredictability (and we all know how important that is for your client-billing software).

    B. They allow us to use leftist café words like *pseudo.*

    C. Games would be impossible without them.

    D. All of the above.

2. How do you prevent the computer from generating the same random numbers over and over?

    A. You plant a random-number seed.

    B. You sow a seed to produce a random-number plant.

    C. You make the computer guess harder by threatening it with a large magnet.

    D. You use a second computer to generate new random numbers.

3. The best way to seed the random-number generator is:

    A. Use the `srand` function.

    B. Use the `srand` function with a random value you type from the keyboard.

    C. Use the `srand` function with a random value stolen from the computer's internal clock.

    D. Use the `srand` function with a random value obtained from your local druggist.

4. Which C language mathematical doojobbie do you use to find the remainder of one number divided into another?

    A. Mogul.

    B. Modus operandi.

    C. Modulus.

    D. Molasses.

5. What is the symbol for the answer to question 4?

    A. %

    B. //

    C. @

    D. |

6. Of the following situation comedies, which one has a theme song most people can sing?

    A. "All in the Family."

    B. "Gilligan's Island."

    C. "Green Acres."

    D. "The Brady Bunch."

Chapter 5 Final Exam

1. Functions in C are necessary because:

   A. They prevent the `main` function from getting too big.

   B. They remove redundancy from your programs.

   C. They just look cool.

   D. All of the above.

2. To make use of the `playAlex()` function, what would you put in your source code?

   A. `playAlex()`'s phone number.

   B. `gosub playAlex();`

   C. `playAlex();`

   D. `call playAlex();`

3. The vernacular for using a function is:

   A. To *call* a function.

   B. To *use* a function.

   C. To *invoke* a function.

   D. To *vernacal* a function.

4. When you define a function, you must:

   A. Give the function a name.

   B. Declare the function to be a specific type.

   C. Surround the function's statements in curly brackets.

   D. All of the above.

5. Why do you prototype a function?

   A. To make the compiler happy.

   B. To formally introduce the function.

   C. To avoid a slew of error messages.

   D. All of the above.

6. The first line in the goofus() function is listed next. What is the proper prototype for this function?

```
void goofus(void)
```

A. goofus();

B. void goofus(void);

C. void goofus(void)

D. int goofus(void)

7. Associate the antique computer software with its application category:

A. WordStar   Word processor

B. Reflex   Database

C. VisiCalc   Spreadsheet

D. Framework   Integrated

8. Suppose that the main function uses a variable X and that the disaster() function also uses a variable X. What will happen?

A. The FCC will notify you of a conflict of interest.

B. Nothing. The two variables, though they're named the same, are independent of each other.

C. Whatever the disaster() function does to the variable X will affect the variable X in the main function as well.

D. Core meltdown!

9. If you want to share a variable between all your functions, what type of variable do you create?

A. A shared variable.

B. An int, char, or long variable.

C. A global variable.

D. A universally galactic variable.

10. Declaring variables in any function works just the same as it does in the main function: True or false?

11. How do you send a variable or value off to a function?

A. You put it in the function's parentheses when you call the function. To wit: goofus(7);

B. You define the function to accept one or more values in its parentheses.

C. You use the variable's value inside the function.

D. All of the above.

12. The following statement appears in the function `main`:

    ```
    goofus(80);
    The goofus() function is defined as follows:
    void goofus(int silly)
    ```

    How is the value 80 used inside the `goofus()` function?

    A. It is affected by whatever statements inside the `goofus()` function manipulate that value.

    B. As the `silly` variable.

    C. The value 80 is unchanged.

    D. It's impossible to predict because, like *duh,* you haven't shown us what's inside the `goofus()` function.

13. Match the old place name with the new place name:

    A. Ceylon   Sri Lanka

    B. Formosa   Taiwan

    C. Rhodesia   Zimbabwe

    D. Dutch Guiana   Suriname

14. Keeping in mind the same conditions from question 12, what can you say about the following statement in the `main` function:

    ```
    goofus(ugh);
    ```

    A. The value of `ugh` is represented by the `silly` variable inside the `goofus()` function.

    B. The value of `ugh` is unchanged by the `goofus()` function.

    C. The function doesn't work because `goofus()` must be called with a value.

    D. None of the above (so turn to Appendix A to discover what's really going on).

15. In order for a function to return a value, what must go on?

    A. The function must be declared like a variable, as an `int`, `char`, whatever.

    B. The function uses the `return` keyword to send a variable back.

    C. The function must sign a noncompete waiver.

    D. A and B.

16. Functions can return more than one value: True or false?

17. What is wrong with the following C language statement:

```
putchar(getchar());
```

A. Nothing is wrong.

B. The getchar() function works first because it's inside the parentheses.

C. The compiler errors because the putchar function requires a character value or variable.

D. You have not shown me the putchar thing yet.

18. Which of the following is required for a DOS or BIOS function to work in C?

A. union REGS regs;

B. <include dos.h>

C. int86(0x21,&regs,&regs);

D. regs.h.al = 0x30;

19. Which three steps are required in getting a random number below six in C?

A. Write a program early; work all day; stop before 6 p.m.

B. Seed the randomizer gears; call the rand function; modulo the result with six.

C. Ask the user to type a number between zero and five.

D. Obtain a large submarine; insulate your attic; draw up invasion plans for Monaco.

20. Ginger or Mary Ann?

A. Ginger.

B. Mary Ann.

C. Neither.

D. Gilligan!

The 5th Wave

By Rich Tennant

"IT'S NOT THAT IT DOESN'T WORK AS A COMPUTER, IT JUST WORKS BETTER AS A PAPERWEIGHT."

Chapter 6
Honing Your C Skills

● ●

Lessons In This Chapter
▶ The stuff that comes first (the anything-that-follows-an-# lesson)
▶ Oh, let me tell you (or getting input from your user)
▶ Stealing from the DOS prompt (or getting command-line input)
▶ Even more `if`s
▶ More on variables
▶ Another chapter on numbers (primarily that hex thing)

Programs In This Chapter
HTEST1.C	HTEST2.C	PODEBT.C	GUESS.C
ARGUEL.C	ARGUE2.C	REPT.C	MOON.C
WISE.C	CONFUSE.C	GOOFY.C	NONEGS.C
PODS.C	DECHEX.C	INCODD.C	DECODD.C

Vocabulary Introduced In This Chapter
#include	argc	*argv[]	&&

● ●

*T*he style of this book is to toss a lot of concepts your way but explain only a few of them, saving some advanced or curious topics for later. Well, later has arrived. It's time to discuss some of the funkier aspects of C, including many things you may have witnessed thus far but have been given the excuse of "refer to Chapter 1 Zillion for a definition."

Up for discussion in this chapter is the topic of the #includes, which is something you've seen in all your source code thus far, plus some expansion on other basic C statements, more variables, and more numbers in C, which I'm saving for last because it should be just about nap time when you get to it.

Lesson 6-1: The Stuff That Comes First (the Anything-That-Follows-A-# Lesson)

In case you haven't noticed, there seems to be a lot of detritus piling up at the head of your C programs. Go on and take a gander at some of them (BOMBER.C, ZAPSCRN2.C, RANDOM4.C) or peer at the sample programs in Appendix D. The stuff piling up is possibly one of several things:

❑ The #includes

❑ The #defines

❑ Function prototypes

❑ Global variable declarations

❑ Other garbage

Some of this stuff has been explained to you. Other stuff is familiar and accepted but may still have you scratching your head. Specifically, it's the "stuff that starts with a pound sign" items, those screwy lines that don't end in semicolons, and, I admit, I haven't quite cleared up what they're about or why bother. Fear not, the time has come.

❑ This lesson is specific to the # things, primarily the #include fracas.

❑ An introduction to the #define thingy was provided in Lesson 3-4.

❑ Prototyping functions was covered in Lesson 5-1.

❑ Global variables were mulled over back in Lesson 5-2.

❑ Other items that may appear at the beginning of your C code include external and public variable declarations. These are used when you write several source code "modules," which is an advanced topic, fully covered in *C For Dummies,* Volume II.

Please don't leave me out!

So what exactly does the following mean?

```
#include <stdio.h>
```

This is an instruction for the compiler to do something, to actually *include* a special file on disk, one named STDIO.H, in with your source code. Figure 6-1 illustrates the concept for the STDIO.H file, and Figure 6-2 shows how several lines of #includes work.

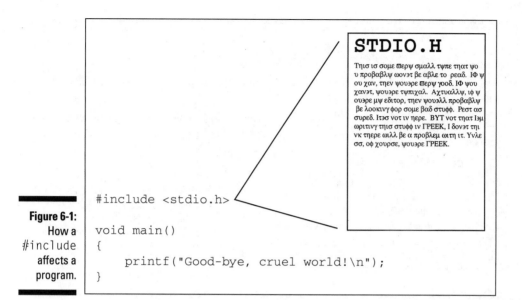

Figure 6-1:
How a
#include
affects a
program.

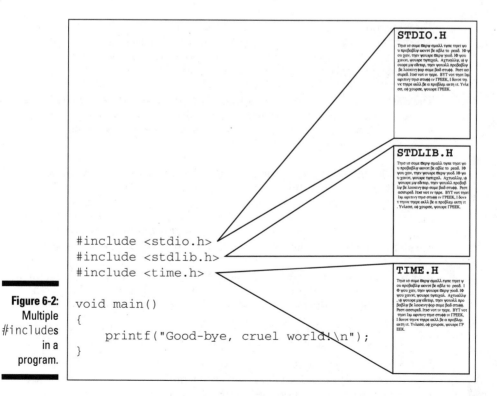

Figure 6-2:
Multiple
#includes
in a
program.

Construction #include

The #include construction is used to tell the compiler to copy lines from a *header file* into your source code. This technique is required when you're using many of the functions included with your compiler. Here is the format:

#include <*filename*>

Type #include, a space, and then a left angle bracket, which is also known as the less-than symbol. That's followed by the header *filename*, which must be in lowercase and typically (though it's not a rule) ends with a little *h*. Then comes the right angle bracket (greater than), and then you whack the Enter key.

Don't type a semicolon to end this line!

A second format is used when you want to include a header file you make yourself or when you're using a header file not found in the compiler's INCLUDE directory:

#include "*filename*"

The format is essentially the same except that the header filename is enclosed in double quotes rather than in angle brackets. The compiler looks for the header file in the same directory as your source code file.

The common #include <stdio.h> thing forces the compiler to look on disk for a file named STDIO.H and copy every line from that file into your source code. No, you don't see that done; it happens as your source code is converted to object code. (See the sidebar called "Long, tedious information you'll want to miss.")

The STDIO.H part is the name of a special file on disk, called a *header* file. This is where the little *h* comes from; H means Header. It also explains why the #include stuff comes first: The files are *headers,* like titles or headers in a word-processing document. The nearby box has the official format for #include.

Header files are necessary to help the compiler properly create your programs. Remember that the C language contains only some 33 keywords (see Table 1-1 in Lesson 1-6). Everything else — printf, getchar, etc. — is a function. Those functions are defined in the various header files you include at the beginning of your programs. Without the header files, the compiler doesn't recognize the functions and may display oodles of error messages.

✔ You'll know when to use a certain header file by looking up a function in your C language library reference. The header file is listed along with the format for the function that needs it.

✔ The STDIO.H header file is the most common one. It's the *s*tandard *i*nput/*o*utput header file, which is where they pull stdio from.

✔ Always use lowercase when you're writing out an include directive. Remember that it doesn't end in a semicolon and that the angle brackets are required around the header filename.

✔ It's possible to write your own header files. This is often necessary, especially for large programming projects. This topic is discussed in the next section, "Writing your own dot-H file."

✔ You have to specify a header file only once, even if two different functions require it. For example, the RANDOM.C suite of programs from the last chapter required the STDLIB.H header for both the rand and srand functions, yet only one #include <stdlib.h> directive is required at the beginning of the program.

✔ You probably have seen the effects of including a header file; have you ever wondered why your compiler often says "435 lines compiled" when your source code is only 20 or 30 lines long? Those extra lines come from the #include file (or files).

✔ Header files are located in a special subdirectory installed on your hard disk with your C compiler. The subdirectory is named INCLUDE, and it contains all the *.H files that came with your compiler. These are all text files, and you can look at them by using a file viewer or your editor. (But please don't change the files!)

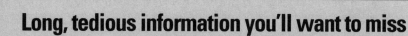

Long, tedious information you'll want to miss

Remember back in Lesson 1-2, which discussed how a text file becomes a program? Remember the section called "The compiler"? Probably not. Anyway, I lied in there. I omitted a step that was kinda superfluous at the time. Before your compiler actually compiles, it takes a quick look at your source code and runs it through a gizmo called the *preprocessor*.

The preprocessor doesn't compile anything. Instead, it scopes out your source code for any line beginning with a pound sign (#). Those lines are actually secretive instructions to the preprocessor, telling it to do something or make something happen.

The compiler recognizes several preprocessor directives. The most common directives are #include and #define. Others are used for something called "macros," which have nothing to do with macros as you know and love them in Lotus 1-2-3. The macros here tell the compiler whether to compile certain parts of your source code — sort of like "If such-and-such is true, ignore the following several lines." This is stuff you can freely ignore, unless you get really geeky with the C language.

Writing your own dot-H file

There is absolutely no need to write your own header file. Not now, not ever. Of course, if you dive deeply into C, you may one day write some multimodule monster and need your own custom header, one you'll proudly show your fellow C Masters, one they'll ponder and say, jealously and guardedly, "I wish I could do that."

To get a feel for it and because this chapter would be unduly short otherwise, create the following header file, HEAD.H, in your editor. Type the lines exactly as written, matching lowercase for lowercase and uppercase for uppercase. (Yes, you can do this by using your compiler's built-in editor.)

Name: HEAD.H

```
/* This is my wee li'l header file */

#define HAPPY 0x01
#define BELCH printf
#define SPIT {
#define SPOT }
```

Save the file to disk as HEAD.H. You have to type in the dot-H, lest your editor saves it to disk with a C, TXT, or DOC extension.

You don't compile or "run" a header file. Instead, you have to include it in a program. Such a program is listed next. Granted, this may not look at all like a C program. In fact, you may just shake your head in disgust and toss the book down right now. Please, I beg, give me a few moments before you run off all huffy to Mr. Software and buy a copy of a Turbo Pascal book.

Name: HTEST1.C

```
#include <stdio.h>
#include "head.h"

void main()
SPIT
     BELCH("This guy is happy: %c\n",HAPPY);
SPOT
```

Start over on a new slate in your editor. Type the preceding source code exactly. The second #include is what brings in your header file; note how it has HEAD.H in double quotes. That's how the compiler finds your header file instead of looking for it with the other, traditional headers. Also, don't let the SPIT, BELCH, SPOT stuff toss you. It is explained later.

Discovering the secrets of HTEST1.C

The second #include (line 2) brings into your source code the HEAD.H file you created earlier. All the instructions in that file are magically included with your source code when HTEST1.C compiles (as are the instructions from the standard I/O header file, STDIO.H).

```
#include "head.h"
```

Inside the HEAD.H header file are a few of those #define directives, which tell the compiler to substitute certain characters or C language words with happy euphemisms. (Refer to your HEAD.H file if you need to.) For example, the word SPIT was defined as equal to the left curly bracket. So SPIT is used in the program rather than the first curly bracket in line 5:

```
SPIT
```

The word BELCH was defined to be equal to the word printf, so it serves as a substitute for

that function as well in line 6, and in line 7 you see the word SPOT used instead of the final curly bracket.

So far, all the #defines have been rather silly. There is no reason to redefine C language words and functions (unless you want to goof someone up). However, the first #define in HEAD.H sets the word HAPPY equal to the value of the PC's happy-face character, 0x01. (That's a hexadecimal number whose value is 1, so I could have just put 1 there, but I thought *naaaah*.)

The following line is in the true spirit of writing your own header files:

```
BELCH("This guy is happy:
   %c\n",HAPPY);
```

Can't remember the code for the happy face? Then #define it in your own header file and use it instead, which is what is done here.

Save the file to disk and name it HTEST1.C. Compile and run. Don't be stunned if you find no errors. Believe it or not, everything should work out just fine. Here's a peek at what the output should look like:

```
This guy is happy:  ☺
```

Mr. HAPPY is happy. And you'll be happy too, after reading the Blow-by-blow sidebar that explains how it all went.

 ✔ Mostly, any header file you write yourself contains a lot of #defines. A doozy I wrote for one program, for example, listed all the #defines for strange key combinations on the keyboard. For example:

```
#define F1 0x3B00
```

This line allows me to use the characters F1 rather than have to remember (or constantly look up) the ugly hexadecimal value the computer understands as the F1 key.

✔ Just about anything in a C program can wend its way into your own, personal header files. #define statements are the most popular. Also allowed are comments, variable definitions, advanced things called *structures,* and even source code (though that's rare). Remember that because it's eventually copied into your source code, anything that normally would go there can also go into a header file.

✔ I'd like to thank my editor for allowing me to use a total of six commas in this section's third sentence.

What the defines are up to

The #define directive is another one of those things the compiler eats before it works on your source code. Using #define, you can set up some handy, clever, and memorable word equivalents to big numbers, constant values, or just about anything that appears in your C source code.

The full scope of the #define "construction" was offered back in Lesson 3-4. Since I'm on an antiredundancy campaign, I'm not going to repeat it here. I will add, however, that #define is the most popular item placed into a header file. Edit your HEAD.H file, in fact, and add the following two lines:

```
#define TRUE 1            //Something is true
#define FALSE (!TRUE)     //Something isn't
```

Save HEAD.H back to disk with these modifications.

What you've done is to create a shortcut word, TRUE, that you can use as a "true" condition. This word becomes handy as you explore some strange C language loops in Chapter 7.

The FALSE shortcut word is defined as being "not" true. The exclamation point in C means not (see Table 4-1 in Lesson 4-1). So the value of FALSE is obviously !TRUE. (It works out to be zero; no big deal.)

To make immediate use of the two new shortcut words (though this isn't the world's best example), type the source code for program HTEST2.C, as shown next.

Name: HTEST2.C

```
#include <stdio.h>
#include "head.h"

void main()
{
      if(TRUE)
```

```
                          printf("Must be true!\n");
        if(FALSE)
                          printf("Never see this message.\n");
}
```

Carefully type this source code into your editor. Save it to disk as HTEST2.C.

Compile HTEST2.C.

In Borland C, you see a bunch of warning-type error messages that are undeniably true. This is the compiler being smart again; it recognizes the certainty of the `if` keyword's "comparison" and tells you whether it *is always true* or *is always false*. It even points out that, because the second `if` is always false, its `printf` statement isn't executed. Big deal. Run the program anyway.

The output looks something like this:

```
Must be true!
```

Granted, this is a wee bit pointless at this stage. The best time for using the TRUE or FALSE shortcut words is when you create a `while` loop, which is still a while off.

- Refer to Lesson 4-1 if you need some brushing up on the `if` keyword.

- I didn't use any curly braces around the `if` keyword's statements in HTEST2.C. Because there is only one statement that belongs to each `if`, the braces are optional.

- In the C language, the value 1 is taken to be `true`, and 0 is `false`. This makes absolutely no sense now, but it will in just a few lessons.

- Some C programmers prefer to define TRUE and FALSE as follows:

```
#define FALSE 0
#define TRUE (!FALSE)
```

Whatever. This book defines TRUE as 1 and FALSE as "not true," which works out to 0. If you see the preceding `#define`s in a program, everything will still work as advertised. Just don't let it throw you.

Avoiding the topic of macros

Though there's no reason to describe what they are in detail and because I'm not crazy enough to waste time with an example, you may see even more pound-sign goobers in someone else's C program. Pick any from the following list:

- ❏ #if
- ❏ #else
- ❏ #endif
- ❏ #ifdef
- ❏ #ifndef

These are also instructions to the C compiler, designed primarily to tell the compiler whether a group of statements is to be compiled or included with the final program.

For example:

```
#if GRAPHICS
      //do graphical wonders here
#else
      //do boring text stuff here
#endif
```

Suppose that GRAPHICS is something defined earlier in the program or in a header file — #define GRAPHICS 1, for example. If so, then the compiler compiles the statements only between the #if GRAPHICS and #else lines. Otherwise, the statements between #else and #endif are compiled. The result? A potential two different programs using one source code.

Crazy! Why bother?

Actually, I've used this trick only once: I wrote a program that had two versions, one that ran on color PCs and a second that ran on monochrome systems. On the color PCs, I had statements that displayed text in color, which doesn't work on monochrome monitors. Therefore, I used the #if goober so that I needed to write only one source code file to create both versions of the program.

- ✔ There is really no need to bother with this stuff. I'm mentioning it here because it fits in the lesson title and because some C poohbah somewhere would chastise me for ignoring it.

- ✔ The #if thing is followed by a shortcut word defined elsewhere in the program with the #define construction. If it's value isn't zero, then the #if condition is true and the statements between #if and #endif are compiled. Oh, and there's an #else in there too, which serves the same purpose as the C language else word. (See Lesson 4-2 for more information about else.)

✔ You may see some of the #ifdef or #ifndef things in various header files. I have no idea what they're doing in there, but they look darn impressive.

✔ Another #-goober is #line. It's rarely used. Supposedly what it does is force the compiler to report a unique line number just in case there's an error. (Don't worry, I don't get it either.)

Lesson 6-1 Quiz

1. What is a dot-H file?

    A. A "header" file.

    B. A file containing extra instructions for the compiler.

    C. A required doogiggle for using some C language functions.

    D. All of the above.

2. What happens when you #include <stdio.h>?

    A. The compiler looks for a file named STDIO.H and laughs at it.

    B. The compiler looks for a file named STDIO.H and sticks it into your source code.

    C. The compiler looks for a file named INCLUDE and laughs at it.

    D. It's just the required first step for any C program.

3. Suppose that you're going to use the blorf function and that it requires the #include <wiggy.h> directive. But you're also using the pest function, and it too requires the WIGGY.H file. What are you going to do?

    A. Specify #include <wiggy.h> twice, once for each function.

    B. Specify #include <wiggy.h> only once.

    C. Look up the answer in Appendix A.

    D. Oh, I just won't bother with the pest function because the topic confuses me.

4. Bill wrote his own header/include file and wants to use it at the beginning of his program's source code. Which of the following lines should he use, providing that his header file is named GATES.H?

    A. #include <bill.h>

    B. #include <gates.h>

    C. #include "gates"

    D. #include "gates.h"

5. Which of the following TV program spinoff sequences is incorrect?

    A. "Cheers;" "The Tortellis;" "Frasier."

    B. "All in the Family;" "Maude;" "The Jeffersons."

    C. "The Mary Tyler Moore Show;" "Rhoda;" "Phyllis;" "Lou Grant."

    D. "Star Trek;" "Star Trek: The Next Generation;" "Deep Space 9."

Lesson 6-2: Oh, Let Me Tell You (or Getting Input from Your User)

There are lots of ways to read the user's intentions: getting input from the keyboard, reading from an external input device (like a mouse), or clairvoyance. Of these, reading the keyboard is the traditional method used in most C programs.

C has an armada of functions that can read the keyboard. So far in this book, you've been exposed to a smattering of functions, each of which is listed in Table 6-1. The only toughie of the group is scanf, though because it's very picky about what it reads, it's easy for an innocent mistake to make a user-friendly program turn stubborn as a bigot.

Don't write off scanf just yet! It does have the handy capability to read values directly into numeric variables. This is something that requires some hoops and whips with the other get-input functions.

    ✔ An introduction to the scanf function is offered in Lesson 2-2.

    ✔ Lesson 2-4 introduces the gets function.

    ✔ Lesson 3-6 deals with getch, getche, and getchar somewhat.

    ✔ You can use the getch and getche functions only in DOS programs created by using Microsoft Visual C++. If you try to use them in a QuickWin window, the compiler gags.

    ✔ You can also use your PC's BIOS keyboard interrupt, 16h, to read the keyboard at the BIOS level in C. Needless to say, this is hairy and complex, and it's mentioned only in passing in Lesson 7-5.

    ✔ There is a function called getc that sounds like it reads characters from the keyboard but that, in fact, reads characters from a file on disk. That subject is covered in *C For Dummies,* Volume II. Don't try to use getc to read characters from the keyboard!

Table 6-1   Some C Language Keyboard-Input Functions

Function	Duty
scanf	Reads formatted input, numbers, and strings
gets	Reads in a line of text ending with the Enter key
getch	Reads in a single character but does not display the character
getche	Reads in a single character and displays (echoes) the character
getchar	Reads in one character, after which you must press Enter

Using scanf *to read exciting stuff from the keyboard*

The scanf function was first touched on in Lesson 2-2. There, it was used to read in a string of text from the keyboard. The following sample line should refresh your memory somewhat:

```
scanf("%s",&name);
```

scanf works a lot like its cousin, printf. First comes a formatting string, usually a bunch of percent-things in double quotes. Then comes a comma and the variable (or variables) into which keyboard input is assigned. Not the easiest thing in the world to understand, and definitely not the prettiest to look at.

In the preceding format, scanf can (and should) be replaced quite easily by the gets function. Reading in strings of text is not scanf's forte. It does shine, however, when it needs to read in values. This it can do directly, allowing you to read the keyboard for a number and store it directly in a numeric variable. Furthermore, you can use scanf to read in several values at a time — even different types of values.

The program PODEBT.C shows how you can use scanf to read in three different types of values: a number, a single character, and a string. Type this source code into your editor and save it to disk as PODEBT.C. (The PO part means Paying Off.)

Name: PODEBT.C

```
#include <stdio.h>
#include <conio.h>
```

```
void main()
{
    int num;
    char let;
    char name[20];

    printf("Type in a number, a letter and your name:");
    scanf("%i %c %s",&num,&let,&name);

    printf("%s typed in %i and %c.\n",name,num,let);
    printf("This information will be used by the\n");
    printf("government to force you into personally\n");
    printf("paying off the national debt.\n");
    printf("Thank you,\nUncle Sam.\n");
}
```

Compile and run the program. You see the following on your screen:

```
Type in a number, a letter and your name:
```

The computer is waiting for you to type in three items. Go ahead and type a number (an integer), a character, and your name, such as:

```
57 T Dan Gookin
```

Press Enter and you see:

```
Dan typed in 57 and T.
This information will be used by the
government to force you into personally
paying off the national debt.
Thank you,
Uncle Sam.
```

Before puzzling over why your last name wasn't included in the string output, run the program again:

```
Type in a number, a letter and your name:
```

Now type each of your three answers on a line by itself; type a number, press Enter, a letter, press Enter, and then a string of text:

```
57
T
Dan Gookin
```

The output still is the same. (So I guess I'm trying to make a point about something here.) Actually, I'm trying to make several points. Here they are:

- You can specify multiple items for scanf to read from the keyboard. Each one is a %-thing, which tells scanf what to look for.

- scanf expects you to type in each of those items; you can't leave any one "blank." (So if you run the program again, try to press Enter for one of the items, and scanf waits until you type what it wants.)

- You can separate each of the items by putting a space between them, pressing the Tab key, or pressing the Enter key.

- Because there is a space between your first and last names, scanf reads in only your first name; your last name is an "extra item" scanf doesn't know what to do with.

- Honestly, if you need to read in three values in your C programs, my advice is to write three separate input routines. Use scanf if you want, but be informative and really let users know what they have to type rather than assume that they can abide by scanf's quirkiness.

- scanf excels in reading in specific values:

```
scanf("%u",&value);
```

This statement allows you to type in an unsigned integer value, which is stored in the value variable.

- You can use additional formatting doojobbies when you're reading in values with scanf. I wouldn't mess with 'em, but gander at the following:

```
scanf("%2s",&state);
```

This statement reads in a string to be stored in the variable, state. The format %2s means that scanf stores the first two characters of whatever was typed in that variable.

- The %-things are officially called *conversion characters*. A whole table of them appears in Lesson 2-5, in Table 2-2.

- Don't forget the ampersand in front of the variables used in a scanf statement! Without it, the values typed in aren't properly stored in the variables.

- Don't put anything other than %-deals in scanf's formatting string. Any text in there will certainly goof you up as well as potentially foul up your user and the program's input.

The horrid guessing-game example

I promised that I wouldn't do this . . . .

Oh, well. I lied. Next is the source code for GUESS.C, a C language guessing game that uses the scanf function to read in a guess from the keyboard. It also borrows the random-number functions from Lesson 5-7 and shows off a bunch of other concepts this book has introduced.

Name: GUESS.C

```
#include <stdio.h>
#include <stdlib.h>
#include <time.h>

#define RANGE 100               //set guessing range
#define TRIES 6                 //give 'em six tries to guess

int rnd(int range);
void seedrnd(void);

void main()
{
    int guessme,guess,t;

    seedrnd();                  //seed the randomizer
    guessme=rnd(RANGE)+1;       //get the number to guess

    printf("GUESS!?!\nGuess the random number.\n");
    printf("I'm thinking of a number \
between 1 and %i.\n",RANGE);
    printf("Can you guess it in %i tries?\n",TRIES);

    for(t=1;t<=TRIES;t++)       //give them TRIES attempts
    {
        printf("Guess #%i:",t);
        scanf("%i",&guess);  //get their guess

        if(guess==guessme)   //they guess correctly
        {
            printf("You got it!\n");
            break;       //stop here
```

```
            }
        else if(guess<guessme) //guess is too low
                printf("Too low!\n");
        else                    //guess is too high
                printf("Too high!\n");
    }                           //this ends the for loop

    printf("The answer was %i.\n",guessme);
}

/*
Random number generator function. Coughs up a random number
in the range of zero to "range." Refer to Lesson 5-7.
*/

int rnd(int range)
{
    int r;

    r=rand()%range;                 //spit up random num.
    return(r);
}

/*
Random number seeding program. This makes the
number "more" random.
*/

void seedrnd(void)
{
    srand((unsigned)time(NULL));
}
```

Start over with a new slate in your editor and then type in that massive source
code just shown. You can save time by copying and pasting the `rnd()` and
`seedrnd()` functions from the RANDOM4.C program that may already be on
your disk drive.

Double-check everything. It's when you get to programs of this size (64 lines) that you forget silly little things. Missing semicolons are a problem. Not matching up curly brackets, parentheses, and double quotes can be painful as well.

When you're ready, save the source code to disk as GUESS.C.

Compile the program. Fix any errors you may have. Remember that the line number the compiler proclaims may be one notch up or back from where the actual error occurred.

Run the program. Here's kind of how it goes:

```
GUESS!?!
Guess the random number.
I'm thinking of a number between 1 and 100.
Can you guess it in 6 tries?
Guess #1: 86
You got it!
The answer was 86.
```

(Well, maybe you won't guess that lucky.)

- ✔ Refer to the Blow-by-blow box nearby for some pointers on the GUESS.C program.

- ✔ Because this program uses `scanf`, there is no need to convert keyboard input into an integer with the `atoi` function, which is what you've been doing when reading the keyboard with the `gets` function.

- ✔ Of course, the drawback to `scanf` is that it's funky: It doesn't accept just the Enter key to be pressed. `scanf` sits around and waits until a value is typed.

- ✔ You can easily change the range of numbers by editing line 5 and defining a new value for the RANGE. Likewise, you can change the number of guesses users have by changing line 6's value for TRIES.

- ✔ If you're good, you should be able to guess any number between 1 and 100 in seven guesses or less. This is why the number of TRIES is initially set to six.

Some things to note when examining GUESS.C

Three #includes are required to meet the demands of the randomizing functions (see Lesson 5-7). The two #defines set up the RANGE for guessing numbers and the number of TRIES allowed. You can easily alter these two values by modifying either line 5 or line 6.

In line 16, the value of the random number is obtained by calling the rnd() function with RANGE(100). This actually returns a random number between 0 and 99, so the statement adds 1 to the value and places the result in the guessme integer variable:

```
guessme=rnd(RANGE)+1;
    //get the number to guess
```

The printf statement in line 19 is split between two lines by using the backslash character:

```
    printf("I'm thinking of a
        number \
between 1 and %i.\n",RANGE);
```

Remember to type a space before that character. Otherwise, when the program runs, the words number and between don't have a space between them. (And don't indent the line either, or there will be a tab between the words.)

There is nothing odd about line 25:

```
printf("Guess #%i:",t);
```

The %i in there is replaced by the value of the t variable. The other characters (the # and the colon) look meaningful, but they're merely part of the formatted output.

To see whether the proper number was entered, line 25's if comparison checks the value of guessme and guess. If they're equal, then You got it! is displayed, and the break; statement breaks out of the for loop. Remember that it takes two equal signs when comparing values.

The else if statement simply checks to see whether the guess was less than the random number and displays an appropriate message. The final else handles the remaining possibility, that the guess was too high. It also displays an appropriate message.

The final printf statement (line 39) tells the user what the random number was:

```
printf("The answer was
    %i.\n",guessme);
```

This is nice in case users didn't guess, so that they know that the computer isn't jerking them around. It also confirms a correct guess.

Lesson 6-2 Quiz

1. The biggest mistake in the history of the scanf function is:

    A. Using it in the first place.

    B. Forgetting the darned ampersand (&) before the variable name.

    C. Goofing up the formatting, which goofs up the input.

    D. Possibly all of the above.

2. The scanf function can be used to read in more than one value at a time. What separates each value?

   A. A fence.

   B. A thin sheet of Mylar.

   C. The famous C language "white space": spaces, tabs, and the Enter key.

   D. Commas.

3. Define gas:

   A. Neither a liquid nor a solid.

   B. A generic term for a variety of petroleum products.

   C. A generic term for the aftereffects of fast food.

   D. A polite term for Aunt Shirley's alternative means of propulsion.

4. If you wanted to use the scanf function to read in a two-digit integer value, which of the following statements would you use?

   A. scanf("%2",i);

   B. scanf("%2i");

   C. scanf("%",2i);

   D. scanf("%2i",i);

Don't forget to take a break before you begin a new lesson. You can't expect to cram all this stuff into your head at one time.

Lesson 6-3: Stealing from the DOS Prompt (or Getting Command-Line Input)

You may have noticed in your DOS travels that quite a few programs allow you to type stuff after the program name. Even DOS commands pull off this trick. You type certain *options* or *parameters* (or if you can't decide which they are, call them *optional parameters*), and the program or DOS command does something exactly the way you want.

Well, just for the sake of argument, you should call the chunks and chunklettes of text after a program name *arguments*. This isn't my idea. No, it's the way the C language refers to them. They're arguments, or args. Argh! That's what Charlie Brown says when Lucy pulls up the football he's about to kick. You'll know the feeling soon enough.

✔ The following DOS command has one argument:

```
FORMAT A:
```

The command is FORMAT, which is the name of a program on disk. Then comes a space and the first (and only) argument, which is A:. That tells the FORMAT command which disk drive contains a disk suitable for formatting.

✔ This is a hellish UNIX command:

```
grep -i "arg" *.c
```

The GREP command is used to search for text in files — which comes in handy and makes you ponder why they call it grep and not something useful, like findthis or searcher. Here, GREP has three arguments: -i, "arg", and *.c.

✔ Arguments are separated by "white space." That means space characters and tabs (though tabs are rare at the DOS prompt).

✔ The UNIX grep command actually does stand for something. It's *global regular expression print*. Figure that one out on your own time.

No arguments about it — the main *function has arguments*

The main function is a lot like other functions you may create in C. It's a specific type of function and, yes, it can swallow arguments just like the best of them can. Indeed, the full-on, hard-core format — the long and detailed way to declare the main function — is as follows:

```
void main(int argc, char *argv[])
```

Now, perhaps, you're glad that you haven't been typing all that information so far. Indeed, it's optional. You can get by with only the following:

```
void main()
```

If you want to see what users typed at the DOS prompt, however, you're going to need a method to access that text. The method is through two variables that are passed off to the main function of every C program you write:

❑ argc, an integer variable

❑ *argv[], a character variable thing

The value of `argc` is equal to the number of items you typed at the DOS prompt. You can think of `argc` as the *arg*ument *c*ount. The program's name is the first argument; anything you type after it becomes argument 2, 3, 4, and on up. `argc` holds the value of the total number of items typed. Figure 6-3 boldly illustrates this concept.

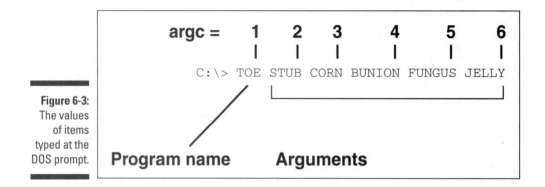

Figure 6-3:
The values
of items
typed at the
DOS prompt.

The `*argv[]` thing is a specific type of character variable. It actually defines a bunch of strings of text or a group of words, as opposed to a single character or one string of text. That's sort of how the asterisk and the empty square brackets fit in there.

My advice is not to dwell on the `*argv[]` thing right this moment. Instead, work through this lesson and agree wholeheartedly with how it's used. Then discover the ugly truth about it in the next volume of this book.

✔ And the ugly truth about the `*argv[]` thing is . . . that it's an *array* of strings. Bold, new concept, that. *C For Dummies*, Volume II actually discusses this stuff in detail.

✔ The program name will always be the first argument, so the value of `argc` will always be at least 1 in any program. The way to test for any "real" arguments is to see whether the value of `argc` is greater than 1. In C, that's done with the following:

```
if(argc>1)
```

✔ I pronounce them "arg-see" and "arg-vee." These could be two dingbat characters from a Dr. Seuss *Cat in the Hat* book.

✔ You don't have to specify the full declaration for the `main` function if you don't plan to examine the command-line arguments. But if you need to, the complete format, as shown in this section, is required.

✔ Chapter 5 was devoted to the topic of creating functions in C. Refer to Lesson 5-4 for information on declaring a function to be a specific type; Lesson 5-4 discusses how options (arguments) are passed to functions.

So, did they type anything?

To see whether any optional parameters were typed after your program's name at the DOS prompt, you need to test the value of the argc variable. When it's greater than 1, optional parameters loom.

The following source code is for the program ARGUE1.C. It tests to see whether anything was typed after the program name, and, if so, a nasty error message is displayed.

Name: ARGUE1.C

```
#include <stdio.h>

void main(int argc,char *argv[])
{
    if(argc>1)                  //if true, they typed something
    {
        printf("ERROR! This program is not designed\n");
        printf("to have anything typed after it's name!\n");
    }
    else
        printf("Pleased to be of service!\n");
}
```

Type the source code for ARGUE1.C into your editor. Watch your typing for the declaration of the main function; it gets a little slick and weavy in there. Save the file to disk as ARGUE1.C.

Compile the program and fix any errors if you need to.

Don't run the program from your integrated environment! Why? Because you can't type any arguments in there. (Like, *duh!*) Instead, quit your C compiler integrated environment program area and snuggle up to the DOS prompt.

Run the program. Type ARGUE1 first by itself, and then type it again, but follow it with a few bits of text:

```
C:\PROGRAMS> ARGUE1 THIS IS A TEST
ERROR! This program is not designed
to have anything typed after its name!
```

- ✔ Obviously this is a job for running your compiler at the DOS prompt. Refer to the instructions offered in Lesson 1-3 for running MSVC at the DOS prompt. Better stick there for this entire lesson.

- ✔ It doesn't matter how many things you type or what you type. Anything (other than a space or a tab) after the program name increases the value of the `argc` variable and causes the program to "error."

- ✔ Boy, are you Borland people in luck. There is an option under the Run menu called — believe it or not — Arguments. If you choose that item, you see a box where you can manually type any command-line options, just as though you were typing them after the program name at the DOS prompt. Neat-o mosquito.

How many things did they type?

The value of the `argc` variable is equal to the number of items typed after the program name at the DOS prompt. The following program, ARGUE2.C, displays that value. (I know, this is rather lame — even for this book. But the program builds into something better in the next section.)

Name: ARGUE2.C

```
#include <stdio.h>

void main(int argc,char *argv[])
{
    printf("argc=%i\n",argc);
}
```

Deftly type the preceding source code into your editor. It's real cinchy. You're just taking the value of the `argc` variable and displaying it in a handy `printf` statement. Nothing big. Save the file to disk as ARGUE2.C.

Compile and run the program. You see something like the following displayed:

```
argc=3
```

The number reflects how many items were typed at the DOS prompt. If you saw only `argc=1`, type some bogus options after ARGUE2 at the DOS prompt. Run the program again and you'll see the proper count.

✔ You may get a warning error here — something about argv not being used. Fine. Ignore it. The compiler is just pointing out that a variable was declared (and space set aside for it), but nothing was done with it. Thank the compiler, but move right along.

✔ The program name is the first argument. Anything typed after that is argument 2, 3, 4, and on up. Refer back to Figure 6-3 if you need to.

Displaying each argument

Counting the arguments is nothing. Displaying them, or at least having a way that your program can see what they are, is way more important. That's done with the *argv[] variable thing, which is a little bizarre and may confuse you, so I'll spend a few paragraphs explaining it in a brief and friendly manner.

What the char *argv[] declaration does is to define an array of text characters or strings. Another way to think of it is as a series of words, each of which is separate from the others. Each of the items typed at the DOS prompt is its own "word," and each word has its own *argv[] variable.

Table 6-2 describes the various values for the argc and *argv[] variables for the command typed in Figure 6-3. The first item is the program name. If that were the only item typed, argc would equal 1. The string variable argv[0] is equal to the program name; if your program wanted to know that, it would use argv[0] just as it would use any other string variable.

Table 6-2	**How** *argv[ ] **Relates to Items Typed at the DOS Prompt**		
Argument	*argc=*	**argv[ ]*	*string, %s*
Program name	1	argv[0]	TOE.EXE
First	2	argv[1]	STUB
Second	3	argv[2]	CORN
Third	4	argv[3]	BUNION
Fourth	5	argv[4]	FUNGUS
Fifth	6	argv[5]	JELLY

Each of the items typed at the DOS prompt has its own argv[] string variable. After the program name, the next item is represented by the argv[1] string variable, and so on for each additional item. Here are a few points to ponder:

✔ Unlike declaring a string variable, with `*argv[]` the number in the square brackets refers to the item number for each argument.

✔ You use `argv[0]` or any of the `argv[whatever]` variables just like you use any other string variable. Each of them represents a complete word typed at the DOS prompt — and argument.

✔ Do not use the asterisk when you're referring to the `argv[whatever]` variables in your source code.

✔ What you're messing with here is technically an array of strings. This brings up a messy issue in C called *pointers,* one I'll save for a lengthy discussion in Volume II of this book.

And now, for the program . . . .

The next program is an addition to the ARGUE2.C program you should already have in your editor on the screen in front of you. This time, a few more goodies have been added, primarily so that you can see each of the items typed at the DOS prompt.

Name: ARGUE2.C

```
#include <stdio.h>

void main(int argc,char *argv[])
{
        int x;

        printf("argc=%i\n",argc);
        for(x=0;x<argc;x++)
                        printf("argv[%i] = %s\n",x,argv[x]);
}
```

Make the necessary modifications to turn the old ARGUE2.C program in your editor into the source code you see here. The only additions are the declaration of the integer variable x and the `for` loop. Save the file to disk; you can use your editor's Save command because the name doesn't change.

Compile and run the program. It works best if you run it at the DOS prompt, where you can type some optional parameters. Your output looks something like this:

```
C:\PROJECTS> ARGUE2 HERE THERE
argc=3
argv[0] = C:\PROJECTS\ARGUE2.EXE
argv[1] = HERE
argv[2] = THERE
```

The `printf` statement displays the contents of each of the `argv[]` string variables. You might want to take another look at Table 6-2 to see how it all works out.

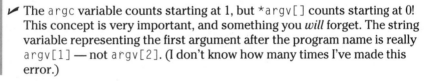

- ✓ Notice how each argument is assigned to its own `argv[]` thing. This is really much better than taking the whole command line and swallowing it as one long string. By splitting it up into words, your program can examine each word and do something with it. Otherwise, your program would have to fish each word out of a longer string, which is very tough.

- ✓ The next two sections in this chapter demonstrate programs that actually do something with the arguments.

- ✓ Don't let the concept of `argv[]` befuddle you. Just accept it for now. It is fully explained in *C For Dummies*, Volume II.

- ✓ The asterisk is not necessary when you're using `argv[]` to display a string. However, you do need the asterisk when you're declaring it in the `main` function.

- ✓ The `argc` variable counts starting at 1, but `*argv[]` counts starting at 0! This concept is very important, and something you *will* forget. The string variable representing the first argument after the program name is really `argv[1]` — not `argv[2]`. (I don't know how many times I've made this error.)

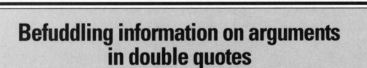

Befuddling information on arguments in double quotes

Occasionally the user may do something dumb, like enclose an argument in double quotes. No need to sound the claxons; there's a reason for this. Primarily, when a single argument is more than one word long, you want to hug it with something that says "these guys belong together." Hence, the double quotes create one argument where the silly computer would think that there were many more. Simple story. Easy proof: Run the ARGUE2.C program again, and type the following line at the DOS prompt:

```
ARGUE2 "this is cool" this is neat
```

The program proclaims that there are five arguments, even though you see seven bits of text. The `argv[1]` argument is `this is cool` — all one argument.

A bizarre aside is that the double quotes aren't saved as part of the argument. This may seem moot right now, but I once wrote a program where I *needed* the double quotes. Solution? I added them manually with a `printf` statement and the `\"` escape sequence. No problem. (Try that with ARGUE2 to see how it works.)

Maybe I should repeat myself . . . .

The following source code is for a program that repeats a single character a specific number of times. You type the character in addition to the number of times it repeats. For example:

```
rept * 10
```

This command repeats 10 asterisks at the DOS prompt. Maybe it's not entirely useful, but it shows you how information can be read from the DOS prompt and used in an interesting way. Also, the program shows you how to test to see whether enough items were typed and to display an ugly error message when things aren't right.

Name: REPT.C

```c
#include <stdio.h>
#include <stdlib.h>

void main(int argc,char *argv[])
{
    int x,r;
    char c;

    if(argc<2)                  //no options typed
    {
            printf("This program requires two options:\n");
            printf("REPT c r\n");
            printf("C is the character to repeat and R is\n");
            printf("the number of times to repeat it.\n");
            exit(0);            //quit the program right here
    }
/*
They typed in both options. argv[1] contains the character
to repeat, and argv[2] is the number of times to repeat it
*/
    c=argv[1][0];               //get the character
    r=atoi(argv[2]);            //get the repeat count

    for(x=0;x<r;x++)
            putchar(c); //display the character
}
```

Type the source code for the preceding program into your editor. It's not as bad as it looks; there are a lot of printf statements up front plus some comments telling you what goes on. Save the source code to disk as REPT.C.

Compile REPT.C. Fix any errors that may occur. With all those printfs in there, you'll probably forget a double quote, a parenthesis, or maybe a semicolon. Also count up the square brackets in the last few statements.

Exit to DOS and run the program. First, try it without any options:

```
C:\PROJECTS> REPT
This program requires two options:
REPT c r
C is the character to repeat and R is
the number of times to repeat it.
```

So far, so good. The program noticed that nothing was typed and displayed the informative error message. Now try it with only one option:

```
C:\PROJECTS> REPT *
```

Press Enter and the same error message is displayed. Excellent. The program is behaving exactly as expected and soon the world will be mine. Mine! *All mine! Bwaaa-ha-ha-ha* . . . .

A-hem. Try typing the following command:

```
C:\PROJECTS> REPT * 10
```

Press Enter and you see 10 asterisks displayed. Wonderful.

- ✔ Though this program checks to see whether they typed enough options (in line 9), it doesn't check to see whether they typed the proper options. Try reversing them to see what happens. (No, the computer doesn't explode, but the program doesn't behave either.)

- ✔ Line 15 contains the exit command, which you haven't seen yet. It allows you to quit a program early on in the main function, similar to the way you use return to leave a function early. (This command is formally discussed in this book's second volume.)

- ✔ Line 21 requires some explaining:

```
c=argv[1][0];                          //get the character
```

The c is a character variable, but `argv[1]` is a string — a bunch of characters marching in a row. You cannot assign a full string to a character variable. So instead the preceding statement fishes out the first *character* of the string `argv[1]`. That's done with the `argv[1][0]` thing. Essentially, that means "the first character of the string," because zero means "first" when it comes to strings in C.

✔ The repeat value is obtained in line 22 by using the `atoi` function. This is just a straight string-to-integer conversion, though the string is held in the `argv[2]` variable.

✔ The `for` loop repeats the character *c* for *r* number of times. Refer to Lesson 4-5 for more information about the `for` keyword.

✔ The single character is displayed on the screen by using the `putchar` function in line 25. You haven't seen this function yet (and that's twice for me to do that in one program); it's formally introduced in *C For Dummies*, Volume II.

Your weight-on-the-moon program

You may be a rotund mass of jiggling belly jelly here on the earth, but on the moon you weigh only one-sixth as much. Forget Susan Powter! Take the next rocket ship to Luna and lose an amazing five-sixths of your bulk! And to get a preview, you can try the MOON program, source code listed next.

Name: MOON.C

```
/*
MOON.C
A program to see how much you'd weigh on the moon.
*/

#include <stdio.h>
#include <stdlib.h>

void main(int argc,char *argv[])
{
    int weight;

    if(argc<2)                              //no options typed
    {
        printf("This program requires you to type your\n");
```

```
            printf("weight after MOON, as in:\n");
            printf("MOON 175\n");
            exit(0);        //quit the program right here
    }
/*
argv[1] contains the user's weight
*/
    weight=atoi(argv[1]);    //get their weight
    weight/=6;               //divide weight by 6

    printf("On the moon, you would weigh %i pounds.\n",weight);
}
```

Type the source code for MOON.C into your editor. You can use the source code for REPT.C as a base because both programs contain similar parts. But save the end result to disk as MOON.C.

Compile the program. Check for any errors. Then exit out to the DOS prompt to run the program. Type a value after MOON, as in:

```
MOON 125
```

Press Enter and you see:

```
On the moon, you would weigh 20 pounds.
```

Go head! Enjoy that thick, creamy shake! You just worked off 105 pounds!

- ✔ This program uses a comment as an introduction. As your programs grow more sophisticated (and useful), you should comment them in this manner — but also include the date you first worked on the program, plus any other useful information that may remind you of something later.

- ✔ Refer to Lesson 4-8 for more information about the `weight/=6;` statement. This statement actually translates into `weight=weight/6;`.

- ✔ Although you may weigh only one-sixth as much on the moon, you still have all your mass. That means that, if you float into a wall, you still have your full earth bulk to deal with on impact.

Making a moon float

Because the MOON.C program uses only integers, the result you see is accurate only to the nearest pound. Suppose that you weigh 125 pounds. On the moon, you would weigh one-sixth of that amount, which is 20.83 pounds, or nearly 21 pounds. Yet the MOON program calculates it out to only 20 pounds. (Integers round *down* in C.)

To solve the problem, you can make the MOON.C program work in floating-point numbers and then display the result to the nearest tenth of a pound. You should make two modifications.

First change line 11 to declare the weight variable as a float:

```
float weight;
```

Then change line 23 so that the atof function is used:

```
weight=atof(argv[1]);
    //get their weight
```

The atof function in there converts a string into a floating-point number. (This also allows the user to type fractions, though people who weigh 150.5 pounds typically say that they weigh only 150.)

Finally, change line 26 so that the printf statement uses the %f placeholder rather than %i to display a floating-point number. You can also specify it as %.1f so that the answer prints out to one decimal place:

```
printf("On the moon, you would
    weigh %.1f pounds.\n",weight);
```

Save the changes to disk and recompile. You then have a more accurate moon-weight program. Sell it to NASA!

Lesson 6-3 Quiz

For the first three questions in this quiz. please refer to the following command line:

```
C:\PROJECTS> POP /ICE /FIZZ "ROOT BEER"
```

1. What would be the value of the argc variable for the preceding command line?

2. Please fill in the blanks for the values of the following various argv[] variables:

   A. argv[0] = _____

   B. argv[1] = _____

   C. argv[2] = _____

   D. argv[3] = _____

   E. argv[4] = _____

3. Which of the following statements tests to see whether there are any optional parameter things typed at the DOS prompt?

   A. `if(argc>0)`

   B. `if(argc<1)`

   C. `if(argc>1)`

   D. `if(argc>=1)`

4. What is the difference between a corn and a bunion?

   A. You can't eat a bunion.

   B. Bunions happen on only the first joint of the big toe; corns can happen on any toe.

   C. Just the opposite of answer B.

   D. "Corn" is a slang term for a bunion.

Lesson 6-4: Even More `if`s

No word takes the blame in the human language like `if`. Of the if-a's, woulda's, and shoulda's in the world, if-a is the worst: If-a only the boss wouldn't have been eavesdropping . . . ."; "If-a I had only played my lottery numbers last week . . . ."; "If-a I'd only bought Microsoft stock back in '86 . . . ." And so on. If. If. If.

Lesson 4-1 introduced the mighty `if` command in the C language. It's what helps your programs make decisions and evaluate things. You set up `if` by presenting it with a condition. If the condition is true, the statements belonging to the `if` are executed; otherwise, they're skipped:

```
if(iq<120)
```

Here, if the value of the `iq` variable is less than 120, the statements belonging to the `if` are executed. When `iq`'s value is 120 or higher, the statements are skipped.

Alas, everything in life just isn't that clean-cut. Usually, there's more than one condition that must be evaluated when you pull an if-a. For example:

```
If I would have been home when the meteor hit my house, I'd be
             dead now.
```

To put this phrase into C-language-spiel, it might look something like this:

```
If(me_home==TRUE && meteor_house==TRUE)
{
    dead();
}
```

This is an example of a *logical* comparison. The && symbol stands for a *logical and*: It means that both conditions must be true for the entire if comparison to be true. Both the me_home and meteor_house variables must be equal to the value of TRUE for the dead() function to execute.

- ✔ As usual, please don't reread the preceding paragraph to attempt to get a grip on this situation. Logical comparisons are the subject of this lesson, and it is thoroughly hashed out over the next few pages. For now, just agree and keep reading.
- ✔ The symbol for the logical and comparison is &&, two ampersands (see Table 6-3).
- ✔ Both me_home and meteor_house are integer variables. Their values are set according to other statements and functions in the program.
- ✔ TRUE is defined equal to 1, maybe with the following declaration at the beginning of the program:

```
#define TRUE 1
```

- ✔ Also refer to Lesson 6-1 for more information about defining TRUE and FALSE values in a program.

Using the if *command to evaluate multiple conditions (AND and/or OR)*

To check out more than one condition with the if command, you use the so-called logical operators. Of course, the bitter truth is that the logical operators are actually an ugly, twisted root of the tree of mathematics. Fortunately, they're also employed (and logically so) in our everyday speech, as was demonstrated at the beginning of this lesson.

Consider the example of the meteor slamming into your house (which probably isn't covered by your homeowner's policy, by the way). Table 6-3 illustrates how the logical AND doowacky works in an if comparison.

Table 6-3	Effects of the && (AND) Logical Operator		
me_home	*Logical Operator*	*meteor_house*	*dead()?*
TRUE	&&	TRUE	YES
TRUE	&&	FALSE	NO
FALSE	&&	TRUE	NO
FALSE	&&	FALSE	NO

This all makes total sense if you sound it out:

❐ If I'm at home (TRUE) and (&&) a meteor hits my mouse (TRUE), then I'll be dead (YES).

❐ If I'm at home (TRUE) and (&&) a meteor does not hit my house (FALSE), then I won't be dead (NO).

❐ If I'm not at home (FALSE) and (&&) a meteor hits my mouse (TRUE), then I won't be dead (NO).

❐ If I'm not at home (FALSE) and (&&) a meteor does not hit my house (FALSE), then I won't be dead (NO).

Of course, in the C language, it would look more like this:

```
if(c=='p' && a=1)
```

If the value of the c variable is equal to the letter 'p' and if the value of the a variable is 1, then the comparison works out and the statements belonging to the if command are executed. But if either one doesn't work out or they both don't work out, the overall condition is false and the statements don't execute. This is what's known as a logical AND comparison, which is represented in the C language by two ampersands: &&.

Another comparison is the logical OR. Consider the following statement:

```
If I win the lotto or my rich uncle wills me a million dollars,
          I'll be rich.
```

Here is the bogus C language comparison:

```
if(win_lotto || inherit_money)
{
    rich();
}
```

The operator symbol for the logical OR condition is | |. That's two vertical bars, or *pipes,* which are on the backslash key on your keyboard. (The pipe symbol is Shift+\.)

Table 6-4 shows how the OR comparison works out. Unlike the logical AND condition, an OR comparison figures out to be true when any one of the things compared is true. This is the essence of the logical OR operation, and it would please Mr. Spock to no end.

Table 6-4	Effects of the && (OR) Logical Operator		
win_lotto	*Logical Operator*	*inherit_money*	*rich()?*
TRUE	||	TRUE	YES
TRUE	||	FALSE	YES
FALSE	||	TRUE	YES
FALSE	||	FALSE	NO

Here is the verbalization of the logical OR comparisons:

❒ If I win the lotto (TRUE) or (| |) I inherit money (TRUE), then I'll be rich (YES).

❒ If I win the lotto (TRUE) or (| |) I don't inherit money (FALSE), then I'll still be rich (YES).

❒ If I don't win the lotto (FALSE) or (| |) I inherit money (TRUE), then I'll be rich (YES).

❒ But if I don't win the lotto (FALSE) or (| |) I don't inherit money (FALSE), then I won't be rich (NO).

✔ It loses something in the English translation, but you can still see how it works out.

✔ The symbol for the logical AND operation is &&.

✔ The symbol for the logical OR operation is | |.

✔ Yes, there are two of each: && and | |. The single & and the single | mean something else in the C language. This would be easy to remember, if you recall that most of the other comparisons in an if statement are pairs as well: l==, l!=, l<=, and l>=.

✔ In actual C programs, the compiler tests each comparison first before doing any logical stuff. The comparison *evaluates* to TRUE or FALSE. For example:

```
if(c=='p' && a=1)
```

If the variable c holds the letter 'p', then that comparison is TRUE; any other letter and it's FALSE. Same with variable a: If it's equal to 1, it's TRUE; otherwise, it's FALSE. Only then does the compiler compare the two TRUE or FALSE conditions and see whether the if comparison passes the test.

✔ When comparing two conditions with && (AND), the if statement is true only if both conditions are true.

✔ When comparing two conditions with || (OR), the if statement is true if either one of the conditions is true.

Who is wiser: Melvin or Poindexter?

To demonstrate the wisdom of the logical if comparisons, I present the following program. It allows you to pick who is wiser, a guy named Melvin or someone named Poindexter. You'll notice that the program actually lacks any logical comparisons. That's coming in a later version.

Name: WISE.C

```
/*
WISE.C - a series of programs to test logical
comparisons: && = AND, || = OR
*/

#include <stdio.h>
#include <conio.h>

#define WISE 1                          //Wise is TRUE
#define SILLY !(WISE)                   //Silly is FALSE

void main()
{
    char c;
    int Poindexter,Melvin;

    printf("Who is wise, Poindexter or Melvin?\n");
    printf("Type P or M:");
    c=getch();                          //get input
    if(c=='p')                          //they typed P
```

```
        {
                    printf("P\n");      //display their input
                    Poindexter=WISE;    //Make 'em wise or
                    Melvin=SILLY;       //silly
        }
    else
        {
                    printf("M\n");      //display input
                    Poindexter=SILLY;
                    Melvin=WISE;
        }

//These comparisons display the results

    if(Poindexter==WISE)
                printf("Poindexter is wise.\n");
    if(Melvin==SILLY)
                printf("Melvin is silly.\n");
    if(Poindexter==SILLY)
                printf("Poindexter is silly.\n");
    if(Melvin==WISE)
                printf("Melvin is wise.\n");
}
```

Carefully type the source code for WISE.C. There are a few if comparisons in there, but nothing logical as of yet. Save it to disk as WISE.C.

Compile the program. Fix any errors or typos you may have included. Then run it. Here is a sample of the output:

```
Who is wise, Poindexter or Melvin?
Type P or M:
```

Make a judgment call here. I'd say Melvin, so I type M. An M appears on the screen and then the following:

```
Poindexter is silly.
Melvin is wise.
```

That's exactly what I thought.

✔ Try running the program again, but type P to make Poindexter the wise guy.

✔ Wisdom and foolishness are defined in this program as follows:

```
#define WISE 1              //Wise is TRUE
#define SILLY !(WISE)       //Silly is FALSE
```

This is the same way TRUE and FALSE were defined in Lesson 6-1. WISE equals 1 in the first definition, and then SILLY equals "not" WISE. That works out to 0, but still — logically speaking — WISE and SILLY are defined as opposites and can be used in the program like TRUE or FALSE conditions.

✔ This program gets either-or input from the user with the following prompt:

```
Type P or M:
```

This could be "Type Y or N" for yes or no or any other either-or type of prompt. It's handled in the program by checking for only one of the keys, if(c=='p') in line 20. Notice two things: First, users don't have to type an M; any character other than 'p' is assumed to mean M. In real life, if you really want to narrow down the choices, you can do so (this subject is covered in Lesson 7-3). Second, the character typed is displayed by a print function (line 22 or 28). This way, it looks to the user as though he pressed the right character no matter what.

✔ I have nothing against people named Melvin or Poindexter. If you'd rather, enter your own pet names for the two gentlemen.

To P or not to P

One big problem with the WISE.C program is that it only checks to see whether you typed a little *p*. Line 20 compares the value of the c character variable only with little *p*. If you run the program again and type a big *P*, it stubbornly assumes that you typed an M for Melvin. This is wrong, but it can be corrected.

With WISE.C still in your editor, change line 20 to read as follows:

```
if(c=='p' || c=='P')
```

Aha! Logic hits the if statement. The preceding comparison says that either a little *p* or a big *P* will match the if condition. (See Table 6-4 to learn how || (OR) works out.)

Save the program back to disk and run it again. Try typing a big *P* or a little *p*. Either way, you'll pick Poindexter as the wise one.

Tricks of the C Masters you don't have to know

The subject of this lesson is logical comparisons, AND and OR. Or is that AND or OR? Anyway, there is another way C programmers use to see whether either a big *P* or little *p* was typed. That's to employ the `toupper` function. What it does is take a letter and make it uppercase. So no matter what a user types, the `toupper` function makes it big.

To use the `toupper` function, modify line 19 in the program to read as follows:

```
c=toupper(getch());
```

This is one of those confounded compound statements I warned you about back in Lesson 5-5; remember that they work from the inside out:

First, `getch()` reads a character from the keyboard. That's passed to the `toupper()` function, which converts said character to uppercase. Then the character is saved in the C variable.

You also have to include the CTYPE.H header file, so add the following line toward the beginning of your source code:

```
#include <ctype.h>
```

Now you can use the following `if` comparison without fear of missing the little *p:*

```
if(c=='P')
```

The final, bloated WISE.C program with almond clusters

Time to drive home the point about logical comparisons. This time, after you choose who's wise and who's silly in the WISE.C program, a few logical `if` statements are used to jump to some conclusions.

Modify the WISE.C program in your editor as follows:

1. Delete lines 35 through 42, the final four `if` statements and their offspring.

2. Replace the lines with the following new text:

```
if(Poindexter==WISE && Melvin==SILLY)
    printf("Poindexter is wise and Melvin is silly.\n");
if(Poindexter==SILLY || Melvin==SILLY)
    printf("Either Poindexter or Melvin is silly.\n");
if(Poindexter==WISE || Melvin==WISE)
    printf("Either Poindexter or Melvin is wise.\n");
```

```
if(Poindexter==SILLY && Melvin==WISE)
        printf("Poindexter is silly and Melvin is wise\n");
if(Poindexter==SILLY || Melvin==WISE)
        printf("Either Poindexter is silly or Melvin is
           wise.\n");
```

Save the file to disk. Compile 'er. Run.

These lines contain quite a few logical comparisons. The effect they have on the program's output is to make it look like an SAT test problem. For example:

```
Who is wise, Poindexter or Melvin?
Type P or M:P
Poindexter is wise and Melvin is silly
Either Poindexter or Melvin is silly.
Either Poindexter or Melvin is wise.
```

The extremely weird ? : operator

Here's a way to really make your programs look nice and cryptic. It's called the *conditional expression operator* because the term "funky question-colon thing" was already used by the Pascal language. Essentially, the ? : operator is a shorthand way of doing a simple if-then statement. Using it is rare, which is why I'm discussing it in this box.

The ? : works like this:

```
(I'm a condition) ? (I'm TRUE) :
   (I'm FALSE);
```

There are three items, separated by the ? and :. The first item is a condition, a comparison like you would find in an if statement, but with an equal sign. The second item is what happens when the condition is TRUE; the last item happens when the condition is false. That's the best I can explain it in two sentences. Here is an example:

```
z=(c>0) ? 1 : 0;
```

This line reads "If C is greater than 0, then z equals 1; otherwise z equals 0. Here are the corresponding statements in normal C syntax:

```
if(c>0)
        z=1;
else
        z=0;
```

I can't really think of any positive application for this, other than a pure lust for crypticness on the programmer's part. Even the examples in other C programming books are equally lame, which kinda drives the point home.

And now for the bad news . . . .

You can do not only two logical comparisons in an if statement, but also three, four, even more. It can truly get quite insane. Here's the longest example I could dream up in the last five minutes:

```
if(a==1 && b==1 && c=='a' && d==1)
```

This if comparison tests four different conditions:

❑ The value of variable a must equal one and

❑ The value of variable b must equal one and

❑ The value of variable c must equal the letter *a* and

❑ The value of variable d must equal one

Only if all four conditions are TRUE are the statements belonging to if executed.

Doing multiple comparisons like this can be hairy. Even worse, some if statements contain compound statements. When that happens, you should begin separating everything by using parentheses. For example:

```
if((c==-1 || c== NAK) && !error_count-)
```

The first logical comparison performed is the OR that tests the value of the c variable. (Remember that the stuff in parentheses is always done first.) If it's equal to –1 or whatever NAK is, fine. Either condition works out to be TRUE. But then the !error_count– monster must also be TRUE because there's a logical AND in there as well. Yoikles!

This is not an example to be memorized. The point here is that you can use parentheses to make one operation work out before another one does — just as you would in a math problem. The parentheses also serve to set off parts of the comparison, which is useful when you have monstrous equations and C language functions embedded in an if statement.

In the My Dear Aunt Sally scheme of things, the && and || operators fall way down toward the bottom of the list. && comes before ||, but just about everything else comes before them. (The last thing in the official order of precedence is the weird ?: operator.) No need to memorize this.

Lesson 6-4 Quiz

1. Which `if` comparison is true when the variable `c` is equal to the letter *K* and the variable `x` is equal to 10?

    A. `if(c=='K' AND x==10)`

    B. `if(c=='K' & x==10)`

    C. `if(c=='K' && x==10)`

    D. `if(c==TRUE && x==TRUE)`

2. Which of the following `if` comparisons is true when either the value of variable `c` is equal to the letter *K* or the value of variable `x` is equal to 10?

    A. `if(c=='K' OR x==10)`

    B. `if(c=='K' || x==10)`

    C. `if(c=='K' AND x==10)`

    D. `if(c=='K' && x==10)`

3. Without running the program, look at the last several statements in WISE.C and predict which lines are displayed if Melvin is WISE and Poindexter is SILLY.

4. Who won the first Super Bowl?

    A. Green Bay Packers.

    B. Kansas City Chiefs.

    C. New York Jets.

    D. Baltimore Colts.

Lesson 6-5: More on Variables

Your knowledge of C language variables up to this point is very good for a beginner. Before giving you a C Variable Diploma, you should brace yourself for two concepts: First comes a full explanation of *type casting*, which was thrown at you in Lessons 5-4 and 5-7, and second comes a decent explanation of why there are `signed` and `unsigned`, `long` and `short`, and even `fair` and `unfair` variables.

Boring. Trite. Definitely vegan fare. But necessary.

Type casting and other acting problems

Remember Adam West? He was TV's Batman (and the only person who could ever play Batman, in my humble opinion). Poor Adam. He did such a good job that no one would hire him for anything other than Batman-like roles. Because of *type casting,* he was doomed to endless nights of dinner theater and "Love Boat" cruises for unappreciative audiences (who still thought of him as Bruce Wayne).

Type casting definitely happened to Bob Denver (née Gilligan). It almost happened to Sean Connery, who was *the* definitive James Bond. It can also happen to your variables in the C language, though it won't ruin anyone's acting career.

✔ Type casting works by placing a variable type declaration before a variable of another type. Suppose that variable i is an integer:

```
(float)i
```

This type cast makes variable i look like a float. (Of course, this would appear in a function or mathematical statement; you can't just typecast a statement by itself — it's like standing in the shower without the water running.)

✔ Type casting is only temporary. It doesn't change a variable's type at all. Only for the brief moment that the type cast appears is the variable treated as another type.

The essence of type casting

Type casting, or *type conversion,* is a C process in which you temporarily fool the compiler into thinking that a variable is of a different type. You can wave a magic wand and make an int into an unsigned or yank up your black cape and an int becomes a float.

Why Bother Reason #1: In Lesson 5-4, you saw how the IQ.C program calculated someone's IQ based on that person's age, weight, and area code. Those are three integer values, but because they were divided, the result would be a floating-point number. Indeed, whenever you divide two integers, you get a float. So the result was type casted into a float as follows:

```
iq=(float)(age*weight)/area;
```

Why Bother Reason #2: Some C language functions may require a certain type of variable as input. To twist the compiler's arm, you can type cast. This was done in Lesson 5-7 with the seedrnd() function:

```
void seedrnd(void)
{
```

```
        srand((unsigned)time(NULL));
}
```

The srand() function requires an unsigned integer value. To ensure that it
always gets one, the (unsigned) type cast is included in the function. This is
the essence of type casting.

The long *and the* short *of it*

There are two sizes for integers: long and short. Normally, you use the short,
which is declared as an int in all your programs. This allows you to play with
values from –32,768 all the way up, passing 0 and collecting $200, and up and up
to 32,767. For most purposes, an int or short does just fine.

Longs are still integers, but they can range up through 2 billion-something. This
gives you far more latitude for playing with big integers. If you're writing a game
in which you kept track of money, for example, you can use a long. That way, it
can hold values up to 2 billion and the players think that they're really accom-
plishing something.

The following program should confuse the heck out of you. It's called
CONFUSE.C, and it contains two loops that count to 1 million by 1,000s. The
first loop uses a short integer (which means that it doesn't ever get to 1 million
because a short isn't that big), and the second loop uses a long integer (better
for counting to 1 million).

Name: CONFUSE.C

```
#include <stdio.h>

void main()
{
        short s;
        long l;

        for(s=0;s<1000000;s+=1000)
                        printf("%i\t",s);

        printf("\nPress Enter\n");
        getchar();

        for(l=0;l<1000000;l+=1000)
                        printf("%li\t",l);
}
```

Enter the source code for CONFUSE.C into your editor. It contains two loops, separated by a "Press any key" function, though since I loathe that message, this one logically says "Press Enter" (which makes you wonder who the heck thought of the "any key" garbage).

Compile the program. You may encounter two warning errors that are OK for now. The first complains that a constant is out of range. I'll explain that in a minute. Another potential warning error may claim that getchar() doesn't do anything. This is true; the compiler is expecting you to save the character that getchar() coughs up, which you don't bother with. No problem with that. Any other errors you get have to be fixed.

Run the program.

Press Ctrl+S to halt the maddening screen. Look at the numbers displayed. You see two chunks: one ranging from large negative numbers to smaller, followed by one ranging from small positive numbers on up to the 32,000 range. Then it repeats.

Press Ctrl+Break to cancel the program. (You may have to press Enter to return to your integrated environment.)

What happens is that the short integer can handle only numbers that range from –32,000-something up to positive 32,000-something. The loop never finishes because the value of the s variable never hits 1 million. The compiler knows this, which is why it warns you that the "constant is out of range"; 1,000,000 is too big of a value for a short integer.

- ✔ Discussion of the CONFUSE.C program picks up again in the next section.

- ✔ You may have to press Ctrl+Break and then Enter to return to your integrated environment.

- ✔ One million is written for us humans like this: 1,000,000. In your C compiler, you don't specify the commas. So 1 million looks like this: 1000000.

- ✔ The s+=1000 thing means s=s+1000, which increments the value of the s variable by 1,000. This is covered in Lesson 4-8.

- ✔ Refer to Table 3-1 in Lesson 3-5 for the limits of the various C language variables.

- ✔ To display the long integer value in a printf statement, the %li placeholder is used (in line 15 of CONFUSE.C). The little *l* means "long," and the little *i* means "integer." This wasn't mentioned in Table 2-3 in Lesson 2-5 because it's confusing and kind of rare; you might want to write it in the blanks at the end of the table right now.

Hopefully less confusion about CONFUSE.C

Because the range of an integer reaches only up to 32,000, edit line 8 of the CONFUSE.C program to read as follows:

```
for(s=0;s<32000;s+=1000)
```

Save the change to disk. Compile and run.

You see the computer count from 0 to 32,000 by 1000s. Then comes the prompt:

```
Press Enter
```

Press the Enter key.

The computer counts to 1 million by 1000s, which takes a while to display. This part of the program works out fine because a long integer can hold such high values (all the way up to 2 billion, according to Table 3-1).

Here are some points to ponder about long and short integers:

- ✔ The int, short, and short int variable types all define the same thing. Most people use int to declare their short integer variables.
- ✔ Use ints whenever you need an integer value. Bother with a long integer only if you need a particularly large value or if a function requires it.
- ✔ To display a long integer value in a printf statement, use the %li placeholder.
- ✔ Remember that you can type cast a short integer into a long with the following:

```
(long)i
```

This line assumes that the variable i is a short integer.

Use a long integer when you need a large value. Theoretically, you could declare all your integer variables as longs. This works, but it adds overhead to the computer's thinking time, so use shorts when you can get away with it.

- ✔ In a printf statement, use the %li placeholder to display a long integer's value.
- ✔ For any values larger than what a long integer can swallow, use a float.
- ✔ The ranges for every type of C language variable can be found in the Range column of Table 3-1, in Lesson 3-5.

Signed, unsigned, soap, no soap, radio

Whenever you declare an `int` or `long` integer, the compiler assumes that you want to deal with both positive and negative numbers. This makes sense; if you're doing math and the result is minus-something, it's breezy to store it in any old integer variable.

The only time the negative numbers may throw you for a loop is in a loop. For example, I wrote a program once that counted from 0 to 127. Over and over. I used a `char` variable because it ranges from 0 to 127 handily, and I stuck it in a `for` loop:

```
for(c=0;c<128;c++)
```

Your logical C programmer mind should deduce that this loop counts from 0 up to 127 and then stops; the value of c starts at 0 and increments (c++) as long as c is less than 128. So it loops around 128 times, which is what I wanted in my program.

But it didn't work! It proved to be an antagonizing bug that took me a while to stomp. The problem was that the character variable c was `signed`, which is demonstrated in the following program, GOOFY.C:

Name: GOOFY.C

```
/* This program demonstrates signed and unsigned
variables and how screwy they can be */

#include <stdio.h>

void main()
{
    char c;

    for(c=0;c<128;c++)
                printf("%i\t",c);
}
```

Type the source code for GOOFY.C into your editor. Save it to disk as GOOFY.C.

Compile the program. You may see a warning error about a value being out of range. Like, *duh!* (If I would have noticed that, it would have saved me a great deal of time and trouble.) Anyway, run the program.

Press Ctrl+S to temporarily freeze the screen. You see numbers ranging from
–128 up to 0 and then 127 and then repeating over and over. The reason is that
if you add 1 to 127 — which is what c++ does in this program's loop — you get
–128. That's how signed integer values work. It doesn't matter whether it's a
char, int, or long; as soon as you add 1 to the highest value in the variable's
range, you get a negative number.

Press Ctrl+Break to halt the program. (You may have to press Enter after
pressing Ctrl+Break.)

The solution is to make the variable an unsigned integer:

```
unsigned char c;
```

Make this change to the program (in line 8) and recompile it. The program runs
as expected.

- ✔ Using unsigned integers seems like the logical thing to do most of the time.
  After all (and referring back to Table 3-1), you get bigger values with
  unsigned integers.

- ✔ Yes, 1 + 127 = –128 in signed land. This takes some getting used to, but
  you can see how it works when you run the program (over and over).

- ✔ Some compilers have the capability to automatically assume unsigned
  integers all the time. That way, everything is always an unsigned value
  and you never have to declare anything as unsigned.

- ✔ Another way to make a variable unsigned is to type cast it, making the
  variable temporarily unsigned. For example:

```
for(c=0;(unsigned)c<128;c++)
```

The (unsigned) type cast inserted into this for loop makes the c variable
in there of an unsigned type, ensuring that it can reach above the value
127. This has the advantage of still letting the variable hold negative
numbers elsewhere in the program, but it can still work out properly in the
loop. (Type casting is covered earlier in this lesson.)

Unsigned variables seem to lack that negative-attitude problem

Quickly type the source code for the following, stupid, silly, little program.

Name: NONEGS.C

```
#include <stdio.h>

void main()
{
    unsigned int a,b,c;

    a=150;
    b=300;
    c=a-b;

    printf("Unsigned C = %u\n",c);
    printf("Signed C = %i\n",c);
}
```

Save the program to disk as NONEGS.C. What it does is demonstrate the signed and unsigned nature of integers and what happens during the struggle to avoid negative numbers.

Compile the program and run it. Here is what the output should look like:

```
Unsigned C = 65386
Signed C = -150
```

What is the true value of the unsigned integer variable c? Well, if you use the %u (unsigned) placeholder to display its value, you get a positive number. Like, duh, since it's an unsigned integer value. (I'll explain in a second how that number got there.)

When the %i placeholder is used, the value displayed is –150, which is what you get when you subtract 300 from 150. So which answer is "correct"?

Unfortunately, both are. Again, it all depends on how you look at the number held in the variable. If you consider it unsigned, it will always be positive. When you subtract 300 from 150, you get –150. The highest value that can be held in an unsigned int is 65,535. Subtract 150 from that and you get 65,385. But because 0 is also a number and the computer counts its value, you add 1 to the result to get 65,386 — which is what the program displayed. (Don't even *try* to understand how that works.)

So the answer to the puzzle is that 65,386 and –150 are both actually the same value. One or the other is displayed depending on whether you use the variable as a signed or unsigned integer. (You might want to read the Techy sidebar "The whole painful spiel on why we have signed integers" in Lesson 3-5 for an explanation of how the heck this works.)

There is no way you should ever memorize this nonsense. I bring it up here only because it may confuse you when you encounter it later or when you get one of those annoying bugs you just can't track down.

Fair and unfair variables

There is no such thing as `fair` and `unfair` variables. No, not in the C language.

Lesson 6-5 Quiz

1. What is type casting?

   A. Temporarily changing a variable type to meet the whims and desires of your program.

   B. Permanently changing a variable type to meet the whims, etc.

   C. Converting one variable into another.

   D. See Adam West in the index.

2. Which of the following films did not star Adam West?

   A. *Mara of the Wilderness*

   B. *Nevada Smith*

   C. *Tammy and the Doctor*

   D. *The Reluctant Astronaut*

3. You need to store the value 4,198,375,123 in a variable. Which of the following declaration or assignment statements meets that end?

   A. `unsigned long i;i=4198375123;`

   B. `int i;(unsigned long)i=4198375123;`

   C. `float i;i=4198375123;`

   D. All of the above.

4. Suppose that n is a `signed` integer variable. If n now equals 32,767, what does n equal after the following statement?

   ```
   n++;
   ```

   A. 1

   B. 0

   C. 32,768

   D. –32,768

5. Your four-year-old son is suffering from nightmares and calls you into his room. After calming him down and getting him a drink of water, and before leaving, you do which of the following?

   A. Casually whisper "He's yours" into the closet.

   B. Pretend that something is pulling you under the bed.

   C. Bulge your eyes and say, "I just saw your teddy bear smile — and *he has long teeth!*"

   D. Sit on the edge of his bed, pat his head, and tell him a Freddy Krueger story.

Lesson 6-6: Another Lesson on Numbers (Primarily That Hex Thing)

There are values and there are numbers. Say that you have these 50 alien pods you have to deliver to San Francisco for the end of human life as we know it. Do you have 50 pods? Or maybe 32 pods? Or 62? Or even 110010? Or how about L pods? How many? The value is still 50, but the number is represented in different ways. Those ways are referred to as a *counting base*.

✔ A *counting base* is merely a way of expressing a value as a number.

✔ The most common counting base is base 10, which is what we humans use.

✔ Computers use counting base 2, known as *binary*.

✔ Binary numbers are composed of 1s and 0s. Because larger binary numbers can get quite chunky, programmers use counting base 16, hexadecimal, as a shortcut for dealing with those numbers.

✔ A counting base used by older computers is base 8, octal. This counting base is actually used by CompuServe's massive on-line computers, which is why you don't see any 8s or 9s in anyone's e-mail ID.

Counting bases has nothing to do with baseball

The counting base humans use is base 10, called the *decimal* system. This is probably because we have 10 fingers (and of course, most Vikings have 12 fingers, so they use counting base 12). Fifty pods in base 10 is written like this: 50. No need to memorize that. It works out to 5×10 and 0×1, which is 50.

The number 365 means 3×100, 6×10, and 5×1. The number 100 is 10 times 10, and 10 is 10 times 1. Ten! Ten! Ten! This is why it's called base 10.

All the numbers you use in C should be in base 10. That's the way the compiler thinks, which is handy because you also think in terms of base 10. No problems there.

What does cause problems are three other counting bases that are known to the computer. They are shown in this list:

❑ Hexadecimal

❑ Octal

❑ Binary

Counting base 16 is called the *hexadecimal* system. The word *hex* comes from the Greek *hexe*, which means "witch" or 16 of something. In that system, you would deliver 32 pods to San Francisco. It works out to 3×16 and 2×1, which is $48 + 2$, which is 50. In hexadecimal, or *hex*, the numbers represent multiples of 16 rather than 10. More on hex in a moment.

Counting base 8 is called the *octal* system. The word *oct* means eight, which is easy to remember because an octopus has eight tentacles and the month October is not the eighth month of the year. In this system, you would send 62 pods over to S.F.: 6×8 and 2×1 equals $48 + 2$, which is 50. In octal, everything is based on the number 8.

Finally, there is *binary*, the native counting mode of all computers. In fact, hexadecimal and octal are merely "shorthand" notations for the binary information computers bandy about like drunken sailors on leave. Heave-ho! In this case, you deliver what looks like the massive sum of 110010 pods to the City by the Bay. However, the binary system uses only 1 and 0 — no other numbers. It works like this:

```
1 x 32
1 x 16
0 x 8
0 x 4
1 x 2
0 x 1
```

That's $32 + 16 + 2$, which is 50 pods on their way to San Francisco.

✔ The letter *L* is 50 in roman numerals, which leads me to the bottom line:

✔ These are all different ways of representing values. C lets you pick any method (except for roman numerals), so you don't have to learn anything. You should learn to recognize other number formats, however, because other manuals may allude to them from time to time.

Spying out hexadecimal numbers

A hexadecimal number is merely a shortcut way of expressing a binary number. I won't go into the details of how that works because it isn't important. What is important is recognizing that you have a hexadecimal number and not a decimal number. From the previous sections, you should gather that although 32 looks like a decimal number, it can be a hexadecimal number. In decimal, its value is 32; in hex, it's equal to 50. Big difference.

In hexadecimal, you count like this:

> 1, 2, 3, 4, 5, 6, 7, 8, 9, A, B, C, D, E, F, 10

After you get to 9, you begin using letters to represent the values 10 through 15. A equals 10, B equals 11, and on up until F, which equals 15. So AF is a legitimate hexadecimal number. Strange, but that's how it works.

The value 10 in hexadecimal is equal to 16 decimal. Then you start over again, counting on up as follows:

> 11, 12, 13, 14, 15, 16, 17, 18, 19, 1A, 1B, 1C, 1D, 1E, 1F, 20

This is where it gets weird because 11 hexadecimal is equal to 17 decimal. But don't sit back and try to figure out what each of the values means. Instead, you need to know how to identify a hexadecimal number. That's what's really important. There are several hints:

- ✔ Hexadecimal numbers contain the letters *A, B, C, D, E,* or *F.*

  This works most of the time, but it isn't foolproof because 185 can be a hexadecimal number disguised as a decimal number.

- ✔ Programmers prefix a hexadecimal number with a dollar sign: $1E or $32.

  This is common in Macintosh land.

- ✔ Programmers postfix a hexadecimal number with an *H:* 32H or sometimes 5Bh.

  The little *h* is very popular, and sometimes they actually spell out *hex,* as in 4A hex.

- ✔ In C, hexadecimal numbers are prefixed with a zero and a little *x:* 0x32 or 0x5A.

  This is how you beat it into the C compiler that you're using hexadecimal numbers. So when you say 32, it knows that you mean thirty-two; and when you say 0x32, it knows that you mean 32 in hexadecimal. No problem.

- ✔ The hexadecimal character escape sequence can also be used: '\x32' or '\x01'.

  The backslash-x thing is an escape sequence which tells the compiler that the following number is a hexadecimal value: 32 hex and 1 hex, as shown earlier.

Table 6-5   Hexadecimal, Binary, and Decimal Values

Hex	Bin	Dec	Hex	Bin	Dec
0	0000	0	8	1000	8
1	0001	1	9	1001	9
2	0010	2	A	1010	10
3	0011	3	B	1011	11
4	0100	4	C	1100	12
5	0101	5	D	1101	13
6	0110	6	E	1110	14
7	0111	7	F	1111	15

✔ Please ignore Table 6-5.

✔ Lesson 5-6 discussed the use of DOS and BIOS functions, which are all listed in hexadecimal. That's one of the rare times you are faced with this type of number.

✔ The \x escape sequence is used sometimes to see whether certain characters were typed at the keyboard — characters you can't normally type, such as the £. That character is 9C hexadecimal. If you want to confirm that the c character variable held the £, you could use the following:

```
if(c=='\x9c')
```

Granted, most of the time it's easier to use 156, the character's decimal value. But there are geeks out there who stick to hex and love it.

✔ A better way is to define the character:

```
#define BRITPOUND 0x9C
```

Then you can use the BRITPOUND shortcut word and never mess with hex again in your source code.

Letters in hexadecimal numbers can be in upper- or lowercase.

✔ Scientific notation also uses the number E, which may make you confuse one of those numbers with a hexadecimal number. The key here is to see the decimal point used in scientific notation: 4.9E3 is scientific notation for the number 4,900 — four-point-nine, E three. But 49E3 is probably a hexadecimal number.

✔ DOS versions 4.0 and later slap a serial number on each disk they format. The serial number is actually a hexadecimal number; type the VOL command to see your disk's serial number and scope out the hexadecimal letters in there.

✔ Several people have tried to come up with alternative symbols for the values 10 through 15 in hexadecimal. They've all failed, primarily because every keyboard has the keys A through F available.

Displaying numbers in strange ways — including hex

A value is a value no matter what its number looks like. Take pods, for example. Since you've been dawdling here, pondering the nature of hexadecimal and other numbers, you've been slacking on your civic duty to replace the population of San Francisco with pod people. You now must take 62 pods to the City by the Bay. Furthermore, your superiors may ask for the number in hexadecimal — or even octal! Be prepared. Enter the program PODS.C into your editor and you'll know for certain.

Name: PODS.C

```
/* This program displays the value 62 three
different ways */

#include <stdio.h>

#define PODS 62

void main()
{
    printf("You must send %i pods to San Francisco.\n",PODS);
    printf("You must send %o (O) pods to San
        Francisco.\n",PODS);
    printf("You must send %x (H) pods to San
        Francisco.\n",PODS);
    printf("You must send %X (H) pods to San
        Francisco.\n",PODS);
}
```

Type the source code for this program into your editor. Save it to disk as PODS.C.

Compile the program. Fix any errors or congratulate yourself if it compiles right the first time.

Run the program. Here is what the output should look like:

```
You must send 62 pods to San Francisco
You must send 76 (O) pods to San Francisco
You must send 3e (H) pods to San Francisco
You must send 3E (H) pods to San Francisco
```

The first line is in English, er, decimal. The second is in octal (O), and the last two are in hexadecimal (H). If you use the little *x* placeholder, the letters in any hexadecimal number appear in lowercase; big *X* makes 'em uppercase, as seen in the last line.

✔ The bottom line? No matter how the number is displayed, its value is still 62.

✔ Because this program uses #define to create the pods shortcut word, you have only to edit line 6 to change the number of pods and see how other numbers are displayed in other bases (or just run the program in the next section).

✔ There is no conversion character (percent thing) to display binary numbers. Oh, that would be fun, but it just isn't there. Unfortunately, many C programming tutorial books include a program that displays numbers in binary format. What joy! Look through the stacks of books you've already bought on learning C and you're bound to find such a program. Impress your friends with it. Really. I'm serious.

A nerdy ASCII-decimal-hexadecimal chart program

As much as it pains me to include useful programs in this book, the following is just that. It displays values from 0 up through 255, in three columns: ASCII character, decimal, and hexadecimal. I'll explain how to use the program in a moment. First, here is the source code:

Name: DECHEX.C

```
/* DECHEX, display ASCII, decimal and hex values
*/

#include <stdio.h>
```

```
void main()
{
    int x;

    printf("A  DEC\tHEX\tA  DEC\tHEX\t");
    printf("A  DEC\tHEX\n");
    for(x=32;x<64;x++)
    {
                printf("%c  %3i\t%2X\t",x,x,x);
                printf("%c  %3i\t%2X\t",x+32,x+32,x+32);
                printf("%c  %3i\t%2X\n",x+64,x+64,x+64);

    }

}
```

Type the source code for DECHEX.C into your editor, watching carefully the tangled mess in all those printf statements. Yikes! (There are two spaces after the big A and the %c in those printf statements.) Refer to the Blow-by-blow box for details on how this contraption works. Save it to disk as DECHEX.C.

Compile! Run!

This program displays the characters and numbers for ASCII codes 32 through 127, which includes all the characters on your keyboard. To use it, you can do one of three things:

❐ Type its name at the DOS prompt:

DECHEX

The program spits out the ASCII characters from 32 up to 128, in three columns. A better way to see the whole thing is with the following DOS command:

MORE < DECHEX

The MORE filter pauses the program's output after the first screenful of text. Press the Enter key to see the last few values in each column.

❐ Send its output to your printer:

Make sure that your printer is on and ready to print. Then type the following command at the DOS prompt:

DECHEX > PRN

After the last line prints, press your printer's Form Feed or Paper Eject button to get a handy, printed copy of the ASCII character table.

❐ Save its output to a file on disk for examination later:

DECHEX > ASCII.TXT

This command saves the output from the DECHEX command into a file on disk named ASCII.TXT. You can then use an editor to examine the file and look up pesky ASCII character codes at your whim.

✔ The DECHEX.C program doesn't worry about translating between ASCII characters, decimal, and hex; all it does is count numbers in a loop. The way the `printf` function displays the values makes the program useful as a reference table.

✔ This program doesn't display ASCII codes 0 through 31 because they do some odd things to your screen and printer, including make them beep!

✔ ASCII codes from 128 to 255 are *extended ASCII* codes, which contain strange characters and symbols. You can modify the program to display them: Change line 12 to read as follows:

```
for(x=128;x<160;x++)
```

Change the \n in line 16 to a \t.

Add a new line 17 as follows:

```
printf("%c  %3i\t%2X\n",x+96,x+96,x+96);
```

Save it to disk as DECHEX2.C. It displays output in four columns, and you have to write a "header" for that fourth column. I'll leave the modifications to line 11 up to you.

The 5th Wave **By Rich Tennant**

5th Wave PowerTip: To increase application speed, punch the Command Key over and over and over as rapidly as possible. The computer will sense your impatience and move your data along quicker than if you just sat and waited. Hint: This also works on elevator buttons and crosswalk signals.

BLOW BY BLOW

How the heck DECHEX.C works

The tricky thing about DECHEX.C is that it displays the ASCII characters and codes in three columns. That's not hard, just tricky. The program can display everything in one column, which is done by first displaying a column heading and then looping through the ASCII code numbers. For example:

```
printf("A  DEC\tHEX\n");
```

This `printf` function displays the column head, the A for ASCII character code, two spaces, DEC, a tab, and then HEX and the newline character. This can be followed by a simple `for` loop to display all the characters and codes from 32 up to 127. (Codes 0 through 31 do funny things to the display, so they aren't displayed).

```
for(x=32;x<128;x++)
```

This `for` loop marches through all the codes, from 32 up to 127.

```
printf("%c  %3i\t%2X\n",x,x,x);
```

This `printf` statement displays the value of the x variable three times: first as a character (`%c`), then as an integer value (`%3i`), and then as a hex number (`%2X`). The 3 in `%3i` formats the output to always be three characters wide, which makes the display look even. The 2 in the `%2X` does the same thing for hex numbers.

Each line `printf` would spit out lists the ASCII character, its code, and its code in hex for all the numbers in the loop, from 32 through 127. Unfortunately, it would take several screens to do this, so in DECHEX.C the program was designed to display three columns. To do that, lines 10 and 11 display three of the headers, one for each column:

```
printf("A  DEC\tHEX\tA
   DEC\tHEX\t");
```
```
printf("A  DEC\tHEX\n");
```

Since there are three columns, each column contains only one-third of the numbers from 32 to 127. (Ugh. Time for math.) Since character 127 is

displayed, you have to use the value 128 for math (just as in the `for` loop): 128 – 32 = 96, and 96 / 3 = 32. There are 32 characters in each column.

So the first column begins with code 32 and contains 32 items. This is how the `for` loop is set up:

```
for(x=32;x<64;x++)
```

The first character is 32, and the loop repeats itself 32 times. The first `printf` statement takes care of items in that column:

```
printf("%c  %3i\t%2X\t",x,x,x);
```

The second column handles the next set of numbers, each of which is 32 greater than those in the first column. This is done with the following `printf` statement:

```
printf("%c
   %3i\t%2X\t",x+32,x+32,x+32);
```

Finally, the third column contains the next set of numbers, which are 32 greater than the second column and 64 (32 + 32) greater than the first column:

```
printf("%c
   %3i\t%2X\n",x+64,x+64,x+64);
```

Each of these `printf` statements prints one after the other on the same line. So the first time through, you get 32 (x=32 from the `for` loop), which the first `printf` statement displays in the first column, 64 in the second column (x+32), and 96 in the third column (x+64).

As the `for` loop repeats, each value in each column gets larger—the magic of the computer! And lo, after 32 times, each column displays its own set of numbers.

I know that this is a strange thing to grasp, and it's not like the program flew out of my fingers and into the editor on the first try. But this does show how information can be displayed in columns. As long as you know how many items are in each column and start the next column as x+that_many_items, as done in DECHEX.C, it works.

Lesson 6-6 Quiz

1. What are some punny titles the author could have used in this chapter?

   A. Go to Hex!

   B. Removing the Hex from Hexadecimal.

   C. Seldom Encountered Numbers, or Hex Rarrison.

   D. Everything You Wanted to Know About Hex (but Were Afraid to Ask).

2. What is the name for base eight?

   A. Octopal.

   B. Eighto.

   C. Octal.

   D. Rectal.

3. Which of the following is not a hexadecimal number?

   A. `51h`

   B. `$42`

   C. `0xFF`

   D. `FACE`

4. You're writing some screwy program that needs to know whether the user typed character `0D` hex at the keyboard. Which of the following `if` comparisons tests for that key, assuming that you read it by using the `ch=getch();` statement?

   A. `if(ch=='\x0d');`

   B. `if(ch=="0x0d");`

   C. `if(ch==0x0D);`

   D. `if(ch=="\x0D");`

5. Using the `rnd()` function from Lesson 5-7, write a program that displays a random number in decimal, hex, and octal formats. You can use the PODS.C program as a base.

Bonus question — worth 10,000 blue points!

Please complete the following dot-to-dot exercise. Note that the numbers are done in hexadecimal. You have two minutes. Begin.

Chapter 6 Final Exam

1. Bill has written his own header file, BILL.H. To include it in his source code, he used the following statement:

```
#include <bill.h>
```

Why doesn't this work?

A. Because Bill is a jerk!

B. Bill did not enclose the header filename in double quotes, which is what you do when you write your own headers.

C. There is no semicolon at the end of the line.

D. It's a trick question; everything is done properly.

2. Two functions in your program require the STDLIB.H header file. What do you do?

A. Use other functions that don't require it.

B. Specify #include <stdlib.h> at the beginning of the source code.

C. Specify #include <stdlib.h> *twice* at the beginning of the source code.

D. Specify #include 2*<stdlib.h> at the beginning of the source code.

3. Which of the following is not a function that can read characters from the keyboard?

A. scanf()

B. gets()

C. getchar()

D. gobblech()

4. Which of the following scanf statements reads a string and a number from the keyboard?

A. scanf("%s %i",st,num);

B. scanf("%si",st,num);

C. scanf("%s",st); scanf("%i",num);

D. The scanf function cannot read two different variable types at once.

5. A strike is scored as follows:

   A. A hit on the target.

   B. Two points for labor, none for management.

   C. Ten points plus your next two balls.

   D. Cutaneous myiasis.

6. What are the two arguments of the `main` function?

   A. `arga` and `argb`

   B. `arg1` and `arg2`

   C. `argc` and `*argv[]`

   D. `void` and `main()`

7. Which of the following `if` conditions is true when someone has typed an option after your program name at the DOS prompt?

   A. `if(argc>0)`

   B. `if(argc>1)`

   C. `if(argc>=1)`

   D. `if(argc>2)`

8. Which of the following `printf` statements displays the first thing typed after the program's name at the DOS prompt?

   A. `printf("%s",argv[0]);`

   B. `printf("%s",argv[1]);`

   C. `printf("%s",argv[2]);`

   D. `printf("%s",argv[argc]);`

9. What are the values of `argc` and `argv[1]` for the following command line?

   ```
   BLORF "DONUT HOLES" COFFEE
   ```

   A. `argc=2, argv[1]=BLORF`

   B. `argc=3, argv[1]=DONUT`

   C. `argc=2, argv[1]="DONUT HOLES"`

   D. `argc=3, argv[1]=DONUT HOLES`

10. What is Maxwell House coffee's slogan?

    A. Good to the last drip.

    B. Good to the last drop.

    C. Good to the last heartburn.

    D. Even the gritty stuff on the bottom tastes like coffee.

11. Which of the following statements tests to see whether the character variable c is equal to either little *p* or big *P?*

    A. `if(c=='p' || c=='P')`

    B. `if(c=='p' || 'P')`

    C. `if(c=='p') || if(c=='P')`

    D. `if(c||'p' == c||'P')`

12. Both Poindexter and Melvin are silly. Which of the following conditions is true?

    A. `Poindexter==WISE && Melvin==SILLY`

    B. `Poindexter==SILLY || Melvin==SILLY`

    C. `Poindexter==WISE || Melvin==WISE`

    D. `Poindexter==SILLY && Melvin==WISE`

    E. `Poindexter==SILLY || Melvin==WISE`

13. Variable i is an integer variable. Which of the following statements works out properly?

    A. `i=(long)2000000;`

    B. `(long)i=2000000;`

    C. `i=(unsigned long)2000000;`

    D. `(unsigned)i=2000000;`

14. What happens when you subtract 1 from a `signed char` variable that's equal to –128?

    A. You get –129.

    B. You get 0.

    C. You get –1.

    D. You get 127.

    E. You get 1.

    F. It cannot be done.

    G. The compiler will cry.

    H. There are too many choices here for me to deal with.

15. Which of the following actors has not received an Academy Award for best actor in a film?

    A. Charlton Heston.

    B. Clark Gable.

    C. Ernest Borgnine.

    D. Sylvester Stallone.

16. Which of the following statements assigns the hexadecimal value 10 to the variable x?

   A. x=10x;

   B. x=10h;

   C. x='\x10';

   D. x=0x10;

Chapter 7
Going Completely Loopy

• •

Lessons In This Chapter

▶ The lowdown on `while` loops

▶ The down-low on upside-down `do-while` loops

▶ The bizarre case of `while true` (and other loopy oddities)

▶ Nested loops and other birdbrain concepts

▶ The sneaky `switch-case` loops

Programs In This Chapter

OUCH2.C	TYPER2.C	BOMBER3.C	COUNTDWN.C
YORN.C	EHD.C	GRID.C	COLORTXT.C
BORC.C	LOBBY1.C	LOBBY2.C	LOBBY3.

Vocabulary Introduced In This Chapter

while	do-while	toupper	tolower
continue	switch	case	default

• •

You're not done looping in C, not by a long shot. The truth is that the `for` loop just can't handle every conceivable loop there is. In fact, I'd venture to say that the most popular type of loop in C is the `while` loop, which can also be a `do-while` loop, but never a `do-waddy-waddy-do-wop` loop. In a way, these loops combine both aspects of a `for` loop and the `if` statement, which you'll discover comes in increasingly handy for large programs that truly do something.

Lesson 7-1: The Lowdown on while Loops

While is one of those words that loses all meaning when you say it by itself over and over. *While. Why-all. Oo-eye-all.* Before losing your mind with that, consider the following:

While you wait for the light to change, keep your foot on the brake.

This is a simple example of a `while` loop in real life. It means, roughly, "While this thing is true, keep repeating this action" (that is, a loop). Your foot is stepping on the brake loop as long as the light hasn't changed. Easy enough.

My son sometimes suffers from a `while` loop when he's thinking of something to say. I call it the Ya Know While Loop. It goes something like this:

> While you're thinking of what to say, repeat "ya know" over and over.

So he sits there and says "Ya know . . . ya know . . . ya know . . . ." until we tell him to start thinking before he starts talking.

There are lots of `while` loop examples in real life. One of them was cited early in this book (in Lesson 4-5) — the shampoo instructions. Here they are again:

1. Wet hair.

2. Pour shampoo on palm of hand.

3. Gently massage lather through hair.

4. Rinse thoroughly.

5. Repeat steps 2 through 4, if desired.

If you were going to rewrite these instructions by using a C-like syntax, it might look like the following:

```
while(desired);
{
        Wet hair;
        Pour shampoo on palm of hand;
        Gently massage lather through hair;
        Rinse thoroughly;
}
```

`Desired` is a condition that can be either true or false — like in an `if` statement. While `desired` is true, the statements held in the `while` loop's curly brackets repeat. When `desired` becomes false, the block of statements is skipped and the next part of the program is run. This is the essence of a `while` loop in C.

Whiling away the hours

As in a `for` loop, you can set up a `while` loop to repeat a chunk of statements a given number of times. Unlike a `for` loop, the `while` loop's controls (the doojabbies that tell the loop when to start and where to finish) are blasted all over the place. This is good because it doesn't mean that everything is crammed into one line, as with a `for` loop. This is bad because, well, I get into that in the next section. For now, busy yourself by typing in the source code for OUCH2.C, a brilliant C program shown right next.

Name: OUCH2.C

```
#include <stdio.h>

void main()
{
     int i;

     i=1;
     while(i<6)
     {
                 printf("Ouch! Please stop!\n");
                 i++;

     }
}
```

Type in this program, which is essentially an update of the earlier OUCH.C program from Lesson 4-5. Both programs do the same thing, in fact, but by using different types of loops. Refer to the nearby Blow-by-blow box if you need extra help. Save the file to disk as OUCH2.C.

Compile. Run.

Here's what the output looks like:

```
Ouch! Please stop!
Ouch! Please stop!
Ouch! Please stop!
Ouch! Please stop!
Ouch! Please stop!
```

Brilliant. Simply brilliant.

✔ Unlike a for loop, the while loop requires extra setup, before and after the loop itself. In OUCH2.C, the variable i is set up (or *initialized*) before the loop and is incremented inside the loop. The while statement itself only cares about when i is less than six.

✔ The statements belonging to the while — those lines clutched by the curly brackets — are repeated only as long as the condition is true. If the condition is immediately false (suppose that the variable i was already greater than six), those statements would be skipped altogether (as in an if statement).

✔ While loops are easy targets for the infinite-loop boo-boo. Because of this, you have to check extra hard to make sure that the condition while tests for eventually becomes false, which makes the loop stop repeating. (You learn more about this over the course of the next few lessons.)

✔ In order for a while loop to quit, something must happen inside the loop that changes the condition while examines.

✔ This is the first time you've seen two different programs tackle the same program: OUCH.C used a for loop, and OUCH2.C uses a while loop. Neither one is better than the other. See the section "Deciding between a while loop and a for loop," later in this lesson, for more information.

Taking baby steps through OUCH2.C

OUCH2.C is a standard repeat-something-x-times program. In this case, you want to repeat a line of text five times, so you need a loop to repeat a printf statement that many times.

The i variable is used as the loop's counter. First, it's set up to be equal to 1 in line 7. This is the first part of the loop (and you should remember that all loops have three parts: starting, while-true, and do-this):

```
i=1;
```

The next part of the loop is the while statement in line 8. This is the loop's last part, the part that tells the computer when to stop looping. In the case of line 8, the loop continues to repeat as long as the value of variable i is less than 6; i already equals 1, so the loop repeats five times: 1, 2, 3, 4, 5, and then stops when i equals 6.

```
while(i<6)
```

After the while comes the statements to repeat, which are enclosed in curly brackets. For OUCH2.C, there are two statements:

```
printf("Ouch! Please stop!\n");
i++;
```

The first statement displays the message Ouch! Please stop!. The second statement increments the value of the i variable by 1. After these two statements are executed, the computer goes back and looks at line 8 to see what the while loop wants done next. The value of the i variable is compared with 6, and if it's still less than 6, the whole deal repeats. This happens five times.

When the while condition becomes false, the statements belonging to the while loop are skipped — just as when the condition in an if statement is false. The program picks up with the next statement (or statements). Since there aren't any in OUCH2.C, the program just ends.

The while *keyword (formal introduction)*

The while keyword is used in the C language to repeat a block of statements. Unlike the for loop, while only tells the computer when to end the loop. The loop must be set up before the while keyword, and when it's looping the ending condition — the sizzling fuse or ticking timer — must be working. Then the loop goes on, la-de-da, until the condition that while monitors suddenly becomes false. Then the party's over, and the program goes on, sadder but content with the fact that it was repeating itself for a while (sic).

While loops have an advantage over for loops in that they're easier to read in English. For example:

```
while(ch!='~')
```

This statement says, "While the value of variable ch does not equal the tilde character, repeat the following statements." For this to make sense, you must remember, of course, that ! means "not" in C. Knowing which symbols to pronounce and which are just decorations is important to understanding C programming.

Keyword while

The while keyword is used to set up a loop in C. It has a group of statements that repeat as long as a certain condition is true. Note that unlike a for loop, the starting and "while looping" conditions are specified before and during the loop. Here's the rough format:

```
starting;
while(while_true)
{
    statement(s);
    do_this;
}
```

First, the loop must be set up, which is done with the starting statement. For example, this state-ment (or a group of statements) may declare a variable to be a certain value, wait for a key-stroke, or do any number of interesting things.

while_true is a condition that while exam-ines. If the condition is true, then the *statements* enclosed in curly brackets are repeated. while examines that condition after each loop is re-peated, and only when it's false does the loop stop.

Inside the curly brackets are statements repeated by the while loop. One of those statements, do_this, controls the loop. The do_this needs to modify the while_true condition somehow so that the loop stops at an appropriate time.

On the downside, while loops must be set up and executed differently. For example, take the program OUCH2.C, earlier in this lesson. The value of the i variable is set before the while loop starts. And as the while loop goes 'round and 'round, i is incremented. This is a must. If i weren't incremented, the loop would be eternal and you would have to shoot the computer to stop it.

- The while_true condition the while loop examines is the same as you would find in an if comparison. The same symbols used there are used with while, including ==, <, >, !=, and so on. You can even use the logical dojabbies && (AND) or || (OR), to make several comparisons (see Lesson 6-4).

- When you apply the language of the while loop's format to OUCH2.C, you get the following:

Starting	Line 7	i=1
While_true	Line 8	i<6
Do_this	Line 11	i++

- Since you're familiar with for loops, see the following section for information about how for and while loops compare.

- Notice that, like the for keyword, while lacks a proper semicolon. It's just followed with a group of statements in curly brackets. This is fine. However, another semicolon format applies in only certain situations:

```
starting;
while(while_true)
    do_this;
```

As long as only one statement is looping with while, you don't need the curly brackets. By combining statements in an unusual and perverse fashion, in fact, it's possible to format a while loop as follows:

```
while((do_this)==TRUE)
    ;
```

Deciding between a while *loop and a* for *loop*

There are many similarities between a while and for loop — so much so that you'd almost seem kooky to use while if you're fond of for and vice versa. As an example, here is the basic for loop from the program 100.C, back in Lesson 4-5:

```
for(i=1;i<=100;i=i+1)
    printf("%i\t",i);
```

This loop counts from 1 to 100 and displays each number. (Refer to Lesson 4-5 if you want a full review of the process.)

Here is the same loop à la `while`:

```
i=1
while(i<=100)
{
      printf("%i\t",i);
      i=i+1;
}
```

See how the `for` loop was broken up and placed into the `while` loop? It's easier to see if I replace the pieces' parts with big, bold letters. Take a look at this:

```
for(A;B;C)
      printf("%i\t",i);
```

becomes:

```
A;
while(B)
{
      printf("%i\t",i);
      C;
}
```

So everything is there, but it looks as though the `while` loop involves even more typing. You could say that if your fingers are tired, you can use a `for` loop. Personally, I like `while` loops because everything isn't jammed into one line. It's easier to see the different parts. Also, it's possible to control the "C" part of the loop in different ways, which I get into in later lessons.

Another advantage of the `while` loop is that it looks more graceful. This is especially true when you're replacing what I think are those ugly `for(;;)` structures. In fact . . . .

Replacing those unsightly `for(;;)` *loops with elegant* `while` *loops*

Several programs in this book have used the following structure:

```
for(;;)
```

This is a `for` loop that repeats forever. Indefinitely. Beyond when the cows come home. Of course, nestled within the loop is a `break` statement that halts it short, such as when some condition is met. But — meeting a condition to halt a loop — doesn't that sound like a natural job for a `while` loop?

Without going through a lot of effort, load the TYPER1.C program into your editor. This program was introduced back in Lesson 4-6 to demonstrate the `break` keyword, among other things. The bulk of the program is the following `for` loop:

```
for(;;)
{
        ch=getche();
        if(ch=='~')
        {
                        break;
        }
}
```

This reads, "For*ever* do the following statements." A character, `ch`, is read from the keyboard and then checked to see whether a tilde was typed. If so (if `true`), the loop stops with a `break` statement.

Now go ahead and delete all those lines. Yank! Yank! Yank!

Replace them with the following:

```
while(ch!='~')
{
        ch=getche();
}
```

Oh, this is too easy! The `for` statement is gone, replaced by a `while` statement that says to repeat the following statement (or statements) as long as the value of the `ch` variable does not equal the tilde character. As long as that's the case, the statement is repeated. And that sole statement simply reads characters from the keyboard and stores them in the `ch` variable.

Save the changed source code to disk as TYPER2.C. Compile it and run.

After you see the `Press the ~ key to stop` message, type away. La-la-la. Press the tilde key to stop.

> ✔ This is an example of a `while` loop elegantly replacing an ugly `for` loop.

> ✔ There is no need for a `break` statement in this loop because `while` automatically halts the loop when `ch` equals a tilde.

Shortcuts you don't need to know about with TYPER2.C

Since the `while` loop in TYPER2.C contains only one statement, you can rewrite it as follows:

```
while(ch!='~')
        ch=getche();
```

There's no need to enclose a single statement in curly brackets in this case. Furthermore, you can make the following, highly advanced shortcut:

```
while(getche()!='~')

        ;
```

This is an example of "C functions work from the inside out" (see Lesson 5-5). The `ch` variable is replaced by the `getche()` function. This has the disadvantage of not saving the character typed in a variable, which would be necessary for more involved programs, plus it has the disadvantage of being highly cryptic and nerdy.

Another example of this type of replacement comes with the BOMBER2.C program, back from Lesson 5-2. In its own ugly way, that program used a `for(;;)` loop to repeat a group of statements and then used the `break` keyword to bust out when a certain condition was met. Again, this is ripe for replacement with a `while` loop.

Load the source code for your BOMBER2.C program into your editor.

Change line 15. It looks like this:

```
for(;;)
```

The ending condition for the loop is when character variable x equals the tilde. So create a `while` loop with the following condition, replacing line 15 in the program:

```
while(x!='~')
```

This means that the program loops as long as the character variable x does not equal a tilde. Fair 'nuff.

Delete the following lines, 20 through 23:

```
if(x=='~')
{
        break;
}
```

Just yank 'em on outta there. They're no longer needed because the `while` loop itself tests for this condition and halts the loop when it happens.

Save the file to disk as BOMBER3.C.

Compile and run.

```
Press ~ to end your mission
Press any key to drop bomb:
```

Press Enter.

Vvvrrrrrrmmmmm . . . .

```
15 people killed!
```

Press ~ to stop. Uh-oh:

Vvvrrrrrrmmmmm . . . .

```
30 people killed!
```

Sorry, folks. Apparently the `while` loop does not replace the `for` loop on equal footing. In this example, the `while` loop continues to work through all its statements, not stopping in the middle with a `break`, as the `for` loop did. This is one of those examples in which the ugly `for(;;)` construction actually works better than the graceful `while` loop does.

- ✔ The condition checked for by the `while` loop is negative. It means to keep looping as long as `ch` does not equal the tilde character. If you had `while(ch=='~')`, the loop would repeat only as long as they kept pressing the tilde key on the keyboard.

- ✔ The comparison for "does not equal" is `!=`, an exclamation point (which means "not" in C) and an equal sign.

- ✔ Also remember to use single quotes when you're comparing character variables.

- ✔ Notice that the program does display the tilde character when you press it. That's because the `ch=getche()` statement is executed before `while` tests the condition.

- ✔ Not that it's worth mentioning, but the endless `while` loop setup, equivalent to `for(;;)`, is written `while(1)`. In either case, the statements belonging to the loop repeat indefinitely or until a `break` statement frees things up.

- ✔ You can still use `break` to halt a `while` loop in the middle. However . . .

- ✔ In the new BOMBER program, you might as well use `for(;;)` because there is no advantage to sticking with `while`.

- ✔ Both this and the preceding program, TYPER2.C, don't bother with any setup before the `while` loop works. This is fine, but note that statements controlling the condition `while` monitors are included with the other statements that repeat.

Not to beat a dead horse or anything . . . .

It's come to this, your first inane programmer joke in C:

```
while(dead_horse)
    beat();
```

Drawing on your vast knowledge of C, you can now appreciate what humor there is in the "no use beating a dead horse" cliché translated into the C programming language. Here are the specifics — providing you can hold your sides in long enough:

- ✔ The `dead_horse` is the name of a variable whose value is either TRUE or FALSE. While `dead_horse` is true, the loop repeats.

- ✔ I've also seen the first line written as follows:

```
while(horse==dead)
```

In other words, "While it's a dead horse . . ."

✔ beat() is a function that repeats over and over as long as the value of dead_horse is true (or as long as horse==dead in the alternative form).

✔ You don't have to enclose beat() in curly brackets because it's the only statement belonging to the loop.

✔ Yuck. Yuck. Yuck.

Lesson 7-1 Quiz

1. Write a modification of the program 1000.C that counts from 5 to 1,000 by fives but uses a while loop rather than a for loop.

2. In the song "Kansas City," from the musical *Oklahoma!,* Will Parker sings about several wondrous things he finds in Kansas City, Missouri, when compared with the Oklahoma territory. Which of the following doesn't he sing about:

    A. They have a building seven stories high.

    B. They have gasoline-powered vehicles.

    C. They have a burlesque theater.

    D. They aren't required to marry their close relatives.

3. What controls how long a while loop loops?

    A. The number in the parentheses tells the computer how many times to repeat the loop.

    B. The loop repeats as long as the computer is happy.

    C. The loop repeats as long as the condition that is specified is true.

    D. The loop repeats until a break statement is encountered.

4. How many times is a while loop guaranteed to repeat itself?

    A. It will repeat at least once.

    B. It won't repeat at all if the condition is false.

    C. Some of the statements will repeat, but only until a break statement is encountered.

    D. The loop repeats at least once, and if it doesn't, you can call Borland or Microsoft to get a small refund.

5. Which part of speech is the word *while?*

    A. It's a noun, usually meaning a slice of time (for a *while*).

    B. It's a conjunction (do this *while* I do that).

C. It's a preposition (she kept smiling *while* he insulted her).

D. It's a verb (don't *while* away your time).

Lesson 7-2: The Down-Low on Upside Down do-while Loops

A while loop may not repeat, no, not ever. If the condition it examines is false before the loop starts, then the block of statements designed to repeat is skipped like so many between-meal snacks would be if you really knew what's in them.

It's completely possible for a while loop to make a judgment and skip its statements, just like a cold, cruel if statement:

```
while(v==0)
```

Here, if v doesn't equal zero, then the statements clinging to the underside of the while loop are skipped, just as though you had written the following:

```
if(v==0)
```

There is an exception, of course. It's the upside-down while loop, called a do-while loop. This type of loop is rare, but it has the charming aspect of always wanting to go through with it once.

The devil made me do-while it!

The following program contains a simple do-while loop that counts backward. To add some drama, you supply the number it starts at.

Name: COUNTDWN.C

```
/* An important program for NASA to properly launch
America's spacecraft. */

#include <stdio.h>

void main()
{
    int start,delay;
```

```
        printf("Please enter the number to start\n");
        printf("the countdown (1 to 100):");
        scanf("%i",&start);

/* The countdown loop */

        do
        {
            printf("T-minus %i\n",start);
            start--;
            for(delay=0;delay<10000;delay++);        //delay loop
        }
        while(start>0);

        printf("Zero!\nBlast off!\n");
}
```

Type the source code for COUNTDWN.C into your editor. The do-while loop is located at the end of the program; details about how it works are offered in the next section.

Save the file to disk as COUNTDWN.C, which is the best way to fit the word *countdown* into an 8-letter DOS filename.

Compile. Fix any errors. Notice that a semicolon is required after the end of the while at the bottom of the do-while loop. If you forget it, you get an error.

Run the program.

```
Please enter the number to start
the countdown (1 to 100):
```

Be a traditionalist and type **10**. Press Enter.

```
T-minus 10
T-minus 9
et cetera . . .
T-minus 1
Zero
Blast Off!
```

✔ You might not notice a delay between the numbers. Indeed, they seem to fly by a bit quickly on some computers. If so, change the value 10000 in line 20 to something bigger, like 32000.

✔ And if you really want a big delay, redeclare the `delay` variable to be a `long`. Remove `delay` from line 8 and insert a new line as follows:

```
int start;
long delay;
```

Then change the for delay loop to read as follows:

```
for(delay=0;delay<1000000;delay++);
```

That's 1,000,000 (1 million). Save the change to disk and run it. If the delay is too slow, change the value to 500000 or so; if it's too fast, try 2000000 instead.

✔ If you're using a Borland compiler, just replace line 20 with the following:

```
delay(1000);
```

That's the word *delay* and then 1,000 in parentheses. The delay function pauses the computer for a given number of milliseconds; 1,000 of them means a one-second pause. You also have to add the following `#include` at the beginning of the program:

```
#include <dos.h>
```

And delete the declaration of the delay integer variable, which will foul up the program to no end if you don't remove it. Compile. Run. Be amazed.

✔ In a `do-while` loop, a semicolon is required at the end of the monster, after `while`'s condition (see line 22 in the program).

✔ Don't forget the ampersand (&), required in front of the variable used in a `scanf` statement. Without that & there, the program *really* screws up. (Refer to Lesson 6-2 for more information about `scanf`.)

✔ That `for` loop ends with a semicolon, meaning that it doesn't "own" any statements which are repeated. Another way to format it would have been:

```
for(delay=0;delay<10000;delay++)        //delay loop
    ;
```

This shows you that the `for` loop doesn't have any statements worth repeating. It just sits and spins the microprocessor, wasting time (which is what you want).

✔ Incidentally, having a `for` loop inside a `while` loop is technically referred to as a *nested loop*. This concept is touched on fully in Lesson 7-4.

Do-while *details*

A do-while loop has only one advantage over the traditional while loop; it always works through once. It's as though do is an order: "Do this loop once no matter what." It's guaranteed to repeat itself. If it doesn't, you're entitled to a full refund; write to your congressman for the details.

The 5th Wave   By Rich Tennant

Re'al Pro'gram·mers

Real Programmers have trouble supressing homicidal tendencies when asked "Are you sure?"

Keyword do-while

do is a keyword belonging to while when the traditional while loop stands on its head. The only bonus here is that the while loop always works through once, even when the condition it examines is false. It's as though the while doesn't even notice the condition until after the loop has wended its way through one time.

Here is the standard format thing:

```
do
{
    statement(s);
```

```
}
while(condition);
```

The *condition* is a true-or-false comparison that while examines, the same type of deal you would find in an if comparison. If the condition is true, the *statement(s)* in the loop repeat. They keep doing so until the *condition* is false, and then the program continues with the next statement. But no matter what, the statements are always gone through once.

The full format of the do-while loop is shown in the preceding box. It always starts with a do, and then the statements to repeat in curly brackets, and then comes the while with the condition for repeating the loop. An important thing to remember here is that the while at the end of the loop requires a semicolon. Mess this up and it's sheer torture later to figure out what went wrong.

One strange aspect of the do-while loop is that it seriously lacks the *starting, while-true,* and *do-this* aspects of the traditional while and for loops. There is no starting condition because the loop just dives right into it. Of course, this doesn't mean that the loop would lack those three items. In fact, it might look like this:

```
starting;
do
{
    statement(s);
    do_this;
}
while(while_true);
```

Yikes! Better stick with the basic while loop and bother with this jobbie only when something needs to be done once (or upside down).

✔ The condition that while examines is either TRUE or FALSE, according to the laws of C, the same as a comparison made by an if statement. You can use the same symbols used in an if comparison, and even the logical doodads (&& or ||) as you see fit.

✔ This type of loop is really rare. In the biblical tome *The C Programming Language,* by Master Kernighan and Saint Ritchie, they claim that only a mere 5 percent of all loops in C are of the do-while variety.

✔ You can still use break to halt a do-while loop. Only by using break, in fact, can you halt the statements in the midst of the loop. Otherwise, as with a while or for loop, all the statements within the curly brackets repeat as a single block.

Exposing the flaw in the COUNTDWN.C program

Run the COUNTDWN.C program again. When it asks you to type a number, enter **200**.

There isn't a problem with this; the program counts down from 200 to 0 and blasts off as normal. But 200 is out of the range the program asks you to type.

Press Ctrl+Break to halt the program now if you typed 200 and want your computer back. (You may have to press Enter after pressing Ctrl+Break to return to the integrated environment.)

What about typing 0 or a negative number? Try that now; run the program and type in **–5**. You see something like this:

```
T-minus -5
Zero
Blast Off!
```

It isn't one of the great boo-boos of modern programming history, but it's bound to startle the astronauts, who are expecting a leisurely though suspenseful takeoff sequence.

The way to guard against this faux pas is to write a special loop which ensures that the value which is typed is kosher. Yes, a kosher number loop. That is handled quite brilliantly by do-while.

The always kosher number-checking do-while loop

One thing you should do in all your programs is — and I put this on a separate line for emphasis — the following:

Check your input bounds!

This makes sense only if you know what *input bounds* are. OK: They're the range of numbers or letters or whatever that your program is looking for. In COUNTDWN.C, they're numbers from 1 to 100. In some database programs, they're the "type in 40 or fewer character" limits. Stuff like that.

You want to ensure that users cannot type a wrong or "illegal" value, one that would screw up your program. You have to make sure that they type only 40 or fewer characters. Any more and your program may die a strange death. You must guard against this — and you can if you write your program correctly.

Traditionally, this type of defensive programming is known as *bulletproofing*. This protects the program from such errors in advance. That's why you check everything the user types to see whether it's kosher. If not, you can either ask politely for input again or just print a rude error message (like DOS does).

To make the COUNTDWN.C program a bit bulletproof, you have to have the program ask for input again whenever the value entered is either less than 1 or greater than 100. A do-while loop does that job nicely, and I'm willing to argue that on two points:

❒ The first argument for do-while is that it repeats itself once no matter what. That way, you can ask the question the first time and it has to be repeated only when the value entered is out of range.

❒ The second argument is that the while part of the loop checks to see whether the value entered (the start variable) was less than 1 or greater than 100.

You don't have to change COUNTDWN.C very much. Just modify the first part of the program to read as follows:

```
do
{
    printf("Please enter the number to start\n");
    printf("the countdown (1 to 100):");
    scanf("%i",&start);
}
while(start<1 || start>100);
```

The do-while loop asks the same question the program asked before. But after a user types a value, the while part of the loop checks to see whether the value of the start variable is less than 1 OR greater than 100. If either condition is true, then the loop repeats, asking the same question over and over until a proper value is entered.

Save the changed COUNTDWN.C source code to disk. Compile the program. Run it.

```
Please enter the number to start
the countdown (1 to 100):
```

Type **0** and press Enter.

Ha! The program asks again. Now type **101** and press Enter.

Golly, this program is smart. Any value outside the range from 1 to 100 causes the program to ask again and again for the proper number to be pressed. That's all made possible with a `do-while` loop.

- ✔ Bounds checking like this is done in just about every professional program. Whenever you're asked to type a value in a certain range or type fewer than so-many letters, a loop is in there making sure that you're doing it right.
- ✔ Refer to Lesson 6-4 for more information about the logical || (OR) comparison.
- ✔ You might want to insert the following comment into your source code, just above the first loop:

```
/* This loop ensures they type in
a proper value */
```

- ✔ As a complete aside, the guy who wrote the famous "Internet Worm" program a few years back used an input-bounds flaw in the Internet mail program to bring down the entire system. In a matter of hours, the program he wrote — the *worm* — siezed hundreds of computers across the USA and almost the entire world! He did this because he knew that some part of the program would accept more characters than you normally type at the prompt. The Internet gurus immediately corrected this flaw by adding an input-bounds check to the mailer program.

Lesson 7-2 Quiz

1. How many times does a `do-while` loop repeat its statements?

   A. Only once.

   B. At least once.

   C. At least once; maybe twice in France.

   D. Anywhere between once and infinity.

2. A common mistake made with `do-while` loops is:

   A. Using them in the first place.

   B. Forgetting to add the semicolon after the `while`.

C. Adding a semicolon after the `while`.

D. Spelling `do` wrong.

3. What is "bounds checking"?

A. Hiring a surveyor so that you'll know exactly where to put the fence on the back 40.

B. A new bank account with a minimum balance but no per-check charge.

C. Determining that the user typed a value in the proper range before moving on.

D. Using the `||` (OR) test to see whether a number is less than or greater than a given amount.

4. In "Star Trek," what was the predecessor of the Federation?

A. NASA.

B. The United Nations Space Agency (USA).

C. The United Earth Space Probe Agency (UESPA).

D. The United Constipation of Planets (UCP).

Lesson 7-3: The Bizarre Case of `while true` (and Other Loopy Oddities)

Personally, I find `while` loops to be the core of my programs more than any other type of loop. Yeah, `for` has its place and purpose. But when you're writing those big, involved programs that do a number of things, you'll discover the elegance and beauty of a `while` loop. (Golly, I must be getting nerdy if I'm waxing poetic about programming code.)

There are a few sample programs in the back of this book that make extensive use of `while` and `do-while` loops. One of the key elements in each program is a `while(TRUE)` trick. To understand how this works, you should consider the sample program in the next section.

YORN.C, as C as the wind blows . . . .

Asking a yes or no question is a common hobby for computer programs. It wasn't always this way. In the olden days, programs just plowed ahead with whatever they did, assuming that you never needed questioning or that some deleterious act shouldn't be confirmed. Even DOS was ill with this sickness. It wasn't until just recently that it formatted a hard disk without so much as a casual "Hey, what you're about to do is dangerous" message.

Name: YORN.C

```c
/* YORN - a program to get a yes or no answer */

#include <stdio.h>
#include <conio.h>
#define TRUE 1              //this is "true" in C
#define FALSE !TRUE         //this is "not true"

void main()
{
    char c;

    printf("Please answer Y for Yes or N for No:");

    while(TRUE)             //this means "loop forever"
    {
                c=getch();
                if(c=='Y' || c=='y')                break;
                if(c=='N' || c=='n')                break;
    }
    printf("%c\n",c);
}
```

Type in the source code for YORN.C, a routine that poses a yes-or-no question and waits patiently for a Y or N key to be pressed on the keyboard. Save it to disk as YORN.C, which is a clever way of writing Y-or-N.

Compile and run the program.

```
Enter your response, please:
Y for Yes or N for No:
```

Be goofy. Type W. Type P. Type Enter. It keeps asking over and over until you give up and type a Y or an N.

- ✔ The program works because of its while(TRUE) evaluation. The loop repeats forever until it's halted by the break statements in line 18 or 19.

- ✔ The while(TRUE) statement actually works out to while(1). This is how you set up an endless while loop in C. Zero is considered false, and a while(0) loop would never repeat.

- ✔ Notice how the question is split in two: First, a printf statement poses the question, and then a second printf statement within the loop explains which keys are being looked for. That way, if they goof, only the "you have these choices" part of the question is repeated. You could repeat the whole thing; it really depends on how smart you think your users are.

- ✔ Using break to exit a loop, as is done in YORN.C, is kinda tacky but often necessary. It's covered in the next lesson if you're interested.
- ✔ Yes, it's true, a for(;;) loop could handle the problem just as well. But things get better. Keep reading in the next section.

Spiffing up YORN.C a tad

This is so redundant:

```
if(c=='Y' || c=='y')        break;
```

Checking for either upper- or lowercase is a true waste of time. A better solution is to use the handy toupper function, which converts any lowercase letter to uppercase. It makes writing these single-key input functions much easier.

To use toupper, you have to make two modifications to the YORN.C program. First, add the following #include thing up near the beginning of your source code:

```
#include <ctype.h>
```

Second, change the meat of the while loop to read as follows:

```
c=toupper(getch());
if(c=='Y' || c=='N')        break;
```

After the printf statement, insert the toupper function into the getch() statement already there (as shown here). Then delete one of the if comparisons and edit the second one as shown here. You're just checking for Y or N now — no lowercase is allowed.

Save the changes to YORN.C to disk. Compile and run. You won't notice any difference in the output, but the program has been made more elegant, and the C lords will smile brightly upon you.

The required information on the toupper function

Shown nearby is the full format of the toupper function. I do this out of politeness because it is a handy function. The only thing you'll forget when you're using it is that you need the darn #include <ctype.c> declaration at the beginning of your source code; without it, the compiler is clueless about toupper's role in life.

Function `toupper`

The `toupper` function converts a single character from lowercase to uppercase. It takes little *a* through little *z* and makes them into big *A* through big *Z*. It ignores any other characters, and it works only with single-character variables or functions that spew such variables as part of their output.

Here is the format:

`c=toupper(a);`

c is a single-character variable; a is another single-character variable. After this statement, c contains an uppercase version of whatever character is stored in a.

If a doesn't contain a lowercase letter, then c equals a.

Another format:

`c=toupper(char_function());`

Here, `char_function` is any C language function that produces a single-character variable, such as `getch()`. The `toupper` function converts its output to uppercase and saves the resulting capital letter in the C variable.

Required in your source code is the inclusion of the CTYPE.H header file; the following line does the trick:

`#include <ctype.h>`

The `toupper` function makes a complete statement in C, and it ends with a semicolon.

Musings on other CTYPE.H functions you may not care about

An entire flotilla of character-conversion functions is in the C library, all of which require the CTYPE.H header: The `isalpha` function checks to see whether a character is A to Z, upper- or lowercase; the `isupper` and `islower` functions check to see whether a character is upper- or lowercase (but they don't convert the character); `isdigit` checks for numbers zero through nine; `ispunct` checks for punctuation marks; `isprint` checks for any printable character; and so on.

For the most part, these functions return TRUE or FALSE values — either 1 or 0, depending on what they find. So this implies that they're used with `if` statements, such as:

`if(isalpha(c))`

This statement checks to see whether character variable c is a character in the alphabet, upper- or lowercase. If so, the statements belonging to the `if` are executed.

- ✔ Remember that C functions work from the inside out. If you use `toupper` to modify the output of the `getche()` function, then `getche()` echoes its letter — upper- or lowercase — `before toupper` converts it.
- ✔ The `toupper` function has a sister function, `tolower`. Its role in life is to convert uppercase letters to lowercase, just the opposite of what `toupper` does. The format is the same, so I'm not adding a separate format box just for it. Oh, and you still need the `#include <ctype.h>` thing at the beginning of your text for `tolower` to work.

The "cook until done" type of `while` loops

Peep at the following:

```
while(!done)
```

This type of loop repeats "while not done." That's how you pronounce the C syntax here; the `!` is "not," and the `done` is an integer variable. This means that, literally, the loop repeats until it's done. That is, until the value of the `done` variable becomes true.

Ah, but what is truth?

There's finally an answer for that question. In fact, you've known it for some time now. It was introduced back in Lesson 6-1, when the subject of header files was discussed. I mentioned that these two items are popular in personal header files:

```
#define TRUE 1            //Something is true
#define FALSE (!TRUE)     //Something isn't
```

Truth, in C at least, is defined as equal to 1. Actually, it's any nonzero value. This is why the following loop goes on forever:

```
while(1)
```

False, on the other hand, is `!TRUE`, or not true. In C, that works out to 0. So truth is 1 and false is 0. And the answer to life, the universe, and everything is 42. But don't let these concepts frazzle your mind. The bottom line is that they're consistent. They work. And it's easy to remember that it all fits in nicely with `while(!done)`.

The following program is an update to YORN.C. The theme is still the same: to weed out a Y or N keypress from the keyboard. But this time a `while(!done)` loop is used.

Name: YORN.C (again)

```
/* YORN - a program to get a yes or no answer */

#include <stdio.h>
#include <conio.h>
#include <ctype.h>

#define TRUE 1              //this is "true" in C
#define FALSE !TRUE         //this is "not true"

void main()
{
    char c;
    int done;

    printf("Enter your response, please:");
    done=FALSE;             //no, we're not done looping

    while(!done)            //loop while not done
    {
            printf("\nY for Yes or N for No:");
            c=toupper(getch());
            if(c=='Y' || c=='N')
                    done=TRUE;
    }
    printf("%c\n",c);
}
```

Update the YORN.C source code in your editor so that it looks like the final product shown here. You're modifying the main loop so that the done variable controls when it will end, making the while condition TRUE or FALSE. Save the changes to disk when you're done editing.

Compile and run the program. You won't notice any difference in the output, but the approach uses the classic while not done loop, which can come in handy for several types of programs.

> ✔ The program's main loop repeats until the value of the done variable becomes FALSE. That happens only under the direction of the if statement.

> ✔ True, there are other ways to write this particular while loop. In larger programs, however, the while(!done) type of loop makes more sense, which you'll witness in a moment.

> ✔ The loop's starting condition is set in line 16, where done equals FALSE. The loop's ending condition is set in line 23, where done equals TRUE.

- ✔ If done equals FALSE when the loop starts, then while(!done) actually works out to while(TRUE). Think about this for a few seconds, and it should make sense.
- ✔ You'll find an excellent example of using while(!done) in Lesson 7-5, on switch-case loops.

Working while not done

I've used the while(!done) trick dozens of times in writing little programs for myself. Basically, most programs (those that actually accomplish something as opposed to the demo programs in this book) work inside a giant loop. The loop repeats and repeats until something happens and the program finishes. In that case, the following statement halts the loop:

```
done=TRUE;
```

"I'm done," it says, cheerfully. At that point, the loop drags on through its last few statements and the program quits. Of course, remember that done=TRUE; is not the same thing as a break; if you ever want a loop to stop at once, always use break to halt it. This subject is touched on in detail in the next lesson.

Right now the while(!done) trick may not make much sense. That's because you need a real, beefy program to have it work out right. Two such programs provide good examples of this technique, in Appendix D, the CRAPS.C and LOTTO.C programs.

The CRAPS.C program uses the following pieces to create a while(!done) loop:

```
YouWannaPlay=TRUE;
```

The YouWannaPlay variable controls the program's main while loop, the one that plays the game. So:

```
while(YouWannaPlay)
```

The loop repeats as long as *you want to play,* or as long as the YouWannaPlay variable is TRUE. Later on, the program changes the variable to FALSE, but only when you're done playing. (The program uses a while(TRUE) loop as well; turn to Appendix D and read the program's comments to see what's going on.)

The LOTTO.C program employs a strange do-while loop that also works off the concept of "loop while true":

```
do
{
```

```
        b=rnd(RANGE);
    }
while(numbers[b]);
```

The loop is used to generate a random number. The rnd() function is from
Lesson 5-7, and it spits out a value in the range of 0 through RANGE (a defined
constant value). The numbers[b] thing will be a value of either one or zero,
which the while statement evaluates as either true or false. The do-while loop
repeats until a zero is returned by the numbers[b] thing. (Refer to the
program's comments in Appendix D to see what's going on in the big picture.)

The point here is not to impress you with tidbits from larger programs. What
you should note is how the larger programs make use of while(TRUE) and
while(!done) types of loops. As you explore on your own (and definitely take
a peek at Appendix D), you discover for yourself how useful these types of
loops can be.

Using YORN as a function

Most of the time, the YORN.C program you've been hassling with will never
exist, not at an entire program. Instead, you'll use the infamous yorn() function. What that does is pose the question and then return either a TRUE or
FALSE value, depending on whether Y (TRUE) or N (FALSE) was pressed.

The following source code is for the EHD.C program, where EHD stands for
Erase Hard Drive. Don't panic; this program is impressive in a visual sense. No
damage will come to your hard drive. The purpose here is to see a yorn()
function in action.

Name: EHD.C

```
/* EHD - Erase That Hard Drive! */

#include <stdio.h>
#include <conio.h>
#include <ctype.h>

#define TRUE 1            //this is "true" in C
#define FALSE !TRUE       //this is "not true"

int yorn(void);

void main()
{
    /* print impressive messages */
```

```
        printf("EHD - Erase Hard Drive Utility\n");
        printf("Version 3.2 (C) BrainSoft Inc.\n\n");
        printf("WARNING: This program might erase your hard
                drive!\n");
        printf("Continue? (Y/N):");

        if(yorn())
                        printf("You're gutsy, kid. Foolish, gutsy.\n");
        else
                        printf("Whew! That was close!\n");
}

/* The yorn() function returns TRUE if Y was
pressed; FALSE for N */

int yorn(void)
{
        int done=FALSE;
        char c;

        while(!done)            //loop while not done
        {
                c=toupper(getch());  //make uppercase
                if(c=='Y' || c=='N') //look for Y or N only
                        done=TRUE;
        }
        printf("%c\n",c);

        if(c=='Y') return(TRUE);                //Y==TRUE
        return(FALSE);                          //N==FALSE
}
```

Type the source code for EHD.C into your editor. It's just a lot of text, plus the vaunted yorn() function doing its thing. Save the file to disk as EHD.C.

Compile and run.

```
EHD - Erase Hard Drive Utility
Version 3.2 (C) BrainSoft Inc.

WARNING: This program might erase your hard drive!
Continue? (Y/N):
```

Press Y or N; and that's all because it doesn't let you type any other key. The program ends with an appropriate message, but no harm comes to the hard drive. (This is why the message is that it *might* erase your hard drive; if you're feeling particularly nasty, delete the might and just say erases instead.)

- ✔ There are two newline characters, \n, at the end of the text the printf function displays in line 16.

- ✔ The yorn() function is called from within an if comparison in line 20. This is possible because C functions work from the inside out: First the call is made to the yorn() function, and then its TRUE or FALSE nature is evaluated by the if statement.

- ✔ Refer to Lesson 5-5 for more information on functions working from the inside out.

- ✔ There's no need to go if(yorn()==TRUE) in line 20 because the yorn() function itself works out to TRUE or FALSE directly.

- ✔ The yorn() function in this program works just like the YORN.C programs demonstrated earlier in this lesson. The difference is that a value is returned, either TRUE or FALSE, depending on which key is pressed.

- ✔ The completely nifty thing about having a yorn() function in your program is that you can use it a number of times. Any spot in which you feel the need to pose to the user a yes-or-no question is ideally suited for the yorn() function.

Final, consoling words on while *loops*

while loops can be very frustrating. Sometimes they just don't work like you think they will, and you get all mad and heaving and scream at the computer. It happens to everyone.

If I could distill the essential information into one key point, it would be as follows:

Remember that the condition while examines must work out to TRUE or FALSE. (One is true and zero is false.)

Try to look at what while is doing and figure out whether it ever becomes one or zero or TRUE or FALSE. Does the stuff that while is holding in its parentheses ever work out that way? Can the same thing work out in an if statement?

If you just can't get it to work the way you want, there is still hope. You can change your while to the following:

```
while(TRUE)
```

Or:

```
while(1)
```

Then use an `if` statement inside the loop — one that you know for certain will work — and use the `break` keyword to bust out of the loop when the time comes. This technique is sneaky. It's underhanded. It's frowned on by college professors who teach C. But it works. So there.

Lesson 7-3 Quiz

1. What does the following loop do?

```
while(TRUE)
```

   A. It lasts but a fraction of a second in Washington, D.C.

   B. It prevents anyone from reading a supermarket tabloid.

   C. It causes a loop to spin forever (until `break` gets you out).

   D. It causes a loop to stop when `TRUE` is `FALSE`.

2. What does the following loop do?

```
while(!done)
```

   A. It waits until the loop is done and then quits.

   B. It waits until the `done` variable becomes `FALSE` and then it quits.

   C. It waits until the `done` variable becomes `TRUE` and then it quits.

   D. It doesn't do anything.

3. What function changes a character *c* to an uppercase letter of the alphabet?

   A. `toupper(c);`

   B. `tobigletter(c);`

   C. `tocaps(c);`

   D. `toshiftkey(c);`

4. Please identify the following features on the sample fish in Figure 7-1:

   A. Dorsal fin(s).

   B. Caudal fin.

   C. Pelvic fin.

   D. Pectoral fin.

   E. Huckleberry fin.

   F. Eyeball.

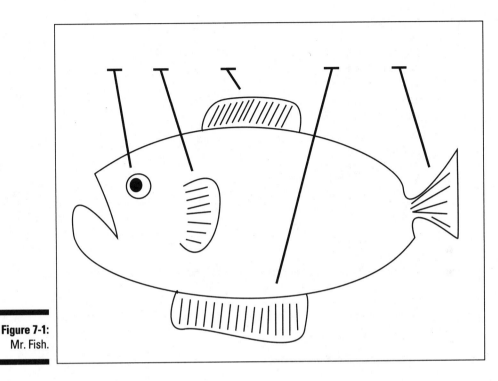

Figure 7-1:
Mr. Fish.

5. What is truth?

    A. Truth is known only to God.

    B. It's up to each person to decide what truth is.

    C. Truth is merely an observation.

    D. Truth is one.

Lesson 7-4: Nested Loops and Other Birdbrained Concepts

Glorious loops within loops, wheels within wheels spinning 'round like some nauseating amusement-park ride with a drugged-out, tattooed guy named Craig asleep at the controls. But that's another subject. In the C programming language, spinning two loops is a cinchy and practical thing to do. It's called making a *nested loop,* nested meaning one loop inside another.

Nested loops are nothing new to you; you've been witness to several of them throughout this book. There's no crime in using them — nothing tricky except identifying the nested loop concept, lest someone accuse you of doing it and you thinking that it's something else entirely.

You have the following nested loop, pulled from the mire of the COUNTDWN.C program (see Lesson 7-2):

```
do
{
        printf("T-minus %i\n",start);
        start—;
        for(delay=0;delay<10000;delay++);
}
while(start>0);
```

To do-while loop is the outside loop because it spins around first. The for (delay) loop is the inside loop, nested inside the do-while loop. It repeats itself ten thousand times each time the do-while loop repeats once. That's the essence of a nested loop, or, more accurately, that's what this type of arrangement is called.

Here are the facts on nested loops:

- A nested loop is basically one loop spinning round inside another loop.

- The first loop, or outside loop, ticks off first. Then the inside loop ticks off, looping as many times as it does. After that, the outside loop ticks off another one, and then the inside loop repeats entirely again. That's how they work.

- Keep the variables associated with one loop or another separate. For example, the following two for loops are nested improperly:

```
for(x=0;x<5;x++)
        for(x=5;x>0;x—);
```

Since x is used in both loops, these nested loops do not behave as you expect. This is an infinite loop, in fact, because both are manipulating the same variable in different directions.

- This disaster probably won't be apparent to you. You'll write some huge program and nest two for loops miles apart without thinking about it, by using your favorite variable x (or i) in each one. Those kind of bugs can really wreck your day.

- The way to avoid messing up nested loops is to use different variables with each one — for example, a or b, or i1 and i2, or even something very descriptive, such as start and delay, used in the COUNTDWN.C example.

The nitty GRID.C of nested loops

Nested loops happen all the time. Most often they happen when you're filling in a grid or an *array* (which is the subject of Chapter 8 in the second volume of this book). In that case, you work on rows and columns, filling up the columns row-by-row one after the other or vice versa. An example of how this is done is shown in the GRID.C program, which displays a grid of numbers and letters.

Name: GRID.C

```
#include <stdio.h>

void main()
{
        int a;
        char b;

        printf("Here is thy grid...\n");

        for(a=1;a<10;a++)
        {
                        for(b='A';b<'K';b++)
                        {
                                        printf("%i-%c ",a,b);
                        }
                        putchar('\n');  //end of line

        }
}
```

Enter the source code for GRID.C into your editor. The program then creates a 10-by-9 square (OK, *grid*) of numbers and letters by using a nested-loop arrangement. Save your efforts to disk as GRID.C.

Compile the program. You'll notice that putting two `for` statements together doesn't cause the compiler to spew errors at you (unless you made a typo somewhere).

Run. Here's what the output should look like:

```
Here is thy grid...
1-A 1-B 1-C 1-D 1-E 1-F 1-G 1-H 1-I 1-J
2-A 2-B 2-C 2-D 2-E 2-F 2-G 2-H 2-I 2-J
3-A 3-B 3-C 3-D 3-E 3-F 3-G 3-H 3-I 3-J
4-A 4-B 4-C 4-D 4-E 4-F 4-G 4-H 4-I 4-J
5-A 5-B 5-C 5-D 5-E 5-F 5-G 5-H 5-I 5-J
```

```
6-A 6-B 6-C 6-D 6-E 6-F 6-G 6-H 6-I 6-J
7-A 7-B 7-C 7-D 7-E 7-F 7-G 7-H 7-I 7-J
8-A 8-B 8-C 8-D 8-E 8-F 8-G 8-H 8-I 8-J
9-A 9-B 9-C 9-D 9-E 9-F 9-G 9-H 9-I 9-J
```

Wow. Such efficiency should please any government bureaucracy.

- The first, outer `for` loop counts from 1 to 10.

- The inner `for` loop may seem strange, but it's not. It's only taking advantage of the dual number/character nature of letters in a computer. The character variable b starts out equal to the letter *A* and is incremented one letter at a time up to letter *K*. Actually, what happens is that b is set equal to letter *A*'s ASCII value, which is 65. It then increments up to letter *K*'s ASCII value, which is 75. Sneaky, but doable.

- The `printf` function displays the numbers and letters as the inner loop spins. You can see this on your screen: The outer loop stays at one number while the letters *A* through *K* print. Then the outer loop increments, and the next row of letters is printed.

- The `putchar` function displays a single character on the screen. In GRID.C, it's used to display a newline character at the end of each row. (This function is "introduced" in the second volume of this book.)

Something special only for Borland compilers

Sorry, Microsoft people and others. You can't work the following program because your compilers are lame-o, *lame-o, LAME-O*. Please observe only or skip ahead to the section titled "`break` the brave and `continue` the fool."

To make the nested loop thing a little more dramatic, not to mention colorful, the following program was concocted. It does the same grid thing as GRID.C, but it displays its results by using every possible combination of color text known to the PC.

Name: COLORTXT.C

```
/* Colorful text program for Borland users only */

#include <stdio.h>
#include <conio.h>

void main()
{
```

```
int foreground,background;

for(foreground=0;foreground<=15;foreground++)
{
                for(background=0;background<=7;background++)
                {
                                textcolor(foreground);
                                textbackground(background);
                                cprintf("TEXT!");
                }
                putchar('\n');
}
}
```

Type this source code into your editor. The integer variables foreground and background are used to set the text foreground and background colors, respectively. Nice, long variable names, eh? No crime, but it makes the source code a little wordy. Save the file to disk as COLORTXT.C.

Compile the program. If you get an error, it's probably because you forgot to include the CONIO.H header file. That contains the prototypes for the textcolor, textbackground, and cprintf functions. Without it, you're doomed.

Run it. You see a colorful grid of the word *TEXT* repeated in 16 rows of 8 columns, one for each foreground and background color combination on the PC's boring old text screen. Remember that it's the nested loop concept that makes such a colorful program possible.

✔ It's the textcolor, textbackground, and cprintf statements that make this program unique to Borland compilers.

✔ The textcolor function sets the foreground color for text on the screen. Colors are set by choosing various numbers, from 0 to 15. (See your reference guide for the color each number represents.)

✔ The textbackground function sets the background color for text on the screen. Colors are chosen by using numbers zero through seven.

✔ The cprintf function is a doppleganger for the printf function. The difference is that the text takes on the colors set by textcolor and textbackground (as well as other text-manipulating functions offered by your compiler).

✔ Your PC uses various number codes to represent text screen colors. Foreground colors range from 0 to 15; background, from 0 through 8. The color numbers and their colors are buried somewhere in your Borland manual. Note that only the cprintf function (and its cputs and other cousins) display text by using the colors you choose.

break *the brave and* continue *the fool*

Two C language keywords can be used to directly control loops in your programs. They are break and continue. The break keyword should be familiar to you, having been introduced in Lesson 4-6 and tossed at you every now and again since then. The continue keyword is a new beast, but it plays an important role — one you may even find handy.

What continue does is to instantly repeat a loop. It works like break in that the rest of the statements in the loop are skipped, but unlike break, the continue command sends the computer back to the beginning of the loop. The fool!

- ✔ Both break and continue are C language keywords and statements unto themselves. They each must end with a semicolon.
- ✔ Both break and continue work inside any C loop.
- ✔ Both break and continue cause horrid errors outside a loop.

Please continue . . . .

The following program is BORC.C, which isn't named after former Supreme Court nominee Robert Bork. Instead, it's an acronym for *b*reak *or c*ontinue, the two keywords this program fiddles with at length.

Name: BORC.C

```
#include <stdio.h>
#include <conio.h>
#include <ctype.h>

void main()
{
    int x=0;
    char c;

    while(x<5)
    {
        x++;                          //loop counter
        printf("\n%i: Press B to break, C to
            continue:",x);
        c=toupper(getch());      //getkey
        if(c=='C')
```

```
                {
                        putchar(c);     //display C
                        continue;       //loop repeats right here!
                }
                if(c=='B')
                        break;          //loop breaks right here!
                printf("%c is not B or C.",c);
        }
}
```

Type the source code for BORC.C into your editor. Save it to disk as BORC.C, which stands for *break or* continue. (If you keep thinking of Robert Bork, you'll save it to disk as BORK.C, which isn't what I'm after.) A nearby Blow-by-blow box and Figure 7-2 explain the details of how this program works.

Compile and run the program.

Here's how it goes:

```
1: Press B to break, C to continue:
```

Press **X**! You'll see:

```
X is not B or C.
2: press B to break, C to continue:
```

Press **C**. This forces the program to execute the continue statement inside the while loop. You see:

```
3: Press B to break, C to continue:
```

The BORC.C program skipped the rest of the lines in the loop and repeated itself again. You can tell because the number that begins each line is incremented by the while loop.

Press **B** to break it. The program ends.

> ✔ When you press **C** to continue, the continue command executes in line 18. It causes the loop to immediately repeat, jumping back up to the while on line 10. The rest of the statements in the loop are skipped.

> ✔ If the x++ statement (the one that increments this loop in line 12) were skipped by the continue command, the loop would become infinite. Watch out for that.

✔ The `putchar` function in line 17 is used to display a single character on the screen. In this case, it displays the character held in the single-character `c` variable. Flip to Volume II of this book gives you the formal introduction.

✔ Refer to Lesson 7-3 for more information on the `toupper` function.

✔ This program's loop repeats five times. The `x` variable counts the loop and it starts out equal to zero (line 7). The loop repeats while `x` is less than five (line 10), and `x` is incremented during the loop (line 12). You can prove that it repeats only five times by running the program and pressing X or some other key each time you're asked. You see lines 1 through 5 displayed. This works because `x` is incremented *after* the `while` statement makes its comparison. Sneaky, but it works.

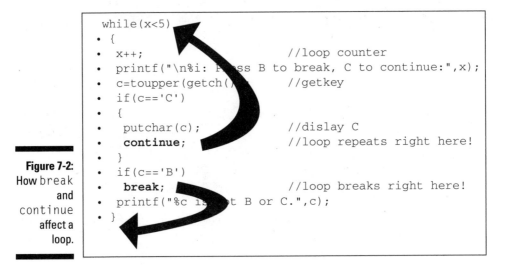

Figure 7-2:
How break
and
continue
affect a
loop.

```
while(x<5)
 {
   x++;                              //loop counter
   printf("\n%i: Press B to break, C to continue:",x);
   c=toupper(getch());              //getkey
   if(c=='C')
   {
     putchar(c);                    //dislay C
     continue;                      //loop repeats right here!
   }
   if(c=='B')
     break;                         //loop breaks right here!
   printf("%c is not B or C.",c);
 }
```

The `continue` *keyword*

Like the `break` keyword, the `continue` keyword is used to affect how a loop loops. This time, the job is to immediately repeat the loop, skipping over the remaining statements and starting the loop over with the first line (the `for`, `while`, or `do` or whatever that started the loop in the first place).

The `continue` command comes in handy when you have statements in a loop you don't want to repeat every time; `continue` just skips over them and starts the loop over at the beginning.

BLOW BY BLOW

How BORC.C does it

The loop in the BORC.C program spins around five times given that you don't press a B or C when it asks. If you do, then a break or continue command alters the loop's spinning, essentially becoming the programming equivalent of Kaopectate or Ex-Lax, depending on how you look at it.

The loop counter comes first at line 12. The next line contains a printf that displays the loop count (it starts at zero and is immediately incremented to one), plus prompts for single-key input:

```
x++;
    //loop counter
printf("\n%i: Press B to break, C
    to continue:",x);
```

Input is gathered in line 14 by using a compound statement: getch() reads a single key from the keyboard, and then toupper converts it to uppercase.

```
c=toupper(getch()); //getkey
```

When C is pressed, the program continues with the continue command in line 18. The rest of the loop is skipped over, and the while condition is immediately examined to see whether the loop should repeat.

```
continue; //loop repeats right here!
```

If B is pressed, the break command in line 21 halts the loop, skipping over the remaining statements in the loop.

```
if(c=='B')
    break; //loop breaks right here!
```

If neither C nor B is pressed, line 22 displays a message and the loop repeats as normal.

Keyword continue

The continue keyword forces the computer to instantly repeat a loop. The rest of the statements in the loop are just skipped, and the loop starts all over.

```
continue;
```

The continue keyword is a C language statement unto itself and must end properly with a semicolon.

Please use continue only within a loop. When you don't, and you just stick continue on a line by itself, rogue and unattended outside a loop, the compiler goes berserk.

Note that continue repeats only the loop its in. If you have a nested loop, keep in mind that continue affects only one loop at a time. Also, continue cannot repeat a while loop when the loop's condition becomes false.

Keep in mind that though continue forces another spin of the loop's wheel, it does not reinitialize the loop. It tells the compiler to "go again," not "start over."

- ✔ The continue command works in any loop, not just in while loops.

- ✔ There are only two real warnings to keep in mind with the continue command: Don't use it outside a loop and don't expect it to work on nested loops, and be careful where you put it in a while loop, lest you skip over the loop's counter and accidentally create an endless loop.

- ✔ Like break, continue affects only the loop it's in.

- ✔ As a final, consoling point, this command is rarely used. In fact, many C programmers may be a little fuzzy on what it does or not know precisely how to use it.

Lesson 7-4 Quiz

1. What is a nested loop?

    A. One loop inside another loop.

    B. Two for loops inside each other.

    C. A loop composed of twigs, straw, and bits of hair.

    D. A loop set off by tabs or indented somehow.

2. What's a good thing to do with nested loops?

    A. Build shelters for homeless avians.

    B. Create grids and fill in tables and arrays.

    C. Write intricate programs without if statements.

    D. There is nothing good you can do with nested loops.

3. Which of the following is not a "land" in Disneyland?

    A. Bear Country

    B. Frontier Land

    C. Jungle Land

    D. Tomorrow Land

4. How would you modify the program BORC.C so that the B key is displayed when you press it?

Lesson 7-5: The Sneaky switch-case *Loops*

Let's all go to the lobby,

Let's all go to the lobby,

Let's all go to the lobby,

And get ourselves a treat!

— Author unknown

And when you get to the lobby, you'll probably order yourself some goodies from the menu. In fact, management at your local theater has just devised an interesting computer program to help cut down on pesky, hourly-wage employees. The program they've devised is shown right here:

Name: LOBBY1.C

```c
/* Theater lobby snack bar program */

#include <stdio.h>
#include <conio.h>
#include <ctype.h>

void main()
{
    char c;

    printf("Please make your treat selection:\n");
    printf("B - Beverage.\n");
    printf("C - Candy.\n");
    printf("H - Hot dog.\n");
    printf("P - Popcorn.\n");
    printf("Your choice:");

/* Now you must figure out what they typed in. */

    c=toupper(getch());                  //get input
    if(c=='B')                           //Beverage
            printf("Beverage\nThat will be $2\n");
```

```
        else if(c=='C')                    //Candy
                printf("Candy\nThat will be $1.50\n");
        else if(c=='H')                    //Hot dog
                printf("Hot dog\nThat will be $4\n");
        else if(c=='P')                    //Popcorn
                printf("Popcorn\nThat will be $3\n");
        else
        {
                printf("\nThat is not a proper selection.\n");
                printf("I'll assume you're just not hungry.\n");
                printf("Can I help whoever's next?\n");

        }
}
```

Type this source code into your editor. Save it to disk as LOBBY1.C. This should brighten your heart because you know that more LOBBY programs are on the way . . . .

Compile. Fix any errors. You may get a few because it's such a long program. Watch your spelling and remember your semicolons. Recompile after fixing any errors.

Run.

```
Please make your treat selection:
B - Beverage.
C - Candy.
H - Hot dog.
P - Popcorn.
Your choice:
```

Press **C** for Candy. Love them Hot Tamales! You see:

```
Candy
That will be $1.50
```

Run it again and try a few more options. Then try an option not on the list. Type **M** for a margarita.

```
That is not a proper selection.
I'll assume you're just not hungry.
Can I help whoever's next?
```

Oh well.

The switch-case *solution* *to the LOBBY program*

Don't all those else-if things in the LOBBY1.C program look funny? Doesn't it appear awkward? Maybe not. But it is rather clumsy. This is because there's a better way to pick one of several choices in C. What you need is a switch-case loop.

Right away, I need to tell you that switch-case is not a loop. Instead, it's a selection statement, which is the official designation of what an if statement is. switch-case allows you to select from one of several items, like a long, complex string of if statements — the kind that is pestering the LOBBY1.C program at present.

Next is the source code for LOBBY2.C, an internal improvement to the LOBBY1.C program. It's internal because you're just messing with the program's guts here — making them more elegant. Externally, the program still works the same.

Name: LOBBY2.C

```
/* Theater lobby snack bar program */

#include <stdio.h>
#include <conio.h>
#include <ctype.h>

void main()
{
    char c;

    printf("Please make your treat selection:\n");
    printf("B - Beverage.\n");
    printf("C - Candy.\n");
    printf("H - Hot dog.\n");
    printf("P - Popcorn.\n");
    printf("Your choice:");

/* Now you must figure out what they typed in. */

    c=toupper(getch());        //get input
    switch(c)                  //find the key they pressed
    {
```

```
            case 'B':   //Beverage
                        printf("Beverage\nThat will be $2\n");
                        break;
            case 'C':   //Candy
                        printf("Candy\nThat will be $1.50\n");
                        break;
            case 'H':   //Hot dog
                        printf("Hot dog\nThat will be $4\n");
                        break;
            case 'P':   //Popcorn
                        printf("Popcorn\nThat will be $3\n");
                        break;
            default:
                        printf("\nThat is not a proper selection.\n");
                        printf("I'll assume you're just not hungry.\n");
                        printf("Can I help whoever's next?\n");

    }
}
```

Keep the LOBBY1.C program in your editor. Use this source code for LOBBY2.C as a guide, and edit what you see on your screen. You're changing all the `if` statements into a `switch-case` thing. Be careful what you type. When you're done, double-check lines 21 through 35 in the program to make sure that you got it right. (The first few lines of the program don't change at all.)

Compile. Fix any errors or typos. Note that those are colons — not semicolons — on the `case` lines. The character constants are enclosed in single quotes. The word *default* also ends in a colon.

Run. There should be no difference in the output. Internally, however, you've converted an ugly string of `if-else` statements into an elegant decision-making structure: the `switch-case` loop (or "thing").

✔ Detailed information on what happens in a `switch-case` loop is covered in the next section.

✔ The `switch` command in line 21 takes the single character typed at the keyboard (from line 20) and tells the various `case` statements in its curly brackets to find a match.

✔ Each of the `case` statements (lines 23, 26, 29, 32) compares its character constant with the value of variable c. If there's a match, the statements belonging to that `case` are executed.

✔ The `break` in each `case` statement tells the compiler that the `switch-case` thing is done and to skip the rest of the statements.

✔ The final item in the `switch-case` thing is `default`. It's the option that gets executed if there is no match.

The old switch-case *trick*

This is really one booger of a command to try to become comfy with. Although `switch-case` things are important, they contain a lot of programming finesse that many beginners stumble over. My advice is to work through the programs in the lesson to get a feel for things and then use the following format box and the check marks in this section for review purposes or to figure out what went wrong when things don't work.

Keyword switch (case **and** default)

The `switch` keyword is used to give your programs an easy way to make multiple-choice guesses. It should replace any long repetition of `if-else` statements you're using to make a series of comparisons.

Using `switch` involves creating a complex structure that includes the `case`, `break`, and `default` keywords. Here is how it might look:

```
switch(choice)
{
        case item1:
                statement(s);
                break;

        case item2:
        case item3:
                statement(s);
                break;

        default:
                statements(s);
}
```

The *choice* is usually a variable, something that can be one of several different things. It can be a key typed at the keyboard, a value returned from the mouse or joystick, or some other interesting number or character the program has to evaluate.

After the `case` keyword come various *items;* item1, item2, item3, and so on are the various items that `choice` can be. Each one is a constant, either a character or a value; they cannot be variables. The line ends in a colon, not in a semicolon.

Belonging to each `case` item is one or more `statements`. The program executes these statements when the item matches the `choice` switch is making — like an `if` statement match.

Typically the last statement in a group of `case` statements is a `break` command. Without the `break` there, the program keeps working its way through the rest of the `case` statements.

The last item in the `switch` structure is `default`. That contains the statements to be executed when there is no match — like the final `else` in an `if-else` structure. The `default` statements execute no matter what (unless you `break` out of the structure earlier).

The most important thing to remember about switch-case is that the program always walks through the entire thing unless you put a break in there when you want it to stop. For example, consider the following program snippet:

```
switch(key)
{
    case 'A':
                printf("The A key.\n");
                break;
    case 'B':
                printf("The B key.\n");
                break;
    case 'C':
    case 'D':
                printf("The C or D keys.\n");
                break;
    default:
                printf("I don't know that key.\n");
}
```

Suppose that key is a single-character variable containing a character just typed at the keyboard. Here are three examples of how this would work:

Example 1. Suppose that the key variable contains the letter *A*. The program works:

```
switch(key)
```

Pick a key! So key equals big A. Mosey on down the case list:

```
case 'A':
```

Yup, we have a match. The value of key equals the constant, big A. Execute those statements:

```
printf("The A key.\n");
```

Message printed. Then:

```
break;
```

Bail out of the switch-case thing. I'm done.

If you didn't bail out at this point, the rest of the statements in the switch-case structure would execute *no matter what*.

Example 2. Now suppose that they press the C key. Here's how that works:

```
switch(key)
```

key is a C. Time to check the case statements for a match:

```
case 'A':
```

Nope! Skip to the next case:

```
case 'B':
```

Nope! Skip to the next case:

```
case 'C':
```

Yup! There is a match. The value of key equals the character constant 'C' right here. What's next?

```
case 'D':
```

The computer just goes ho-hum here. There is no match, but it's still waiting for instructions because it matched the case 'C'. Because the statements after case 'D' are the first it finds, it executes those:

```
printf("The C or D keys.\n");
```

Message printed. Then:

```
break;
```

The rest of the switch-case structure is skipped.

Example 3. This time, the character X is entered at the keyboard. Here's how the switch-case thing works:

```
switch(key)
```

key is an X. The computer wends its way through the case statements for a match:

```
case 'A':
```

Nope! Skip to the next case:

```
case 'B':
```

Nope! Skip to the next `case`:

```
case 'C':
```

Nope! Skip to the next `case`:

```
case 'D':
```

Nope! But all the `cases` are done. What's left is the *default,* which supposedly handles everything else — including the X:

```
default:
```

And the only statement:

```
printf("I don't know that key.\n");
```

The `switch-case` structure is done.

- ✔ The thing in `switch`'s parentheses (`choice`) must work out to either a character or integer value. Usually, most programmers put a character or integer variable there. You can also put a C language statement or function in the parentheses, providing that it works out to a character or integer value when it's done.

- ✔ The `case` line ends with a colon, not a semicolon. The statements belonging to `case` are not enclosed in curly brackets.

- ✔ The last statement belonging to a group of `case` statements is usually `break`. This statement tells the computer to skip over the rest of the `switch` structure and keep running the program.

- ✔ If you forget the `break`, the rest of the `switch` structure keeps running. This may not be what you want.

- ✔ The computer matches each item in the `case` statement with the choice `switch` is making. If there is a match, the statements belonging to that `case` are executed; otherwise, they're skipped.

- ✔ It's possible for a case to lack any statements.

- ✔ The keyword `case` must be followed by a constant value, either a number or a character. For example:

```
case 56:                        //item 56 chosen
```

Or:

```
case 'L':                       //L key pressed
```

You cannot stick a variable there. It just doesn't work.

✔ Most C manuals refer to the command as `switch`, and `case` is just another keyword. I use `switch-case` because it helps me remember that the second word is `case` and not something else.

✔ You don't need a `default` to end the structure. If you leave it off and if none of the `case`'s items match, nothing happens.

The special relationship between while *and* switch-case

Most programs have at their core a `while` loop. But within that `while` loop, they usually have a nice, big `switch-case` structure. That's because you can keep choosing options over and over until you choose the option that quits the program. The over-and-over is a loop handled by `while`, and the selection is done by a `switch-case` structure. To drive this point home, I present the final incarnation of the LOBBY.C program:

Name: LOBBY3.C

```
/* Theater lobby snack bar program */

#include <stdio.h>
#include <conio.h>
#include <ctype.h>

#define TRUE 1              //This is true
#define FALSE !(TRUE)       //This is not true

void main()
{
    char c;                 //their choice
    int done                //while loop ender
    float total=0;          //start their total at zero;

    printf("Please make your treat selections:\n");
    printf("B - Beverage.\n");
    printf("C - Candy.\n");
    printf("H - Hot dog.\n");
    printf("P - Popcorn.\n");
    printf("= - Done.\n");
    printf("Your choice:\n");
```

```
/* Now you must figure out what they typed in. */

    done=FALSE;
    while(!done)
    {
        c=toupper(getch());  //get input
        switch(c)            //find the key they pressed
        {
                    case 'B':   //Beverage
                                printf("B - Beverage\tThat
                                    will be $2\n");
                                total+=2;
                                break;
                    case 'C':   //Candy
                                printf("C - Candy\tThat will
                                    be $1.50\n");
                                total+=1.5;
                                break;
                    case 'H':   //Hot dog
                                printf("H - Hot dog\tThat
                                    will be $4\n");
                                total+=4;
                                break;
                    case 'P':   //Pop corn
                                printf("P - Popcorn\tThat
                                    will be $3\n");
                                total+=3;
                                break;
                    case '=':   //done
                                printf("= Total of
                                    $%.2f\n",total);
                                printf("Please pay the
                                    cashier.\n");
                                done=TRUE;
        }                       //end switch-case
    }                           //end while
}
```

Please type the source code for LOBBY3.C into your editor. You can try editing the LOBBY2.C program if you want, but I've made many subtle changes to the program and wouldn't want you to miss any. So start from scratch if you're willing. A Blow-by-blow box nearby describes the details.

Save the file to disk as LOBBY3.C.

Compile. Fix any errors that may have crept into the code.

Run.

```
Please make your treat selection:
B - Beverage.
C - Candy.
H - Hot dog.
P - Popcorn.
Your choice:
```

The program looks a little different from here on. Press **B** to order a beverage and then **P** to order some popcorn:

```
B - Beverage      That will be $2
P - Popcorn       'That will be $3
```

Now press the equal key (=) to get your total:

```
= Total of $5.00
Please pay the cashier.
```

Amazing piece of work! Think of the money this theater will save on dopey counter employees!

✔ Most programs employ this exact type of loop. The while(!done) spins 'round and 'round while a switch-case thing handles all the program's input.

✔ One of the switch-case items handles the condition when the loop must stop. In LOBBY3.C, the key is the equal sign. What it does is to set the value of the done variable to TRUE. The while loop then stops repeating.

✔ Refer to Lesson 6-1 for more information on the TRUE and FALSE defines at the beginning of the source code. Also see Lesson 7-3 for information on while(!done) loops.

✔ There is no default item in LOBBY3.C's switch-case thing. Honestly, I can't think of anything to say there. Even if you displayed Invalid key or something equally dorky, it doesn't do users any good.

✔ Before the Dopey Movie Theater Counter Employees Union writes me a nasty letter, know that I was once one of your legions. "Would you like buttery-flavored topping on that, sir?" Oh, those were the days . . . .

The `while-switch-case` of it all in LOBBY3.C

The LOBBY3.C program uses three different variables: c holds the key that is pressed; done is set to TRUE or FALSE and controls the while loop; and total keeps track of customers' tabs as they order various items.

```
done=FALSE;
while(!done)
```

With the done variable set to FALSE in line 26, the while loop on the next line repeats over and over until done is set to TRUE again (which happens in line 51, after the equal key is pressed).

Line 29 gets input from the keyboard. A single character is read, converted to uppercase, and then saved in the c variable. That variable is then used in the switch-case thing to determine which key was pressed and to take appropriate action:

```
c=toupper(getch());
switch(c)
```

An alternative way to write these two lines is as follows:

```
switch(toupper(getch()));
```

This method also works because C functions work from the inside out (see Lesson 5-5). It has the disadvantage that the key isn't saved in a variable, but that's OK in this program.

The various case structures then examine the keys that were pressed. For each match, three things happen: The item ordered is displayed on the screen, the total is increased by the cost of that item (total+=3, for example), and a break statement busts out of the switch-case thing. At that point, the while loop continues to repeat as additional selections are made.

Line 48 breaks out of the while loop when the equal key is pressed. The total is displayed, along with other information, and then the done variable is set to TRUE. That stops the while loop.

```
case '=':
        printf("= Total of
            $%.2f\n",total);
        printf("Please pay the
            cashier.\n");
        done=TRUE;
```

The $%.2f\n thing wins the award for being cryptic in this program. The core is the %f placeholder, which prints the floating-point total variable. In that, you'll find a .2, which limits output to only two characters after the decimal point — a properly formatted dollar amount. The $ is just a dollar sign prefix, and \n is the newline character. Altogether, it's pretty imposing.

A function-key menu program

If you want to see another example of a while-switch-case loop in action, turn to Appendix D and check out the FUNMENU.C program. It's a function-key menu program that runs several DOS commands. You can modify it to run other programs on your hard drive as well. But at the core of the program is the while-switch-case loop, so popular in other C programs.

Two funky things happen in the FUNMENU.C program that you may be curious about. The first is how the function keys are read from the keyboard. The second is how the program executes DOS commands.

To read a function key, you have to access the computer's keyboard BIOS; normal C functions such as `getch` and `getchar` just don't cut it. The reason is that those keys produce two characters when you press them. The first character is called a *scan code,* which is a unique number for each key and each key combination (Alt+, Shift+, or Ctrl+) on the keyboard. The second character is the character that appears on the screen when you press that key. C language keyboard functions don't bother with the scan code, so you're stuck with having to access the BIOS to read those keys.

The following function, called `getKey()`, accesses the PC's hardware to read the keyboard directly:

```
int getKey(void)
{
    union REGS regs;

    regs.h.ah=0x00;                 //Read keyboard function
    int86(KEYBOARD,&regs,&regs);    //dial up keyboard BIOS

    return(regs.x.ax);              //Return keyboard "scancode"
}
```

This function returns an integer value (not a character value) that contains both the scan code and character code for each key you press on the keyboard. Hectic stuff! (This function requires the DOS.H header file to work.)

To make things worse, you have to know the scan code values for the various keys. Typically, they're represented as four-digit hexadecimal numbers — which might as well be Chinese, as far as you or I are concerned. Refer to the file FUNCTION.H in Appendix D for a list of the codes generated by the 10 function keys on your PC's keyboard.

The second trick in FUNMENU.C is how DOS commands are run from within a C program. This is known as "shelling to DOS" but in C it's also called creating a "child program." Whatever. The secret is that you can use the `system()` function to have your program "type" anything you can type at the DOS prompt. For example:

```
system("DIR");
```

This command in your C program causes your program to stop, bail out to DOS, run the DIR command, and then return to your program to pick up where it left off. Ingenious stuff, and it's the guts of how a menu program such as FUNMENU.C works.

> ✔ You have to include the STDLIB.H header file in your source code to use the `system()` function.
>
> ✔ The `getKey()` function can also be used to read various Alt+key combinations on the keyboard. These key combinations can be found in other programming reference books.
>
> ✔ See the comments in FUNMENU.C in Appendix D for additional information.

Lesson 7-5 Quiz

1. Define a `switch-case` loop:

   A. It's a thing used to make multiple guesses in a C program.

   B. It handily replaces a long parade of `else-if` things.

   C. It converts uppercase to lowercase and then back again.

   D. Both A and B look right to me.

2. Which of the following is not a British spelling of an English word?

   A. Centre.

   B. Colour.

   C. Mothre.

   D. Theatre.

3. What's wrong with the following statement:

   ```
   case car;
   ```

   A. Nothing's wrong.

   B. The line should end with a colon and not a semicolon.

   C. The `car` variable should be enclosed in single quotes, and you need a colon, not a semicolon, to end the thing.

   D. You cannot use a variable with `case`, and the semicolon should be a colon.

4. If none of the items by the various `case` statements in a `switch-case` thing matches, how can you explain it to the program's user?

   A. Just write a contingency plan for everything and explain it to them that way.

   B. Have the next statement after the `switch-case` thing be a `printf` command saying, "Sorry, I couldn't match that keystroke" or something.

   C. Just put in about 16 `break` statements. That oughtta do 'er.

   D. Use the `default` statement to handle all nonmatches.

5. Where did Lee surrender to Grant to end the U.S. Civil War?

   A. Gettysburg, Pennsylvania.

   B. Appomattox Court House, Virginia.

   C. Richmond, Virginia.

   D. It's a trick question; Lee surrendered to Sherman.

Lesson 7 Final Exam

1. A `while` loop repeats until what happens?

    A. The Second Coming.

    B. Its wife calls it for dinner and then it still takes another 20 minutes before it stops working.

    C. It repeats until the final curly bracket.

    D. It repeats as long as the condition it's clutching in parentheses is true.

2. What is the `while` equivalent of the following `for` loop?

    ```
    for(;;)
    ```

    A. `while(;;)`

    B. `while(TRUE)`

    C. `while(1)`

    D. `while(0)`

3. Define *Mildred:*

    A. A fear of mills.

    B. A fear of mildew.

    C. A temperate hot sauce of a ruddy hue.

    D. The opposite of Derdlim.

4. How many times does the following `while` loop repeat itself?

    ```
    while(6)
    ```

    A. Never.

    B. Once.

    C. Six times.

    D. Forever.

5. In a `do-while` loop, the condition that `while` examines:

    A. Comes last.

    B. Can't stop the loop from repeating at least once.

    C. Is followed by a parentheses and a semicolon.

    D. All of the above.

6. Which of the following is really an official government agency-thing?

    A. The Department of Tourism and Tobacco.

    B. The Consumer Product Safety Commission Lids and Caps Division.

C. National Bureau of Standards Fudge Department.

D. Department of Agriculture Meat and Poultry Hotline.

7. How would you read the following:

```
while(!done)
```

A. `while` I'm excited and then `done`, over and over.

B. `while` not `done`.

C. `while`, exclamation-point thing, `done` in parentheses.

D. Repeat the `while` loop as long as the variable `done` is happy.

8. Which of the following techniques stops a `while(!done)` loop? (Choose two.)

A. The `break` statement.

B. Changing the value of the `done` variable to `FALSE`.

C. Kicking out the computer's wall plug.

D. Pressing Ctrl+Alt+Delete.

9. What do you call one loop inside another loop?

A. A nested loop.

B. A dual loop.

C. A loop-de-loop.

D. A hula-hoop loop.

10. What are loops in loops good for?

A. Filling in arrays and grids.

B. Repeating something twice.

C. Making the computer really sweat.

D. Getting dizzy.

11. How does the `continue` command affect a loop it lives in?

A. Truly it's unnecessary because the loop continues anyway; most programmers don't bother with this statement.

B. `continue` is the opposite of `break` — whatever that means.

C. The `continue` command forces the loop to repeat again, skipping any statements left in the loop.

D. The `continue` command increments the loop counter without forcing the loop to repeat.

12. How many feet should you stay back when following an emergency vehicle?

A. 200 feet.

B. 300 feet.

    C. 500 feet.

    D. 1,000 feet.

13. What usually lives in the heart of a `while` loop?

    A. Mr. Bug!

    B. A `switch-case` thing.

    C. A set of statements that repeat.

    D. A control statement.

For the next few questions, consider the following snippet of code:

```
switch(c)
      case 'A':
      case 'B':
                    printf("A or B!\n");
      case 'C':
                    printf("C here!\n");
                    break;
      case 'D':
                    printf("Must be D!\n");
                    break;
      default:
                    printf("Can't help you.\n");
```

14. If c is equal to A, what is displayed on the screen?

    A. Nothing.

    B. `A or B!`

    C. `A or B!` *and* `C here!`

    D. `Can't help you.`

15. If c is equal to C, what is displayed on the screen?

    A. Nothing.

    B. `A or B!`

    C. `C here!`

    D. `Can't help you.`

16. If c is equal to X, what is displayed on the screen?

    A. Nothing.

    B. `A or B!`

    C. `C here!`

    D. `Can't help you.`

17. Which one of the following cities has the most rainfall, on average, during the months of May and June?

   A. Mobile, Alabama.

   B. San Francisco, California.

   C. Richmond, Virginia.

   D. Seattle, Washington.

Where Do I Go From Here?!?

Sorry to take you just so far with learning C and then leave you stranded. At my publisher's insistence, I had to lop off this book somewhere, and here was the spot. Honestly, there is more to come. This book's second volume picks right up where you left off — right at Chapter 8, in fact. Look for *C For Dummies,* Volume II at your favorite bookstore soon. Until then, please continue to dabble with the concepts offered in this book. Maybe even consider cracking open some of those other C books on your desk. Do something, do anything, but please wait until Volume II comes out sometime soon.

Appendix A

Answers to Exercises

*H*ere are the answers to this book's various lesson quizzes and final exams. So as not to offend anyone or make you feel unduly stupid, here is the way you grade yourself:

- ✔ If you miss zero questions, give yourself a Brown.
- ✔ If you miss one question, give yourself a Yellow.
- ✔ If you miss two questions, give yourself a Gold.
- ✔ If you miss from three to eight questions, give yourself a Blue.
- ✔ If you miss all of the questions, give yourself a button that boasts, "I'm learning" and the state will buy you lunch for life.

Lesson 1-1 Quiz Answers

1. B. The B language came before C.

2. D. B came from Bell Labs.

3. D. Actually, the other language is called C++, which means "one more than C" in nerd-speak.

4. D. C is a mid-level language, so give yourself a point if you chose answer B as well.

Lesson 1-2 Quiz Answers

1. B. By creating a program that lets the user accomplish some task — hopefully, the same task the user wants accomplished.

2. B. The steps required to create a program by using the C language.

3. A-1, B-2, C-3, D-4.

4. A. The source file comes first (STOMP.C), then comes the object file (STOMP.OBJ), and then the final, executable program file (STOMP.EXE).

Lesson 1-3 Quiz Answers

1. C. A source code file is a text file.

2. D. Employee theft is most probably caused by stealing.

3. B. C source code files end with the following filename extension (.C).

4. A. Save it, compile it, link it, run it.

Lesson 1-4 Quiz Answers

1. D. You'll find yourself reediting your source code file because of errors, bugs, improvements, and eternal tweaking.

2. B. Recompile and *then* rerun the program to see whether you fixed the errors. Give yourself half a point for choosing A.

3. C. The capital of Nepal is Katmandu.

4. D. To start a new C language program, you pray for inspiration and then start working on a new source code file.

Lesson 1-5 Quiz Answers

1. D. Error messages contain line numbers, but the numbers offer only a general hint of where the error could be. Most likely, a missing semicolon statement would be an error in the previous line.

2. C. The importance of the semicolon is discussed in Lesson 1-7. Any answer gets you a point with this one.

3. B. The spelling error may be another piece of the program, so when the linker can't find that piece, it displays an error.

4. C. Fix and recompile.

Lesson 1-6 Quiz Answers

1. B. The main function in every C language program is called main.

2. A. C language keywords are the "words" of the C language.

3. D. In addition to the keywords are functions, such as printf, functions that came with your compiler that do all sorts of fun things with DOS and Windows, and functions you can make up yourself.

4. C. Some functions may require parentheses because the parentheses hold various things required by or belonging to the function.

5. D.

```
void main()
{
        printf("Goodbye, cruel world!\n");
}
```

Lesson 1-7 Quiz Answers

1. C. Computers are really about input and output.

2. D. I/O is Input and Output.

3. B. B&O is Baltimore and Ohio.

4. A. When you see an error, compare your source code with the one shown in this book, reedit, save it again to disk, and then recompile.

Lesson 1-8 Quiz Answers

1. A. The compiler creates several files; among them are files ending in C, OBJ, EXE, and maybe BAK.

2. A. The most important files worth keeping are C and EXE because the file ending in C is the source code file, and EXE is the program created from it.

3. B. The capital of the Canadian province of Manitoba is Winnipeg.

4. C. Creating a subdirectory structure for your C programs helps you organize your C programs and keep you sane.

Lesson 1-9 Quiz Answers

1. C. Most likely, you'll forget to end statements with a semicolon.

2. B. Semicolons are required at the end of C language statements.

3. A. Programmers say "A string of text."

4. C. When you see \n, think newline, which means a new line of text (like pressing the Enter key) and not New Line Cinema.

Chapter 1 Final Exam Answers

1. Here is one such program:

```
#include <stdio.h>

void main()
{
        printf("10,000 years of human development so I could\n");
        printf("display this on my computer. Wow!\n");
}
```

2. A. There are lots of ways to write a C program that displays the message in question 1.

3. A. The C programs you've typed in so far begin with #include <stdio.h>.

4. C. The next thing in a C program is typically void main().

5. B. The main function in all C programs is called main.

6. B. Surrounding the main function — holding it together — are curly brackets or braces.

7. D. They can send a man to the moon, so why can't they make a decent decaffeinated coffee? (Actually, most decaffeinated coffee today is much better than the strained weeds they had when this slogan was popular.)

8. A. C is composed of words, statements, functions, and other stuff.

9. C. Statements in C, similar to sentences in a human language, end with a semicolon.

10. A. Text enclosed in double quotes is referred to as a string of text.

11. D. C programs start out as a text file.

12. D. The text file is also known as a source code file.

13. C. The compiler converts the source code file into an object file.

14. A. The linker creates the final product, the EXE program file.

15. B. The best way to deal with errors is to reedit the source code file and recompile.

16. C. The sample printf statement displays two lines of text. The /n thing in the middle of the string breaks the one line in half, which makes for two lines of text displayed.

Lesson 2-1 Quiz Answers

1. Something like this would do:

```
#include <stdio.h>

void main()
{
```

```
        printf("Goodbye? Ha! This is DOS. You can never leave!\n");
}
```

The key is the `printf` function, which displays the message.

2. D. An escape sequence is a method of putting special characters into a text string.

3. Here is what the STOOGES.C program might look like:

```
#include <stdio.h>

void main()
{
        printf("Larry\nMoe\nCurly");
}
```

The key here is to put \n escape sequence dealies in the string so that each word appears on a different line. There must be a \n between `Larry` and `Moe` and between `Moe` and `Curly`.

4. Here is the modified STOOGES.C program:

```
#include <stdio.h>

void main()
{
        printf("\"Larry\"\n\"Moe\"\n\"Curly\"");
}
```

Gads! What a mess.

5. D. Actually, could be any old "Star Trek" episode.

Lesson 2-2 Quiz Answers

1. D. You can use the `printf` and `scanf` functions to read a line of text from the keyboard and display it.

2. D. `char menutext[48];` creates a string variable `menutext` that has room enough to store 48 characters.

3. Here is such a program:

```
#include <stdio.h>

void main()
{
        char name[20];

        printf("What is your name?");
        scanf("%s",&name);
        printf("%s? My name is %s too!\n",name,name);
}
```

4. A. The %s in a `printf` function means that there must be a corresponding string variable later in that same `printf` function.

5. C. Any quoted string of text is a literal string.

Lesson 2-3 Quiz Answers

1. D. Comments in a C program are silly little things you write to yourself that are ignored by the compiler.

2. D. The characters that begin and end a comment are traditionally /* and then */ to end. You can also use // to stick a comment on only one line (which ends when you press the Enter key).

3. D. The comment begins and ends with the wrong characters. Comments begin with /* and end with */.

4. A. Commenting out is the art of disabling part of your program by hugging it as a comment.

Lesson 2-4 Quiz Answers

1. D. gets is to scanf as puts is to printf.

2. A. gets(firstname); and scanf("%s",firstname); both do the same thing.

3. Here is such a program:

```
#include <stdio.h>

void main()
{
    puts("This is the first line\nThis is the last line");
}
```

The point here is that you can stick a \n (newline character) into any string, even one displayed by puts.

4. puts(jerk); matches printf("%s\n",jerk);

and

puts("Bletch!") matches printf("Bletch!\n");

5. Here is the updated MADLIB1.C program rewritten with gets statements:

```
/*
MADLIB1.C Source Code
Written by (your name here)
*/

#include <stdio.h>

void main()
{
    char adjective[20];
    char food[20];
    char chore[20];
    char furniture[20];
```

```
/* Get the words to use in the madlib */

    printf("Enter an adjective:");     /* prompt */
    gets(adjective);                   /* input */
    printf("Enter a food:");
    gets(food);
    printf("Enter a household chore (past tense):");
    gets(chore);
    printf("Enter an item of furniture:");
    gets(furniture);

/* Display the output */

    printf("\n\nDon't touch that %s %s!\n",adjective,food);
    printf("I just %s the %s!\n",chore,furniture);
}
```

Lesson 2-5 Quiz Answers

1. D. Any of the statements works.

2. C. A conversion character begins with a % (percent sign), such as %s or anything listed in Table 2-2.

3. B. An escape sequence in a string is \ followed by a character, used to insert secret codes and stuff into a text string.

4. A. Only the double quote (") requires an escape sequence (\") if you're to include it with printf.

Chapter 2 Final Exam Answers

1. Stick in the backslashes as shown here:

```
printf("Please enter \"your name,\" last name first:");
```

2. B. Tell Earl that you just stick two backslashes into a string: \\. The computer displays only one of them.

3. Here is one such program:

Name: HEYBABE.C

```
#include <stdio.h>

void main()
{
    char me[20];

    printf("What is your sign?");
    scanf("%s",&me);
```

```
        printf("Hey, babe! I'm a %s too!\n",me);
}
```

The ampersand (&) before the me variable in the scanf statement is optional.

4. Here is how you would rewrite the HEYBABE.C program to substitute the gets command for scanf:

Name: HEYBABE.C

```
#include <stdio.h>

void main()
{
        char me[20];

        printf("What is your sign?");
        gets(me);
        printf("Hey, babe! I'm a %s too!\n",me);
}
```

5. C. The universe is almost as big as the media's ego.

6. C. The /* and /* mark the starting and ending points for a comment in the C language.

7. B. The evil nested comment rears its ugly head!

8. C. Anti-lamination reduces atmospheric friction but is a tremendous drain on reserve fuel.

9. B. The following two statements produce the same output:

```
printf("Cough up the money for this program or I'll erase your
        data.\n");
```

```
puts("Cough up the money for this program or I'll erase your data.");
```

Answer C lacks a semicolon at the end of the statements. (Gotcha!)

10. C. The following two statements do the same thing:

```
scanf("%s",city);
```

```
gets(city);
```

11. C. The puts function always sticks a newline character after its output.

12. D. To reduce the U.S. deficit, the government should cut spending. This is only common sense, and anyone who tells you otherwise is profiting from our current malaise.

13. D. The following printf statement makes noise because of the \a escape sequence. That sequence sounds the PC's speaker (the "bell"):

```
printf("\arghghgh!\n");
```

14. D. OK. They're really all escape characters, though Steve McQueen isn't officially recognized by printf.

15. D. Same reason as for #14.

Lesson 3-1 Quiz Answers

1. A. They're called variables because their contents can change.

2. B. Variables can contain strings of text or numbers. They don't "change constantly," though their contents can be changed.

3. A = `char` to define string or text variables

   B = `int` to define numeric variables

4. D. An integer is a number without a fraction or decimal part between –32,000-something and 32,000-something.

5. B. Values are assigned to numeric variables by using an equal sign.

6. A. You can't assign a string variable by using the equal sign; it works only with numbers.

7. A simple modification to the METHUS2.C program would work as follows:

```
#include <stdio.h>
#include <stdlib.h>

void main()
{
    int age;
    char years[8];

    printf("How old are you?");
    gets(years);
    age=atoi(years);
    printf("Golly, %i is awfully old.\n",age);
}
```

8. B. St. Redundancy is proclaiming "ASCII to integer! ASCII to integer!" (and he's saying it as "a-to-i," not "a-toy! atoy!").

Lesson 3-2 Quiz Answers

1. C. The unique little symbols you use to add, subtract, multiply, and divide numbers, values, variables, and stuff in the C language are called operators.

2. A. +   Addition

   B. -   Subtraction

   C. *   Multiplication

   D. /   Division

3. D. All the statements place a value into the `attempts` variable. The strange one appears to be option C:

```
attempts=tries+attempts;
```

   However, this just increases the value of the `attempts` variable by the value of the `tries` variable. This subject, which I call the "art of incrementation," is covered in Lesson 4-7.

4. A. Only the value 969 is a constant.

5. C. For the `atoi` function to work properly, you must add the `#include <stdlib.h>` thing at the beginning of the program.

Lesson 3-3 Quiz Answers

1. A. Declaring your variables is almost as important as flossing. And if you didn't know that, you should dial 1-800-DENTIST and find a dentist near you whose dental hygienist will scold you for it.

2. C. The `naughty` variable name is rather nice.

3. D. Item D is a string constant, not a variable. You might have thought that item B was wrong too, but the `33` is part of the variable name.

4. D. With few exceptions, the evil Captain Kirk wears the eyeliner, though arguments can (and will) be made for the other choices.

Lesson 3-4 Quiz Answers

1. A. The value π is a constant.

2. A. Throughout the course of your program, a constant would never change its value.

3. D. The advantage of the `#define` thing is that you can set up a constant value once and then use a shortcut word to represent the value elsewhere in your program and that changing a constant value is as easy as editing the `#define` thing. It also makes your programs look more cool, though that wasn't the answer I was looking for.

4. D. No more degrading IQ comments. At least not for a few more lessons.

5. D. You know, I'm very fond of Chinese food and especially enjoyed the real Chinese food I got to eat when I visited China in 1980. Answer A is usually what I say when reading my fortune cookie for everyone; answer B is my sarcastic remark after returning from the john; answer C was actually uttered by a co-worker of mine when I worked in a steakhouse restaurant in the late '70s. That leaves answer D as the correct one.

Lesson 3-5 Quiz Answers

1. B. The compiler works with different types of numbers differently, which is why we must deal with numeric data types.

2. A. The Ints (integers) and Floats (floating-point numbers) are the two basic types of numbers in the C language.

3. D. Integers are really the most popular type of number: easy for the computer to digest, quick, and ideal for small values.

4. D. Floats handle very large or very small values and any value that must be precise.

5. A. "Float" is short for floating-point number.

6. A. An unsigned integer variable would never be negative. Nope, not never.

7. Here they are:

A. 98.6	9.86E1
B. 2001 a Space Odyssey	2.001E3
C. 1,500,000,000,000	1.5E12
D. 0.000001 (one millionth)	1E-6

Incidentally, 1.5E12 is the dollar amount of the 1995 federal budget for the United States. In a few years, this value may actually seem cheap!

8. D. Double-precision numbers hold larger values and are more precise, but you pay a price in speed for using them.

Lesson 3-6 Quiz Answers

1. A. The `char` keyword creates single-character variables.

2. D. The `char key;` statement simply declares the variable `key` but doesn't put anything into it. In answer C, the `francis_scott` thing is a variable, which contains a value, which winds up in the `key` variable.

3. C. It would take a lot of balloons to hoist a cat.

4. D. The `getche()` function echoes the character.

Lesson 3-7 Quiz Answers

1. As follows:

   A. + Addition

   B. − Subtraction

   C. * Multiplication

   D. / Division

   E. ≅ Confusion

2. B. Adding 1 to a number is referred to as incrementation.

3. A. This is the proper way to increment `incme`: `incme=incme+1;`

4. B. After Mr. B comes Mr. B+1, which has nothing to do with the C language, but I wanted to include a Hazel joke in this book somewhere.

Lesson 3-8 Quiz Answers

1. B. The order of precedence refers to the way math is done in a C language program.

2. C. My Dear Aunt Sally is a mnemonic for Multiplication, Division, Addition, and Subtraction, the order in which long math problems are done in C programs.

3. C. Carefully placed parentheses will foil the desires of My Dear Aunt Sally every time.

4. A. The answer is 42.

5. A. In C, math works inside the parentheses first; multiplication and division first and then addition and subtraction sections; work from left to right.

Chapter 3 Final Exam Answers

1. C. Variables are used in C to store numbers (values) and text that can change.

2. A. Declare a variable before you use it.

3. B. Numeric variables hold numbers or values.

4. A. The `int` variable holds only integer values or whole numbers.

5. C. The `float` variable holds fractions or numbers with a decimal part and very large and very small values.

6. Here is such a program:

Name: IQ.C

```
#include <stdio.h>
#include <stdlib.h>

void main()
{
```

```
        int age;
        float hat_size;
        float iq;
        char input[4];

        printf("Enter your age:");
        gets(input);
        age = atoi(input);

        printf("Enter your hat size:");
        gets(input);
        hat_size = atof(input);

/* The atof function is used to convert strings
   to floating point values */

        iq = age*hat_size;
        printf("You have an iq of %.2f.\n",iq);
}
```

Since you didn't know about the `atof` function, I'll cut you some slack on your solution. If you used `atoi` to convert the hat size, all that means is that people with in-between hat sizes get cheated on their final IQ value.

7. C. The `char` variable holds characters and strings of text.

8. D. The ugly truth is that Soylent Green is made of people — people like Edward G. Robinson, to be exact.

9. D. Don't use an equal sign in a constant definition or end the line with a semicolon.

10. A. The `atoi` function converts numbers typed at the keyboard (and stored in a string variable) into values.

11. Like this:

    A. Multiplication   *

    B. Division   /

    C. Addition   +

    D. Subtraction   -

12. C. Incrementation is adding something to a variable's value, increasing it by about yay much. If you answered B, you're only half right because you can increment by values more than 1.

13. A, B, and C only. *Boobyprize* is the most popular *Starship Enterprise* pseudonym in *Mad* magazine.

14. A The `getch` function reads a single character typed at the keyboard. Answer D is correct, but the function isn't really designed to make the computer wait (there are functions, such as `sleep` and `delay`, that do that in Borland C).

15. Here is such a program:

Name: GET2.C

```
#include <stdio.h>
#include <conio.h>
```

```
void main()
{
    char a,b;

    printf("Type a character:");
    a = getche();

/* Start this next line with a \n */

    printf("\nType another character:");
    b = getche();

    printf("\nYou typed a %c and a %c.\n",a,b);
}
```

16. C. The order of precedence means that multiplication and division are done first and then addition and subtraction.

Lesson 4-1 Quiz Answers

1. D. The `if` keyword does it all.

2. C. When the thing `if` compares is true, then the statement (or statements) belonging to the `if` keyword are executed.

3. D. You use two equal signs to see whether two values are equal.

4. As follows:

A.	`<`	Less than
B.	`==`	Equal to
C.	`>`	Greater than
D.	`<=`	Less than or equal to
E.	`>=`	Greater than or equal to
F.	`!=`	Not equal to

5. True.

Lesson 4-2 Quiz Answers

1. D. If-else structures handle either-or decisions in the C language.

2. D. The second `printf` statement is executed when the value of variable `var` is greater than or equal to 3.

3. A. In any if-else structure thing, one or the other set of statements will be executed.

4. B. For now, use an initial `if`, then `if-else` commands, and finally an `else` to handle several conditions. (In the future, you use a `switch-case` loop to do the same job.)

5. D. Ever try teaching "incorruptible" moral values to anyone?

Lesson 4-3 Quiz Answers

1. A. The if statement compares two characters by using their ASCII code values.

2. C. Single quotes for single characters.

3. B. A and B are equal, A==B.

4. D. Unless you're in a water boat, there is no such thing as a "water landing."

Lesson 4-4 Quiz Answers

1. C. Formatting your C code makes it more readable.

2. B. Wo you Tsign Dao pi-jou.

3. C. White space includes tabs, spaces, blank lines, and other "airy" aspects of C language source code.

4. C. No body lice here.

Lesson 4-5 Quiz Answers

1. A. All loops have a beginning, middle, and end.

2. B. The for keyword sets up a simple loop (and it also confuses the heck out of everyone).

3. B. It loops around 10 times, from 0 through 9.

4. Here is a possible solution:

```
#include <stdio.h>

void main()
{
    int i;

    for(i=1 ; i<100 ; i=i+1)
    {
        printf("Ouch!\t");
        printf("%i\n",i);
    }
}
```

Lesson 4-6 Quiz Answers

1. C. Table 3-1 in Lesson 3-5 shows the range for an unsigned char variable to be 0 to 255. If it were signed, the range would go up to only 127. Lesson 6-6 runs on and on about this concept, if you care to delve into it.

2. D. (Though all answers are technically correct.)

3. B. Loops must have an exit point or else they loop eternally.

4. A. The break keyword is used to stop any loop, even those run amok.

Lesson 4-7 Quiz Answers

1. B. The ++ operator is the incrementation operator.
2. A. They can count forward and backward.
3. A. Counting backward in C is achieved by subtracting, or decrementing, in a loop.
4. A. Decrementing is the art of decreasing a variable's value.
5. I'll assume that you managed to rewrite 100.C by using the sample for loops provided.
6. D. The Adam's apple always gives them away.

Lesson 4-8 Quiz Answers

1. C. The i=i+2 part of the for loop ensures that it will count by twos.
2. B. But give yourself a credit for any answer.
3. Just change the i=i+5 part of the for loop to read i=i+5.
4. D. They multiply it by whatever shortcut is *=.

Chapter 4 Final Exam

1. D. If makes its decision based on a comparison.
2. A. The greater-than equal symbol is >=, just like it sounds. Notice that the => is not the same thing.
3. D. These are not the only signs that someone is choking.
4. D. If and else handle an either-or type of decision in the C language.
5. A. If compares two character's ASCII values.
6. B. If a > b you get Wambooli!
7. A. If a < b you get Blorf!
8. D. If a = b you get Fragus!
9. F. It's not true; both men and women have the same number of ribs. However, men can usually eat more ribs than women can.
10. B. It loops ten times, from 0 through 9.
11. D. The break keyword stops any loop.
12. A. The ++ is the incrementation operator.
13. A. The -- is the decrementing operator.
14. B. The proper salutation for the Pope in a letter is Most Holy Father.
15. A. It's the only for statement that decrements the variable by fives.
16. Here you go:

    A. x=x+ 1; x++;

    B. x=x*5; x+=5;

    C. x=x-5; x-=5;

    D. x=x-1; x--;

    E. x=x/5; x/=5;

Lesson 5-1 Quiz Answers

1. A. Functions unclutter the `main` function and help avoid redundancy in your programs.

2. A. Or B. Either one. Don't bother counting off if you get this one wrong.

3. B. Answer A defines "nausea"; answer C stems from not having a life (I mean, the people at the convention don't even watch the whole thing); and answer D defines "boredom." This leaves B.

4. D. Can't think of anything clever to say here.

5. A. The vernacular is to *call* a function.

6. B. The `eatPet` function comes from a game where you must eat one of Satan's pets to defeat the goddess of the First Amendment.

7. B. Prototyping tells the compiler about your functions (and answer C counts as well).

8. C. As in:

```
void jerk(void);
```

9. B. Van Wolverton's first name is Van.

Lesson 5-2 Quiz Answers

1. D. Each function can use its own variables.

2. A. Variables inside other functions are declared just as they are in the `main` function.

3. D. Two variables in two different functions can share the same name.

4. D. Though the other answers suffice.

5. C. There are only global and local variables.

6. A. *Jailhouse Rock* is pretty much even with *Flaming Star* as two of Elvis' best films, with *Jailhouse Rock* slightly in the lead. *Viva Las Vegas* is also a good Elvis film, pairing him with the energetic Ann-Margret. *Change of Habit,* on the other hand, is almost universally regarded as the worst Elvis film of all time.

Lesson 5-3 Quiz Answers

1. B. Only in B is the variable defined as a `float`.

2. D. You can pass either a function a value in a variable or a value directly.

3. B. This is really up to you, though I prefer to listen to Frank's '50s work. The early stuff is too much music and not enough singing. And, well, heck, all of it is good. Give yourself a point no matter what.

4. D. To make a prototype for any function, stick a semicolon at the end of the line that defines the function.

5. D. The integer value passed to the `taxes()` function is represented by the `income` variable inside the function. Answer B also works, though it's very specific.

Lesson 5-4 Quiz Answers

1. B. Functions must be defined as the type of value they return (or produce).

2. C. An `int` function returns integer values.

3. D. You can use `return` to return a value from a function or to "bail out" of a function before the final curly bracket.

4. A. Type casting temporarily (one time only) changes a variable's type, typically from `int` to `float`.

5. A. Suriname is located in South America.

Lesson 5-5 Quiz Answers

1. A. C functions work from the inside out.

2. C. The `getchar` function goes first.

3. Like this:

```
return(garlic());
```

4. A. Blood type O is the universal donor.

5. D. Blood type AB is the universal recipient.

6. Counting this question, the phrase "inside out" was used 13 times in this lesson.

Lesson 5-6 Quiz Answers

1. D. It's more answer A than the other two, but each one is an example of "reinventing the wheel."

2. D. Hold the onion, Reggie.

3. D. I'd also include anyone from my family, though you don't know them personally and wouldn't get the reference.

4. As follows:

   A. `regs.h.al`   AL

   B. `regs.x.cx`   CX

   C. `regs.h.dh`   DH

   D. `regs.h.dl`   DL

5. A. Personally, the Doublemint song does me in every time. If you have another song you can't get out of your head, please write me in care of the publisher, whose address is in the front of this book.

6. A. On a computer screen, home is the upper left corner of the display.

Lesson 5-7 Quiz Answers

1. D. Most importantly, answer C.

2. A. The random-number seed allows Mr. Computer to grow new, unique random numbers.

3. C. Most programmers use the computer's clock to seed the random-number generator.

4. C. It's Dr. Modulus!

5. A. The modulo symbol is the percent sign (%).

6. D. Most people over 25 can sing at least some of the "Brady Bunch" theme song; a few of us may know some of the bawdier lyrics.

Chapter 5 Final Exam Answers

1. D.

2. C. To call a function, just name it as a statement in your source code.

3. A. In C, we *call* a function.

4. D. You also must prototype the function.

5. D.

6. B. Here is the proper prototype for the `goofus()` function:

```
void goofus(void);
```

7. As follows:

WordStar Word	processor
Reflex	Database
VisiCalc	Spreadsheet
Framework	Integrated

8. B. Both variables are "local" to their functions and operator-independent of each other.

9. C. Global variables can be shared between all your program's functions.

10. True. You declare variables in your functions just as you do in the `main` function.

11. A. Put the value or a variable holding that value into the function's parentheses.

12. B. The value will be used inside the function as the `silly` variable.

13. As follows:

Ceylon	Sri Lanka
Formosa	Taiwan
Rhodesia	Zimbabwe
Dutch Guiana	Suriname

14. A. Whatever `ugh` equals, it is treated as the variable `silly` inside the `goofus` function.

15. D.

16. F. Functions return only one value. In this book's second volume, you discover how that one value can be a key to unlock more values.

17. A. Nothing is wrong — it's an example of how C functions work from the inside out.

18. B. Technically, only B is required. Answer A has been used, but it's not required (and can be formatted differently), and the other answers are very specific. Give yourself a point if you feel that this question was a gyp.

19. B. Sounds easy, huh?

20. B. Obviously Mary Ann. Gilligan was not an option!

Lesson 6-1 Quiz Answers

1. D. Call them "header files," not "H files."

2. B. The `#include <stdio.h>` means that the compiler will look for a file named STDIO.H and stick it in your source code.

3. B. You need to `include` a header file only once, no matter how many functions require it.

4. D. You use double quotes around a header file you created yourself.

5. D. In each case, the spinoffs were created by using characters appearing in the original: "The Tortellis" featured Carla's ex-husband, who appeared in a "Cheers" episode *first*. The same with "Frasier," "Maude," "Rhoda," et al. In the case of the "Star Trek" lineage, the new shows weren't spawned from the old ones based on characters who appeared in the original; even if you call the *Enterprise* a "character," the new one wasn't seen in the original series. (Another spinoff from "All in the Family" was "Good Times," but it's actually a spinoff of "Maude" — a spinoff of a spinoff.)

Lesson 6-2 Quiz Answers

1. B. The biggest mistake is definitely forgetting the ampersand (&) before the variable name.

2. C. Use white space to separate the values.

3. A. Gas is neither a liquid nor a solid.

4. D. This statement will read a two-digit integer value into variable i:

```
scanf("%2i",i);
```

Lesson 6-3 Quiz Answers

1. Four.

2. As follows:

    A. argv[0] = POP

    B. argv[1] = /ICE

    C. argv[2] = FIZZ

    D. argv[3] = ROOT BEER

    It's "ROOT BEER" because it's enclosed in double quotes.

3. C. If the argument count is greater than 1, there are optional parameters.

4. B. Bunions happen on only the first joint of the big toe; corns can happen on any toe.

Lesson 6-4 Quiz Answers

1. C. The && (double ampersands) are used to make logical AND comparisons.

2. B. The || (double whatevers) are used to make logical OR comparisons.

3. Here's what you would see (and I hope that you didn't cheat):

```
Either Poindexter or Melvin is silly.
Either Poindexter or Melvin is wise.
Poindexter is silly and Melvin is wise.
Either Poindexter is silly or Melvin is wise.
```

4. A. The Green Bay Packers won 35 to 10 over Kansas City in the first Super Bowl, January 1967.

Lesson 6-5 Quiz Answers

1. A. Type casting *temporarily* changes a variable type.

2. D. Adam was not in *The Reluctant Astronaut* — though it sounds like one of his films.

3. A. Only A meets the end. For answer B, you don't get an error, but the value stored isn't what you expect; Answer C may seem to work, but it creates a float, which is accurate to only seven digits, so it doesn't store the entire number properly.

4. D. Add 1 to a signed integer equal to 32,767 and you get –32,768.

5. My wife would kill me if I did *any* of those things. Just sit and talk with the kid. Eventually he'll roll back to sleep.

Lesson 6-6 Quiz Answers

1. B. I've actually used the heading "Removing the hex from hexadecimal" in several books. Yeah, I probably stole it from somewhere to boot!

2. C. Base eight is octal.

3. D. Item D could be a hexadecimal number, but it has no doodad to clue you (or the compiler) in to that. In fact, your compiler would flag it as a linker error or something.

4. A. The character 0D hex is written as '\x0d' in an if comparison. Remember: Single quotes!

5. Here is one such program:

Name: PODSNRD.C

```
/* Display random number in several counting bases */

#include <stdio.h>
#include <stdlib.h>
#include <time.h>                        //for seeding randomizer

int rnd(int range);
void seedrnd(void);

void main()
{
     int r;

     seedrnd();
     r=rnd(32000);

     printf("You must send %i pods to San Francisco.\n",r);
     printf("You must send %o (O) pods to San Francisco.\n",r);
     printf("You must send %x (H) pods to San Francisco.\n",r);
     printf("You must send %X (H) pods to San Francisco.\n",r);
}

int rnd(int range)
{
     int r;

     r=rand()%range;                     //spit up random num.
     return(r);
}

void seedrnd(void)
{
     srand((unsigned)time(NULL));
}
```

Chapter 6 Final Exam Answers

1. B. Always enclose your own, pet header files in double quotes rather than in angle brackets.

2. B. You have to specify a header file only once in your source code.

3. D. I have no idea what the `gobblech()` function does.

4. A.

5. C. I'm talking about bowling here. A strike is 10 points plus the total points of your next two balls. This is archaic information no longer required in the age of automatic bowling-score machines.

6. C. `argc` and `*argv[]` are the two arguments of the `main()` function.

7. B. If someone has typed an option after your program name at the DOS prompt, the value of `argc` will be greater than 1.

8. B. The string variable `argv[1]` holds the first thing typed after the program's name at the DOS prompt.

9. D. The double quotes around DONUT HOLES makes it one (1) item. Therefore, the `argc` variable will equal 3, and `argc[1]` is equal to DONUT HOLES.

10. B. The slogan, coined by President Theodore Roosevelt, is "Good to the last drop."

11. A.

12. B. Only `Poindexter==SILLY || Melvin==SILLY` holds true if both of them are silly. Every other option produces a FALSE overall result.

13. Actually, all the statements work out improperly. Because type casting is a one-time thing, the value two million is never stored in the `i` integer variable.

14. D. Subtract 1 from a signed `char` variable equal to -128 and you get 128. Weird, but that's the way it works.

15. D. Sylvester Stallone was nominated for *Rocky* in 1976 but lost. The rest are all winners: Charlton Heston for *Ben Hur* (1959); Clark Gable for *It Happened One Night* (1934); and Ernest Borgnine for *Marty* (1955).

16. D. Answer C also works.

Lesson 7-1 Quiz Answers

1. Here is one such program:

Name: 1000W.C

```
#include <stdio.h>

void main()
{
    int i;

    i=5;
    while(i<=1000)
    {
            printf("%i\t",i);
            i+=5;
    }
}
```

2. D. No one is required to marry a close relative in Kansas City.

3. C. A `while` loop loops as long as the condition specified is true.

4. B. A `while` loop won't repeat at all if the condition is false.

5. C. If C were a human language, `while` would most likely be a preposition.

Lesson 7-2 Quiz Answers

1. B. A `do-while` loop repeats its statements at least once.

2. B. Don't forget to put a semicolon after the `while` in a `do-while` loop.

3. C.

4. C. Captain Kirk refers to the UESPA ("*Yoo*-spuh") in the first few episodes of the old "Star Trek" series.

Lesson 7-3 Quiz Answers

1. C. Assuming that TRUE equals 1, the loop spins forever until you *break* out of it.

2. C. The `while(!done)` loop repeats until the `done` variable becomes TRUE; it's already FALSE and the ! (not) reverses that when the loop starts (so the loop is TRUE). Strange. Reread the section if you need brushing up.

3. A.

4. As shown below:

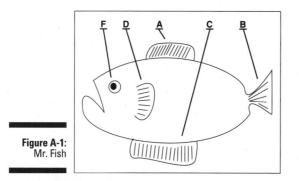

Figure A-1:
Mr. Fish

5. C. Truth is 1, at least in C.

Lesson 7-4 Quiz Answers

1. A. A nested loop is one loop inside another.

2. B. Nested loops are used primarily to create grids and fill in tables and arrays. Stuff like that.

3. C. Jungle Land is officially called Adventure Land. It's known as Jungle Land by almost everyone because it contains the amusing Jungle Boat tour. Also included in Adventure Land is the tepid, though Enchanted, Tiki Room "ride" and the Swiss Family Robinson "Tree" House. The treehouse, which is actually made of some form of *igneous disneylandius* compound, sits ungeographically correct opposite the Pirates of the Caribbean ride (which is in New Orleans Square-Land). I know this for a fact, having stood in line for Pirates some two-and-a-half hours one August.

4. Just make that if statement look more like the preceding one for the character 'C'. To wit:

```
if(c=='B')
{
    putchar(c);          //display B
    break;               //loop breaks right here!
}
```

Lesson 7-5 Quiz

1. D.

2. C. They may do some things strange, but *mother* is spelled the same on both sides of the pond.

3. D. Variables cannot be used with case. Also, there needs to be a colon ending that line and not a semicolon.

4. D. The default part of the switch-case thing handles situations in which there aren't any other matches.

5. B. Lee surrendered to Grant at Appomattox Court House, in Virginia, on June 9, 1865.

Lesson 7 Final Exam Answers

1. D. A while loop repeats until the condition it's clutching in parentheses is true.

2. C. A while(1) loop repeats forever, just like a for(;;) loop does.

3. B. Mildred is a fear of mildew.

4. D. The while(6) loop repeats forever because its condition is interpreted as always true by the compiler. (A break will get you out of it.)

5. D.

6. D. There really is a Department of Agriculture Meat and Poultry Hotline.

7. B. while(!done) means *while not done.*

8. A and B.

9. A. One loop inside another loop is a nested loop.

10. A. Nested loops are used for filling in arrays and grids.

11. C. The continue command forces the loop to repeat again, skipping any statements left in the loop.

12. B. Stay back at least 300 feet.

13. C. Though I'll give you credit for answer B as well.

14. C. Because there is no break statement after the printf("A or B!\n");, the next few lines are executed as well.

15. C.

16. D. Because there are no matches, the default condition takes over.

17. A. Mobile, Alabama wins, with 5.3 inches of rain, followed by Richmond, Virginia. Your probable first guess, Seattle, gets only 1.5 inches of rain during May and June. (The most rainy months in Seattle are November and December.) San Francisco gets only a paltry 0.2 inches of rain in May and June.

Appendix B
ASCII Table

ASCII	Character	Hex	Binary	Notes
0	^@	00	0000-0000	Null character, \0
1	^A	01	0000-0001	
2	^B	02	0000-0010	
3	^C	03	0000-0011	
4	^D	04	0000-0100	
5	^E	05	0000-0101	
6	^F	06	0000-0110	
7	^G	07	0000-0111	Bell, \a
8	^H	08	0000-1000	Backspace, \b
9	^I	09	0000-1001	Tab, \t
10	^J	0A	0000-1010	
11	^K	0B	0000-1011	
12	^L	0C	0000-1100	Form feed, \f
13	^M	0D	0000-1101	Enter key, \n (or \r)
14	^N	0E	0000-1110	
15	^O	0F	0000-1111	
16	^P	10	0001-0000	
17	^Q	11	0001-0001	
18	^R	12	0001-0010	
19	^S	13	0001-0011	
20	^T	14	0001-0100	
21	^U	15	0001-0101	
22	^V	16	0001-0110	
23	^W	17	0001-0111	
24	^X	18	0001-1000	
25	^Y	19	0001-1001	
26	^Z	1A	0001-1010	DOS "end of file" character
27	^[	1B	0001-1011	Escape
28	^\	1C	0001-1100	
29	^]	1D	0001-1101	
30	^^	1E	0001-1110	
31	^_	1F	0001-1111	
32		20	0010-0000	Space
33	!	21	0010-0001	
34	"	22	0010-0010	
35	#	23	0010-0011	
36	$	24	0010-0100	
37	%	25	0010-0101	
38	&	26	0010-0110	
39	'	27	0010-0111	
40	(	28	0010-1000	
41	)	29	0010-1001	
42	*	2A	0010-1010	
43	+	2B	0010-1011	
44	,	2C	0010-1100	
45	-	2D	0010-1101	
46	.	2E	0010-1110	
47	/	2F	0010-1111	
48	0	30	0011-0000	
49	1	31	0011-0001	
50	2	32	0011-0010	
51	3	33	0011-0011	
52	4	34	0011-0100	
53	5	35	0011-0101	

ASCII	Character	Hex	Binary	Notes
54	6	36	0011-0110	
55	7	37	0011-0111	
56	8	38	0011-1000	
57	9	39	0011-1001	
58	:	3A	0011-1010	
59	;	3B	0011-1011	
60	<	3C	0011-1100	
61	=	3D	0011-1101	
62	>	3E	0011-1110	
63	?	3F	0011-1111	
64	@	40	0100-0000	
65	A	41	0100-0001	
66	B	42	0100-0010	
67	C	43	0100-0011	
68	D	44	0100-0100	
69	E	45	0100-0101	
70	F	46	0100-0110	
71	G	47	0100-0111	
72	H	48	0100-1000	
73	I	49	0100-1001	
74	J	4A	0100-1010	
75	K	4B	0100-1011	
76	L	4C	0100-1100	
77	M	4D	0100-1101	
78	N	4E	0100-1110	
79	O	4F	0100-1111	
80	P	50	0101-0000	
81	Q	51	0101-0001	
82	R	52	0101-0010	
83	S	53	0101-0011	
84	T	54	0101-0100	
85	U	55	0101-0101	
86	V	56	0101-0110	
87	W	57	0101-0111	
88	X	58	0101-1000	
89	Y	59	0101-1001	
90	Z	5A	0101-1010	
91	[	5B	0101-1011	
92	\	5C	0101-1100	
93	]	5D	0101-1101	
94	^	5E	0101-1110	
95	_	5F	0101-1111	
96	`	60	0110-0000	
97	a	61	0110-0001	
98	b	62	0110-0010	
99	c	63	0110-0011	
100	d	64	0110-0100	
101	e	65	0110-0101	
102	f	66	0110-0110	
103	g	67	0110-0111	
104	h	68	0110-1000	
105	i	69	0110-1001	
106	j	6A	0110-1010	
107	k	6B	0110-1011	
108	l	6C	0110-1100	
109	m	6D	0110-1101	
110	n	6E	0110-1110	
111	o	6F	0110-1111	
112	p	70	0111-0000	
113	q	71	0111-0001	
114	r	72	0111-0010	
115	s	73	0111-0011	
116	t	74	0111-0100	
117	u	75	0111-0101	
118	v	76	0111-0110	
119	w	77	0111-0111	
120	x	78	0111-1000	
121	y	79	0111-1001	
122	z	7A	0111-1010	
123	{	7B	0111-1011	
124			7C	0111-1100	

ASCII	Character	Hex	Binary	Notes
125	}	7D	0111-1101	
126	~	7E	0111-1110	
127		7F	0111-1111	
128	Ç	80	1000-0000	(Extended ASCII characters)
129	ü	81	1000-0001	
130	é	82	1000-0010	
131	â	83	1000-0011	
132	ä	84	1000-0100	
133	à	85	1000-0101	
134	å	86	1000-0110	
135	ç	87	1000-0111	
136	ê	88	1000-1000	
137	ë	89	1000-1001	
138	è	8A	1000-1010	
139	ï	8B	1000-1011	
140	î	8C	1000-1100	
141	ì	8D	1000-1101	
142	Ä	8E	1000-1110	
143	Å	8F	1000-1111	
144	É	90	1001-0000	
145	æ	91	1001-0001	
146	Æ	92	1001-0010	
147	ô	93	1001-0011	
148	ö	94	1001-0100	
149	ò	95	1001-0101	
150	û	96	1001-0110	
151	ù	97	1001-0111	
152		98	1001-1000	
153	Ö	99	1001-1001	
154	Ü	9A	1001-1010	
155	¢	9B	1001-1011	
156	£	9C	1001-1100	
157	¥	9D	1001-1101	
158		9E	1001-1110	
159	ƒ	9F	1001-1111	
160	á	A0	1010-0000	
161	í	A1	1010-0001	
162	ó	A2	1010-0010	
163	ú	A3	1010-0011	
164	ñ	A4	1010-0100	
165	Ñ	A5	1010-0101	
166	ª	A6	1010-0110	
167	º	A7	1010-0111	
168	¿	A8	1010-1000	
169		A9	1010-1001	
170	¬	AA	1010-1010	
171	½	AB	1010-1011	
172	¼	AC	1010-1100	
173	¡	AD	1010-1101	
174	«	AE	1010-1110	
175	»	AF	1010-1111	
176	▒	B0	1011-0000	
177	▓	B1	1011-0001	
178	█	B2	1011-0010	
179	│	B3	1011-0011	
180	┤	B4	1011-0100	
181	╡	B5	1011-0101	
182	╢	B6	1011-0110	
183	╖	B7	1011-0111	
184	╕	B8	1011-1000	
185	╣	B9	1011-1001	
186	║	BA	1011-1010	
187	╗	BB	1011-1011	
188	╝	BC	1011-1100	
189	╜	BD	1011-1101	
190	╛	BE	1011-1110	
191	┐	BF	1011-1111	
192	└	C0	1100-0000	
193	┴	C1	1100-0001	
194	┬	C2	1100-0010	

ASCII	Character	Hex	Binary	Notes
195	├	C3	1100-0011	
196	─	C4	1100-0100	
197	┼	C5	1100-0101	
198	╞	C6	1100-0110	
199	╟	C7	1100-0111	
200	╚	C8	1100-1000	
201	╔	C9	1100-1001	
202	╩	CA	1100-1010	
203	╦	CB	1100-1011	
204	╠	CC	1100-1100	
205	═	CD	1100-1101	
206	╬	CE	1100-1110	
207	╧	CF	1100-1111	
208	╨	D0	1101-0000	
209	╤	D1	1101-0001	
210	╥	D2	1101-0010	
211	╙	D3	1101-0011	
212	╘	D4	1101-0100	
213	╒	D5	1101-0101	
214	╓	D6	1101-0110	
215	╫	D7	1101-0111	
216	╪	D8	1101-1000	
217	┘	D9	1101-1001	
218	┌	DA	1101-1010	
219	█	DB	1101-1011	
220	▄	DC	1101-1100	
221	▌	DD	1101-1101	
222	▐	DE	1101-1110	
223	▀	DF	1101-1111	
224	α	E0	1110-0000	
225	ß	E1	1110-0001	
226	Γ	E2	1110-0010	
227	π	E3	1110-0011	
228	Σ	E4	1110-0100	
229	σ	E5	1110-0101	
230	µ	E6	1110-0110	
231	τ	E7	1110-0111	
232	Φ	E8	1110-1000	
233	Θ	E9	1110-1001	
234	Ω	EA	1110-1010	
235	δ	EB	1110-1011	
236	∞	EC	1110-1100	
237	φ	ED	1110-1101	
238	ε	EE	1110-1110	
239	∩	EF	1110-1111	
240	≡	F0	1111-0000	
241	±	F1	1111-0001	
242	≥	F2	1111-0010	
243	≤	F3	1111-0011	
244	⌠	F4	1111-0100	
245	⌡	F5	1111-0101	
246	÷	F6	1111-0110	
247	≈	F7	1111-0111	
248	°	F8	1111-1000	
249	·	F9	1111-1001	
250	·	FA	1111-1010	
251	√	FB	1111-1011	
252	ⁿ	FC	1111-1100	
253	²	FD	1111-1101	
254	■	FE	1111-1110	
255		FF	1111-1111	Blank character

Appendix C

Contending with Borland C++ 4.0

*B*orland C++ Version 4.0 (and possibly later versions) is radically different from Borland's earlier C language packages. Primarily, Borland C++ 4.0 is a Windows-only thing. It only creates Windows programs. And unlike Microsoft Visual C++, it's extremely unforgiving if you intend to write a meek, old DOS program.

Oh well. Complaining aside, you have Borland C++ 4.0 and you want to learn how to write programs as told by this book. To do so, you have to use Borland C++ at the DOS prompt. Forget Windows. Forget the pretty Borland C++ program. Forget what you spent for this turkey.

Before starting, make sure that you include Borland C++'s subdirectory on DOS's search path. The directory you want is \BC4\BIN. So if that directory is on drive C, you want to have a search path that looks like the following:

```
path=c:\dos;c:\util;c:\bc4\bin
```

The second thing to do is create a batch file that will help you automatically compile your programs. Use your favorite text editor, such as DOS's Edit program, to create the following file in your Borland C++ \BC4\BIN directory:

```
@ECHO OFF
BCC -IC:\BC4\INCLUDE -LC:\BC4\LIB %1
```

The first line is an @ sign, followed by ECHO, a space, and then OFF.

The second line is BCC, followed by a space, a minus sign, and a capital I. It *must* be a capital *I,* not lowercase. Follow that by the drive letter for Borland C++. Drive C is used in the preceding lines. It's followed by a colon and \BC4\INCLUDE. Then comes another space, another minus sign, and a capital L. Again, this must be a capital *L.* Follow that by the drive letter for Borland C++ (C is used in the preceding lines) and then a colon and \BC4\LIB. Then type another space, a percent sign, and the number one (1). Press Enter to end this line.

Save this file as CC.BAT in the \BC4\BIN directory. You're now ready to use the compiler at the DOS prompt. The steps for creating the GOODBYE.C program are listed next.

Steps: Creating the GOODBYE program with Borland C++ 4.0

Step 1. Using a text editor, such as DOS's EDIT program, QEdit, or something similar, type in the GOODBYE.C source code, as shown at the beginning of Lesson 1-3.

You can follow the instructions in Lesson 1-3, in the box titled "Entering the GOODBYE.C program's source code," if you need a little more help.

Step 2. Save your work to disk in a file named GOODBYE.C.

You have to refer to your editor's documentation for the proper Save commands.

Step 3. Quit your editor and return to the banal DOS prompt.

Step 4. At the DOS prompt, use the CC command to compile and link your program.

CC is actually the name of the batch file that will run the Borland C++ compiler for you — plus smooth out a few potential ruffles.

Step 5. Type the following line:

```
C> CC GOODBYE.C
```

Remember to specify the full filename for the source code: GOODBYE.C. If you forget the dot-C, the final program is not created.

Step 6. Press Enter.

The CC batch file runs Borland C++'s compiler, which both compiles and links the source code. If everything goes as planned, you see something like the following displayed:

```
Borland C++ Version 4.00 Copyright (c) 1993 Borland Interna-
        tional
goodbye.c
Turbo Link  Version 6.00 Copyright (c) 1992, 1993 Borland
        International
```

Congratulations! It worked.

If you get an error message, return to your text editor and double-check your work. Lesson 1-5 offers more information about dealing with the heartbreak of errors.

The C compiler has created a program named GOODBYE.EXE. That's your program.

Step 7. To run it, type GOODBYE at the DOS prompt, just as you would run any other program:

```
C> GOODBYE
```

Step 8. Press Enter and you see the program's output displayed. It should look like this:

```
Goodbye, cruel world!
```

The message displayed is the fruit of your labors. It was produced by a program you created and built yourself. The program file GOODBYE.EXE is now permanently stored on your PC's hard disk and can be run from now until the earth's magnetic poles shift late next year and destroy all the data stored on our hard drives.

Step 9. Go back to Lesson 1-3 and begin reading at the section titled "Save it! Compile it! Link it! Run it!"

Refer to *DOS For Dummies* for more information about the PATH command. *MORE DOS For Dummies* has additional information about the PATH command in addition to a smattering of info about batch files. Both are available in your grocer's freezer.

"THE ENTIRE SYSTEM IS DOWN. THE COMPUTER PEOPLE BLAME THE MODEM PEOPLE WHO BLAME THE PHONE PEOPLE WHO BLAME IT ON OUR MOON BEING IN THE FIFTH HOUSE WITH VENUS ASCENDING."

Appendix D
Potentially Fun Programs

*T*his appendix contains some sample programs you should feel free to type in and experiment with. References to relevant lessons in this book are offered in each program's comments. (You don't have to type all the comments, especially the long ones.)

Name: DIBBLE.C

```c
/*
This program displays some happy faces at random spots on
the screen. It uses the cls() and locate() functions from
Lesson 5-6 and the rnd() and seedrnd() functions from
Lesson 5-7. Other than that, it's pretty silly.
*/

#include <stdio.h>
#include <stdlib.h>
#include <time.h>
#include <dos.h>

#define FACE 0x01              //Face character number
#define LOOP 100               //number of faces to display
#define PAUSE 150000           //pause time (0-16,000,000)
#define VIDEO 0x10             //Video interrupt
#define COLS 80                //Screen width
#define ROWS 25                //Screen rows

void cls(void);
void locate(int col,int row);
int rnd(int range);
void seedrnd(void);
```

```
void main()
{
     int t,x,y;
     unsigned long p;          //p=pause loop

     cls();                    //clear the screen
     seedrnd();                //set randomizer

     for(t=0;t<LOOP;t++)
     {
          x=rnd(80)+1;         //random column
          y=rnd(25)+1;         //random row
          locate(x,y);         //move cursor there
          putchar(FACE);       //be happy
/*
The following statement is a pause loop, delaying the program for
a few seconds. Values for the PAUSE constant can range from 0 (fast)
up to 16,000,000, which is really slow. Values will differ depend-
ing on how fast your PC is.
The Borland C++ compiler has two pausing functions built-in, both
of which are better than relying on a for loop. The sleep() func-
tion pauses for a given number of seconds; the delay() function
pauses for a given number of microseconds. So sleep(1); pauses for
one second, as does the delay(1000); statement.
*/
          for(p=0;p<PAUSE;p++);     //pause

     }
}

void cls(void)
{
     union REGS regs;

     regs.h.ah=0x06;          //call func 6, scroll window
     regs.h.al=0x00;          //clear screen
     regs.h.bh=0x07;          //make screen "blank" color
     regs.h.ch=0x00;          //Upper left row
     regs.h.cl=0x00;          //Upper left column
     regs.h.dh=ROWS-1;        //Lower right row
     regs.h.dl=COLS-1;        //Lower right column
     int86(VIDEO,&regs,&regs);
```

```
        locate(0,0);                    //"Home" the cursor
}

void locate(int col,int row)
{
     union REGS regs;

     regs.h.ah=0x02;                    //video func 2, move cursor
     regs.h.bh=0x00;                    //video screen (always 0)
     regs.h.dh=row;                     //cursor's column position
     regs.h.dl=col;                     //cursor's row position
     int86(VIDEO,&regs,&regs);
}

int rnd(int range)
{
     int r;

     r=rand()%range;                    //spit up random num.
     return(r);
}

void seedrnd(void)
{
     srand((unsigned)time(NULL));
}
```

Name: DRUNK.C

```
/*
This program tries to prove the old "drunk and the lamppost"
problem. A character starts out in the middle of the screen
and then moves in random steps: up, down, left, or right.
Theoretically, he will always return to the lamppost, never
venturing far away. Will he?
This is based on the DIBBLE.C program, with only the main
function changed, plus a few new DEFINEs.
*/
```

```
#include <stdio.h>
#include <stdlib.h>
#include <time.h>
#include <dos.h>

#define FACE 0x01                    //Face character number
#define BACKSPACE 0x08               //Backspace character
#define BLANK 0x20                   //Blank character number
#define LOOP 100                     //number of faces to display
#define PAUSE 150000                 //pause time (0-16,000,000)
#define VIDEO 0x10                   //Video interrupt
#define COLS 80                      //Screen width
#define ROWS 25                      //Screen rows

void cls(void);
void locate(int col,int row);
int rnd(int range);
void seedrnd(void);

void main()
{
    int t,x,y;
    unsigned long p;                 //p=pause loop

    cls();                           //clear the screen
    seedrnd();                       //set randomizer

// start at the center of the screen
    x=COLS/2;                        //half screen width
    y=ROWS/2;                        //half screen height

//Move the drunk LOOP number of times
    for(t=0;t<LOOP;t++)
    {
            locate(x,y);             //move cursor
            putchar(FACE);           //be happy
            for(p=0;p<PAUSE;p++);    //pause
/*
The following two statements move the drunk one position
up, down, right, or left. The rnd() function returns a random
value between 0 and 2. When you subtract 1 from that value,
you get -1, 0, or 1, which moves the drunk left or up (-1) or
```

```
right or down (1) or keeps him in the same spot (0).
*/
                        x+=(rnd(3)-1);          //new random X
                        y+=(rnd(3)-1);          //new random Y
/*
The following four statements ensure that the drunk doesn't
migrate off-screen. If the X coordinate is less than 1, it's
changed to 80 and vice versa. That way, he'll move in the same
direction, but won't "disappear." Likewise for the value
of Y.
*/
                    if(x<1) x=80;              //wrap to the left
                    if(x>80) x=1;              //wrap to the right
                    if(y<1) y=25;              //wrap to the bottom
                    if(y>25) y=1;              //wrap to the top


/*
It's by erasing the drunk that the animation illusion
is created. First you must back up, and then display a blank
character where the drunk was. (The next statement in
the for loop will redisplay the drunk in his new
position.)
*/
                    putchar(BACKSPACE);        //back up and
                    putchar(BLANK);            //erase drunk

    }
}


void cls(void)
{
    union REGS regs;

    regs.h.ah=0x06;              //call function 6, scroll window
    regs.h.al=0x00;              //clear screen
    regs.h.bh=0x07;              //make screen "blank" color
    regs.h.ch=0x00;              //Upper left row
    regs.h.cl=0x00;              //Upper left column
    regs.h.dh=ROWS-1;            //Lower right row
    regs.h.dl=COLS-1;            //Lower right column
    int86(VIDEO,&regs,&regs);
```

```
        locate(0,0);                  //"Home" the cursor
}

void locate(int col,int row)
{
    union REGS regs;

    regs.h.ah=0x02;                   //video function 2, move cursor
    regs.h.bh=0x00;                   //video screen (always 0)
    regs.h.dh=row;                    //cursor's column position
    regs.h.dl=col;                    //cursor's row position
    int86(VIDEO,&regs,&regs);
}
int rnd(int range)
{
    int r;

    r=rand()%range;                   //spit up random num.
    return(r);
}

void seedrnd(void)
{
    srand((unsigned)time(NULL));
}
```

Name: CRAPS.C

```
/* Program to simulate the exciting and confusing game
of casino craps.
Basically, you roll two dice and total the number. If it's
a 7 or 11, you win; 2, 3, or 12 and you lose. Easy enough.
If you roll any other number, 4, 5, 6, 8, 9, or 10, it
becomes your "point." You must roll that number again to
win, but if you roll a 7 before that, you lose.
Confused? Play it awhile.
This game only plays pass; no other fancy bets that would
confuse you anyway and make it harder to program. */

#include <stdio.h>
```

```c
#include <conio.h>
#include <stdlib.h>
#include <ctype.h>                          //for the toupper() function
#include <time.h>                           //for seeding randomizer

#define TRUE 1                              //It's true!
#define FALSE !TRUE                         //It's false!

int rnd(int range);
void seedrnd(void);
int roll(void);

void main()
{
    int x,YouWannaPlay,pot,bet,point;
    char c;

/* Setup */

    seedrnd();                             //randomizer
    printf("\nVegas Craps!\nThe dice game no one
           understands.\n\n");
    YouWannaPlay=TRUE;
    pot=100;                               //start with $100

/* Play the game main loop*/

    while(YouWannaPlay)
    {

/* First get their bet in a do-while loop. The bet must be
greater than $2 and can't be greater than their pot (total).
If the bet is less than 2, the if statement displays a rude
message. */

        do
        {
            printf("You have $%i in your pot.\n",pot);
            printf("Enter your bet: $");
            scanf("%i",&bet);
```

```
            if(bet<2)
            printf("Hey! You wanna do that lowball stuff, go
        downtown!\n");
        }
    while(bet<2 || bet>pot);

    x=roll();        //roll the dice
    printf("\tThe roll was %i.\n",x);
```

```
/* The switch-case loop thing handles all rolls of
the dice: 7 and 11 to win and double your bet,or 2, 3, or
12 to lose and lose your bet. */
```

```
    switch(x)
    {
            case 7:
            case 11:
                    printf("\tYou win!\n");
                    pot+=bet;
                    break;
            case 2:
            case 3:
            case 12:
                    printf("\tCraps! You lose!\n");
                    pot-=bet;
                    break;
            default:            //everything else
                    point=x;  //set point
                    printf("\tYour point is now %i.\n",point);
```

```
/* The while(TRUE) loop loops forever, but breaks within
the loop get you out of it. Basically, you're looking for
x=point, rolling the point again, or x=7, which means that
you lose. Both conditions are handled by if statements
within the loop, which adjust the pot and break out of
the loop as necessary */
                    while(TRUE)
                    {
                            x=roll();   //roll the dice
                            printf("\tYou rolled %i, point is
                                %i.\n",x,point);
                            if(x==point)
                            {
```

```
                                                printf("\tYou win!\n");
                                                pot+=bet;
                                                break;
                                        }
                                        if(x==7)
                                        {
                                                printf("\tSeven out, you
                                                        lose!\n");
                                                pot-=bet;
                                                break;

                                        }

                                }

                }

/* Game over stuff */
/* At this point, you've either won or lost, but you're still
in a while loop. First tell users how much is in their pot.
Then, if the pot is empty, you need to end the game.
Otherwise, ask if they want to play again and repeat the
loop. */

        printf("You now have $%i in your pot.\n",pot);
        if(pot==0)                              //outta money
        {
                printf("You're broke!\n");
                printf("Get outta here!\n");
                break;                          //quit the loop and the game
        }
        printf("Play again Y/N?");

/* This chunk of code gets Y or N input and quits the loop if
N is pressed. toupper converts the keystroke into uppercase.
If they type an N, it's displayed and YouWannaPlay is set to
false, which ends the loop. Otherwise, the program assumes that
you pressed Y and the loop repeats.*/

        c=toupper(getch());
        if(c=='N')
        {
                printf("N\n");                  //display input
                YouWannaPlay=FALSE;
        }
        else
                printf("Y\n\n");                //assume Y pressed
```

```
    }

/* Exit routines (there aren't any, but here is where they'd go) */

}

/* The roll function rolls the dice and returns the total */

int roll(void)
{
    int dice1,dice2;

/* One is added to the value rnd() returns since it returns
values from 0 to 5. */

    dice1=rnd(6)+1;            //get random number between 1 and 6
    dice2=rnd(6)+1;
    return(dice1+dice2);
}

/* Generate a random value */

int rnd(int range)
{
    int r;

    r=rand()%range;            //spit up random num.
    return(r);
}

/* Seed the randomizer */

void seedrnd(void)
{
    srand((unsigned)time(NULL));
}
```

Name: LOTTO.C

```c
/* This program is designed to pick out random lotto numbers
from 1 to RANGE, as defined below.
Normally, you would think that drawing random numbers in a lottery
wouldn't be a problem; however, you cannot draw the same number
twice. So there must be a mechanism to make sure that the numbers
already drawn are excluded from the pool of available numbers.
Here I solve the problem by building an array -- essentially
an array of lotto balls. The array is initialized to zeroes,
and when a ball is drawn, a 1 is stuck in its place. When
future balls are drawn, the program checks the array to see
whether a 1 is in that ball's position. If not, the ball can be
drawn. */

#include <stdio.h>
#include <stdlib.h>
#include <time.h>                //for the seedrnd() function

#define RANGE 50                 //number of numbers
#define BALLS 6                  //number of balls to draw
#define DELAY 1000000            //delay interval between picks

int rnd(int range);
void seedrnd(void);

void main()
{
    int numbers[RANGE];      //array that holds the balls
    int i,b;
    unsigned long d;         //delay variable

/* set things up */

    printf("L O T T O   P I C K E R\n\n");
    seedrnd();                   //seed the randomizer

/* Initialize the array by filling every element with
a zero. This means none of the balls have been drawn
yet */
```

```
        for(i=0;i<RANGE;i++)         //initialize the array
                    numbers[i]=0;

    printf("Press Enter to pick this week's numbers:");
    getchar();

/* draw the numbers */
    printf("\nHere they come: ");
    for(i=0;i<BALLS;i++)
    {
        for(d=0;d<=DELAY;d++);           //pause here

/* The do-while loop picks a random number, b=rnd(RANGE),
as its only statement. The while part checks to see whether a
1 is in that ball's position in the array. Since 1=TRUE,
the loop repeats until a number/ball is drawn with zero
in the array. 0=FALSE, so the loop stops. */

        do
        {
            b=rnd(RANGE);        //draw number
        }
        while(numbers[b]);        //already drawn?

/* After the ball is drawn, a 1 is stuck in its position
in the array. The b+1 in the printf statement accounts for
the fact that the array starts at zero. In real life, there
is no zero lotto ball, so we add 1 to that number to get
1 as the lowest ball. Everything else falls into place. */

        numbers[b]=1;        //mark it as drawn
        printf("%i ",b+1);  //add one for zero

    }
    printf("\n\nGood luck in the drawing!\n");
}

/* Generate a random value */

int rnd(int range)
{
    int r;
```

```
        r=rand()%range;          //spit up random num.
        return(r);
}

/* Seed the randomizer */

void seedrnd(void)
{
        srand((unsigned)time(NULL));
}
```

Name: FUNMENU.C

```
/* A Function Key Menu Program
This program uses a while-select-case loop to run a
little menu program. The system() function is used
to execute a DOS command in this program's doDOS
function. Various function keys are used to select
the commands.
Many of the function keys have been left blank for
you to fill in with your own commands if you like.
It's cinchy.
*/

#include <stdio.h>
#include <conio.h>
#include <stdlib.h>          //for executing system() function
#include <dos.h>             //For DOS function calls
#include "function.h"        //Function key definitions

#define VIDEO 0x10           //Video interrupt
#define KEYBOARD 0x16        //Keyboard interrupt
#define COLS 80              //Screen width
#define ROWS 25              //Screen rows
#define TRUE 1               //This is true
#define FALSE !TRUE          //This is not true

void screenSetup(void);
void doDOS(char *command);
int getKey(void);
```

```c
void cls(void);
void locate(int row,int col);

void main()
{
    int done=FALSE;         //while loop variable

    screenSetup();          //Set up the screen

/* The program's main loop is a while-select-case
loop. It scans the keyboard, looking for one of
the 10 function keys to be pressed.
Refer to the getKey and doDOS functions later in
the source code for a description of how they work */

    while(!done)
    {
        switch(getKey())    //read in a key
        {
            case F1:  //Go to DOS
                      locate(0,24);
                      puts("Type EXIT to return to the menu.");
                      doDOS("COMMAND.COM");
                      break;
            case F2: //Format a disk
                      doDOS("FORMAT A:");
                      break;
            case F3:      //[blank] (fill in later)
/*
To add your own functions, stick in a doDOS call, putting the
DOS command in the parentheses in double quotes. Remember to
change the proper menu item in the screenSetup() function to
reflect your new command.
*/
                      break;
            case F4:      //[blank]
                      break;
            case F5:      //[blank]
                      break;
            case F6:      //Check disk
                      doDOS("CHKDSK");
                      break;
```

```
                    case F7:          //DIR command
                                doDOS("DIR /P");
                                break;
                    case F8:          //[blank]
                                break;
                    case F9:          //[blank]
                                break;
                    case F10:         //Quit
                                done=TRUE;
                                break;
            }
        }
    locate(0,24);
    puts("Bye!");
}


/* Set up the screen function
By putting all these commands here in their own function,
you make the main function more readable */

void screenSetup(void)
{
    cls();                          //Clear the screen
    locate(20,3);                   //Move the cursor to x,y
    puts("Function Key Menu Program");
    locate(10,5);
    puts("F1 - Go to DOS");
    locate(10,7);
    puts("F2 - Format a disk");
    locate(10,9);
    puts("F3 - [blank]");
    locate(10,11);
    puts("F4 - [blank]");
    locate(10,13);
    puts("F5 - [blank]");
    locate(40,5);
    puts("F6 - Check disk");
    locate(40,7);
    puts("F7 - DIR command");
    locate(40,9);
    puts("F8 - [blank]");
```

```
        locate(40,11);
        puts("F9 - [blank]");
        locate(40,13);
        puts("F10 - QUIT");
        locate(20,16);
        printf("Your Choice:");          //don't display ENTER char here
}


/* This function runs a DOS program or command.
The command is in the string "command" passed to this
function. The system() function prototype is found in
the STDLIB.H header file. It sends whatever text is in
the parentheses to DOS, just as though you typed it at
the prompt. Here, the text is passed in the command
string variable.
Note that the getchar() function by itself will produce
a warning error. It's a nevermind warning error. */

void doDOS(char *command)
{
        locate(0,24);
        system(command);          //run the command
        locate(0,24);
        printf("Press ENTER to return to the menu:");
        getchar();                //press ENTER
        screenSetup();            //repaint the screen
}


/* Read the BIOS key function (to read function keys).
Unfortunately, getch() doesn't read function keys. To do
that, you need to phone up the PC's keyboard BIOS interrupt
and get the keyboard character's secret code. The code is a
four-digit hexadecimal number unique for each key and key
combination on the keyboard. The KEYBOARD.H file contains
the codes for the functions.
You cannot use this function to read regular keys; use
getch instead. (Well, you can use this function, but it's
really tricky, and I may get into it in Volume II.) */

int getKey(void)
{
        union REGS regs;
```

```
        regs.h.ah=0x00;                 //Read keyboard function
        int86(KEYBOARD,&regs,&regs);    //dial up keyboard BIOS

        return(regs.x.ax);              //return keyboard "scan code"
}

/* Clear Screen Function (from ZAPSCRN2.C in Lesson 5.6) */

void cls(void)
{
        union REGS regs;

        regs.h.ah=0x06;                 //call function 6, scroll window
        regs.h.al=0x00;                 //clear screen
        regs.h.bh=0x07;                 //make screen "blank" color
        regs.h.ch=0x00;                 //Upper left row
        regs.h.cl=0x00;                 //Upper left column
        regs.h.dh=ROWS-1;               //Lower right row
        regs.h.dl=COLS-1;               //Lower right column
        int86(VIDEO,&regs,&regs);

        locate(0,0);                    //"Home" the cursor
}

/* LOCATE Function (also from Lesson 5.6) */

void locate(int col,int row)
{
        union REGS regs;

        regs.h.ah=0x02;                 //video function 2, move cursor
        regs.h.bh=0x00;                 //video screen (always 0)
        regs.h.dh=row;                  //cursor's row position
        regs.h.dl=col;                  //cursor's column position
        int86(VIDEO,&regs,&regs);
}
```

Name: FUNCTION.H

```
/* Function key header file */

#define F1 0x3b00
#define F2 0x3c00
#define F3 0x3d00
#define F4 0x3e00
#define F5 0x3f00
#define F6 0x4000
#define F7 0x4100
#define F8 0x4200
#define F9 0x4300
#define F10 0x4400
```

Index

Notes

Notes

Notes

Notes

Notes

Notes

Notes

Notes

Notes

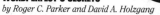

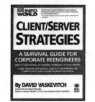

IDG BOOKS

Order Form

Order Center: (800) 762-2974 (8 a.m.-5 p.m., PST, weekdays) or (415) 312-0650

For Fastest Service: Photocopy This Order Form and FAX it to: (415) 358-1260

Quantity	ISBN	Title	Price	Total

Shipping & Handling Charges

Subtotal	U.S.	Canada & International	International Air Mail
Up to $20.00	Add $3.00	Add $4.00	Add $10.00
$20.01-40.00	$4.00	$5.00	$20.00
$40.01-60.00	$5.00	$6.00	$25.00
$60.01-80.00	$6.00	$8.00	$35.00
Over $80.00	$7.00	$10.00	$50.00

In U.S. and Canada, shipping is UPS ground or equivalent.
For Rush shipping call (800) 762-2974.

Subtotal _____

CA residents add applicable sales tax _____

IN and MA residents add 5% sales tax _____

IL residents add 6.25% sales tax _____

RI residents add 7% sales tax _____

Shipping _____

Total _____

Ship to:

Name _____

Company _____

Address _____

City/State/Zip_____

Daytime Phone _____

Payment: ❑ Check to IDG Books (US Funds Only) ❑ Visa ❑ Mastercard ❑ American Express

Card# _____ Exp._____ Signature_____

Please send this order form to: IDG Books, 155 Bovet Road, Suite 310, San Mateo, CA 94402.

Allow up to 3 weeks for delivery. Thank you!